Electronic Mediations

Katherine Hayles, Mark Poster, and Samuel Weber, Series Editors

Digitize This Book!

The Politics of New Media,
or Why We Need Open Access Now

GARY HALL

Electronic Mediations 24

University of Minnesota Press
Minneapolis • London

Earlier versions of some of the material in this book have been previously published as "The Cultural Studies e-Archive Project (Original Pirate Copy)," *Culture Machine* 5 (2003); "Digitize This," *Review of Education, Pedagogy, and Cultural Studies* 26, no. 1 (January–March 2004); and "IT, Again: How to Build an Ethical Virtual Institution," in *Experimenting: Essays with Samuel Weber,* eds. Simon Morgan Wortham and Gary Hall (New York: Fordham University Press, 2007).

Produced by Wilsted & Taylor Publishing Services
Copyediting by Nancy Evans
Design and composition by Yvonne Tsang

Published by the University of Minnesota Press
111 Third Avenue South, Suite 290
Minneapolis, MN 55401-2520
http://www.upress.umn.edu

LIBRARY OF CONGRESS CATALOGING-IN-PUBLICATION DATA

Hall, Gary, 1962–
  Digitize this book! : the politics of new media, or why we need open access now / Gary Hall.
      p. cm. — (Electronic mediations ; 24)
  Includes bibliographical references and index.
  ISBN 978-0-8166-4870-2 (acid-free paper) — ISBN 978-0-8166-4871-9 (pbk. : acid-free paper)
      1. Open access publishing. 2. Scholarly electronic publishing. 3. Communication in learning and scholarship—Technological innovations. 4. Internet—Political aspects. I. Title.
  Z286.O63H35 2008
  070.5´7973—dc22   2008011042

Printed in the United States of America on acid-free paper

The University of Minnesota is an equal-opportunity educator and employer.

15 14 13 12 11 10 09 08   10 9 8 7 6 5 4 3 2 1

CONTENTS

ACKNOWLEDGMENTS

I'm going to keep this short and simple. A lot of people have provided me with help and support of one kind or another during the writing of this book. Among them, I'd especially like to thank Doug Armato, Clare Birchall, Dave Boothroyd, Paul Bowman, Timothy Clark, Jeremy Gilbert, Henry Giroux, Steve Green, Lawrence Grossberg, Ian Hall, Sigi Jöttkandt, Kembrew McLeod, Angela McRobbie, David Ottina, Paul Patton, Mark Poster, Nina Sellars, Steven Shaviro, Stelarc, Sandy Thatcher, Joanna Zylinska.

This one is for Ian (the original digitizer).

Another University Is Possible

University-Generated Media

What kind of university is desirable, or even possible, in the age of digital reproduction: CDs, DVDs, cell phones, computers, laptops, printers, the World Wide Web, the Internet, e-mails, text and picture messages, e-books, open-source and free software, blogs, Google, MP3 files, BitTorrent, podcasts, Bluetooth, Wikipedia, MySpace, Facebook, Flickr, YouTube, Second Life, Kindle, and so on?[1] It is an understatement to say that many of the changes introduced in the university in recent years have met with a fairly unfavorable response from both academics and nonacademics alike.[2] These changes include:

- The establishment of an internal market within higher education, as different institutions, and even different courses within the same institutions, are forced to compete nationally and internationally for limited resources in terms of faculty, staff, students, funding, and more
- The increase in student numbers, as well as faculty administrative, bureaucratic, and managerial responsibilities and workloads
- The further concentration of research in a small number of older, prestigious (some would say more conservative), "research-intensive" institutions: Harvard, Princeton, Yale, Oxford, Cambridge, Melbourne, and so forth[3]
- The declining security of university employment via the increase in fixed-term and hourly paid contracts—something which, alongside the concentration of research in fewer institutions, is turning many academics into "precarious" and "semi-precarious" proletarianized laborers, often forced to work for free both within

1

and without the institution in order to carry out the kind of research that interests and excites them

- The introduction of a host of micromanagement practices such as audits, inspections, monitoring, league tables, and performance-related pay, all designed to ensure economic efficiency and "value for money"[4]

- The lack of support for, and in some instances eradication of, departments, disciplines, and areas of study that have as part of their tradition the critique of capitalism, or (even worse) that are not easily commercially exploitable: cultural studies, English literature, philosophy, medieval history, and so on

- The conversion of students into customers, not least by coercing them to exercise consumer choice over the cost and place of their education[5]

- The use of students—who need either to pay off the debts incurred during their time in college by taking out loans, or to at least to keep their debts to a minimum—as a reliable source of cheap labor for other parts of the economy

Yet for all the introduction and subsequent pushing through of these reforms, and the very real sense of disappointment and frustration that has on occasion been engendered by what we might call this "neoliberal turn" in higher education, I am convinced that the university remains worth defending.[6] In fact, it is *precisely because of* these developments that I want to reaffirm a commitment on my part to the idea of the university: not only because "there is nothing outside the university,"[7] but also because, if universities are to continue to be capable of functioning "albeit in conditions of adversity . . . as places of dissent" (although universities are of course not the only such places), then we need to defend them, in some form at least (McRobbie 2000, 219).

The problem is, if we disagree with the way in which the forces of capitalist free-market economics are increasingly transforming higher education into an extension of business, and at the same time do not wish to propose a return to the kind of paternalistic and class-bound ideas associated with F. R. Leavis (1943), Matthew Arnold (1868), and John Henry Cardinal Newman (1858) that previously dominated the university—ideas that view it in terms of an elite cultural training and reproduction of a national culture, with all the hierarchies and exclusions around differences of class, race, gender, ethnicity, and so forth that those terms imply—then how do we want the university to be? Moreover, how is it possible to defend the university without appearing to advocate one of these two models?

This is an extremely important question—all the more so considering that the inability to articulate an effective alternative vision for the future, for all their criticisms and complaints in the media, higher education press, and scholarly research literature, appears to have left the majority of academics and institutions with very few options for resisting or even redirecting such changes (other than saying "no" from time to time).

So how do we want the university to be?

We need to explore and experiment with this question if we are to challenge what Bill Readings (1996) so memorably characterized as the University of Excellence. It is this question—how is it possible to defend the university, and to do so without advocating one of the above two models?—that I have been creatively exploring and experimenting with in my work for some time now. Obviously, I have not been able to experiment with new forms of academic institutions by establishing my own university, my own "counter-institution," as it were. (Even if I had access to the kind of funding required, which I do not, the government would be unlikely to give me accreditation.) What I have been able to do is help set up some smaller, "minor," experimental projects; projects that may enable us to make an institutionally pragmatic, "tactical use of the space of the university," and so begin to think of the institution differently and otherwise (Readings 1996, 18).[8]

One of these university-generated media projects is *Culture Machine*. *Culture Machine* is an umbrella term for a series of experiments in culture and theory. At the moment it includes the *Culture Machine* open-access (OA) electronic journal of cultural studies and cultural theory I co-founded and co-edit.[9] Another more recent project has involved setting up the first (to my knowledge) open-access archive for cultural studies and cultural theory: the Cultural Studies e-Archive, or CSeARCH.[10] (By open access, I mean access that is digital, online, and free of charge to those able to connect to the Internet, without having to pay subscriptions either to publish or to [pay per] view, in its purest form, anyway. This in turn means free to upload to and download from, read, print, reproduce and distribute copies, and also free of most licensing and copyright restrictions.)[11] Devised and constructed by myself and Steve Green, and launched in March 2006, the aim of CSeARCH is to provide cultural studies with something like an equivalent to the arXiv.org E-Print Archive, the open-access archive for physics currently located at Cornell University in the United States.[12] This book constitutes, at least in part, an attempt to think through some of the potential implications of ongoing experiments with open-access publishing of this kind: implications for the institution of the university, but also for cultural studies, for scholarly writing and research, and for our ideas of ethics, politics, and culture.[13] (I will say more later in this book about the importance of focusing on projects with which I am involved when I talk about the specificity and singularity of new media.)

From Knowledge Economy to Academic Gift Economy

The digital reproduction and publication of academic research and scholarship in open-access journals and archives is particularly interesting in the context of the paradigmatic shifts that are currently taking place within higher education. As is now well known, governments all over the world have come to regard the management of knowledge and information as increasingly important. Whereas previously economies were understood as being driven by the manufacture of goods and services, these days it is knowledge and its successful commercial exploitation by business that is often held as the key to a society's success and future economic prosperity. Joseph Stiglitz, a Nobel Prize winner for economics and ex-senior vice president and chief economist at the World Bank, describes the situation as follows: "Knowledge and information is being produced today like cars and steel were produced a hundred years ago. Those, like Bill Gates, who know how to produce knowledge and information better than others reap the rewards, just as those who knew how to produce cars and steel a hundred years ago became the magnates of that era" (Stiglitz 1999, n.p.). As Stiglitz's reference to Bill Gates indicates, new or emerging media is perceived as playing a vital part in the development of what has come to be known as the "knowledge economy," helping to transform traditional modes of production, consumption, and distribution, and creating in their place new types of firms, products, and markets based on the commodification and communication of knowledge and information. Universities and academics are also assigned an important role in this vision of society: both in producing economically "useful" knowledge and research, which can then be commercially exploited through the establishment of links with business and industry; and in educating and training the more flexible, constantly creative, imaginative, and dynamic entrepreneurial labor force of highly skilled "knowledge workers" or "immaterial laborers" that this new economy requires.[14]

But the digital reproduction and publication of academic research is also worth exploring in the context of the debate on the current state of academia because, as Michael Hardt and Antonio Negri make clear, if knowledge, information, and "communication [have] increasingly become the fabric of production, and if linguistic co-operation has increasingly become the structure of productive corporeality, then the control over linguistic sense and meaning and the networks of communication becomes an ever more central issue for political struggle" (Hardt and Negri 2000, 404). In short, information and communication have become a principal terrain through which power relations are established today.[15] Some have even gone so far as to argue that, whereas in the past "the factory was a paradigmatic site of struggle between workers and capitalists," today it is the university that is a "key space of conflict, where the ownership of knowledge, the reproduction of the labour force, and the creation of social and cultural stratifications are all at stake" (edu-factory collective 2007). Certainly, one of the principal reasons I am interested in the digital reproduction and publication of scholarship and research is because this is one arena where some academics *have* challenged the forces of neoliberal free-market economics in a reasonably effective manner (even if this has not always been as a result of conscious or overtly radical political intentions on their part). Let me explain.

Earlier I listed a few of the elements of the "neoliberal turn" in higher education, whereby universities are acting as if they were for-profit businesses rather than not-for-profit institutions serving the public interest. However, this marketization and managerialization of the university has also been accompanied by a radical change in the world of academic publishing.

Open Access

The system of higher education that operates in many countries today has seen an expansion of the student population accompanied by a decline in the number of books provided per student by institutional libraries. Sharp reductions in public funding for universities together with the growing concentration of academic publishing within profit-driven transnational media conglomerates have combined to create a situation in which it is increasingly difficult for libraries to be able to afford to stock books, and for students to be able to afford to purchase them. To provide an example from the United States, whereas previously the University of California would have bought a copy of a particular book for each of its eight campuses—UCLA, Berkeley, Irvine, etc.—in 2002 it made a decision to purchase only one copy to share across all of them (Phillips 2002, 18). The response of many academic publishers has been to cut back drastically on their lists and to concentrate on producing readers and introductions for the relatively large undergraduate core courses. Consequently, although now more books than ever are being published by university and trade presses—certainly in the United Kingdom, where the number of new volumes published in 2005 was 206,000 (Bowker 2006)—a great many academic titles are merely repeating and repackaging old ideas and material. All of which means it is getting harder and harder for junior members of the profession to publish the kind of research-led books and monographs that often enable them to secure their first full-time position, let alone establish a reputation for originality of thought. Yet it is not just those in the early stages of their careers—whose institutions are in effect now letting decisions concerning hiring, tenure, and promotion be made for them by scholarly presses on primarily economic grounds—who should be concerned. The current state of academic publishing makes it difficult for nearly everyone (apart from a few "stars") in those fields where the full-length book is the most valued mode of publication to continue to produce certain kinds of research: research that is intellectually ambitious, challenging, even if at times difficult and time-consuming to read, and that is therefore not always particularly accessible and student friendly. If publishers cannot sell such research in sufficient amounts, they are increasingly making the decision not to publish it at all, and to focus their efforts on products that are more financially profitable instead. As a result, not only are the careers of a generation of younger scholars in danger of being damaged, but also the whole of academia risks being intellectually impoverished, as research that breaks new ground and develops new insights and understanding is rejected for publication, and hence dissemination, in favor of publications that concentrate on introducing or collecting the work of previous generations.

This situation is *not* likely to be altered by the Google Book Search project first announced in December 2004. Google's plan is to scan

digitally the books of a significant number of major research libraries—including (at the time of writing) those at Harvard University, Oxford University, Princeton University, Stanford University, the New York
Public Library, the University of Michigan, the University of California,
the University of Wisconsin–Madison, the University of Texas at Austin,
the University of Virginia, the University Complutense of Madrid, the
National Library of Catalonia, the Bavarian State Library, the University Library of Lausanne, the University of Mysore, the University of
Ghent, and Keio University—and make their contents available online
for full text searches. The aim is to eventually produce a "universal virtual library" of available knowledge to rival that constructed at Alexan-
dria around 300 B.C., which at the time was estimated to contain between 30 and 70 percent of all known books. However, at present Google
is making available only those books that are out of copyright and in
the public domain, or for which their publishers/copyright holders
have given permission; for those still within copyright, if their publishers or authors have joined Google's Partner Program, then anything
from a few sample pages to the entire book may be available, otherwise
Google will show only snippets. But even if Google *were* intending to
make all of the texts they are digitizing available for free in their en-
tirety, a book still has to be published first in ink-on-paper form for
Google to digitize it. This in turn means that, more often than not
these days, a book still has to be capable of generating a financial profit
for its initial publisher before it can appear as part of the Google Book
Search Project.[16]

A number of scholars have responded to the growing corporatization of both the academic book and journal markets by developing
open-access archives of electronically reproduced academic research.
Successful repositories of research papers have been in operation for
some time now at, among other places, Cornell University (arXiv.org)
in the United States and the University of Southampton (Cogprints) in
the United Kingdom.[17] In fact, many universities nowadays provide opportunities for staff to publish their research electronically via local
repositories,[18] and to access other stores held by institutions participating in the Open Archives Initiative (OAI) and the Scholarly Publishing
and Academic Resources Coalition (SPARC), a project designed to reduce the cost of published research work and bypass commercial publishers of increasingly expensive journals, whether printed or electronic.[19] These digital archives furnish academics with a means of

publishing their research, and making it widely available immediately upon completion to anyone who can access it, regardless of how much particular publishers decide to charge for their books and journals, and how much individual institutions and libraries can afford to pay for them. Accordingly, these archives, together with open-access electronic journals,[20] are perceived as offering a solution to many of the problems currently confronting scholars as a result of the decline in state funding for higher education and the increasingly market- and profit-driven nature of the academic publishing industry. They do so by providing an alternative model for the sharing and exchange of knowledge to that afforded by capitalist neoliberalism: one in which participants are able to give and receive information at comparatively little cost; and in which decisions over the publication and distribution of research can be made, not by the market on the basis of a text's ability to make a financial profit for its author or publisher, but according to other criteria, not least its *intellectual value and quality.*

Open Access + : Or, What's Next for Open Access?

The ramifications of "digitization"—especially the possibility of making all the research literature open access and thus available at very low cost to researchers, teachers, students, and the public, on a global scale—have been hotly debated within scientific, technical, and medical circles. Over the years vigorous discussions have taken place in high-profile organs such as *Nature, Science, American Scientist, The Times Higher Education Supplement* and even *The Guardian.*[21] For some (and this is understandably an attractive route to take, strategically or otherwise, when applying for public funding), the open-access approach is presented as providing value for money for taxpayers by ensuring they do not have to pay twice for the same piece of research: once for academics to carry out the research; and then a second time to access it in the form of journal subscriptions or book cover prices.[22] For others there is a certain amount of concern and anxiety over whether open-access publishing can be sustained as a business model, and especially over how academic standards of "quality" can be maintained in the transition to the digital mode of reproduction. Still others see open access as a means of democratizing knowledge and research by making not just journal, books, and databases, but also the computing technology that is required to develop and support them, available to those who cannot afford to invest in such resources themselves. John Willinsky refers to this as "the access principle": "namely, that a *commitment to the value and quality of research carries with it a responsibility to extend the circulation of this work as far as possible, and ideally to all who are interested in it and all who might profit by it*" (2006, 5 [emphasis in original]). From this standpoint, open access has consequences not just for academics and academia: it has potential benefits for the public and indeed democratic societies at large.

For Stevan Harnad, for example, who has long been one of the most vocal proponents of open-access archiving, the digitization and self-archiving of the refereed research literature will make:

The entire full-text refereed corpus online
On every researcher's desktop, everywhere
24 hours a day
All papers citation-interlinked
Fully searchable, navigable, retrievable
For free, for all, forever (2001/2003, n.p.)

The idea that is being promoted here is for every digital repository to join up as part of the Open Archives Initiative, which is described (somewhat problematically in my view) as being in effect one "global," "virtual archive" of jointly searchable academic work. This global archive would then provide anyone, at any networked desktop, with "seamless" access to what are called e-prints across the whole of the network (see Harnad 2001/2003, n.p.).[23] By allowing easy access to research and publications in this way—not just for academics, researchers, teachers, and students, but for editors, publishers, consultants, policy analysts, investigative reporters, union organizers, NGOs, political activists, and protest groups, too, even the general public—open access becomes a means for the free and fair distribution and exchange of knowledge and information on a worldwide scale.

In many ways the above take on the free and fair exchange of knowledge is as radical as the majority of works on open access get. Nor should the significance of this position be underestimated. Proposing a model for challenging the "complacent and comfortable habits of scholarly publishing" (Willinsky 2006, xiii), one with the potential to have a public and democratic impact that stretches far beyond the confines of the academy, and which even comes replete with a whole philosophy as to how to transform the institutions of academic publishing and research libraries on an economic basis, is obviously no mean feat.[24] Still, the fact remains that the rapidly increasing process of digitizing the academic research literature tends to be regarded for the most part as having merely a prosthetic effect on the performance of our existing disciplines and "paper" forms of publication. It is understood largely in terms of providing an increase in the amount of material that can be stored, the number of people who have access to it, the potential impact of that material, the range of distribution, the ease of information retrieval, reductions in staffing, production and reproduction costs and so forth. The argument then usually focuses on whether different aspects of this transformation can be considered to be a "good" or a "bad" thing. David J. Solomon (2006), for instance, taking as his case study the open access journal *Medical Education Online* he founded and edits, emphasizes how a system for managing the peer-review process of an open-access journal can be almost completely automated using the Internet, thus significantly reducing the costs and effort involved. Within the scientific, technical, and medical fields especially, which is where these debates have featured most prominently,[25] there has been relatively little *rigorous* or *detailed* consideration of the way in which digital texts—with their lack of "fixity" (Eisenstein 1979), stability, and permanence relative to time and place, their undermining of the boundaries separating authors, editors, producers, users, consumers, humans and machines, and their ability to incorporate sound (MP3, WMA) and still and moving images (JPEG, MPEG, streaming video)—contain the potential, not merely to *remediate* older media forms, and thus deliver a preexisting and more-or-less unchanged content, albeit in a new way, but to *transform fundamentally that content, and with it our relationship to knowledge.*[26] Neither has there been much discussion of the radical ethical and political questions digitization raises for academic and institutional authority and legitimacy. As well as advocating for open access to the scholarly research literature, then, *this book is attempting to explore and experiment with some of these latter, potentially even more uncomfortable issues and questions.*

That said, I want to make it quite clear that whatever problems and weaknesses I may locate in the ideas of those who have tried to provide a philosophy for the open-access publication of scholarly research literature, it is not my intention in this book to decry the accomplishments of Paul Ginsparg (who founded the arXiv.org E-Print Archive), Stevan Harnad, Jean-Claude Guédon, Peter Suber, John Willinsky, or any of the others who have advocated long and hard on the issue. I consider their achievements in generating interest and support for open access, not least at governmental and institutional levels, while often countering entrenched corporate and commercial interests, to have been immense. As I said earlier, one of my reasons for writing this book is certainly to advocate for open access to be adopted more extensively, particularly in the humanities.

Thus, I have focused here mainly on the consequences for academic book publishing of the neoliberal marketization and managerialization of the university, and the potential impact open access, and particularly open-access archives, can have on this. Since open access has been taken up and debated most extensively in the so-called exact sciences, most writing on the subject has presented it as a solution to the rise in prices and extremely high cost of scientific, technical, and medical (STM) journals. The adoption of this particular stance toward open access can be partly explained by the fact that prestigious, international, peer-reviewed journals are the most valued mode of publication in the sciences. Even John Willinsky, who is a professor of literacy and technology, perceives the issue predominantly through an STM lens, as it were, depicting the open-access movement in his book *The Access Principle* as a response to two "conflicting current events":

> The first of these events is a steady escalation in journal prices, with the rate neatly summarized by Peter Suber (2004) . . . as "four times faster than inflation for nearly two decades." The second event is the advent of the Internet and digital publishing, which in a decade has transformed how readers access journals and created a viable alternative to a publishing model that, as a result of the first event, was otherwise rendering more and more of the literature affordable to fewer and fewer institutions. (Willinsky 2006, xiii)

Willinsky thus argues for open access in terms that are either specific to the sciences—as he admits (147), the majority of his examples, *PloS Biology*, National Institutes of Health (NIH), *Nature*, Kenya Medical Research Institute (KEMRI), BioMed Central, and so on, are drawn from the sciences and to a lesser extent the social sciences (although Virginia Woolf, Samuel Johnson, and Jacques Derrida all get a mention)—or quite general, without going into any real detail when it comes to considering the many differences that exist between the various fields and disciplines that make up the academy. Since I am more concerned in *Digitize This Book!* with the potential impact of open access on the humanities, however, I have concentrated on changes to the world of academic book publishing and the promise offered by open-access archives. I have done so because in the humanities—and especially in those areas in which I work: cultural studies, continental philosophy, English literature, media studies, new media studies—it is books published by respected international presses, rather than journals, that are the most valued and prestigious mode of publication, functioning as the main criteria for tenure and promotion. And unlike open-access journals, open-access archives *can* include books.[27] Therefore, in arguing for the acceptance of open access in the humanities, it seems the effective tactic is to approach the issue from this more book- and archive-oriented angle.

Yet pragmatic decisions about the object of study are not the only thing that is a little different and even novel about the argument I am making here. *Digitize This Book!* also arises from my concern that a number of extremely important ethical and political questions that are being raised by digitization concerning our relationship to knowledge, and concerning academic and institutional authority and legitimacy, are, at best, being taken for granted and treated comparatively superficially and lightly, and, at worst, marginalized or even ignored by arXiv .org, Harnad, Willinsky, and others. My argument in this book is that it is imperative to address issues of knowledge and its authority and legitimacy in the context of digitization; and that doing so will enable us to see that the ethical and political consequences of open-access publishing extend far beyond, and in excess of, those anticipated and intended by the majority of people who have written about this subject to date.

Cultural Studies in the Age of Its Digital Reproducibility

Let me stay for a moment with my concern that a number of extremely important ethical and political questions that are being raised about our relationship to knowledge, and about academic and institutional authority and legitimacy by digitization, are being taken for granted and treated "complacently and comfortably" by most of those who have championed open access to date. Significantly, there has so far been relatively little explicit research carried out on the potential impact of digital reproduction, publication, and archivization either *on* or *by* cultural studies—as distinct from producing analyses of digital culture, cyberspace, virtual reality, techno-science, the "knowledge economy," "immaterial labor," biotechnology, the Internet, networked connectivity, or "Web 2.0" conducted from a cultural studies perspective. Granted, much of what I want to say in this book regarding digitization is more or less applicable to other fields. Still, cultural studies has for some time now arguably been the means by which the university thinks about itself—because of the field's concern for anti- and interdisciplinarity, its self-reflexive relation to culture, the everyday, and the other (seen in terms of sexuality or gender, race or ethnicity, etc.); its tradition of engaging with the new, the different, the marginal, the excluded, and the unusual as well as apparently useless, trivial, and unimportant forms of knowledge; its willingness to be "adventurous" and "ambitious" and to use "continental theory" to innovate "outside the scholarly tradition" (McRobbie 2000, 214); and its awareness of the aporia of authority at the heart of academic legitimacy (Rifkin 2003, 104–5). Indeed, cultural studies has for many replaced philosophy and literary studies in this respect, at least in the United Kingdom and the United States.[28] Cultural studies therefore appears to offer a privileged mode of access to questions of knowledge, ethics, politics, and the university in a way that, for example, the sciences (which have had open-access e-print archives for quite some time), and even literary studies and philosophy, do not.[29] Admittedly, as Caroline Bassett notes, "within writing that explores techno-culture . . . an increasingly influential body of work that finds its roots in medium theory and media philosophy has rejected cultural studies more or less entirely" in favor of the German media theory of Friedrich Kittler, Niklas Luhmann, and Bernhard Siegert, the philosophy of Gilles Deleuze and Félix Guattari, and the cybernetics and information theory of Claude Shannon and Norbert Wiener (Bassett 2006, 221). Nevertheless (and despite the fact that I want to draw on some of this work here, too, particularly that associated with "net criticism" and tactical media), cultural studies for me continues to provide a valuable means of, and space for, inventively reflecting on and affirmatively engaging with practices, policies, and issues concerning the university, academic authority, and institutional legitimacy as well as the consequences of digitization for our relationship to knowledge.

At the same time, in thinking about the future of the university, I want to supplement my cultural studies approach by drawing on the thought of Jacques Derrida and, to varying degrees and extents, a number of other writers who have been influenced by his work, in particular Samuel Weber, Bill Readings, Bernard Stiegler, Ernesto Laclau, and Chantal Mouffe. I want to provide this theoretical supplement for a number of reasons.

First, because the intersection of philosophy and literature associated with Derrida and "deconstruction" is one of the places where questions of ethics have been thought about most rigorously. To a large degree this has been carried out under the influence of Derrida's reading of the philosophy of Emmanuel Levinas (which is in turn indebted to Edmund Husserl's phenomenology and his view of consciousness as an intentionality that is always situated in connection to objects outside of itself). Derrida, following Levinas, defines ethics not according to traditional moral philosophy, with its predefined codes and norms, but rather as an infinite and aporetic responsibility to an "unconditional hospitality" to the other (2000, 147). Cultural studies, by contrast, although it cares deeply about "the other" and puts issues of respect, responsibility, and difference firmly on its agenda, has rarely addressed the question of ethics explicitly. This has been evident in its sometimes too quick conceptualization of who its "other" is, as well as in cultural studies' promotion or even celebration of difference at the expense of the interrogation of the ontological conditions of this difference (see Zylinska 2005).

Second, because deconstruction is one of the places where questions of politics have been thought about most rigorously, too. Even though cultural studies has nearly always defined itself as explicitly political, it has, in recent years especially, too often left the question of politics unaddressed (G. Hall 2002). Rather than endeavoring to make a responsible decision that would remain open to the specific and contingent demands of each singular conjunction of the "here" and "now"—precisely the kind of openness that one could argue resulted in the singular, "original" work and ideas that led to the emergence of cultural studies in the first place—cultural studies has tended to fetishize the politics associated with its "founding" thinkers (Raymond Williams, Stuart Hall, the Birmingham School, and so forth), their followers and interpreters, and its established canon of texts. In other words, it has frequently made decisions regarding its politics and what "the political thing to do" is based upon and derived from conceptions of politics and the political that were first produced and established in a very different historical moment and social and cultural conjuncture. This fetishization has enabled cultural studies to make seemingly endless proclamations about what politics *is* and *is not* (it *is* about action and consensus and engaging with the often unpleasant realities of the world around us, but *is not* about thinking too much about what cultural studies, or ethics, or politics is—that is boring and detracts from the real task in hand). It has also led to moralistic condemnations of other forms of and possibilities for politics on this basis, without (and indeed perhaps precisely to avoid) opening itself to the "real antagonism and dissent"—including that over ideas of what politics is and what it means to be political—that Derrida and others show is necessary for politics.[30]

Third, because having learned from Derrida the necessity of thinking about the university (see Derrida 1983; 1990; 1992a; 1992b; 2001c; 2002a; 2004), Samuel Weber and Bill Readings especially are among the most important and influential of recent writers on the authority and legitimacy of the contemporary institution.

Fourth, because the kind of analysis of ethics, politics, and the institutional structures of academic discourse they and Derrida have provided over the course of the last twenty years and more has tended to be dismissed, overlooked, or at best kept within specific limits by cultural studies. One of the reasons for this is that such theoretical meta- or self-reflection is often considered too abstract, conceptual, and naively elitist, too bound up with the very values of the university cultural studies is supposed to place in question, and therefore as taking away from the *proper* business of cultural studies, which concerns understanding and engaging in the struggle over practical, material, social, political, and economic issues in the world that lies beyond the institution. Another reason is that deconstruction is also mistakenly presented as part of the "linguistic turn" that was taken in the humanities and social sciences in the latter half of the twentieth century, a turn that we now have to move on from toward "the material" and "the real."

The above four points are in many ways interconnected. For instance, as we have seen, one of cultural studies' most influential and deeply cherished beliefs is the idea that, if cultural studies is to have any sort of politics worthy of the name, it needs to be committed to social, historical, and political movements wider than itself. From this position, in order to be political and to *do politics*, those of us within cultural studies who work in universities need to be attempting to forge hegemonic links with social movements, struggles, and forces "outside" the university. Only by doing so, it is claimed, only by moving beyond the institutionalizing and disciplining effects of the university, can cultural studies hope to achieve the sort of political impact on both society and the university it seeks.[31]

Cultural studies' somewhat moralistic insistence on engaging with the harsh realities of the world around us and associated suspicion of the institution as something that threatens to tame and discipline its otherwise radical political potential (hence cultural studies' concern with inter- and anti-disciplinarity, marginalized and excluded forms of knowledge, and so forth) has led it to pay comparatively little attention to the university in general, and the digital reproduction of academic scholarship in particular. In this respect, cultural studies has not always been as political as it thinks. Because of the emphasis that, as a result of its desire to be politically committed, cultural studies has placed on the importance of examining and engaging with "real world," pragmatic, empirical, ethnographic, and experiential issues—war, poverty, immigration, the environment, climate change, the Israel/Palestine conflict, the effects of Hurricane Katrina, and so on—many of those in cultural studies have spent relatively little time examining and engaging with the "real world" pragmatic, empirical, ethnographic, and experiential context of their own situation, which more often than not involves the university. As Alan O'Shea and Ted Striphas acknowledged in 1998, "for all the vigorous debate" that has taken place within cultural studies over the question of institutionalization, "little attention has been paid to its own institutional practices," or its own "existing institutionalizations," for that matter (O'Shea 1998, 513; Striphas 1998, 453). The absence of work on the digitization of cultural studies scholarship would be one contemporary instance of this; the relative lack of cultural studies writing on the academic publishing industry—of which Striphas's own research is an obvious exception—another (Striphas 2002, 2003; Striphas and McLeod 2006).[32] Instead, the politico-institutional forces that have determined much of the work that has been carried out in cultural studies have too often remained unexamined, precisely in favor of focusing on whatever "our current world crisis" is perceived to be at any particular time. They have therefore been left to shape and control a cultural studies that has often proceeded to act, in this respect at least, in a less-than-responsible ethical and political fashion.

That said, there are signs that things have begun to change to a certain extent. Following the increasing corporatization of the university that occurred in the 1990s and early 2000s, and often working, if not under the direct influence of Bill Readings's *The University in Ruins* (1996) and the renewed interest in the idea of the university generated by that book, then certainly in its wake, a number of people associated with cultural studies *have* turned their attention to the institution in recent years.[33] Yet even here cultural studies has tended (albeit in different ways and to differing extents) to persist in placing at least two significant limits on its own otherwise important thinking of the university.

On the one hand, cultural studies has in the main continued to adhere to conceptions of politics and the political that are decided according to the most obvious and easy-to-identify signs and labels. To be political from this point of view is still very much to be concerned with left politics, with hegemonic struggle, with forging connections with social, historical, and political movements external to the university, with engaging with pragmatic, empirical, ethnographic, and experiential issues and their articulation with broader structures, processes, and formations, and so on. So even when cultural studies *has* turned its attention toward the university—as with its longer-standing history of work on education and pedagogy[34] or its more recent analyses of the neoliberal corporatization and managerialization of the institution—this has most often been justified as an attempt to enable it to move beyond such disciplining and institutionalizing—and now corporatizing and managerializing—effects, and to connect with "real people" outside the university, and thus with cultural studies' larger democratic political project proper. The problem with this approach is that it represents a refusal to make a responsible decision as to what "the political thing" is to do in the here and now of the contemporary conjuncture. Indeed, I would argue that positions of this kind involve resorting to precisely the kind of fetishization of politics I described above. It is a fetishization where, as Slavoj Žižek points out in connection with the concept of "interpassivity" or false activity, "you think you are active, while your true position, as embodied in the fetish, is passive" (1997, 21).

On the other hand, this fetishization of politics and its placement in a transcendental position where the last thing that is raised in all this discussion of politics *is the question of politics*, has at the same time often resulted in cultural studies continuing to, at best, downplay and keep within specific limits, and at worst marginalize and even remain blind to, other means, spaces, and resources for politics and for being political. In particular, it has led to the overlooking or "forgetting" of positions that may not subscribe to cultural studies' melancholia for the politics of a past era, and that therefore cannot necessarily be recognized according to the most common-sense, taken-for-granted labels. Included in this are many political resources that are associated with the university, such as the kind of analysis of various aspects of the institutional forces, practices, and structures of academic discourse that has been provided by deconstruction.[35] Consequently, while cultural studies may on occasion have directly or indirectly drawn on the influence of a number of thinkers associated with Derrida's philosophy in recent years (Readings especially), at least enough to focus more on the university, it has tended to do so very much on its own terms. While cultural studies has incorporated those aspects of this philosophy that it can include in its already established political project, those elements that might have fundamentally challenged cultural studies, and forced it to radically rethink its politics and ethics, have by and large been marginalized or ignored. Cultural studies has deradicalized deconstruction, in other words, rather than being open to the possibility that deconstruction might radicalize it.

This is another reason I want to draw on thinkers such as Derrida, Weber, Readings, Stiegler, Laclau, and Mouffe in this book. Their work on ethics, politics, and the contemporary academic institution and its relation to emerging media technologies can help me shift cultural studies beyond some of the limits the latter has set to its own important work on and in the university. Indeed, if Derrida makes a right to philosophy crucial to the future of the university and the humanities within it, I would argue that cultural studies, since it has replaced philosophy as a means of thinking the university, is now just as vital in this respect, if not more so. Admittedly, if cultural studies is to respond responsibly and do justice to this role, we may have to be capable of imagining and inventing new forms of cultural studies—what we might call cultural studies 2.0 or, far better, next-generation cultural studies. Creating opportunities for doing so, however, is partly what this book is about.

Notes on Creating
Critical Computer Media

> *Metadata* (Greek: meta- + Latin: data "information"), literally
> "data about data," is information that describes another set of data.
> A common example is a library catalog card, which contains data
> about the contents and location of a book: It is data about the
> data in the book referred to by the card. . . . Another important
> type of data about data is the link or relationship between data. . . .
> Since metadata is also data, it is possible to have metadata of
> metadata—"meta-metadata."
>
> Metadata that is embedded with content is called *embedded
> metadata*. A data repository typically stores the metadata *detached
> from the data*.
>
> —*Wikipedia*, 2006d

A Pragmatic Institution?

Another way of thinking about this book is that it concerns some of the
stories and narratives we tell ourselves about new or emerging media.[1]
Obviously, digitization—the conversion of media that previously existed
in analogue forms (books, newspapers, films, and so forth) into digital
data that can be dealt with by computers as a series of numbers in a
binary system—is central to a lot of new media technology. But I am also
arguing for the importance, within this, of paying attention not just to the
specificity, but also the singularity of new media.[2] Which is why I am
working through a specific instance—or example or case study, to use
social science terminology (which is not, however, without problems, as
we shall see below)—in this book.

By commenting on these stories, I am of course producing yet another narrative, rearranging the discursive networks to tell a different

story, one that is woven through a number of nodal points, including capitalist free-market neoliberal economics, the "knowledge economy," "deconstructive pragmatics," papercentrism, the "crisis in tenure and publishing," the "academic gift economy," the institution of the university, academic legitimacy, authority, disciplinarity, judgment, knowledge, cognition, ethics, politics, tactical media, and post-politics. Not that the narrative I am constructing with this book is necessarily better or more true; but it is at least a story that is more attuned to questions of ethics, politics, and academic and institutional authority and legitimacy—questions that, as I shall demonstrate, have always been an important part of discourses around new media. In the process, I am creatively experimenting with the work of writers such as Jacques Derrida, Samuel Weber, and Bernard Stiegler who are operating at the intersection of philosophy and literature associated with deconstruction. These writers, in one way or another, have long been thinkers of ethics, politics, the university, media, and technology (if not necessarily in the most obvious or conventional of fashions). However, they are also thinkers of narrative and text, and as such are highly attentive to the "materiality" of language, too (even if some of them have not always paid as much attention to specific forms and practices of new media as they might).[3]

Given my mention of deconstruction, it is no doubt worth clarifying that I am *not* trying to present my interest in open-access digital publishing as an affirmative, creative, practical response on my part to the kind of criticisms that have been leveled at both cultural studies and the thought of Jacques Derrida in recent years. The argument is by now familiar: that cultural studies and deconstruction have in their different ways both been too theoretical, too philosophical, too transcendental and self-reflexive, too concerned with language and linguistics and producing texts critiquing other texts rather than dealing with concrete, practical, real life, material issues.[4] Following this line of thought, whatever problems and weaknesses *Digitize This Book!* may identify in the ideas of those who have tried to give the movement toward the open-access publication of the scholarly research literature a philosophy, the Cultural Studies e-Archive could be positioned as an actual, pragmatic, "deconstructive" institution, constructed using the Internet, the World Wide Web, HomeSite, Adobe Photoshop, VBScript, JavaScript, Microsoft SQL Server and Microsoft Windows 2000 Server, and operating within the specific material and economic context of the contemporary university and late capitalism.[5] As such, it could be presented as providing one way of answering the question that is often raised around the relation of Derrida's philosophy to the university: "How might it help launch practical initiatives for institutional transformation, taking shape in the gaps, margins, or spaces 'in-between' the contemporary situation of the university?"[6] At the same time it could also be seen to serve as a practical, pragmatic response on my part to the kind of calls that have regularly been made over the last twenty years or so for cultural studies to move away from the "high theory" that dominated the field in the 1980s and early 1990s, and return to material reality and the sort of politically engaged commitments that are regarded as lying at its roots.

Yet, for me, there are a number of question marks that would need to be placed against any attempt to portray either *Digitize This Book!* or the CSeARCH open-access archive in this fashion. It is some of these I want to draw attention to now.

The Prosumer Revolution Will Not Take Place

The first issue I want to draw attention to concerns the way in which ideas of this kind rest on certain notions of production and consumption that a lot of new media may actually be involved in challenging. To be sure, such arguments hold a certain attraction for many academics working on new media. This is because scholars can be positioned in this scenario as moving from *thinking to doing, and with it from negativity to positivity, criticism to affirmation.* Instead of offering yet more theoretical critiques of digital culture, net critics are able to depict themselves as having taken the mode of production into their own hands in order to actually *create* new media: in the form of photographic essays, digital films, CD-ROMs, personal homepages, weblogs, wikis, MySpace and Facebook pages, Second Life presentations, podcasts, even pieces of "critical software."[7]

Now, as I say, making a move of this kind from critique to creation is an extremely common fantasy among academics, and those working in media studies in particular. Yet they are not alone in thinking in this way. The notion that digital technology enables people to shift from passivity to activity, to the point where producers and consumers are one and the same, is actually fairly common in contemporary culture. Nowhere can we see this more clearly than with idea of the "prosumer." The story here is as follows. Previously, society was structured in terms of two more or less separate and distinct groups. On the one hand there were the professional producers, who could create, copy, and distribute media and cultural objects such as books, films, and TV programs. On the other there were the domestic consumers who could not. They could only use the media and cultural objects created for them by the professional producers; and they could only do so relatively passively. They could not reproduce, copy, alter or circulate them, or change them into something new, at least on a large scale. At the most they could only do so with regard to their own individually purchased and owned copies. The development of "prosumer" technologies changed all this. Originating in the video industries, these are technologies of a high enough technical standard to be able to produce work that can be recorded, broadcast, and distributed at a professional level, yet at the same time they are cheap enough to be affordable to most amateur consumers. The result is that now the consumer no longer needs to occupy a predominantly passive relation to media and cultural objects. They, too, can not only consume such objects, but also actively create, reproduce, copy, change, and circulate them on something approaching a mass-produced, professional scale in the guise of the prosumer. In their book New Media, Martin Lister et al. provide a number of examples of prosumer technologies which they present as having led to the breaking down of the "professional/amateur category" and of "the distinction between producer and consumer." These include digital video cameras (whereas once "'broadcast standard' cameras and editing equipment would . . . cost around £50,000 for a standard Betacam and Avid set up," equipment that is "'broadcast acceptable'" can now be acquired for a "tenth of that figure"), the apparatus of music production and the Web site homepage, to which we could these days also add the blog, vblog, and podcast ("anyone with an online account can now potentially publish") (Lister et al. 2003, 33). Interestingly enough, however, given our concern here with scholarly production and creation, they cite as "the ultimate figure of media 'prosumer' technology" the personal computer. "It is a technology of distribution, of consumption, as well as a technology of production. We use it to look at and listen to other people's media products, as well as to produce our own, from ripping CD compilations to editing videotape, mixing music or publishing websites" (Lister et al. 2003, 34).

The issue around ideas of this kind for me is not that digital technology does not enable a good many people, including academics, to become involved in creating media and cultural texts in this way. It does. Indeed, as I made clear earlier (and will proceed to say more about in chapter 2), whereas up until now scholars and researchers have given their work away for free to publishers who publish it only to then charge other academics fees to access it, either in the form of the cover price on books and CD-ROMs, or the cost of subscribing to journals and online databases, one of the things that is interesting and important about open-access journals, and particularly archives, is the way they provide academics with an opportunity to take control of the means of production and reproduction and publish their research themselves, using just personal computers and broadband Internet connections. In so doing, they are able to cut out the middlewomen and middlemen of the publishing industry, and in the process make their work readily available to all those who wish to access it—if not entirely for free, then certainly at a much reduced cost. My problem with the concept of the prosumer instead concerns the way in which it maintains and reinforces certain notions of production and consumption—even as it claims these distinctions are being "broken down"—that I would argue new media have helped to undo. For far from blurring these categories, the whole idea of the prosumer depends for its very existence on quite fixed, and somewhat unsophisticated conceptions of "production" and "consumption," as well as the relation between them. After all, production and consumption can be brought together like this in the guise of the prosumer only if they are positioned as having somehow been separate and distinct in the first place—which they generally are in narratives of this kind. As a range of cultural studies thinkers have insisted for some time now, however, production and consumption are much more complicated and less stable concepts than a lot of erstwhile cultural analysis has seemed to allow. Meaghan Morris wrote way back in 1988 that "in an era of deindustrialisation and increasing integration of markets and circuits alike, the problem of theorising relations between production and consumption (or thinking 'production' at all) is considerably more complex than is allowed by the reduction of the effort to do so" to what are for Morris already "anachronistic terms" (1988, 24). If this was the case in 1988, it is even more so today in the era of the "knowledge economy" and what Phil Graham has termed "hypercapitalism":

> In a technologically mediated global economy, the largest sector of which produces abstract financial instruments designed to be continually exchanged but never "consumed," questions about precisely *what* is being produced and consumed, and by whom, become

quite difficult to answer. A knowledge economy implies that the production of particular mental predispositions has become a central focus for globalised productive processes. In a system with such a singular and abstract focus, production, consumption, and circulation become an inseparable whole, and "value creation" becomes an immediate, continuous process that unites the formerly separable spheres of production, consumption, and circulation (Barlow 1998).

> Thus there can be no distinct analytical usefulness in separating these spheres within hypercapitalist political economy because the boundaries—conceptual, physical, and temporal—between them are dissolved by new media's ubiquity; by the work habits engendered by new media; and by the mass, and more importantly, the immediacy of hypercapitalist exchanges. (Graham 2002b, 9)

The problem of theorizing relations between production and consumption, and even thinking "production" and "consumption," is rendered even more complicated by the manner in which, as Hardt and Negri show, the dominant form of labor today—what they refer to as "biopolitical production" and "immaterial labor," by which they mean precisely that which creates "immaterial projects, including ideas, images, affects, and relationships"—involves not just the "production of material goods in a strictly economic sense." It "also touches on and produces all facets of social life, economic, cultural, and political" including life itself (that is, the production of consumers themselves) (2004, xvi).

The Digital Dialectic

All of this relates to a second problem I want to draw attention to regarding any positioning of open access, and CSeARCH in particular, as enabling the philosophy of Jacques Derrida or Samuel Weber, or myself, to be moved away from a concern with producing a theoretical critique (or even a theoretical "critique of a critique") of texts and on to practical, creative, material production. This has to do with the way in which ideas of this kind set new media theory up in a relation of contrast to new media practice.

Dichotomous relations between theory and practice can be found in many accounts of new media. Even those deemed most radical and theoretically sophisticated are frequently based on what Peter Lunenfeld has termed "the digital dialectic." Lunenfeld's eponymous book is structured around just such a series of tensions: between the "real and the ideal," the "body and the machine," the "medium and the message" and the "world and the screen" (2001a). The central dialectic for him, however, is that between theory and practice, Lunenfeld defining the digital dialectic precisely as "grounding the insights of theory in the constraints of practice" (Lunenfeld 2001b, xv):

> A critical theory of technological media will always be in inherent conflict with the practice of creating these very media. For if theory demands from its objects a certain stability, theory is itself free to break the tethers of its objects, to create a hermetically (and hermeneutically) sealed world unto itself. The pressures of the market and the innovations of the laboratory combine to make stability impossible within the practice of digital media, however. Yet both the market and the technologies themselves are bound by a series of constraints that theoretical texts can elide with fuzzy forecasting and the bromides about the future. The digital dialectic offers a way to talk about computer media that is open to the sophisticated methodologies of theory without ignoring the nuts and bolts or, better yet, the bits and bytes of their production. To repeat, the digital dialectic goes beyond examining what is happening to our visual and intellectual cultures as the computer recodes technologies, media, and art forms; it grounds the insights of theory in the constraints of practice. (Lunenfeld 2001b, xviii–xix)

Lunenfeld is far from alone in seeing computer media in these terms. Geert Lovink states in the introduction to *Dark Fiber*, his book of "practice-driven Internet theory," or what he calls " 'net criticism' " (2003, 17), that throughout his study the key axiomatic as far as he is concerned resides "in the feedback between theory and practice." "The emerging discipline of Internet studies, if it wants to be innovative, has to be enriched with a critical involvement in both technical, user-related matters and content matters," Lovink writes, before proceeding himself to quote from Lunenfeld on the "digital dialectic" (2003, 8).

Now I can perfectly understand why digital artists, designers, programmers, hackers, hacktervists, and others involved in writing their own software and creating their own computer programs might, when it comes to the study and understanding of new media, want to place more emphasis on practice. And of course the concept of the "digital dialectic," in which practice is given "equal weighting" to theory, allows them to do just this. I can also see a number of other advantages to treating open access in this fashion. Among them is the way such an approach aligns itself with the current interesting and at times quite useful impetus in certain strands of new media criticism to move away from the broad, hyperbolic, "the future is now" theories that for many characterized so much of the field in the mid-1990s, and toward the development of a more focused, detailed, and specific analysis of media objects, platforms (cell phones, MP3 players, Personal Navigation Devices), and software (compilers, program text editors, operating systems, application programs—Windows Media Player, VideoLAN Client, MPlayer, and so on). N. Katherine Hayles argues along these lines in her 2002 book, *Writing Machines*: "We are near the beginning of a theory of media-specific analysis in literary studies," she writes. "Many people . . . are now . . . moving from print-orientated perspectives to frameworks that implicitly require the comparison of electronic textuality and print to clarify the specificities of each" (2002, 106).[8] It is an approach that takes far more account of the specific *materiality* of new media (even though it may see that materiality as an "emergent property" [Hayles 2002, 33]), and that engages with media technologies, as Matthew Fuller puts it, not on the "basis of a category or class of objects" but rather with "specific instances of that class" (Fuller 2003, 16).

In this respect I believe it is important that *Digitize This Book!* takes as part of its focus a subject drawn from my own, "personal," "practical" experience as a new media writer, editor, publisher, and open-access archivist. Not least because this enables me to respond to Jeffrey Sconce's point that "so much of the writing on new media [is] concerned with other writing on new media rather than new media itself" (2003, 189); and also to Mark Poster's criticisms of Derrida's own account of new media technologies, and virtual reality especially, in *Specters of Marx* (Derrida 1994a). For Poster, despite sensing the "need to account for differential materialities of the media," Derrida "tends to preserve the philosopher's taste for the general over the cultural analyst's penchant for the particular," providing "strings of hyphenated terms, 'tele-technology' or 'techno-scientifico-economico-media,' that vaguely point .in a direction without guiding the virtual traveller in any particular direction" (Poster 2001a, 140–41). Certainly, one of the main criticisms anyone dealing with the impact of digital technology risks facing nowadays *is* that he or she is talking about some rather vague and general possible future consequences of new media, without examining particular material instances of digital culture in detail; or, in this case, without pointing to what a *digital cultural studies* (as opposed to yet another cultural studies analysis of the digital) or a *digital institution* might actually look like, what forms it could actually take.

Still, even though I am sympathetic to some strategic uses of the argument concerning practice and the need to explore and engage with it in the study of new media, I want to make it quite clear that this book should not be taken as:

1. A case study—since that would imply I already have my theory of new media worked out and decided in advance, and that I am merely using open-access publishing and archiving, and with them CSeARCH and *Digitize This Book!*, as a means of illustrating this theory. Any such new philosophy of new media would fail to remain open to the singularity either of CSeARCH, or of *Digitize This Book!*, or to the affective performativity of their functioning. In other words, such a "case study approach" would take little or no account of the way in which, as I argue in this book, the ethics and politics of open-access publishing and archiving do not simply come prepackaged, but have to be creatively produced and invented by their users in the process of actually using them.[9]

2. A form of digital dialecticism—at least of the kind Peter Lunenfeld refers to, where a focus on analyzing how these "media are created and work" is utilized to avoid the danger of slipping into some theoretical fantasy land, where the focus is on "the implications of technologies (especially where something could go)," rather than the "technologies themselves" (2001b, xix).

For me, thinking about new media and open access raises a number of issues and problems for the concept of the digital dialectic.

The Street Life of Computers

One particular concern I have is that an emphasis on practice almost invariably results in a lack of rigorous attention being paid to the theory that underpins and helps to shape approaches to new media. The digital dialectic as described by Lunenfeld, Lovink, and others is no exception to this. In fact, this idea, that theory should be positioned in a dialectical relation to practice, is itself a classical theoretical idea. Granted, it may well be suggested that a lot of attention *is* being paid to theory in the digital dialectic. Yet while it may *appear* as if theory is being assigned an equal role and status in the relationship with practice here, it is actually being kept within certain limits. For one of the things theory frequently does, in some of its guises at least, is bring into question notions of practice, *and indeed theory,* as well as any simplistic conceptions of the dialectical relation between them. So it is only by marginalizing or ignoring this important aspect of theory that an attempt to combine new media theory with new media practice in this fashion can be made.

Whether it is immersed in the cultural and media theory of Guy Debord, Vilém Flusser, Michel de Certeau, Marshall McLuhan, Gilles Deleuze, Félix Guattari, Michel Foucault, Jean Baudrillard, Donna J. Haraway, Paul Virilio, Friedrich Kittler, and others or not, a dialectical approach to net criticism is, in effect, a way of positioning theory, if not in terms of what Homi Bhabha referred to as the "damaging and self-defeating" notion that has often and elsewhere afflicted it—that is, that theory is "necessarily the elite language of the socially and culturally privileged" (1994, 19)—then certainly as a potential threat to, or distraction from, the *real* job of "net criticism." The real job, as we have seen, tends to be very much "grounded in the constraints of practice" and presents itself as "practice driven." As a result, the concept of practice continues to function as something of a fetish, similar to the way politics, activism, and "the street" do in other media and cultural studies–related discourses (see Bowman 2006b; Dean 2005), where it is important to talk about being practical, about engaging with those who make policy decisions, about getting involved with political activists, relating to the kids on the street, and so on, because all this is held as having to do with actual, concrete, political materiality. So talking about practice feels, you know . . . well, *really real.*

Of course, when it comes to much new media criticism, the dialectical nature of their relation means that theory is to all intents and purposes assigned a place where it should be able to help us think through some of these ideas regarding practice, or at least act as a brake on and counterbalance to this fetishistic tendency. In order for practice to take place and even exist as "practice" at all in this dialectical sense, however, it is necessary for theory's capacity to rigorously interrogate accepted ideas of theory and practice, as well as the dialectic between them, to be placed within specific limits. Which means that, despite the manner in which it is apparently positioned in the digital dialectic, *theory can never be taken on board sufficiently to bring such fundamental notions of the identity, role, place, and purpose of new media practice into question.* As a result, for all that the dialectical nature of their relation means that each side is *supposed* to be capable of interrogating the other, there is still the very real danger of conveying the impression that to be involved with the actual specifics of creating with computer media —with software production, programming, coding, and so on—is somehow more material, more political, more *real*; that it, too, is to be involved with action, with "concrete-reality," with a "street-knowledge of the net," as it were.

We Have Never Been Practical

Efforts to set up new media theory and practice in a dialectical relation by attempting to integrate some of the concerns of each—"the sophisticated methodologies of theory" together with "the bits and bytes" of computer media production, as Lunenfeld puts it—also risk underestimating the degree to which each position is already implicated in the other so that they do not represent contrasting options in the first place. I am thinking, not so much of the by now more or less banal point that there can be no pre-given or essentialist opposition between theory and practice, as theory is already being placed in a supplementary relation to practice here; that it is only by opposing him or herself to the new media theorist that the digital dialectician can establish and define him or herself as different.[10] The reason new media theory and practice do not represent contrasting options for me has more to do with the way in which each side in this relation contains, and is made up of, many elements that are otherwise described as belonging to the other. What I mean by this is not just that a lot of new media theory *has already* been concerned with the hard-edged "materiality" of particular instances of digital technology—although I would argue that it has. I am also referring to the performative aspect of many so-called theoretical texts. I have in mind not just the writing of such texts but also the publishing, marketing, selling, and reviewing of them. Such supposedly "theoretical" texts, I would maintain, are capable of functioning as singular, active, affective, affirmative, "practical" events, gestures, and interventions into the here-and-now space of history, culture, and the institution of the university. Moreover, this is the case not just with regard to works reproduced in the digital medium, but also with regard to those in ink-on-paper form. (One need only think of many of the works of Jacques Derrida, Gilles Deleuze, and Félix Guattari to see that. In this respect it is a shame that some of those who are advocating for more attention to be paid to specific "material" forms of new media do not also pay more attention to specific "material" forms of theory.)

By the same token, new media practice is not something that exists outside of and that comes only *after* the moment of theorization. Nor is practice something that comes *before* theory, something that the latter then merely provides an explanation of. There can be no new media practice without theory. In a sense new media practice has never been "practical": not only because the practices of new media production—the work of coders, programmers, designers of human-computer interfaces, and so on—are invariably informed and underpinned by theory and theoretical investments of some sort, whether consciously or not, dialectically or not (so there is no easy distinction that can be made between theory and practice); but also because the practical—along with other sociopolitical referents such as the people, the activist, the street, the community, the multitude—is *constructed* in and through theory, through strategies of writing, textuality, language, and discourse. New media practice, then, has *always* been a matter of theory.

I mention all this not to suggest that new media theory and practice are the same: they of course have their different operational qualities, modalities, expository purposes, and effects.[11] Nor do I want to simply repeat the "post-structuralist" cliché that practice, production, and the material are not pre-given and do not exist outside of language and the text in some essential, naturalistic sense. I am mentioning it rather to emphasize the manner in which the fact that new media practice has never been simply practical requires us to undo and reconceive the relation between "writing on new media" and "new media practice," not least to take account of the force and effect of new media theory as a productive discourse: one that *creates* and defines (rather than simply reflects) the practical, and simultaneously renders it available as an article or aim *for* practice.

This is a significant point. Unless it is understood, and the complexity of the relation between theory and practice and what is meant by practice—and theory, for that matter—is thought through accordingly, there is every likelihood of producing rather uninteresting, confused, and contradictory theoretical and/or practical work. One of the places where this can indeed be seen to be the case is precisely with the fetishization of practice within a lot of recent new media studies. Here, the emphasis on practice, on doing something active, creative, affirmative, or pragmatic, frequently prevents "something" active, creative, affirmative, or pragmatic from "really" happening, from actually taking place. Too often the technology acts merely as a screen onto which the fantasy of action, of doing something practical and having an effect, is projected.[12] In fact, I would suggest that, of the two, far from being something that needs to be kept within certain limits, it is actually theory that is capable of being the more effective (and affective) practically—at least to the degree that it is more likely to take into account the metaphysical ideas and philosophical beliefs that affect the operation and development of "net criticism" (including the fetishization of theory in turn), and thus less susceptible to being blindly shaped and controlled by them.

I want to develop a similar case for the emphasis within new media criticism that is often placed on supporting and valuing "amateur practice." This is something Critical Art Ensemble (CAE) do, for instance, in their account of tactical media (with which Geert Lovink is also associated, and which I discuss in more detail in chapter 4). Amateur practice is important to Critical Art Ensemble because, for them, "amateurs have the ability to see through the dominant paradigms, are freer to recombine elements of paradigms thought long dead, and can apply everyday life experience to their deliberations. Most importantly, however, amateurs are not invested in institutionalized systems of knowledge production and policy construction, and hence do not have irresistible forces guiding the outcome of their process such as maintaining a place in the funding hierarchy, or maintaining prestige-capital" (Critical Art Ensemble 2001, 9). Now, while I would go along with much of CAE's stress on adopting a critical approach to dominant paradigms and institutionalized systems of knowledge, there is a danger with this kind of privileging of amateurism of slipping over into a lack of rigor, and of tactical media activists remaining unwittingly trapped in the very discourses they are trying to elude (as we shall see in chapter 4). This is because the attempt to be "freer" from such forces by situating ourselves outside professions and institutions can lead to us being recuperated by them without being aware of it—not least in terms of the "specialisms" that are often associated with the practices of tactical activism and CAE. As I pointed out in my Introduction, this suspicion of the institution as something that threatens to tame and discipline the otherwise radical political potential of a given discourse or practice too often results in insufficient attention being paid to institutions in general and the university in particular. Yet the university is one of the main sites for the professionalization of critical discourses and media practice;[13] and the university is also where many tactical media activists find employment from time to time, something that, as Andreas Broeckmann acknowledges, is "no doubt necessary for creating a sustainable practice and infrastructures" (Garcia and Lovink 2001, n.p.). Furthermore, as Peggy Kamuf points out, "the call to 'leave the university behind' like this also abandons this institution as itself an important site for direct political action and intervention" (2004, n.p.).[14] Certainly, my concern is that the emphasis on practice that is such a characteristic feature of the thought of those who situate their work in terms of the digital dialectic will result in downplaying (and at worst marginalizing and even remaining blind to) other means and resources for practice and for being political, both inside and outside the university—including those creative experiments and innovations in thinking and writing that often take place in, or are placed under the name of, theory, and that may not be regarded as either practical or political so long as the latter are to be recognized only with the help of the most obvious signs and labels.[15]

The Creative Industries Ideology

Regardless of whether it is combined in a dialectical relationship with theory or not, then, we should be wary of assuming that, because it *appears* to be more *active, affirmative, creative, pragmatic, material, or real*—new media practice is per se a more effective, radical, and subversive thing to do than, say, writing an academic journal article or publishing an ink-on-paper book. Indeed, I offer what initially might sound like a rather odd and counterintuitive hypothesis: that practice can often be quite conservative. I say this because, as the university becomes more and more commercially oriented, far from challenging capitalist free-market neoliberalism and its emphasis on instrumentalism, on vocationalism, and on being useful to business and industry, being "practical" and "practice driven" often goes along with the discourses of the new economy and their regular attacks on philosophy and cultural studies alike for being too critical and for not being useful or vocational enough. As Clare Birchall and I have shown elsewhere, universities have been placed under increasing pressure to attract financial support from external sources other than public funding. As a result, they have had to devote large amounts of time and attention to addressing practical questions and achieving instrumental outcomes of a kind that do not always sit easily with more "theoretical," less goal-oriented research. In particular, academics have been encouraged to deliver research that serves the neoliberal economy: research that is considered economically and socially productive, that is accessible and useful to a wider audience outside the university, and that is thus potentially supportable and fundable, not just by government and the research councils, but also by those in business, industry, the media, charities, and policy institutes. What is more, this state of affairs has affected not just those more obviously practical areas of study and research that are most explicitly associated with the knowledge economy: business, management, science, technology, computing engineering, and so on. There has been a related effect within the arts and humanities as well, as academics specializing in humanist discourses involved with creativity and invention now find themselves in favor with research councils, university managers, and students-as-paying-customers alike.[16] This is not simply a one-way street, where those aspects of the arts and humanities deemed important and useful in the global economy are extracted and incorporated into more commercially profitable areas of study. Terry Flew writes of "a feedback loop in operation, where discourses identified as having their origins in the arts have filtered through to business, and now returned to artistic and cultural practice through the concept of the 'creative industries,' where artists are increasingly expected to view themselves as *cultural entrepreneurs* ['involuntary entrepreneurs,' as others have described it], managing their creative talents, personal lives and professional identities in ways that maximise their capacity to achieve financial gain, personal satisfaction and have fun" (Flew 2004, 2; quoted in Hall and Birchall 2006a, 9).[17] This approach has been dubbed by Danny Butt and Ned Rossiter as "the Queensland ideology" with regard to the situation in Australia, owing to the emphasis placed on the vocational preparation of students for employment in the cultural and creative industries by the Creative Industries Faculty at Queensland's University of Technology in particular. And it has been criticized accordingly: for its "lack of critical attention to the new economic regimes underpinning the contemporary cultural field," as well as to problems of "uneven development, Intellectual Property Regimes, and the capacity," or lack of it, "for universities to compete effectively with corporations." "By failing to attend to broader social and economic contexts," Butt and Rossiter write, "the Queensland Ideology has hitched the value of academic labour to the value of the market . . . with little leverage to shape the overall forces determining cultural production" (2002).[18]

Digital Deconstruction

I should emphasize that, for all my suspicion of the current fetishization of practice and emphasis on the "creative industries" and "creative economy," I am not suggesting that those of us who are interested in new media *should not* try to "do practice," or get personally involved in making digital films, online journals, personal homepages, weblogs, vblogs, wikis, podcasts, and open-access repositories, or in analyzing particular Web browsers, search engines, open-source code, communication protocols, file structures and so on, and that we should *just* "do theory" instead and speculate over the future implications of digital media in a manner that remains free from the constraints produced by the "pressures of the market and the innovations of the laboratory." Nor, for all my emphasis on the philosophy of Jacques Derrida, am I implying that what we really need to do is just work on some transcendental or *meta* level. I am certainly not advocating that the need to think and to be as theoretically rigorous as possible should be used as an excuse for a failure to pay attention to the "nuts and bolts" of new media production. We still have to be "practical." After all, in setting up the Cultural Studies e-Archive I have been involved in the creative production of what for some could be termed a pragmatic, political institution, constructed using digital technology and invented and designed to take an affirmative ethical and political position with regard to academic publishing and the institution of the university.

My point—which is a multiple one—is rather that:

1. There are many more forms of engaging with new media than theory and/or practice (even if this proposition might initially sound counterintuitive or absurd).
2. Many of the effects of these different forms are likely to be rendered invisible if they are to be recognized only in terms of "theory," "practice," or some dialectical combination of, or relation between, the two.
3. If our understanding and analysis of new media is to be effective, we need to be able to "do" *both* theory *and* practice, while

simultaneously challenging any simple differentiation between them (which is perhaps not too far off from what I am doing with this book and CSeARCH).

So, as I say, I am not arguing against practice, or against getting involved in creating with computer media; nor am I saying that "theory" cannot learn from "practice," or that practice cannot lead us to new ways of thinking and theorizing. What I *am* trying to emphasize is that, for "Internet theory," or "new media studies" (or whatever you want to call it) to be "practically" effective, it also has to be capable of placing such conceptions of practice at risk: of questioning and critiquing and experimenting with them. We need to refuse to place a limit on theory and its questioning of practice and ask: What is meant by theory and practice here? In particular, as far as the kind of emphasis on practice that is common in new media circles is concerned, we need to ask: What is practice? Is practice self-identical? Is practice always and everywhere the same?[19]

Reformatting the Political

I want to conclude this introductory section by noting a number of final problems concerning the idea that open-access publishing and archiving makes it possible for me to move my "deconstructive" philosophy away from a concern with producing a "critique of a critique" of texts and on to practical, positive, material production—in this case of a pragmatic, political institution, constructed using HomeSite, Adobe Photoshop, VBScript, and JavaScript, and designed to facilitate the creation of a "global information commons," a new, revitalized form of public sphere, or an academic "high-tech gift economy" (see chapter 4).

One further difficulty with this position is that it risks implying that other forms of deconstruction (those apart from mine that *do not* involve the creation of a material/virtual institution) *are* just a negative form of transcendental critique, which is far from the case. There is also a related danger of suggesting that, in contrast to what I am doing here, other forms of deconstruction are *not* concerned with the institution. Yet deconstruction, for Derrida at any rate, is a constant taking of an affirmative position, with regard to the institution especially (Derrida 1992a).

A still further problem with adopting an approach of this kind is that to argue that open access is political in this explicit, a priori way, would be to give the impression that it is so simply because it conforms to some already established and easily recognized criteria of *what it is to be political*. As Richard Barbrook writes with regard to the music business, however, as far as digital culture is concerned, what *appears* to be the most political thing to do is not always necessarily the case:

> The music business has long prided itself in its skill at spotting the latest trends and its ability to make money out of the most subversive forms of youth subculture. Back in the 1960s, the hippie generation had called for political revolution—and broke almost every aesthetic and social taboo. Yet the music industry was still able to profit from its cultural creativity. Compared to their predecessors, the ambitions of the Napster generation seemed much more modest: sharing cool tunes over the Net. Ironically, it was this apparently apolitical youth subculture which—for the first time—confronted the music industry with an impossible demand. Everything is permitted within the wonderful world of pop with only one exception: free music. (2002, n.p.)

In other words, politics would be reduced to just the rolling out of a political plan, project, or program that is already known and decided upon *in advance*. As such, little or no account would, or could, be taken here of the possibility that politics on the Internet—like digital texts themselves (at least as I describe the possibilities in chapters 2 and 3)—may be different, new, innovative, exceptional, surprising; or of the way in which (as we shall see in chapters 4 and 5 and in my Conclusion), the net has the potential to change the very nature of politics and how we understand it, especially its current "modern" basis on notions of citizenship, the public sphere, and democracy. There would be no responsible or ethical opening to the future, the unknown, uncertain, unseen, and unexpected (as I describe it in chapters 2 and 3), at least in terms of any understanding of Internet politics. Instead, to take this approach would imply that what politics is, what it means to be political, is already more or less known—whereas deconstruction, very much like the Internet for Mark Poster, is rather "hyperpoliticizing" (as we shall see in chapters 4 and 5 and my Conclusion): "Politicization never ceases because undecidability continues to inhabit the decision" (Mouffe 1996, 136).

I. INTERNETHICS

Why All Academic Research and Scholarship Should Be Made Available in Online Open-Access Archives—Now!

In 2000, for the first time in over a decade—some say for the first time ever—worldwide sales of music compact discs (CDs) fell. The decline continued the following year. The sale of CD singles in the United States, for example, dropped by almost 40 percent in 2000, and fell a further 10 percent in 2001 (Harmon 2002).[1] For a while, only France and Great Britain bucked this global downward trend, in the latter's case partly thanks to the huge success of artists such as Robbie Williams and Dido (remember her?). Yet with the value of United Kingdom music shipments dropping by 3.7 percent to £1.2 billion in 2002, even the previously buoyant British market soon went into decline (Cassy 2003, 22).[2] This left many music industry chiefs frantically scrabbling for explanations. Among the most popular put forward were the slowing down of the world economy, the increase in popularity of CD "rewriters," which enable individuals to make their own CDs, the fact that most people had by then long since replaced their old vinyl recordings with compact disc versions, and the preference among young people to spend their money on ring tones for their mobile phones instead. But there was another explanation, one with far more profound potential consequences for the music industry: Napster.

Software Communism?

Napster was originally a software tool for sharing MP3 files.[3] It was written in 1999 by a then nineteen-year-old student, Shawn Fanning, and was given its title after his nickname at school—he had short, very tight, curly hair. Specially designed for the Web, MP3 files allow users to make free digital copies of their vinyl and CD collections to a very high standard of sound quality. At first MP3 represented merely a technological update on home cassette taping and the associated debates of the 1970s. MP3 is open standard, without copyright protection. That makes it hard for music companies to prevent people from copying and distributing their products without paying for them first. Initially, the big difference between home taping and MP3 lay in the ease and scale with which the copied recordings could be shared. In marked contrast to cassettes, MP3 files can be transmitted from user to user over the Internet, stored on their computer hard drives, and then played back either on their computers or MP3 players. In the early days of MP3 this was not seen as *too* much of a problem. That is because, as with home taping, people tended to exchange these files mainly on an individual basis: among family, friends, and work colleagues. Until Napster, that is. Napster transformed the situation by organizing the process of exchange, simultaneously increasing, *vastly*, the amount of recorded material available. The process works as follows. When a person logs on to Napster, the software reads the hard disk of his or her computer for music files and adds them to its central directory. All anyone looking for free music then has to do is search Napster's directory for the artists or songs they want and download them from there.

Now when it comes to "music piracy"—or "software communism," as some prefer to see it—Napster is pretty old hat these days. I have begun with Napster because it is referenced as the "first" and "groundbreaking" phenomenon in most accounts of file-sharing.[4] Successfully sued for violation of copyright in July 2000, Napster has long since been forced to remove all copyrighted files from its database. In late 2000, in an attempt to reinvent itself as a legitimate business, Napster even signed a deal with Bertelsmann, one of the world's leading music and entertainment companies (who, together with Universal Music, the Recording Industry Association of America [RIAA], Sony Music, AOL Time Warner, and EMI, originally filed the lawsuit against Napster), to access their music catalogue, and subsequently proceeded to operate on a monthly subscription basis. It has not been particularly successful in this respect, however. According to one report, whereas in "the summer of 2000, the peer-to-peer music company had more than 67m registered users swapping files free of charge—an internet phenomenon," by May 2001 it was on the verge of bankruptcy until the Bertelsmann media conglomerate stepped in, its subsequent "transition from a free service to a subscription model" causing users to abandon it en masse (Abrahams and Harding 2002). Napster's site did indeed close down for a while. Then in November 2003 a version of Napster was relaunched by Roxio, who had initially bought Napster's unsuccessful legal competitor, Pressplay. In 2002 Roxio also bought the Napster brand name, a move that subsequently enabled them to rebrand and relaunch the unsuccessful Pressplay as the more competitive and "net-cred" Napster.

But the story does not end, or even begin, with Napster. As Napster was struggling through the courts, Grokster (which was itself closed down in November 2005), Kazaa (subsequently sued and forced to op-erate on a more legitimate, legal basis), Gnutella, eDonkey, FastTrack, eMule, BitTorrent and a range of other unauthorized free music down-load sites and file-sharing networks, applications, and protocols all took its place on the Internet.[5] All of which has led to a whole series of argu-ments and disputes. Do Napster, eDonkey, FastTrack, Gnutella, and others provide a model for revolutionizing the music industry? Or are they examples of the general failure of so much digital culture to es-cape big media's power of incorporation for any significant length of time? Witness the establishment by companies such as Apple, HMV, and Virgin of Web sites for legal digital music downloads (i.e., iTunes, HMV Digital, and Virgin Digital), where, for a relatively low price—which always seems cheap until one remembers that the cost of repro-duction is next to nothing—music lovers can choose from thousands of available online tracks and download them directly onto their comput-ers and portable media players, such as Apple iPods or Creative Zens, without ever having to set foot in a record store.[6] Sales of downloaded tracks are now even allowed to count alongside record and CD sales in the charts' ranking of the most popular music. Moreover, recent years have seen the development of "Web 2.0," "Live Web" or "social network-ing" sites—MySpace and Facebook are perhaps still the most well-known in the United States and United Kingdom—where musicians can promote, distribute, and even sell their music direct to their fans, often bypassing the big music companies altogether.[7] The Arctic Mon-keys, Gnarls Barkley, and Lily Allen are the artists most frequently cited as having come to success in this way—although it has to be said a lot of people regard this idea as yet more hype promoted by the record companies.[8]

But let's hold off with the usual debates around Napster, peer-to-peer file sharing and Web 2.0 for the moment (though I return to them in chapter 4) and play a game of science fiction instead. Let's imagine that at some point in the not too distant future it is going to be possible to have an academic equivalent to Napster, eDonkey, Gnutella, Fast-Track, and BitTorrent.

Academic Publishing 2.0?

As I imagine the majority of those who have recently either taught or studied in a university will be only too aware, the system of higher education that operates in many countries today is one in which an expansion of student numbers has gone hand in hand with a decline in the number of books per student that are provided by university and college libraries. Severe cuts in funding, brought about by the attempts of successive governments to compete in the global marketplace by reducing their state budget deficits through decreases in public spending, not least on higher education, have produced a situation in which it is increasingly difficult for libraries to afford to stock books, and for students to be able to buy them. Not just teaching and learning have been affected. Building a career, even simply surviving as an academic, is today more than ever dependent on publications. Yet as both institutions and students have found it harder and harder to purchase texts, the traditional market for the scholarly book has been substantially eroded. This fact, together with the acquisition and merger of many publishing houses by transnational media conglomerates who frequently expect their publishing divisions to operate according to the same kind of profit margins as other areas of their business (such as music, film, and television),[9] has led a number of publishers of academic texts to cut back sharply on their commissions. In some areas, many publishers have decided to focus on introductions and readers for the relatively large (and so more profitable for their shareholders) first-year undergraduate "core course" markets, and hardly produce books for second- and third-year students, let alone research monographs or even edited collections of original scholarship aimed at postgraduates and other researchers, at all. So bad has the situation become in the United States that in May 2002 Stephen Greenblatt, president of the Modern Language Association (MLA), produced an open letter calling for "Action on Problems in Scholarly Book Publishing":

> [O]ver the course of the last few decades, most departments of language and literature have come to demand that junior faculty

members produce, as a condition for being seriously considered for promotion to tenure, a full-length scholarly book published by a reputable press. . . . The immediate problem, however, is that university presses, which in the past brought out the vast majority of scholarly books, are cutting back on the publication of works in some areas of language and literature. Indeed, we are told that certain presses have eliminated editorial positions in our disciplines. . . .

Some junior faculty members who will be reviewed for tenure in this academic year . . . find themselves in a maddening double bind. They face a challenge—under inflexible time constraints and with very high stakes—that many of them may be unable to meet successfully, no matter how strong or serious their scholarly achievement, because academic presses simply cannot afford to publish their books. . . .

We are concerned because people who have spent years of professional training—our students, our colleagues—are at risk. Their careers are in jeopardy, and higher education stands to lose, or at least severely to damage, a generation of young scholars. (Greenblatt 2002)

Of course, such problems have been offset *to a degree* by the seemingly endless stream of new journals that are being created to meet the demand from academics for ever more "research impact," Research Assessment Exercise (RAE), and Research Quality Framework (RQF) submittable publishing opportunities. The *International Journal of Cultural Studies*, the *European Journal of Cultural Studies*, *Cultural Studies<=>Critical Methodologies*, the *Journal of Visual Culture*, the *Journal of Consumer Culture*, and *Crime, Media, Culture* are just some of the titles that have appeared in the cultural studies field in recent years from Sage alone. Still, a shortage of funds produced by decreasing budgets and the rapidly increasing costs of scientific, technical, and medical journals has meant that, far from expanding the number of periodicals they take, many university libraries are unable to sustain their current holdings. So even if authors do manage to get published in one of these organs, the chances of anyone having access to their work, let alone reading it, are not necessarily growing; indeed, according to some they are becoming slimmer all the time.[10] (As an academic one regularly hears rumors that the average readership for a journal article is, frighteningly enough, somewhere between just three and seven readers.) The fact that the major book chains are increasingly reluctant to stock academic titles—journals especially, but also books—only exacerbates the situation, as does the fact that more and more independent bookstores are closing because of competition from Amazon.com at one end of the market and the likes of (in the United Kingdom) Tescos, Asda, and Waterstones at the other, with even branches of the latter shutting up shop on university campuses (including Goldsmiths, Brunel, and Royal Holloway in London) in 2006.

But, as I say, let's play a game of science fiction and imagine for a moment: What would it be like if it *were* possible to have an academic equivalent to the peer-to-peer file sharing practices associated with Napster, eMule, and BitTorrent, something dealing with written texts rather than music? What would the consequences be for the way in which scholarly research is conceived, communicated, acquired, exchanged, practiced, and understood?

For one thing, a free academic text download (and upload) site of this kind would provide a way around some of the problems created by the kind of restrictive copyright regulations that enable the publishing industry to limit the number of photocopied texts (and the percentage of those texts) university lecturers can give to their students (I will come to the legalities of all this in a moment). Academics could provide their classes with as many copies of books and journal articles as they liked, simply by supplying students with an address where they can find them on the net and download them for free. By "splicing and dicing" from other texts, tutors could even put their own readers together in this fashion, and ensure that they are constructed to suit the exact requirements of their specific courses (rather than having to rely on those huge doorstoppers that are produced by other people with their own courses in mind, and which never quite seem to do the job), while simultaneously meeting the demand for prepackaged material created "partly because of student poverty and partly because of the rise of the student as customer" (Midgley 2002, 15). Most important of all, perhaps, at least as far as many of those working in the humanities are concerned (where, in contrast to the "hard" or "exact" sciences, more importance tends to be attached to writing academic monographs than to publishing in peer-reviewed journals), academics and researchers would no longer need to worry about whether their next project was going to appeal to a publisher as something that could be marketed and sold. They could forget about this, secure in the knowledge that as soon as they have finished slaving over their text it can be made readily available—to anyone, anywhere in the world (provided, of course, that that person has a computer and access to the Internet). What is more, their text can remain available for as long as they wish—so they never again need to suffer the indignity of having their work go out of print after only eighteen months because their publisher only brought out a hardback book version, which cost £50/$US99 apiece and which few people except institutional libraries could afford to purchase.[11]

Knowledgedroppers of the World Unite!

Now I realize that at this point some people may be thinking: "Yeah, yeah, more *cyberbabble!*" Despite what I said earlier about science fiction, however, this is all not as far-fetched and utopian as it sounds. There are already a number of "free text," open-access sites similar to this in operation on the Internet. Perhaps the best-known and most influential of these is the arXiv.org E-Print Archive, which was founded in 1991 by Paul Ginsparg and originally based at the Los Alamos National Laboratory before moving to Cornell University in December 2001.[12] Initially established for high-energy physics—although it has since expanded to encompass other areas of physics, as well as mathematics, computer science, and quantitative biology—this archive had by August 2006 carried more than 379,940 submissions, deposits of a further 54,000 per year, and was receiving 270,000 connections daily at fourteen mirrored sites worldwide. The arXiv.org E-Print Archive works as follows. Whenever a scholar in one of the fields covered by the archive is about to submit a paper to a refereed scholarly journal for publication, he or she sends what is called a preprint copy to arXiv.org. This self-archived preprint is then made available to any researcher, scholar, or student who wants it, without charge. All the reader has to do is download the file from the archive.

Nor does copyright present a problem. One way in which the e-print archiving system is able to avoid falling foul of copyright agreements where necessary (that is, where the publisher's policy or copyright agreement does not already allow the archiving of the final version of the text in an open-access repository), is by means of what is called the "Harnad/Oppenheim preprint and corrigenda strategy" (see Harnad 2001/2003), as an article in *The Times Higher Education Supplement* verified some time ago:

First the author posts a pre-print of his or her paper on the web. Then they submit the paper to a refereed journal. The author makes amendments in light of referees' and editors' comments, then signs the publisher's copyright agreement. . . . The author then posts a note onto the web pre-print, pointing out where areas of correction might need to be made, in effect turning the pre-print into a version of the draft refereed paper. [According to the authors of this strategy], "[i]f these steps are followed, the author has done nothing wrong, has broken no law and has not signed a contract he or she should not have signed." (Patel 2000, 12; see also Oppenheim 2001, 2004)[13]

This last point—that the author is not doing anything illegal by publishing open access in this fashion—is important, as it highlights one of the major differences between the open-access archiving of e-prints and the original Napster, and thus provides a means of overcoming what is, potentially, a major hurdle to making such a free academic text download site a real possibility (instead of a mere science-fiction fantasy).[14] After all, Napster was sued because it infringed upon the rights of music companies and musicians to own and profit from their music.[15] Archiving academic texts electronically in the manner described above, however, is not illegal because of the specific way in which academia works. Unlike Sony, the Motion Picture Association of America,[16] Metallica, Sting, Eminem, Britney Spears, Madonna, or even most authors of other forms of writing (novels, plays, screenplays, newspaper and magazine articles, computer programs . . .), academics tend not to be too concerned about getting paid a fee for, or receiving royalties from their research publications. (They're in the wrong business if they are.) As Stevan Harnad, one of the coauthors of the Harnad/Oppenheim preprint and corrigenda strategy, and himself a vociferous advocate of the e-print archiving system, has emphasized, the main priority of most academics is to have their research read by as many people as possible, in the hope, not only of receiving greater levels of feedback and recognition for their work, and thus an enhanced reputation, but also of having the biggest possible *impact* on future research, and perhaps even society. So they are perfectly willing to in effect *give their work away for free* to anyone who can bring this about. In fact, this is often how academics derive their income—from "how much they are read, cited, and built-upon by other researchers"—as this tends to lead, either directly

or indirectly, to greater reputation and recognition, and thus employment, career advancement (including tenure), salary increases, job offers, promotions, speaker fees, consultancies, the awarding of grants
and funding, and so on (Harnad 2001/2003). One of the things that
makes e-print archiving (often referred to as "self-archiving" or the
"green road" to open access) and open-access publishing in general so
attractive to many academic authors is therefore precisely the extent to
which, by rendering their work easily available to all those who can access it—rather than restricting access merely to those who can afford to
pay for it—they *can* make reaching a relatively large audience a very real
possibility.[17] Figures variously suggest that research published open access is somewhere between two and four times more likely to be read
and cited than if it is just published in ink-on-paper form.[18] So open access is good for the researcher. But it is also good for institutions, especially in the era of the RAE (in the United Kingdom—soon to become
the REF, or Research Excellence Framework) and the RQF (in Australia), since it helps to raise staff profiles, reputations, and indicators
of esteem.

To provide an example of what is achievable, even on a small scale, most
cultural studies journals, even quite well-established ones, have circula-
tions of only 400–600 copies internationally.[19] Compare this to the
fact that *Culture Machine*, the open-access online journal I cofounded
and coedit, was able to achieve a circulation of 6,500 (at least 10 times
the typical amount) in the first ten months of its existence alone, and
only three years later (2001–2002) was receiving as many as 375,000
hits per annum, which works out at somewhere between 40,000 and
50,000 individual accesses, or approximately 4,000 readers a month on
average.[20]

Nor should those authors who *do* want to profit directly from their
work automatically dismiss the potential benefits of open-access self-
archiving. A study of writers by The Society of Authors a few years ago
found that most had to supplement their very low annual earnings with
other forms of work and that "only a handful of writers earn the huge
advances which take up so many column inches in the press. Indeed, in
writing, five per cent earn on average over £75,000 and 'three quarters
of members earned less than the national average wage; and two-thirds
less than half the average wage and one half less than the minimum
wage'" (McRobbie 2002, 111; quoting Pool 2000). This is backed up by

a 2007 study for the Authors' Licensing and Collecting Society (ALCS) by the Centre for Intellectual Property Policy and Management at Bournemouth University. They found that the average author in the United Kingdom earns one-third less than the national average wage, that "typical earnings of a British professional writer aged 25–34 are only £5,000 per annum," and that "only 20% of writers earn all their income from writing" (2007). So the argument that writers of for-profit texts risk losing money, or not making it all, by archiving their work and making it open access does not really apply. Unfortunately, most authors simply have little or no money to lose. Like academics, many of them, too, could gain from the increase in potential readers and exposure that open access brings.

Digitize This!

By now the impact that an open-access repository similar to that at Cornell, or to the Cogprints archive that has been put together for cognitive psychology at the University of Southampton by Stevan Harnad, could potentially have on cultural studies is, I hope, becoming clear.[21] A few years ago *Culture Machine* decided to establish just such a cultural studies open-access repository—the Cultural Studies e-Archive (CSeARCH)—to create a space where research in the field can be published, disseminated, and accessed for free.

Launched in March 2006, CSeARCH enables those in the field to, among other things:

- *Publish their research, and therefore make their research findings widely available, immediately upon completion*—before it appears in either journal or book form (which can take between nine months and two years from submission of the final manuscript, sometimes longer); even before it has gone through the peer-review process if they choose, as that can also take a considerable amount of time.
- *Expand the size of their readership* (and hence potentially both the amount of feedback and recognition they receive and the size of their reputation)—an increasing number of studies suggest that research published as open access is much more likely to be read and cited than if it is published in ink-on-paper form only.
- *Attach a record of all the various stages of the research they wish to record*—from pre-refereeing, through successive revisions, to the submit-

ted, refereed, edited, and journal/publisher-certified published versions, including any subsequently corrected, revised, or otherwise updated drafts. As Kathleen Fitzpatrick quite rightly puts it:

> It makes no sense for electronic texts to mimic print by becoming fixed; electronic texts should be free to continue to grow and develop over time, but that change should somehow be marked within the text, made visible to readers. In this fashion, by enabling an author to continue working on a text even after its publication, but by making the history of changes to that text available, the process of an argument's growth and change could become part of the text itself. This would enable, in conjunction with commenting technologies, the processes of academic publishing to be radically changed, allowing authors to get new material into circulation much sooner. Scholars would no longer be at the mercy of the often appalling time-lags between a text's submission and acceptance, and between acceptance and publication. Instead, articles and monographs could be posted relatively early in their life-spans, as pre-prints or even submissions—perhaps with some indication of that status—and then the debate and discussion that they produce, and the shifts in the author's thinking that result, could take place in the open, as part of the process of the work itself. (Fitzpatrick 2006a, n.p.)

- *Link to underlying, background, and related research*—featured on blogs, wikis, and on individual and institutional Web pages.
- *Make their work available to anyone who can access it*—and not just to those who can afford to pay to read it via journal subscriptions, book cover prices, interlibrary loans, photocopying or the cost of accessing online databases and so forth. This is crucial to what is often designated "the developing world." To have your research recognized as legitimate, you need to be able to situate it in the context of other research that is perceived as important. This requires access to that research, which in turn requires money. If you are going to write about power or biopolitics, for example, then an understanding of the work of Michel Foucault would be regarded by many (not least among them peer-reviewers) as essential. But to acquire this knowledge often requires Foucault's writings to have been translated into a language you can read,

and for your institution or library to be able to afford to purchase those texts if you cannot do so yourself. Yet as Solomon emphasizes, "in the developing world, which includes approximately 80 percent of the world's population, even modest charges for access or publication can be beyond the economic means of libraries and individuals who wish to access the material or who wish to publish their material" (2006, n.p.). The open-access approach to scholarly publishing is important not just for the developing world, however, or for those in smaller and less wealthy institutions, or for those who are not attached to institutions at all. As Stevan Harnad points out, obviously "[r]esearchers in developing countries and at the less affluent universities and research institutions of developed countries will benefit even more from barrier-free access to the research literature than will the better-off institutions, but it is instructive to remind ourselves that even the most affluent institutional libraries cannot afford most of the refereed journals! None have access to more than a small subset of the entire annual corpus" (Harnad 2001/2003, n.p.).

- *Make their work easily accessible, from (almost) any desktop, in any home, university, library, or school, twenty-four hours a day*—when commenting on what value new technologies enable providers to add to content John Thompson puts it like this:

> In traditional systems of content provision, access to content is generally governed by certain spatial and temporal constraints—libraries and bookstores, for instance, are located in specific places and are open for certain hours of the day. But content delivered in an online environment is no longer governed by these constraints: in principle it is available twenty-four hours a day, seven days a week, to anyone who has a suitable internet (or intranet) connection. . . . The personal computer, located in a place or places which are convenient to the end user, becomes the gateway to a potentially vast body of content which can be accessed easily, quickly, and at any time of the day or night. (Thompson 2005, 318–19)

- *Provide their audience, including fellow writers and researchers, postgraduate and undergraduate students, and the general public, with as many copies of their texts as they need*—simply by supplying their readers with the URL address where they can find them on the

net and download them for free or print them off if they prefer.
(So it doesn't matter how many paper copies of your publications
your institutional library can afford to buy—ten, five, one, or
none—students will still be able to access and read the texts you
assign them.)

- *Link their teaching more closely to their research*—this can be done
  again simply by including the relevant references and URL ad-
  dresses in lectures, teaching materials, lecture handouts, and as
  part of online teaching resources.
- *Advertise and promote their texts for free*—all authors need to do is
  send out the relevant URLs by e-mail. This enables individual
  writers to be far more accurate and precise when targeting an
  audience for their works than has otherwise generally been the
  case. For instance, they can send details *directly* to those people
  and groups whom they know will be interested: students, colleagues, peers, and so forth.
- *Potentially increase reading figures, feedback, impact, and even sales of
  their paper publications*—rather than detracting from sales, as many
  commercial publishers fear, publishing on the Web frequently increases sales of paper copies, as the (now ex) chairman of Faber
  and Faber, Matthew Evans, acknowledged in a conference address
  (2002). This point is also accepted by Penguin, the publishers of
  Lawrence Lessig's *Free Culture* (2004). Penguin has made this book
  available online for free to prove their—and Lessig's—case.[22]
- *Publish books and journals that have too small a potential readership or
  too long a "tail" in sales terms to make them cost effective for a "paper"
  publisher to take on*—because they are perceived as being too difficult, advanced, specialized, obscure, esoteric, or avant-garde, or
  because they are written in a minority language or emerge from
  a culture or subculture that has a relatively small population.
- *Make their research "permanently" available*—so authors no longer
  need concern themselves with the thought that their work may go
  out of print or become otherwise unavailable.[23]
- *Republish texts that are rare, or forgotten, or out of print*—and this applies to journal articles as well as full-length books.
- *Revise and update their publications whenever they wish*—so authors
  need no longer be anxious about their work going out of date.
- *Distribute their texts to an extremely wide (if not necessarily "global") audience*—rather than reaching merely the specific audiences their

publishers think they can market and sell their work to—in the case of cultural studies, often primarily the United States, United Kingdom, and Australia. As a posting to the nettime list concerning another free electronic publishing venture, the Global Text Project,[24] emphasized with regard to textbooks (and CSeARCH is open to textbooks, too), these may be "considered expensive in Europe and the U.S., but they are far beyond the reach of many in developing economies. For example, a $108 biology textbook sells for $51 in Africa, but the U.S. GNI per capita is $41,400, and the figure for Uganda is $250. Obviously, the developed world's textbook business model does not meet the needs of those in the developing world. We need a publishing model that can meet the needs of Uganda and the many other countries that are not among the World Bank's high-income countries (those with GNI per capita above $10,066)" (McCubbrey and Watson 2006).

- *Provide a means of opening out and continuing the discussion of their research*—by using blogs, wikis, social networking sites like MySpace and YouTube, virtual environments such as Second Life and other tools.

- *Encourage browsing by enabling even those readers who still prefer to purchase a paper copy to read the texts concerned first*—this is increasingly difficult in the conventional bookselling market, as bookstores are taking fewer and fewer academic titles. As a result, the element of chance and serendipity traditionally associated with browsing in a bookshop is brought back. (Both Amazon.com's "Search Inside the Book" and Google Book Search with its "Partner Program" have been explicitly conceived to provide a service of this kind, not least with a view to acting as a marketing tool for book sales.)

- *Easily and quickly fulfill their obligations to funding bodies*—in 2006 the United Kingdom Economic and Social Research Council (ESRC) followed the lead set by the likes of the U.S. National Institutes of Health (NIH), the European Organization for Nuclear Research (CERN), and the Wellcome Trust, who have for some time now requested that researchers make their research available on an open-access platform. The ESRC made the depositing of research outputs in an open-access repository a mandatory condition of the award of funding from October of that year onward.[25]

In addition, authors have all the advantages associated with electronic publication, including ease of navigation and searching, speed of access, ability to link citations to other electronic pages, texts, sites, and resources (online encyclopedias and bookstores such as Wikipedia and Amazon, for instance, or relevant e-mail lists and discussion forums), and to connect their texts to other multimedia material in general, including video, streaming video, and audio files. To provide just one quick example: individual journal articles are rarely included in library catalogues. Digital texts, however, can be indexed even to the level of specific words and phrases, and the content of whole collections searched on a speed and a scale that is unthinkable in a non-digital context.

All this is available for free—to both authors and their readers. Just go to this address: http://www.culturemachine.net/csearch.

What is more—and it is no doubt worth emphasizing this point—thanks to the Harnad/Oppenheim preprint and corrigenda strategy, it is still perfectly possible for cultural studies writers and scholars to go on to publish research placed in the archive in preprint form as journal articles, and in many cases book chapters, or indeed academic monographs; and to do so without fear of infringing copyright agreements. According to Harnad, a variation on this strategy even works retrospectively for research literature that has already been published—something that is likely to be of particular interest to those in cultural studies and in the humanities generally. Of course, the publisher's policy, license, or copyright agreement may already explicitly permit the self-archiving of either the final edited and published version of the text, or of the refereed but unedited "post-print," as it is called. Happily, this is becoming increasingly the case, especially as more and more institutions and funding bodies are, as I say, making it mandatory for researchers to deposit the research they support on an open-access platform either immediately upon publication or after a specified period of time (usually somewhere between six months and two years). But if the publisher's policy, license, or copyright agreement does not allow this, or if the author is simply not sure, or for whatever reason does not feel comfortable about doing so just yet, then as a last resort Harnad advocates putting together "a revised 2nd edition! Update the references, rearrange the text (and add more text and data if you wish). For the record, the enhanced draft can be accompanied by a '*de*-corrigenda' file, stating which of the enhancements were *not* in the published version" (Harnad 2001/2003, n.p.).[26] In fact this last point—regarding the ability to self-archive open-access versions of texts that have already been published, or that have already been accepted for publication (as is the case with some permissions around postprints)—may be almost as important as far as cultural studies is concerned as the capacity to circumvent many of the restrictions copyright agreements place on access via the posting of preprints. It certainly has the potential to render open-access archiving even more applicable and appealing to a field that—partly because it does not place so much emphasis on the speed with which the results of research are shared, published, and communicated—lacks the history and culture of the preprint exchange of many science disciplines.

Despite everything I have said so far, however, the advantages this process offers to cultural studies teaching and research are not the only reason I am interested in open-access archiving. I am also interested in it because of the ethical and political questions open-access archiving raises for academic and institutional authority and legitimacy, and the way it promises to transform and redefine our relationship to knowledge.

2

Judgment and Responsibility in the Wikipedia Era

> One speaks often today, perhaps too often, of the cutting edge.
> We should never forget, however, that to cut, that edge must cut
> in more than one direction: not merely into the unknown, but
> into established knowledge as well.
>
> —*Samuel Weber, "The Future Campus:*
> *Destiny in a Virtual World," 1999*

A Section in Which the Author Explains Why So Many Academic Electronic Journals Remain to All Intents and Purposes Predigital

As the reader may have gathered, it is not my intention here to provide a broad account or detailed history of the development of open access, its philosophy, the associated legal disputes and debates, and the case for its economic, social, and intellectual benefits. A number of texts available both online and off already cover these topics.[1] Besides, for all that I have written *Digitize This Book!*, at least in part, to advocate for open access to be adopted more extensively, in the humanities especially, I am not interested in open access so much for its own sake; my concern here is more with the way it provides us with a chance to think the university otherwise, both ethically and politically. In this respect I want to concentrate on two key issues.

Much of the debate surrounding the digital reproduction, publication, and archivization of the academic research literature has been taken up with two main areas of concern. The first of these is that of copyright, which I discussed in chapter 1; the second is quality control—not in the sense of the standard of the technical reproduction, publication, and archiving of texts, or their accessibility to the reader, but the quality of the archived work itself: how the established standards of scholarship and research, and thus the identity and coherence of a given field of study, can be maintained after the transfer, *translation*, or, better, transcoding of scholarship into the digital medium. The status and authority of scholarly work *is* regarded as somehow being placed in question by the digital mode of reproduction; there is even a certain *anxiety* and *apprehension* attendant on this change in the material support of knowledge.[2] And, to be sure, as J. Hillis Miller remarks in an article from 1995 on "The Ethics of Hypertext," by positioning the normal and the usual in a "strange and disorientating new context," new digital media technologies *do* encourage us, or at least provide us with a chance (which is also always a risk), to see academic scholarship and research again, "in a new way," as if for the first time, and so account for it and judge it anew (Miller 1995, 32, 35).

For example, the process of establishing an open-access archive (as we shall see, the establishment of an open-access archive is very much a *process*) immediately raises some intriguing questions. How is it to be decided what is to be included in such an archive and what is not? What factors lead to a particular text or work being valorized as worthy of inclusion? In short, what is going to constitute a "proper" piece of, in this case, cultural studies writing or research? With what authority, according to what legitimacy, can such decisions be made? On what criteria are they ultimately to be based?

Currently, an academic text acquires a certain amount of authority and legitimacy in two primary ways. The first, perhaps the easiest to deal with in this context, is by being "published." Any number of people can write a book-length text and print it up, but if a work is "published" it means a professional press considered that text of sufficient value and quality to be worth bringing out in book form—which, as we have already seen, nowadays means more and more that they thought they would be able to successfully market, distribute, and sell it. It is important to emphasize that things have not always been like this. In a guide to some of the perils of publishing for graduate students written back in 1998 Meaghan Morris notes that:

> There was a time [and Morris is only talking about the mid-1980s] when academic books were published by heavily subsidized university presses and a few commercial publishers prepared to carry a prestige list at a loss. This system materially sustained the ethos of

"knowledge as intrinsically valuable"; a good book, containing original thought and research, carefully reviewed by experts and duly revised (often several times) for publication, could usually expect to find a home irrespective of its chances of making money. This is no longer the case. By the end of the 1990s, academic publishing was an industry dominated by a few transnational corporations (Routledge [since purchased by Taylor and Francis] is the best known) and a smallish number of large university presses either forced to live without subsidy, or drawing up plans to do so. Exceptions, like small presses, do remain. On the whole, most academic publishers are increasingly expected to be self-sustaining, and therefore make a profit. (Morris 1998, 501–2)

The kind of open-access archive I am talking about here, however, is effectively free to the reader, so whether a particular text will sell or not is no longer a consideration. Someone can write a book on a subject so marginal and obscure it may be of interest to only one other person in the world—what you might call a real micro-public or nanoaudience— yet it might still be worth including in such an archive. Consequently, the economics of publishing is no longer such an important factor when it comes to deciding what an open-access archive of cultural studies– related material should contain.

The second, and more problematic (at least as far as I am concerned here), way in which the value and quality of an academic piece of writing or research is determined is by peer review. Given the fact that some form of peer review usually constitutes part of the process of getting published in both book *and* journal article form, one could say that this is *the* main way in which the worth of an academic text is measured.[3] (Changes to the academic publishing industry, however, mean that the rigor of peer review can vary; the newer "for-profit" commercial publishers are often tempted to spend less time and care on editing and revising a text than the older "not-just-for-profit" or "not-necessarily-for-profit" university presses.) With peer review, authors submit their work in the first instance to an editor (who will most likely be an employee of the publisher in the case of book publishing, a fellow academic in that of the scholarly journal, or perhaps some combination of both with regard to an edited book series).[4] If the editor considers the submitted piece to be potentially interesting and strong enough to be appropriate for publication, the advice of specialists in the field—

peers—is sought. They review the text in question and report back to the editor as to whether it is suitable for publication in its current form; suitable for publication only after appropriate revisions are made; or not suitable for publication at all. Only once the piece has passed through the peer-review process to the satisfaction of both editor and referees is it accepted for publication.

Yet the change from paper to digital raises questions for this rigorous system of quality control. As anyone who has spent even a small amount of time online can confirm, it is often hard to tell when surfing the Web what exactly *is* legitimate knowledge and what *is not*. This is because electronic publications do not have the same aura of authority as a professionally produced paper text. As long as they possess a basic level of technological know-how, almost anyone can publish on the Web and make it look reasonably impressive to a degree they could not with a self-published printed paper text, since the latter will tend to lack the quality of paper, typography, illustrations, and general all-around "glossiness" of a professionally produced title. Most academic online-only journals have responded to this challenge to their authority by imitating their paper counterparts:[5] in their "page" layout; their publication of material in the form of "essays" or "papers" written in a linear, sequential form; their size and length; their reliance on international editorial boards of established academics who have already proven themselves in the "paper" world; and most especially in their peer-reviewing and certification processes. They have done so in order to try to reassure the university about something that is still relatively new by demonstrating that they are providing recognizable forms of quality control and editorial legitimacy within this new medium. (*Culture Machine*, the open-access journal I coedit, is as guilty of this as any other journal, because if it weren't the likelihood is people wouldn't treat it particularly seriously.)[6]

The problem with the attempt to maintain academic authority in this manner *after* the transition to the digital medium is that, first, it positions electronic publishing merely as a prosthetic extension of print—albeit one offering an improved level of performance in terms of the speed of production, the amount of material that can be stored, the ease of information retrieval, the geographical range of distribution and dissemination, reductions in cost for reproduction and staffing, and so on. (It is not just academic texts that do this, of course. Since the invention of the Web in the mid-1990s, perhaps the majority of digital publications have mimicked the form of the print magazine page: the BBC's Web site being just one of the most well-known examples.)[7] Second, it assumes, even as we move (albeit not in any simple, linear, or teleological way) from an epoch of ink-on-paper reproduction to one that operates increasingly in terms of bits, pixels, and computer files, that academics are going to continue to take paper more or less as their model. Put another way, it presupposes that academic texts will maintain their traditional, predigital form, as derived from the attributes of writing, marking, or tracing on paper, *even when these texts are reproduced digitally*; and that these texts will therefore continue to be recognizable as proper, legitimate, academic pieces of work as these terms are defined in and by the code or language of "paper." Third, the attempt to maintain academic authority in this manner upholds the belief that digital academic texts *can*, and indeed *should*, therefore continue to be judged according to systems of peer review—complete with their social, cultural, and economic hierarchies and filters, standards and values, rules and procedures—that have their basis, if not their origins, in the ink-on-paper world.

Papercentrism

The above no doubt explains why many digital journals—including a good number of open-access publications—remain in effect largely *predigital*, tied to the ink-on-paper template. Such "papercentrism" is not confined to the production of online academic journals, however. A similar set of assumptions underpins many of the better-known open-access archiving models.

Take Stevan Harnad's influential account of how self-archiving in the likes of the arXiv.org E-Print Archive and Cogprints can "free" the research literature. According to Harnad, the way to "distinguish self-publishing (vanity press) from self-archiving (of published, refereed research)," and thus establish the latter's legitimacy and authority, is precisely by means of peer-review. Because he is working in the sciences, where the priority is to publish articles in the most respected journals, it is the prestige journal publisher and reviewer whom he sees as providing this element of quality control:

> The essential difference between unrefereed research and refereed research is quality-control (peer review, Harnad 1998/2000) and its certification (by an established peer-reviewed journal of known

quality). Although researchers have always wished to give away their refereed research findings, they still wish them to be refereed, and certified as having met established quality standards. Hence the self-archiving of refereed research should in no way be confused with self-publishing, for it includes as its most important component, the online self-archiving, free for all, of refereed, *published* research papers. (2001/2003, n.p.)

The publisher and referees of the prestige journal supply control quality, then; the archive itself is perceived as merely providing access to the already-certified data. Indeed, for Harnad, who for all his talk of "Subversive Proposals" (1994a) admits to advocating "a very conventional form of quality control" (1994b), this is the "only essential service still provided by journal publishers . . . peer review" (2001/2003, n.p.).

Note the point Harnad makes in parentheses when he writes that the "essential difference between unrefereed research and refereed research is quality-control (peer review) and its certification (by an established peer-reviewed journal of known quality)." Online-only academic journals are for the most part still considered too new and unfamiliar to have gained the level of institutional recognition required for them to be thought of as being "established" and "of known quality."[8] The relatively few online journals that have acquired such a status have almost invariably been able to do so only by mimicking their traditional printed paper counterparts, especially and above all in their peer-review processes. As Harnad emphasizes, such conventional and "conservative" (1998/2000, n.p.) forms of quality control are essential to their being certified as "established" and "of known quality" in the first place. "Peer review itself is not a deluxe add-on for research and researchers: This quality-control service and its certification is an essential (Harnad 1998/2000). Without peer review, the research literature would be neither reliable nor navigable, its quality uncontrolled, unfiltered, un-sign-posted, unknown, unaccountable" (2001/2003, n.p.). So for "established peer-reviewed journal" we can really read established peer-reviewed paper—or at least *papercentric*—journal. Harnad's emphasis on accreditation by established peer-review journals of quality means, in effect, that the legitimacy and authority of a digitally self-archived academic text is derived from and has its basis in the world of hard-copy, ink-on-paper publishing. What is more, this is the case regardless of whether this happens directly, by means of the sort of peer-review service provided by an actual *paper* journal, or indirectly, via that of an online-only journal "of known quality." For although the medium of the latter may be digital, according to what is (as we shall see) a quite traditional paradox of authority, its quality control procedure (and hence the online journal itself) is necessarily dependent for its legitimacy on a system of peer-review that has its "origins" in the paper world, and which is in turn dependent on that world for its own authority and legitimacy. That changes in the material support of knowledge from "hard" to electronic will, according to Harnad, "make it possible for journals to implement [peer-review procedures] not only more cheaply and efficiently, but also more equitably and effectively than was possible in paper," does nothing to alter this state of affairs. Such changes represent merely a prosthetic extension and improvement of the existing "paper" practices of peer review, as opposed to a rethinking and a working out of what modes of legitimation might actually be needed to respond to the specificity and singularity of digital modes of publication.

Limited Ink: From the Database to Hyperness, by Way of Codework and Wikified Texts

All of this has significant consequences for the way in which a proper, legitimate piece of digitally reproduced academic writing is conceived, defined, and understood; and thus how one might decide or choose what to welcome into an open-access archive and what to cast out, what is deemed important, relevant, and valuable, and what unimportant, irrelevant, and worthless. At this point questions of ethics—understood, according to the philosophical tradition of Jacques Derrida and Emmanuel Levinas, as a duty and responsibility to what the latter terms "the infinite alterity of the other" who places me in question and to whom I have to respond—come to impose themselves (although they were never really absent).[9] For in both the models of electronic publishing we have looked at so far in which peer review is used as a means of sustaining academic authority—that of open-access journal publishing (the "golden road" to open access) and open-access self-archiving (the "green road")[10]—we can see that a papercentric, if not indeed the literal ink-on-paper form, is clearly being *imposed* onto writers of scholarly texts. What is more, this is so even if a text is not destined to appear in print at all, but is to be published directly on the Web in an online journal, or deposited straight from the author's personal computer into an e-print archive. Even if there is *no* original, ink-on-paper version—never has been and never will be—academic texts still have to be written in such a way that they *can* be published in hard form (at least potentially) if they are to be capable of going through the peer-review process and receiving accreditation. Witness the example Harnad provides of those papers ("no one knows how many," he writes in parentheses) initially deposited in arXiv.org as unrefereed preprints, but whose authors never replaced them with the final revised and published draft, either because they could not be bothered or because the pieces in question were never in fact actually accepted for publication. "The 'Invisible Hand' of peer review is still there," Harnad insists, "exerting its civilising influence," since in the open-access e-print archiving system as it currently exists these texts are still written with a view to appearing in a peer-reviewed journal at some stage in order to receive accreditation, even if they never actually do:

> Just about every paper deposited in Los Alamos is also destined for a peer reviewed journal; the author knows it will be answerable to the editors and referees. That certainly constrains how it is written in the first place. Remove that invisible constraint—let the authors be answerable to no one but the general users of the Archive (or even its self-appointed "commentators")—and watch human nature take its natural course, standards eroding as the Archive devolves toward the canonical state of unconstrained postings: the free-for-all chat-groups of Usenet http://tile.net/news/listed.html, that Global Graffiti Board for Trivial Pursuit—until someone re-invents peer review and quality control. (Harnad 1998/2000, n.p.)

In order to be recognized as legitimate and gain accreditation, then, academic electronic texts are operating on the principle of "limited hospitality": they are in effect being limited and restricted to that which can be reproduced on paper. Consequently, if there is little evidence of cultural studies academics producing texts, or even journals, specifically designed to exploit the unique properties of the Internet and World Wide Web, as some have indeed claimed,[11] this may have as much to do with the way in which writers of scholarly digital works are being required, disciplined even, to seek certification in a form that is not necessarily their "own," but which is imposed on them by the academic institution, with its already-established rules and procedures of legitimation, as with any lack of imagination or technical ability on their part.[12]

Yet must we *really* insist that digital texts conform to the standards and hierarchies of the paper world so that we might be able to understand and judge them and hence possibly include them in a cultural studies open-access archive? Is this not to take too little account of the ways in which electronic writing and publishing may differ from that of ink-on-paper, and thus risk restricting the production, publication, and even understanding of electronic texts to that which is merely a repetition of the same, or at least the very similar? Is there not a very real danger here of ignoring or excluding anything that is new, different, innovative, or exceptional, any heterogeneous excess that cannot be recuperated within the logic of identity? To understand the potential of, and the possibilities created by, digital modes of reproduction and publication, shouldn't we also require a certain openness to alterity, to the unknown, the unpredictable, and unexpected, to precisely that which *cannot* be recognized and subsumed under the familiar?

What happens if and when writers and researchers stop attempting to transfer print-based aesthetics into the electronic medium and, as is already happening to a certain extent in the sciences and humanities (and in some contributions to *Culture Machine*), *produce* work that, although not entirely new or different, is nevertheless specific to the digital mode of publication; texts that are not restricted to the book or essay format, but that are "born digital," and are therefore perhaps not even recognizable as texts in the ink-on-paper sense? Without going into interactive artworks and the hypertext of Bolter (1991) and Kolb (1994, 2000), which in many ways seems rather dated now (no offense intended); nor into the many opportunities that are created by the integration of other types of material support, including audio and images, both moving video clips and still photographs and pictures—here are just a few of the many possible easily identifiable examples of what can happen "if and when."

The Database

What happens if and when "writers" take the database, not necessarily as Lev Manovich has suggested, as the "new symbolic form of [the] computer age . . . [and as] a new way to structure our experience of ourselves and of the world"? To my mind that would be to take insufficient account of the many divergences between different types of new media.

(As Manovich acknowledges, not all new media objects are characterized by an absence of linear narrative, even if "underneath, on the level
of material organization, they are all databases"—although, as N. Katherine Hayles points out, Manovich appears here to be both contradict-
ing his claim elsewhere that "not all new media objects are explicitly
databases" [Manovich 2001, 221], and conflating databases with da-
tastructures [Hayles 2005, n.p.].) It would also be to overlook the many
similarities that exist between "new" and "old" media. But what happens when writers take the database at least as a model for structuring
texts that "do not tell stories; they do not have a beginning or end; in
fact, they do not have any development, thematically, formally or otherwise that would organize their elements into a [fixed] sequence. Instead, they are collections of individual items . . . on which the user can
perform various operations: view, navigate, search" (Manovich 1998,
n.p.; 2001, 218–19). It is certainly not hard to imagine a situation where
Digitize This Book! and the Cultural Studies e-Archive, instead of being
separate, as they supposedly are now—the book and the archive, the
"textual" and the "real," the "theoretical" and the "practical" (a state of
affairs that reinforces those academic hierarchies that privilege the
paper means of material support over the digital through the greater
status awarded to the former when it comes to publishing journals, attracting funding, making academic appointments, and so on)—are
combined to form a multiplicitous text/database/institution that is indeed "born digital."

Codework

What happens if and when texts are produced in which the technical
and cultural practices of electronic writing are combined, as in the case
of codeworks? Here notions of authorship are problematized, as codeworks are produced by entities or avatars such as Mez, Antiorp, and
JODI, which may or may not be machinic, and which blur the boundaries between art and writing, poetic language and computer code.[13]

Blogs

What happens if and when academics publish their research and ideas
in the form of weblogs? Of course, for large numbers of academics weblogs amount to little more than online diaries and scrapbooks. For increasing numbers of others, however, they are coming to be regarded
as a highly effective means by which writers and researchers can access

people in the community at large, thus entering the public sphere of debate and enabling them to become, in effect, a form of public intellectual for the twenty-first century.[14] That said, even the most ardent of advocates would acknowledge that publishing in an academic blog is very different, in terms of its status and credibility, to publishing in a refereed academic journal, simply because the two modes of reproduction are not subject to the same kinds of peer review. Indeed, for all their burgeoning popularity with academics—Michael Bérubé, Jodi Dean, Melissa Gregg, and Ted Striphas are just a few of those in the cultural studies field experimenting with the form[15]—it remains unclear as to exactly how academic blogs are to be evaluated and assessed. When blogging is undertaken by academics, should it be considered a private, amateur hobby, part of their professional responsibility as publicly funded scholars, or as something in between? This question takes on an even greater urgency when it comes to hiring and promotion committees, as the case of Juan Cole testifies. In July 2006 *The Chronicle of Higher Education* published a discussion among seven academic bloggers provoked by speculation that Cole had failed to acquire a position at Yale University because of his blogging activities. Should academics who publish their ideas and research in the form of blogs, and are able to reach a large audience in doing so (Cole's blog is reported to receive 200,000 viewers a month), expect to have such work taken into account in the same way as those who publish predominantly in books and refereed journals?[16]

Wikified Texts

What happens if and when texts are coauthored by large groups of often anonymous people (from a certain perspective at least) using wikis, free content, and open-editing principles?[17] Without doubt Wikipedia is the most well known of these, but there is also Digg, the news site where the community of readers themselves donate news stories they have found on the Web, in blogs, podcasts, Web sites, and so forth, and other readers then vote on them; the story that receives the most votes is then put on the front page.[18] In a move directly inspired by Wikipedia, The Institute for the Future of the Book also put McKenzie Wark's then work-in-progress *GAM3R 7H3oRY* (2006) online in a series of Web pages, each of which contained a paragraph from the book and a box where people could post their responses to and comments on Wark's writing. Wark's project was more a form of open peer commentary and open peer review (or even peer-to-peer review) than an instance of the kind of open editing found on Wikipedia; of potentially more interest, the writer Douglas Rushkoff was reported to be exploring writing a wikified doctoral dissertation at Utrecht University in which either the basic skeleton of his thesis is built upon by volunteers, or his original content is "nested within layers of material contributed by collaborators" (Vershbow 2006).[19]

Hyperness

What happens if and when the very concept of "text" becomes, as Andy Miah has argued, "increasingly uninteresting or useless"?—as writers use software, such as Macromedia's Flash, which has the effect of rendering the text more as "image than text, ungraspable and flat, layered with a virtual and invisible hyperness . . . [and] the sub-level of hyperness, which is really what is of interest when discussing hypertext, derives from the nature of the browser, rather than some new characteristic of text" (2003).[20]

A New Code of the Digital?

One does not even have to resort solely to such avant-garde texts to draw attention to this issue. Audio and video interviews or recordings of conference talks and proceedings can be found on many academic-related Web sites. These, too, do not conform to the traditional format of academic scholarly writing; nor do the videos of university lectures that are increasingly appearing on YouTube. Indeed, the same problematic is a feature of even the most conventional digitally reproduced online academic journal, as the very web-like structure of the Web often makes it difficult to determine where texts end—or begin, for that matter. All the cutting and pasting, grafting and transplanting, internal and external linking involved means that the boundaries between the text and its surroundings, its material support, are blurred and can become almost impossible to determine online—just as the boundaries separating authors, editors, programmers, producers, consumers, users, and commentators/critics are blurred. "All this may sound fine and largely innocuous but scholars and researchers stake their career on well-defined products, that is to say objects endowed with stability relative to time and place. . . . In going digital, texts lose this physical stability, this guarantee of permanence. Again, this may look somewhat inconsequential until we stop and think that the whole idea of the author depends on it" (Guédon and Beaudry 1996, n.p.). (Certainly, this aspect of new media—its challenging of the author function—is more likely to create problems for copyright, it seems to me, than the "academic gift economy" [Barbrook 1998] and the open-access publishing and archiving of research and publications per se.)

How, then, are such texts to be judged and assessed? *Are* they to be judged and assessed? Or are they simply to be dismissed as being somehow improper or illegitimate because they cannot easily be reproduced in ink-on-paper form, and so are incapable of receiving accreditation by the established peer-review processes?[21] On what basis can we make such decisions? Are the pre-established paper standards and criteria for judging, reviewing, and certifying academic work sufficient for responding responsibly and doing justice to digitally reproduced texts; texts whose fluid, unfinished, networked form means they might never be read—or be written, for that matter—in the same way twice, and which often render highly problematic the distinctions on which critical interpretation traditionally depends: reader/writer, inside/outside, beginning/end, human/machine and so forth? Or does the (potentially) radically different nature of electronic publishing require the invention of new standards and criteria for the maintenance of "quality control"? Perhaps we need a new knowledge, a new grammar, a new language and literacy, a new visual/aural/linguistic code of the digital that is capable of responding to the specificity and indeed singularity of such texts with an answering singularity and inventiveness?[22]

The Parasite and the Guest

Now you will notice I am not suggesting that all judgment and decision-making—or peer review, for that matter—be somehow done away with. If people are able to self-archive, to upload material into an open-access repository of this kind themselves (which, as far as both the arXiv.org E-Print Archive and the Cultural Studies e-Archive are concerned, they are),[23] if they are able to do so before peer review (ditto), if they are able to do so even without ever finally submitting their work for peer review (likewise), how is the "parasite" to be distinguished from the "guest," the welcome contribution to the field—in this case that of cultural studies (but we could raise similar questions regarding literary studies, philosophy, and indeed the humanities and knowledge in general)—from the unwanted, the illegitimate, the unimportant, the irrelevant, the unworthy, that which is without quality or merit? Traditional moral philosophy teaches us that we can only make such ethical decisions if we have a law, rule, or set of procedures that enact a limiting jurisdiction, that allow us to choose, to judge, to discriminate, to determine value and worth, and consequently to sort, reject, eject, or exclude. Certainly, when it comes to questions of disciplinarity, institutionalization, and of archiving, it is still necessary to choose, to judge, and to make decisions; to elect, filter, and select what is to be contained in the archive and what is not; a certain exercise of power, and with it a certain injustice, thus takes place immediately when an archive is founded.[24] In fact the responsibility of choosing or judging I am referring to is inescapable. This responsibility certainly cannot be eluded by refusing to choose or to decide; by trying to have a completely open system (as if such a thing were possible) with no form of peer review or other means for the assessment of contributions at all. For one thing, that would leave the space of judgment empty and thus available to being filled in and occupied by the returning dominant modes of power, judgment, authority, and legitimation. For another, it would in no way free us from the responsibility of making a decision, as such a refusal would still be a decision, only a poor one, since it would not be consciously assuming the responsibility of deciding.[25]

But if responsibility cannot be eluded by refusing to judge or decide, neither can we rid ourselves of the responsibility of judging and of making a decision by deciding once and for all what the rules and values governing our choices and decisions are—that they are going to be those of the system currently used with regard to ink-on-paper publishing, peer review; or the procedures of peer review *and* peer commentary that Stevan Harnad oversaw at the peer-reviewed paper journal of "open peer commentary" he founded and edited until 2001, *Behavioral and Brain Sciences,* and the online-only peer-reviewed journal of open peer commentary he still edits, *Psycoloquy;* or the system of peer-to-peer review advocated by Kathleen Fitzpatrick and The Institute for the Future of the Book—and that these rules and values are going to apply to everything, in all foreseeable circumstances.[26] As Jacques Derrida quite rightly says in a text that, like this one, is very much concerned with the pragmatics of deconstruction (although which of Derrida's isn't?), "if you give up the infinitude of responsibility, there is no responsibility" (1996a, 86).

We Have Always Been Digital

Judgment and decision-making, then, cannot be abandoned or done away with. The problem is rather with the authority of any such judgment and its mode of performance. The rules, procedures, standards, and criteria by which judgments, interpretations, selections, and decisions are made in the paper world regarding certification and accreditation cannot simply and unquestioningly be extended and applied to electronic texts. This is why it is not sufficient to respond to Greenblatt's (2002) request for solutions to the problem of the decline in academic monograph publishing by calling, as some have done, for research to be put on the Internet, and for equal value and status to be attached to peer-reviewed online publications.[27] Digital publishing cannot automatically be assumed to be merely a prosthetic extension of ink-on-paper publishing. That would be to take too little account of the potential difference and specificity of the electronic medium, its material form and properties, as represented by the hardware, software, operating system, browser, programming code, graphical interface, icons, frames, hyperlinks, location-sensitive pull-down tables, multiple-windowed screens and the ability to add, copy, delete, refresh, and reformat content (to provide just a few of the most obvious examples).[28] In fact, it could be argued that no decision or judgment would be made here at all, that it would represent a refusal of responsibility. For if one already presumes to know the rules, laws, values, and procedures by which something is to be decided and assessed, if one imagines that one is already familiar with that which is to be judged—again, in this particular case, cultural studies, what it is, what form it takes, how it is to be recognized, and thus what is worth including in a cultural studies open-access archive and what is not—then there is no judgment or decision. Its place is taken by the mere application of a rule, law, or program. In order for there to be a decision, the identity of cultural studies cannot be known or decided in advance. As Derrida puts it a little earlier in the same text, "if there is a decision, it presupposes that the subject of the decision does not yet exist and neither does the object. . . . Every time I decide, if a decision is possible, I invent the who, and I decide who decides what" (1996a, 84). I would even take this so far as to insist that this injunction applies not just to "new" cultural studies texts: those that have yet to be published or receive academic accreditation; or those that emanate from formations of cultural studies outside the Anglo-American/Australian nexus—from places such as Canada, Holland, Finland, Turkey, South Africa, Brazil, Taiwan, Singapore, South Korea, Japan, Poland—and that therefore do not always necessarily look like "cultural studies" as it has been traditionally defined, perhaps because they do not share the former's antiestablishment beginnings, or concerns with a notion of politics and social justice based on economic equality. I would argue that it applies to the "whole" of the cultural studies corpus or canon, to the history of what is thought or understood to be cultural studies. In short, and shocking as it may be to some, regardless of the copyright issues, we cannot deposit digitized versions of, say, Raymond Williams's *Culture and Society* (1958) or Stuart Hall et al.'s *Policing the Crisis* (1978) in the archive, confident in the knowledge that the authority and legitimacy of these texts as classic works of cultural studies is already assured: by history, the field, the discipline. We cannot do so for the simple reason that this would again be to merely apply a pre-given rule or program. (Which is not to say such classic texts would *not* be included, just that this decision cannot be made automatically, in advance.)

Still, if judgment cannot be avoided, neither can the question of the status and legitimacy of digital academic work be resolved, as one might initially be tempted to think, through the development of decision-making systems, peer-reviewing procedures, and rules for the provision of certification and accreditation catering specifically for texts that are born digital. It is not a matter of electronic publishing simply being *different* from paper publishing, in a manner akin to the way in which many people have pointed out that to teach online you need to do more than merely put your course materials on the Web, experiment with "course-casting"—using webcasting and podcasting to record lectures as audio or video files and then make them available for students to download onto their computers or iPods—or hold seminars in Second Life.[29] The problem goes much deeper than that, to the extent that the digital mode of reproduction raises fundamental questions for what scholarly publishing (and teaching) actually is; in doing so it not only poses a threat to the traditional academic hierarchies, but also tells us something about the practices of academic legitimation, authority, judgment, accreditation, and institution in general. In fact, echoing a critique of the structure of the sign that was first produced by Derrida some years ago and that has more recently been replayed by Bernard

Stiegler (2002), I want to risk the following proposition or hypothesis: that academic authority is already "digitized"; that it is in a sense always already in a similar condition to that which is brought about by the process of digitization.

The *Process* of Institutionalization

No doubt at first blush my last point may seem bizarre. To explain what I mean, let me turn to one of the places where questions of institutional judgment, legitimacy, and responsibility have been most powerfully articulated in recent years.

In what is still his best-known and most influential book, *Institution and Interpretation*, Samuel Weber shows how institutionalization can be construed rather differently from how it has traditionally been conceived. "The dominant tendency," Weber writes, following the work of René Lourau, "has been to reduce the concept to only one of its elements: the maintenance of the status quo, and thereby to eliminate its dynamic, transformative aspect" (Weber 1987, xv). In other words, institutionalization has been taken for granted; it has been perceived as something that already exists and is established and that just needs to be described, rather than as a *process* to be understood. Weber, by contrast, puts forward a notion of institutionalization "in which *instituted* organization and *instituting* process are joined in the ambivalent relation of every determinate structure to that which it excludes, and yet which, qua excluded, allows that structure to *set itself apart*" (xv).

Weber's analysis of the *process of institutionalization* (expounded in a number of books and articles, including a recently reprinted and expanded [2001] version of *Institution and Interpretation*), is too rich and multifaceted to enable anything more than a partial account of it to be provided here.[30] Besides, it is perhaps sufficiently well known by now, and has become so absorbed into the mainstream of literary and cultural theory (even if the "origins" of this kind of institutional analysis with Weber are, ironically enough, not always explicitly acknowledged or even recognized), as to make any attempt at a comprehensive summary superfluous. So let me just replay a few of what I take to be its most pertinent features, at least as far as the question of the maintenance of academic quality and legitimacy is concerned.

Of particular interest from the point of view of rethinking the university is the way in which a discipline, for Weber, can only institute itself by aid of what lies outside it, by distinguishing itself from that which it is not, what it excludes or expels from its limits. He identifies this procedure as being "highly characteristic of the organization of knowledge in modern society," and notes that it "has developed with problematic intensity in what we call the humanities" (137–38) (itself a concept currently in the process of being replaced for many commentators by cultural studies, although Weber's chief concern here lies with that part of the humanities "dedicated to literary studies").[31] Significantly, this process of delimitation and demarcation, which enables the discipline to establish the difference of its own identity as a self-contained, independent, and autonomous domain of knowledge, does not entail the complete and total rejection of what it is not; "*rather, the exclusions persist qua exclusions*, and they must be so maintained if they are to delimit what falls within the scope of [the discipline's] determinations" (1987, 145). Instead of being able to forget about what it has expelled and go about its business, then, the discipline has to continually refer to that which lies outside its limits. This results in what Weber terms the "*ambivalence of demarcation*": "The demarcation is ambivalent because it does not merely demarcate one thing by setting it off from another; it also de-marks, that is, defaces the mark it simultaneously inscribes, by placing it in relation to an indeterminable series of other marks, of which we can never be fully conscious or cognizant" (145).

At this point it becomes possible to detect a certain instability in the process of institutionalization (an instability that I want to argue creates our first problem when it comes to thinking about what to include in a cultural studies open-access archive).[32] For if a discipline is dependent for its identity on what it is not, on what it expels outside its borders, if it can delimit its internal coherence as an identifiable, recognizable, and autonomous body of thought only by means of this "'exclusionary' activity" (138), then it cannot be either self-identical, independent, autonomous, *or* self-contained. What is more, this irreducible complication in its identity does not come along *after* the formation of the discipline in its ideal, self-contained purity and unity. Rather, this relation, this contamination by the other, by what is positioned as being outside and heterogeneous to it, is *originary*: it comes *before* the establishment of the discipline's identity and is in fact what makes the discipline and its founding possible (and simultaneously impossible). The discipline is thus always opened to its others: other academic disciplines and other forms of knowledge, both legitimate and illegitimate or not yet legitimate; but also other forms of what for short might be called "non-knowledge" (although this term is not without problems).

Now, according to Weber, this process of *de-markation* effectively never ends. Nevertheless, if it is to take place at all it must be brought to a halt: "We must both refer the defining terms to other marks that can never be fully defined for us and at the same time—but this precisely fractures the Sameness of that Time—we must 'forget' this irreducibly undefinable vestige, this set of exclusions that is neither entirely indeterminate nor fully determinable" (145). In this way, Weber's analysis helps us to recognize that any such differentiation or de-markation that goes to institute a discipline—the judgment or decision as to what to include and what to exclude, what should be taken inside and what expelled—is an inherently unstable and irreducibly violent one: the violence inherent in this de-markation, the forceful arrestation of the inherent instability of the discipline's limits, can never be disarmed; the instability can never be removed once and for all: only degrees of more or less control are possible.

What we can also see from the above is that at the discipline's founding there is an *aporia of authority*. For where does the authority to stop this endless process of de-markation and establish—institute—a discipline by setting itself apart from others, from what it is not, come from? A discipline cannot found itself. That would require it to already possess such authority. This authority *must* come from somewhere else, somewhere that is outside the discipline and that precedes it. A discipline is thus indebted to some other, external authority for its legitimacy. And yet the search for origins and legitimacy does not end, or begin, there. For even if this external authority were examined in turn it would not enable the discipline to escape the aporia that lies at its heart. For where would *that* authorizing authority gain *its* authority? It would have to come from outside that authorizing authority, whose authorizing authority would in turn come from outside its authority, in a process leading to a series of infinite regressions. As far as the university is concerned—which is where disciplines do gain much of their authority—its accreditation, its legitimacy as a seat of learning, its power to award titles of competency, *does* comes from elsewhere, from outside: this authority is granted to the university by the state, via accrediting agencies. (In Britain these include the Quality Assurance Agency and the British Accreditation Council.) But from where does the state gain *its* authority?[33]

Of course (and continuing to move quite quickly across Weber's various analyses in *Institution and Interpretation*, for reasons of economy), in order to function as a legitimately instituted field of knowledge the discipline must in effect overlook or forget all this, and act instead as if it is beholden to no one but itself for its authority—although it cannot forget its indebtedness entirely, since it is upon the ambivalence of demarcation and the aporia of authority that the discipline is founded.[34] The discipline thus seeks to overcome its unstable and violent nature by performatively producing a set of "founding" principles and procedures for the institution and reproduction of itself and its original guiding idea. These principles and procedures form the basis of the various rules, regulations, laws, norms, protocols, and conventions concerning the identity of its founding thinkers, their followers and interpreters, its canon and pedagogical techniques, as well as its various forms and styles of writing, publication, research assessment, and so on that go to make up the discipline, defining its sphere of competence and providing the means by which it develops. The problem is that as the discipline does proceed to develop, increasingly little attention is paid to the violent and paradoxical authority on which it is based. Describing some of the distinctive features of the "culture of professionalism" as they appear within the university, Weber puts it like this:

> The university, itself divided into more or less isolated, self-contained departments, was the embodiment of that kind of limited universality that characterised the cognitive model of professionalism. It instituted areas of training and research which, once established, could increasingly ignore the founding limits and limitations of individual disciplines. Indeed, the very notion of academic "seriousness" came increasingly to exclude reflection upon the relation of one "field" to another, and concomitantly, reflection upon the historical process by which individual disciplines established their boundaries. Or the historical dimension was regarded as extrinsic to the actual practice of research and scholarship: history itself became one discipline among others. (1987, 32)

It is not surprising that professional scholars and academics have for the most part followed these procedures with regard to founding principles and disciplinary borders. After all, to do otherwise would involve them in bringing their own legitimacy, based on what Weber analyzes

as the *"professionalist paradigm of knowledge,"* into question: "The regula-
tive idea of this paradigm is that of the *absolute autonomy of the individual
discipline*, construed as a self-contained body of investigative procedures
and of knowledge held to be universally valid within the confines of an
unproblematized field" (147).[35] However, as I say, it means little attention is paid to the irreducibly paradoxical and inevitably violent nature
of the discipline's own foundation. Whenever the issue of its legitimacy
is raised, the discipline merely resorts to narrative myth-making of one
sort or another, (re)telling the story of its foundation, and thereby generating effects of legitimacy through repetition that can only ultimately
be maintained through violence and force.

The University Lives On/Online

Returning to the subject of open access and the archive, we can see that
nowhere are the implications of Weber's analysis of the institution and
of the process of instituting more apparent than with regard to the
question of the maintenance of academic quality control and certification. Who now qualifies as a *bona fide* peer-reviewer, referee, funding
application assessor, RAE panelist, or hiring, tenure, or promotion
committee member? And with what legitimacy are they able to make
the decision as to what to privilege and what to denigrate or exclude
from a given institution, discipline, journal, or archive? On the basis of
their membership in the profession? Their publication record? Their
completion of a certified course of training? Their position in a recognized university department? As Geoffrey Bennington has noted when
commenting on the manner in which "the legislator is always, undecidably, also a charlatan," at the time of the legislator's "coming, it is impossible to decide as to his legitimacy—in view of quite traditional paradoxes of authority, the final establishment of that legitimacy can only
be projected into an infinite future. The radically performative laying
down of the law by the legislator must create the very context according
to which that law could be judged to be just: the founding moment, the
pre-, is always already inhabited by the *post-*" (1990, 132, 131–32).

   In this respect, Weber's analysis provides at least one means of explaining some of the problems Stevan Harnad gets himself into regarding the open-access self-archiving of e-prints. Indeed, Harnad's attempt
to institute and institutionalize the self-archiving of e-prints appears to
offer an almost exemplary illustration of Weber's analysis. Witness the
way in which the academic legitimacy provided by the established pa-

percentric system of peer review is what underpins the mechanism of quality control in the open-access self-archiving system for Harnad: this enables the field of e-scholarship to distinguish between that which is legitimate and that which is not, and thus maintain order and standards. At the same time the legitimacy of this "established" peer-review system is rarely thought about, interrogated, or discussed in Harnad's work on open access. What is important to Harnad, for all his talk about the importance of peer review (1998/2000; 2001/2003), is not the taking of this issue seriously, but the taking of it for granted. Yet how are the judgments, decisions, and choices inherent in peer review to be distinguished from mere prejudice, bias, whim, fantasy, projection, or transference if their authority and legitimacy are not rigorously examined, discussed, and determined? Such questions are indeed "irrelevant to immediate concerns" as far as Harnad is concerned. He is not interested in where this legitimacy comes from or on what it rests, so much as with repeating, reproducing, and replicating this legitimacy in the world of open-access journal publishing and self-archiving.

My point in arguing that at the origins of the academic institution there lies an aporia of authority is not connected to some naïve idea of bringing it crashing down. This "deconstructive pragmatics of institutions," to adopt Weber's terminology, is not a *destruction* in that sense. If we acknowledge that violence is intrinsic to authority, we must—to follow both Weber and Derrida—resort to rules, conventions, and stabilizations of power. This is precisely the moment of the emergence of politics. Deconstruction, for Derrida, is a way of showing that, "since convention, institutions and consensus are stabilizations," they must be seen as fixing in place something intrinsically *unstable* and chaotic. "Thus, it becomes necessary to stabilize precisely because stability is not natural; it is because there is instability that stabilization becomes necessary; it is because there is chaos that there is need for stability" (1996a, 83–84). Derrida perceives this chaos and instability as a threat *and* a promise; it is the condition of both the possibility and impossibility of ethics and politics, as well as of the decision. "[T]his chaos and instability . . . is at once naturally the worst against which we struggle with laws, rules, conventions, politics and provisional hegemony, but at the same time it is a chance, a chance to change, to destabilize. If there were continual stability, there would be no need for politics, and it is to the extent that stability is not natural, essential or substantial, that politics exists and ethics is possible" (1996a, 84).

My point in illustrating the aporia of disciplinary legitimacy and institutional authority is rather to emphasize this chance—which is always also a risk, a promise, an opportunity, a loss—to rethink or think otherwise, and hence to *change* the manner in which the academic institution *lives on.*[36] If Bernard Stiegler is right when he remarks that a change or development in technology suspends or calls into question a situation "which previously seemed stable" (2002, 149), then it is this chance, this opportunity, if only we can take it, that the transition to the digital mode of publication opens up, via its exposition of the instituting process. And we have to take this chance *now* perhaps. For once all this settles down and is no longer quite so new, maybe this opportunity will have been lost. As Carolyn Marvin observed some time ago now in *When Old Technologies Were New,* "the introduction of new media is a special historical occasion when patterns anchored in older media that have provided the stable currency of social exchange are re-examined, challenged and defended" (1988, 4).

Of course, the ethical problem I am describing here—of infinite responsibility to an unconditional hospitality to the other and the necessity of responding, of making a decision—is not new. It certainly did not originate with the invention of information technology. As Weber has shown, a delimitable space such as a discipline or field of study (such as cultural studies) cannot be constituted without also opening it up to that which lies outside it—that which is not that discipline, but also that which is "not knowledge." A discipline has to have a certain relation to others—of both inclusion and exclusion—in order to be a discipline. And disciplines have always been structured like this, even when they were conceived, as they were by more "traditional" and "professional" modes of thought, as being autonomous and self-contained. *This is what I meant when I suggested earlier that academic authority is already digitized; that it is in a sense always already in a similar condition to that which is brought about by the process of digital reproduction.*[37] What *is* new (and what is thus historically specific to this particular moment in time) is the extent to which new media technology makes it possible to multiply, to a perhaps unprecedented extent, the permeability of this border, this frontier control, and thus bring the problem of what, in this case, can and cannot be legitimately included in cultural studies *as cultural studies* to attention and thematize it.[38] For while disciplines have always attempted to police their borders, and have always been more or less violent and lacking in any original founding authority when doing so, digital reproduction, not least because of its speed, the number of texts that can be produced, published, archived, preserved, and stored, the geographic range over which those texts can be distributed, and the relative ease and low cost of all this, together with the lack of stability, "fixity," and permanence of digital texts themselves, has the effect of highlighting the irreducibly violent and aporetic nature of any such authority, making it much more visible.

Another Cultural Studies Is Possible

In this respect the open-access reproduction and publication of the scholarly research literature provides an opportunity for cultural studies to take on, rather than merely act out, the effects of the ambivalence Weber describes in *Institution and Interpretation*, thus demonstrating that it is possible to envisage at least one alternative form of institutionalization or "counter-institution" for cultural studies of the kind Weber looks toward at the end of the book when he talks about conceiving "institutionalized practices of a 'discipline' that would assume the ambivalent demarcations that make it, and them, possible" (1987, 149).[39] What is interesting about open-access archiving in particular is precisely the extent to which it brings into question "the existing definition and delimitation of knowledge, as well as the conditions of its practice: in short, the *discipline* and the *university*" (49). In doing so it enables us to *conceive of a future for the university* in terms other than: either going along with the forces of capitalist neoliberal economics that are increasingly turning higher education into an extension of business; or, alternatively, advocating a return to the kind of paternalistic and class-bound ideas associated with Leavis, Arnold, and Newman that previously dominated the university, and which viewed it in terms of an elite cultural training and the reproduction of a national culture. This is what I meant when I said that the "strange and disorientating new context" of open-access archiving may offer us a chance to see cultural studies again "in a new way," as if for the first time, and so account for it and judge it anew.

(I would even go so far as to suggest that the digital or digitized cultural studies text judged anew like this would be the only one that *is* capable of claiming a certain legitimacy. To be sure, those assessed according to the rules and conventions of the paper peer-review system are not, because, as we have seen, that system operates merely by adhering to predetermined and unquestioned categories. So the digital cultural studies text in this scenario is in a way actually the only one that *is* being responded to responsibly. Contrary to the manner in which they are generally positioned, then, there is not first, and most authoritatively, ink-on-paper academic writing and publishing, and then a secondary and inferior digital copy of this written and published "language." Rather than coming after and being placed in a secondary position to the ink-on-paper text, when it comes to the question of legitimacy the digital text now somewhat paradoxically appears to come first and have priority—and not just in the sense that most academics nowadays write using personal computers.)

In this respect a cultural studies open-access archive promises to "be more than a base of *data*, a repository of the given" (Foster 1996). It is not *just* a "museumification" of cultural studies—to borrow a word of Steve Dietz's I like very much (1999): a means of reproducing and confirming existing conceptions of cultural studies; of collecting, gathering together, interpreting, filtering, and classifying what cultural studies already is or is remembered and perceived as having been (the work of Raymond Williams, Richard Hoggart, Stuart Hall, Lawrence Grossberg, Paul Gilroy, Meaghan Morris, Angela McRobbie, Kuan-Hsing Chen, bell hooks, Tricia Rose; and before that, of Antonio Gramsci, Louis Althusser, F. R. Leavis, Matthew Arnold, and so on). A cultural studies open-access archive will of course be partly that. But it is also a means of *producing* and *performing* what cultural studies is going to be in the past (a past that is still very much "to come," to borrow Derrida's phrase); *and* therefore what there is a chance for cultural studies to have been in the future.

Print This!

About the Book

Digitize This Book! develops an argument I laid out in an earlier book, *Culture in Bits* (2002). There I showed, first, how for many cultural studies had become too concerned with producing abstract Foucauldian, Derridean, or Lacanian readings of cultural images and texts that are far removed from the practical, political, material realities of power and oppression. What cultural studies needed from that standpoint—and needs even more so today post–September 11, July 7, and the attacks on Afghanistan and Iraq—is far more social, economic, and political analysis emphasizing the importance of the empirical, the material, and the concrete.

Second, I showed how this had led cultural studies to become caught in a struggle with political economy;[1] a conflict in which, despite various efforts to transcend it by means of a dialectical combination of the two,[2] cultural studies remained—and, indeed, to a large extent remains—trapped, unable to think its way out.

Third, I showed how the work of theorists associated with the philosophy of Jacques Derrida, such as Bill Readings, Robert J. C. Young, J. Hillis Miller, and Samuel Weber—work which, as Young observes, "does not merely *recognize* mutual incompatibilities, but shows how they can operate in relation to one another in a productive economy" (R. Young, 1996b)—can help us think through this impasse in the study of culture.

Culture in Bits thus argued for a reimagining or reinvention of the relation of cultural studies to what is often called "Theory": a reinvention that avoids the simple binarism of efforts to "connect or culturally translate between theory and practice" (McRobbie 1997, 182); and that instead draws attention to some of the ambiguities that both radically disrupt cultural studies and expose it to forms of knowledge and analysis cultural studies can comprehend only by placing its own identity in question, at least potentially.[3]

Digitize This Book! pursues this argument further and takes it into a new terrain by focusing on one such form or branch of knowledge in particular: that associated with new or emerging media technologies. This book looks most closely at the aspect of new media concerned with the digital reproduction, publication, and archivization of cultural studies itself. Picking up where the final chapter of *Culture in Bits* left off, *Digitize This Book!* endeavors to demonstrate that, as Walter Benjamin (1973) and, more recently, Bill Readings (1994) and Jacques Derrida (1996b) have reminded us, these new, digital media technologies not only change the process of accessing, communicating, exchanging, classifying, storing, and retrieving knowledge, but they also change the *very content and nature of that knowledge.* It follows that the consequences and implications of digital media for research into cultural studies themes, problematics, and questions cannot be explored simply by using the recognized, legitimate, preconstituted, disciplinary forms of knowledge: literary studies, philosophy, sociology, history, psychoanalysis, and so on. Digital media change the very nature of such disciplines, rendering them "unrecognizable," as Derrida says of psychoanalysis.

What this means as far as cultural studies specifically is concerned is that, as I put it by playing on a much-cited passage from Derrida's *Archive Fever,* cultural studies would not have been what it was when, say, Richard Hoggart wrote *The Uses of Literacy* (1957), if digital media technology had existed then. From the moment this new media became possible, cultural studies could in the future no longer take the form that Hoggart and so many other practitioners of cultural studies envisaged for it.[4]

In particular, *Digitize This Book!* investigates how new media technologies promise to change the very content and nature of cultural studies. It thus approaches new media through the question of the difference the medium itself makes, and then tracks some of the changes different digital communication technologies are making in and of themselves—as opposed to analyzing how new media merely remediate older media forms, and deliver a preexisting and more or less unchanged content, albeit in new ways. By exploring the potential for a *digitized cultural studies* and analyzing some currents in digital media development that call for new ways of thinking, *Digitize This Book!* attempts to open cultural studies to the possibility of discovering new objects and new forms of knowledge: not just in the gaps and margins between the already constituted disciplines that make up cultural studies' interdisciplinary repertoire; but objects and forms of knowledge that require the development of new methods and conceptual frameworks, new tools and techniques of analysis—something that may indeed render cultural studies "unrecognizable" *as cultural studies.*

It is with this uncertain, unknowable, unforeseeable future—a future that has profound and far-reaching implications for how we understand not only cultural studies but also scholarly writing, publishing, and research, the institution of the university, even culture, politics, and ethics—that this book is experimenting.

About CSeARCH: *Call for Contributions*

Culture Machine is currently seeking contributions to an open-access archive for research and publications in cultural studies and related fields, including literary, critical and cultural theory, new media, visual culture, communication and media studies, philosophy, psychoanalysis, science and technology studies, feminist theory, and post-colonial theory.

The archive, called CSeARCH, which stands for Cultural Studies e-Archive, is free to download from and upload to.

You can find CSeARCH at: http://www.culturemachine.net/csearch.

Here you can browse the archive and read and download its contents.

To upload work into the archive go to the "Submit" page. Fill in the brief details and you will then be sent a login name and password via e-mail, together with a direct link. Click on the link and you will be there—no need to login at that point the first time. (The password merely ensures no one but you can edit your entries.)

Anything that is already in digital form, be it Word, pdf, and so on, can be uploaded into the archive quite easily and very quickly (in minutes, in fact). So early and/or hard to come by texts, including out-of-print books, book chapters, journal editions or articles that can be scanned or otherwise digitized can all be made available this way. However, the idea of the archive is not just to preserve documents from the past, but also to make recent and even current work widely available open access: both that which has already been published and that which is awaiting publication.

More information about the CSeARCH open-access archive is available on the CSeARCH Web site. If you have any questions or problems, please e-mail me at: gary@garyhall.info.

Google These!

Affect	Hakim Bey
Aporia	Jacques Derrida
BitTorrent	Lawrence Grossberg
Codework	Jean-Claude Guédon
Copyleft	Stevan Harnad
Counter-institution	N. Katherine Hayles
Creative Commons	Douglas Kellner
Critical Art Ensemble	Geert Lovink
The "Golden Road"	Lev Manovich
The "Green Road"	Mark Poster
GREPH	Eric Raymond
Hactivism	Bill Readings
Mash-up	Richard Stallman
Napster	Peter Suber
Neoliberal	E. P. Thompson
Open Content	Samuel Weber
Open Editing	
Open Source	
Re-mix	
Responsibility	
RT@mark	
Singularity	
Tactical Media	

If You Like This Book, You Might Also Like . . .

Giorgio Agamben, *Remnants of Auschwitz: The Witness and the Archive*

Nicholson Baker, *Double Fold: Libraries and the Assault on Paper*

Walter Benjamin, *Walter Benjamin's Archive: Images, Texts, Signs*

Jorge Luis Borges, "The Library of Babel"

Timothy Clark, *The Poetics of Singularity: The Counter-Culturalist Turn in Heidegger, Derrida, Blanchot and the Later Gadamer*

Jacques Derrida, *Geneses, Genealogies, Genres, and Genius: The Secrets of the Archive*

Michel Foucault, *Archaeology of Knowledge*

Sigmund Freud, "A Note upon the 'Mystic Writing Pad'"

Jürgen Habermas, "The Idea of the University: Learning Processes"

N. Katherine Hayles, *Writing Machines*

Thomas H. Huxley, *Science and Education*

Lewis Hyde, *The Gift*

Jean-Noël Jeanneney, *Google and the Myth of Universal Knowledge*

Adrian Johns, *The Nature of the Book: Print and Knowledge in the Making*

Peggy Kamuf, *The Division of Literature: Or the University in Deconstruction*

Immanuel Kant, "On the Wrongfulness of Unauthorized Publication of Books"

Søren Kierkegaard, *Repetition*

F. R. Leavis, *Education and the University: A Sketch for an "English School"*

Sylvère Lotringer and Christian Marazzi, eds., *Autonomia: Post-Political Politics*

Marcel Mauss, *The Gift: The Form and Reason for Exchange in Archaic Societies*

John Henry Cardinal Newman, *The Idea of a University: Defined and Illustrated*

Friedrich Nietzsche, "On the Future of Our Educational Institutions"

Jeff Noon, *Pixel Juice: Stories from the Avant Pulp*

Avital Ronell, *The Telephone Book: Technology, Schizophrenia, Electric Speech*

F. W. J. Schelling, *On University Studies*

Gayatri Chakravorty Spivak, "The Rani of Sirmur: An Essay in Reading the Archives"

E. P. Thompson, *Warwick University Ltd.: Industry, Management and the Universities*

John Willinsky, *The Access Principle: The Case for Open Access to Research and Scholarship* alt. Archives

The arXiv.org E-Print Archive, http://www.arXiv.org
The Atlas Group Archive, http://theatlasgroup.org/aga.html
BioMed Central, http://www.biomedcentral.com
DAREnet, http://www.darenet.nl/en/page/language.view/home
Directory of Open Access Journals (DOAJ), http://www.doaj.org
Directory of Open Access Repositories OpenDOAR, http://www
    .opendoar.org
European Archive, http://europarchive.org
Flinders Academic Commons, http://dspace.flinders.edu.au/dspace
Gallica, http://gallica.bnf.fr
Internet Archive, http://www.archive.org
Open Journal Systems, http://pkp.sfu.ca/ojs
Project Gutenberg, http://www.gutenberg.org
Public Library of Science (PLoS), http://www.plos.org
PubMed Central, http://www.pubmedcentral.nih.gov

3

IT, Again; or, How to Build an Ethical Institution

Our challenge in this new century is a difficult one: to prepare to defend our nation against the unknown, the uncertain, the unseen, and the unexpected.

—*Donald Rumsfeld, former U.S. Secretary of Defense, 2002*

By now I hope to have persuaded you, dear reader, of the importance of digitizing academic research and scholarship and publishing it open access, even of creating open-access journals and open-access archives.[1] None of this is especially difficult to do. Nowadays a significant number of universities provide the means for their staff to both publish their research electronically via local repositories and access other stores held by institutions participating in the Open Society Institute (OSI) and the Scholarly Publishing and Academic Resources Coalition (SPARC) international initiatives. SHERPA (Securing a Hybrid Environment for Research Preservation and Access) has also set up a number of institutional archives of open-access research with, in August 2006, thirty-seven universities in the United Kingdom being listed at its site.[2] In fact, according to a Joint Information Systems Committee (JISC) Open Access briefing paper of April 2005, "by the beginning of 2005, there were almost forty Open Access archives in the UK" alone;[3] while in October 2006 the Directory of Open Access Repositories (Open-DOAR) was able to produce a quality-assured list of 798 repositories.[4] Likewise, it is possible to create and run an open-access journal or archive with very little by way of funding (something that is certainly the case as far as both *Culture Machine* and CSeARCH are concerned). As Solomon emphasizes, "all that is needed are e-mail for correspondence

[and] a Web server for content distribution. These are available to virtually any university faculty member through their institution or they can be purchased for less than $US50.00 from a commercial Internet service provider" (2006, n.p.). There is even available on the Web free and open-source software that makes it possible for institutions and individual researchers to create their own archives.[5] All that is really required is time, energy, and enthusiasm.

But when it comes to open-access archiving, this is in many ways the easy part. That is, it is fine so long as your ambition does not extend much beyond reproducing the current paper system in the digital medium. The last chapter, however, has drawn attention to some of the ethical problems with that. What, then, if we want to do more than just publish our "papercentric" research open access or construct an open-access repository of our own to rival that of the arXiv.org E-Print Archive at Cornell? What if we want to explore the possible forms that an ethically just and responsible open-access archive might take?

So far we have seen how digitization provides us with an opportunity, if only we can take it, to think the institution of cultural studies, and with it the university, differently, and thus to change the manner in which they live on. Assuming that we do want to make the most of this opportunity, how are we to decide what to welcome into a cultural studies archive? How are we to make a responsible ethical decision in a situation that, as we have seen, is marked by an irreducible ambivalence of disciplinary delimitation and an aporia of institutional authority? For help in answering these questions I want to return to the work of perhaps the most influential of recent thinkers on the idea and legitimacy of the institution of the university: Samuel Weber. I begin by turning, not to what in the circumstances might appear to be Weber's most obviously relevant texts, *Institution and Interpretation* (1987/2001) and *Mass Mediauras* (1996), nor even to his more recent essays on the future of the university, "The Future Campus: Destiny in a Virtual World" (1999) and "The Future of the Humanities: Experimenting" (2000), but to a lesser-known early essay in which Weber discusses another form of IT. This is *iterability*, a concept he repeats after Derrida and to which he ascribes the nickname "*it*."[6]

it

In "Signature, Event, Context" Derrida shows how, if it is to function as writing, it must be possible for communication to be "repeatable—

iterable"—legible, in the absence not only of its "original" meaning, context, referent, and of "every determined addressee," but also in the "absence of a determined signified or current intention of signification" (Derrida 1982a, 315, 318). "This iterability (*iter*, once again, comes from *itara*, *other*, in Sanskrit, and everything that follows may be read as the exploitation of the logic which links repetition to alterity), structures the mark of writing itself, and does so for no matter what type of writing (pictographic, hieroglyphic, ideographic, phonetic, alphabetic, to use the old categories). A writing that was not structurally legible— iterable— . . . would not be writing" (1982a, 315). Replicating Derrida's account of iterability in "It," Weber focuses on how the process of cognition (also) always involves repetition (iterability/alterity). "In order for a mark to function, it must be recognized—that is repeated," Weber writes, *pace* Derrida. Indeed, it "is only in and through such repetition . . . that the identity of the mark constitutes itself as that which stays the same and is recognized as such" (Weber 1978, 6). And "if identity is a product of recognition, and hence of repetition," Weber proceeds to argue, it follows that "there is no consistent possibility of recognizing an identity independent of and prior to such repetition" (1978, 7). Hence the way in which, in order to be able to *cognize* something, we already have to be able to *re-cognize* it, that is, *re-peat* it, see or take it *again*. To know and understand an object (for instance, a piece of original, digital, cultural studies writing or research), to perceive, conceptualize, interpret, judge, or assess it, to determine what it is, and just as important what it is not, we need to be able to compare and assimilate this "new" object to that which is already known and understood. Iterability is thus necessary when it comes to thinking about the production of knowledge, for Weber, since it is only through such repetition that the object in question can be measured against an earlier already known and familiar instance, and, by means of that comparison, established and recognized as the same or at least similar. So much so that, as he later makes clear in *Institution and Interpretation*, it is difficult to conceive of a relation to something which is "'absolutely incognizeable.'" This would appear to entail a "contradiction in terms, since there is no way of conceiving or conceptualizing alterity except as the other of cognition, which is nothing but a negative mode of knowledge. To generalize this other, to transcendentalize it, is to assert that we can know what we cannot know, which is unacceptable" (Weber 1987, 11).

The question of iterability also lies at the heart of the transition from paper to electronic publishing (from "it" to IT), I want to argue. In a further repetition of his analysis of iterability, this time, appropriately enough, in the context of a discussion of "the future of the humanities" and, indeed, the university, Weber acknowledges that

> wherever it is a question of repetition, technology and telecommunication are never very far away. Why? Because, as Benjamin was perhaps one of the first to clearly state, the mode of being of modern technology is *repetitive* and *reproductive*. The "work of art," so Benjamin insists, must henceforth be discussed with respect to its intrinsic "reproducibility." And such reproducibility involves inscription: the tracing of traits: photography, cinematography and now, we might say, videography. (Weber 2000, n.p.)

Yet viewing cognition in terms of a process of repetition and comparison with an earlier instance constituted as the selfsame is only one aspect of the acquisition of knowledge. Any act of intellection also has another dimension, one that, although it can never be entirely absent or removed from the scene, is often excluded, repressed, ignored—or indeed taken for granted. For if cognition involves a process of reducing what is unknown to what is familiar, it also involves remaining open to what cannot be assimilated, but instead transforms the familiar into something that is decidedly less so. To put it another way, while the act of intellection denies the object in question its newness, its difference, its heterogeneity, this act must also establish contact with something that is precisely new, different, foreign, other. Otherwise, how are we able to distinguish between knowledge and mere misunderstanding or illusion?

> How is it possible to "know" for certain that in thereby assimilating the hitherto unrecognized "object" to what is familiar, we are not abandoning or losing precisely that which makes it different, other. In short, that which makes it a potential *ob-ject* of knowledge. For if knowledge is to distinguish itself from hallucination, projection or mere phantasm, it must retain a relationship to that which *resists* subsumption under the familiar. The process of discovery, the production of knowledge, must thereby always entail a transformation

of what has hitherto been familiar, taken for granted or considered as "knowledge" into something less self-evident—just as inversely it transforms the hitherto unknown into something more familiar. (Weber 2000, n.p.)

In fact heterogeneity, difference, alterity, otherness are introduced into the act of intellection by the very process of repetition and comparison out of which recognition, and hence the acquisition of knowledge, emerges. The "alterity" presupposed by all repetition can never be entirely absorbed into the identification of the same. There will always be "excess, remainder, left-over" (Weber 1978, 12). This logic, which we have seen Derrida refer to, links repetition to alterity and distinguishes iterability from mere repetition (Derrida 1982a; see also Derrida 2001d, 76). What is more, "this holds not simply for the identification of an object, but for the structure of *consciousness* that such an object implies," as Weber makes clear in "It," when he writes: "Iterability, then, is what, for Derrida at least, precludes consciousness from ever becoming fully conscious of its object or itself. If something must be iterable in order to become an object of consciousness, then it can never be entirely grasped, having already been split in and by its being-repeated (or more precisely: by its *repeated being*)" (Weber 1978, 7). All of which has significant consequences for the process of "reading"; and also that of peer review, since it is not just the identity of the text or object being read, repeated, judged, or assessed that is "split" and no longer self-identical, but also that of the consciousness or subject that is doing the reading, repeating, judging, or assessing.

Any attempt to know and understand an object through perception, conception, interpretation, judgment, or assessment must by necessity proceed by means of two "distinct, if interdependent operations": the one involving a certain closure whereby that which has already been *re*-cognized is incorporated into our already existing systems of knowledge and understanding; the other involving an openness to that which, in its very newness, alterity, difference, and heterogeneity, requires an alteration and transformation of these systems in order for it to be capable of being understood (Weber 1978, 2).[7] The question that remains to be answered is: How are we to do both at the same time? This "problem and its implications have constituted one of the major occupations and preoccupations of Western thought," according to Weber (1978, 3). As in the case of disciplinary identity (but really we are talking about the same thing, this "tension between openness and closure [also characterizing] the university both in its social function and its epistemic practice" [see Weber 1999, n.p.]), in order to be able to know and identify something we cannot place limits on the process of cognition; yet at the same time we have to place limits on it.[8] We do not know where to stop or call a halt to this process; but if we want to *know*, we have to arrest it somewhere:

> For once we have conceded that our knowledge, our coming-to-know presupposes a prior knowing, it is difficult to *know* where to stop. And yet, if we cannot know where to stop, then the very notion of knowledge itself becomes questionable. If the *re-* of recognition cannot be grounded in an original, self-contained cognition, then there are no reasonable grounds for asserting that cognition itself—that is, true knowing—is possible. Instead, we are faced with an intrinsically open-ended process of repetition: the cognitive act can only accede to its object by reproducing an earlier cognition, which itself is only related to *its* object through another repetition of an earlier cognitive act . . . and so on. (Weber 1978, 3)[9]

As in *Institution and Interpretation*, we find ourselves faced with a situation in which we are unable to envisage an institution, a discipline, or even in this case the very act of acquiring knowledge, without limits and hence some form of closure. Given that, as far as cognition is concerned, like judgment and decision making, the operation of re-cognition, assimilation, and reduction of the unknown to that which is similar and familiar cannot be avoided, any more than it is possible to think of a "'text' *without* limitation . . . [o]f writing without some sort of closure," the question here too becomes not "*whether*" such limitations are to be imposed on this process, "but *how?*" (Weber 1987, xvi). To reiterate Weber, it is not so much the existence and survival of closure as such that needs to be explored, "but rather the manner in which it lives on; not whether or not such an assumption must be made, but rather *how* it is *performed* and with what consequences" (1987, xix). In particular, what all this does is help us to think about knowledge and understanding differently. For "if iterability makes recognition and understanding possible, it also makes them possible only as forms of misrecognition or misunderstanding, since the object recognized or understood will never be fully present to consciousness, nor entirely identical to itself.

This, of course, endows the notion of 'misunderstanding' with a status quite different from that traditionally ascribed to it, as long as it is considered to be simply the opposite or other of understanding. As an ineluctable aspect of iterability, misunderstanding no longer excludes understanding" (Weber 1978, 7).

We can therefore see that misunderstanding cannot be removed from the process of cognition in order to make the act of perception, conception, interpretation, judgment, or assessment more legitimate and authoritative, thus helping to establish the identity and difference of a particular discipline as a legitimate and accredited field of knowledge. Misunderstanding is part of what makes the process of cognition possible. All of which immediately raises questions for ideas concerning the legitimacy and authority of academic scholarship. What now is the status of that knowledge by which the other is to be understood if misrecognition, error, projection, hallucination, and illusion cannot be denied or excluded from the analysis, but are all terms for that which makes it possible in the first place—"'the structure of iterability,' in short" (1978, 9). This question becomes even more pertinent to the case in hand (that is, the digital reproduction, publication, and archivization of the cultural studies research literature) when one considers that this problem is something that new media, with their opening up of the academic institution's space of authority and legitimation to intrusion, transformation, and reconfiguration, make increasingly apparent. As Weber makes clear in another analysis concerned with both repetition and the future of the university:

> The very notion of scholarship tends to take for granted the enabling exclusions and limits through which any field of knowledge is constituted as a closed and self-contained area. In a world of increasing virtualisation, taking such exclusions for granted is less and less effective, and perhaps also less and less efficient. It is not a mere accident that the vocabulary imposed by the computerisation of information is one that stresses dynamic relations, rather than static fields. The Internet consists of web sites, of links and networks, not of self-contained realms or fields. And the economic value of commodities, as is well known, is not inherent in their physical makeup nor accessible in their immediate manifestation, but rather a function of complex relations. Both economic and technological factors thus contribute to a virtualisation of reality which can no longer be

effectively articulated by traditional notions of knowledge, based on a criterion of truth as the adequation of thought to its object. In the face of virtualisation there is a tendency which by no means is unmitigated to reconstrue the relation of knowledge to the unknown. Hitherto, one could say, the unknown was regarded, from the point of view of academic scholarship, primarily as the other or negative side of knowledge: as the not-yet-known. But in the light of virtualisation, the unknown becomes as it were the element or medium of knowledge, not merely its negative other. Virtuality emerges not as a possibility to be realized or actualized, but as the dynamic tendency of a network of links, out of which knowledge emerges as nodes or clusters of connections, which in turn are always subject to transformation by further exploration or development of the network or networks. (Weber 1999, n.p.)

Again it seems the legislator is always, undecidably, also a charlatan.

Is this a proper analysis? Have we really built such a cultural studies open-access archive? Am I only joking? Are you sure? Can you tell?

Apprehension and Anxiety

Weber's argument in "It" proceeds from a discussion of a "certain *closure*" in the strategy of deconstruction (1978, 13); to a connection between iterability, apprehension, anxiety, and Freud; and from there, in later texts, to a discussion of Kierkegaard, "experimenting," the university in a "virtual world" (1999), and, indeed, the very future of the humanities (2000). Now there is a lot to say here about Weber's analysis of apprehension and anxiety in "It": his account of the emergence of professionalism as an "effort to establish a measure of self-control . . . on the part of . . . a group, seeking to define and to maintain a certain identity in the face of an extremely dynamic, unsettling, and powerful reorganization and transformation of society" in *Institution and Interpretation*; and the apprehension and anxiety apparent in much of academia over the possible effects of digital reproduction on scholarship (1987, 27).

For instance, apprehension, Weber writes in "It" (and it is worth quoting him at length):

> marks that initial, "original" contact with the object that all cognition
> —and recognition—necessarily presumes. It seems of some inter-

est, therefore, that this word, even today, is anything but univocal. For apprehension, of course, also means: *anxiety*. It signifies the act of understanding, of recognition, of perception: an act by which we catch the meaning of a phrase or ascertain the existence of a thing; and yet also signifies the concern with or expectation of something adverse, uncertain, and possibly dangerous.

Is apprehension, then, perhaps just what we have been looking for—from the very beginning? Does it mark the place *of* that beginning, precisely in *dividing it?* And if this equivocation makes us *curious*, we will not be disappointed by certain of its other meanings: for instance, to apprehend someone is, of course—in the "physical" sense—to *arrest* that person, in the name of the *law* (in order that he be brought to judgement). (Weber 1978, 17)

Later in "It" he puts it this way:

It is as anxiety that the ego apprehends "the presence of danger," determining *it* as *its other*: as the loss of its object, as separation, as privation. As anxiety, the *act* of apprehension . . . is reinscribed as the re-action determining what cannot fully be determined, but what is also never entirely indeterminate. . . . [I]sn't "reading" just another name for what I have tried to describe as *apprehension*: that ambivalent effort to get it together by holding it in *abeyance*, by *arresting* its movement, *re-acting* (to) it—as though it were dangerous, threatening. (Weber 1978, 21–22, 22)

Can the institution's desire to ultimately locate the authority of digitally reproduced texts in the paper world (as we have seen with the example of Harnad) not be read as an attempt to "establish and to institutionalize" a "system of defense" (Weber 1987, 30); and thus as a response to its anxiety over the shift from ink-on-paper to digital publishing and, in particular, the fear that academic texts reproduced using IT may not be so easy to understand or judge? In other words, is this desire on the part of the institution a means of coping with, and establishing a measure of control over, a prospective crisis in academic authority that is being brought about (to a certain extent at least) by the rise of the knowledge economy? Mark Poster has written on the subject of how "digitalization has radically altered the conditions of culture," and how, "in response, the RIAA has exerted enormous influence on politicians to pass laws, including the DMCA [Digital Millennium Copyright Act of 1998], to extend copyright to cover digital products. In this way the RIAA hopes to maintain control over cultural objects," Poster asserts (Poster 2005, n.p.). Could it not be argued that the academic institution is trying to do something analogous with scholarly texts and open-access publishing and archiving in terms of peer review? There are certainly a number of definite advantages as far as the institution is concerned in regarding digital texts as merely a prosthetic extension of paper (as we saw is so often the case with regard to the electronic reproduction, publication, and archivization of the academic research literature). Indeed, from a certain perspective, far from being a problem, this restriction of electronic publishing to the familiar appears to be part of the point of a lot of this discussion and debate. After all, if electronic texts were to be positioned as too different, this would place them beyond the reassuring control of the peer-review system: they would consequently then appear neither "reliable nor navigable, [their] quality uncontrolled, unfiltered, un-sign-posted, unknown, unaccountable" (Harnad 2001/2003, n.p.). As such they would create a sense of anxiety in their audience. Are they legitimate or not? How can we be sure? How can we tell?

From this position, the peer-review system appears as a means of coping with a certain anxiety and apprehension that digital publications may be out of the control of the institution: it is a means of disciplining such texts, keeping them within defined and measurable (i.e., assessable) limits. We could speculate that one reason Harnad is so reluctant to make the leap further into the digital and take what I have characterized as a responsible, ethical decision concerning the standards and criteria for the judging, reviewing, and certifying of academic work on which an open-access archive could be based, is because doing so would force him to address the uncomfortable question of scholarly legitimacy in general—a question that "in the face of an extremely dynamic, unsettling, and powerful reorganization and transformation of society," he has tried so hard to keep closed. For if Harnad were to acknowledge that scholarship on the net is so new that the old "paper" standards of peer review do indeed no longer necessarily apply, not only would this place in question his own competence and authority to read, apprehend, arrest, and judge; it would (as we can now see, following Weber) threaten the status and identity of his discipline and profession. Is this the reason Harnad's work often appears so obsessed with peer review? Does Harnad realize, consciously or unconsciously, that this is a weak spot? Is this why he has had to repeatedly support and defend it in article after article, e-mail after e-mail, and argue that the priority is to make 100 percent of the research literature open access, with anything else, including issues around the legitimacy of peer review, acting merely as a delay or distraction? As Weber makes clear, this level of anxiety (often evident in discussions of the implications and consequences of new media technologies) about maintaining legitimacy via peer review, lest we fall into anarchy and chaos, only indicates that the belief in the importance of peer review may be an effort to cope with the anxiety rather than "an objectively grounded cognition" (Weber 1978, 4).

Now I realize that by raising these issues I risk being regarded (by whom? Harnad? those in cultural studies? by the institution?) as somewhat unreliable, unaccountable, uncontrollable, dangerous, mad, crazy even; as someone who is threatening to bring the whole system of academic validation and accreditation crashing down around our ears; or at least as someone wanting to make it difficult for the system to carry on as it did before, as it has for so many years now. While not wanting to position myself in some romantic, heroic role, this is undoubtedly the risk one must take in order to address, responsibly, questions concerning the legitimacy of the institution. For is the above not the way in which the institution so often attempts to protect itself from such questions—by excluding them in advance as the work of the dangerous or the mad, and thus as illegitimate or inappropriate, before the question of legitimacy has even begun to be raised. Indeed, precisely because the question of institutional legitimacy is on the verge of being raised. . . .

But since I have to stop the chain or network of links and connections somewhere, I think I will end it here for now and bring this chapter to a close with some final remarks on the possible consequences of Weber's analysis for a cultural studies open-access archive and from there a re-thought institution.

The Exception

To sum up (and again moving very quickly): what Weber's work on "it" helps us to understand is that knowledge, understanding, and judgment involve "the aporetic possibility of remaining open to the trace of the other in repetition even while confronting the same. This possibility is aporetic insofar as this opening to the other can never be free of a degree of closure, of assimilation and appropriation" (Weber 2000, n.p.). What this means for cultural studies is that in order to understand itself after the invention of the Internet—but not just *after* the Internet, since iterability is an intrinsic feature of all judgment and understanding—for it to be able to judge and decide on the status of texts that are "born digital," cultural studies must consist of a nondialectical (or not simply dialectical) aporetic "opening *of* and *toward*" that which is different, new, foreign (2000, n.p.).

In the context of a cultural studies open-access archive, this obviously suggests an opening of and toward:

- Those "legitimate" branches of knowledge that are traditionally included in the interdisciplinary repertoire of cultural studies: those encompassed by disciplines such as sociology, philosophy, art history, literary theory, and so forth
- More marginalized forms of knowledge, such as those associated with differences of gender, sexuality, race, or ethnicity
- As well as, increasingly, those forms of knowledge found in formations of cultural studies outside the Anglo-American/Australian nexus—including Poland, Finland, Turkey, South Africa, Brazil, Taiwan, Japan, Singapore, and South Korea

This aporetic possibility also includes that legitimate knowledge ascribed to disciplines that have been marginalized or excluded from cultural studies: some of the more commercially profitable areas of study associated with science, technology, electronic and computer engineering, health, hospitality, sport, tourism, leisure studies, and so on —which are privileged within the contemporary university for meeting the needs of industry and society in the new global economy, but which are often found wanting when judged according to the more politically committed and interrogative criteria of cultural studies—could all possibly be included in this category. So, too, could the likes of political economy, social policy, and anthropology, albeit to varying degrees and extents, depending on the particular situation and circumstances.

Rather less obviously, Weber's work on "it" suggests an aporetic opening toward:

- Forms of knowledge that are not, or not yet, regarded as legitimate: including not just many of those associated with IT (e-mails, e-mail lists, blogs, wikis, wikified texts, Web 2.0—the kind of thing I have been quoting from in this book, in fact) that are not recognizable as legitimate if judged by the rules and conventions of the paper world,[10] but certain ways of being ethical and political, too

- What might be called "non-knowledge"—the apparently useless, unimportant, irrelevant, obsolete, worthless, senseless, trivial, or mistaken (hypnosis, for example, or projection, hallucination, illusion, transference, naffness, phantomism)

More radically still, it suggests an opening toward that which refuses to fit into cultural studies; that which is not cultural studies' other, but is "*other than the other itself*" (Weber 1987, 11), and which rather resists cultural studies as new, different, foreign, heterogeneous, and, resisting it, pushes cultural studies into adopting new forms and inhabiting new spaces in which it may no longer recognize itself *as cultural studies*. In other words (and to reiterate Weber once again), cultural studies must be rethought from the point of view of the "exception; which is to say, from the perspective of what refuses to fit in, what resists assimilation, but what, in so doing, reveals the enabling limits of all system, synthesis and self-containment" (Weber 2000, n.p.). For there is a paradox or contradiction or, indeed, *aporia* in the relation to the "other" or the "outside" of knowledge. Identifying and naming these non-knowledges (even as misunderstanding, misrecognition, error, illusion, projection, hallucination, hypnosis, transference, naffness, death, or whatever) is what makes this relation possible. It is only by identifying and naming them that we can have any such relation to these non-knowledges. At the same time it is also that which renders this relation impossible, because this relation is in effect only being extended to that which *can* be named and identified; whereas the difference between non-knowledge and the other of knowledge is that the latter cannot be named or identified—it is rather that which knowledge cannot or does not know, and which is therefore indeed the other of knowledge. The aporetic relation to non-knowledge thus involves a break with knowledge, with what can be known. It requires that we open knowledge up, not only to that which can be named and identified as the other of knowledge (as non-knowledge, or *not yet* knowledge, or knowledge-to-come), but also that which cannot. In the context of a cultural studies open-access archive, it requires that we open ourselves to the absolute, unknown other; that we be prepared to let it in, to receive it without necessarily asking it to respond reciprocally, by identifying or naming itself, not just as legitimate or not-yet-legitimate, but even as non-knowledge or the unknown. For in even requesting contributors to identify themselves and their research by title, author, publication, date, subject area, abstract, keywords, and so forth we are not being open to the other but are asking them, demanding of them, that they conform to certain preestablished rules, laws, and criteria.[11] Witness the way in which the arXiv.org E-Print Archive was (unsuccessfully) sued by an independent researcher and an American creationist, both of whom made separate claims to the effect that their civil rights had been infringed by the archive moderators' decision not to publish their work in the archive on the grounds that neither is affiliated with a recognized physics institution (*Times Higher Education Supplement* 2002, 4).[12]

Granted, there is a risk (which is of course also an opportunity) that as a result the contents of any such cultural studies "open" archive will not look too much like cultural studies, or academic scholarship, or knowledge, even, at least as these are currently commonly conceived and most easily recognized (and especially as they are understood according to the conventions of ink-on-paper publishing). Yet at the same time this questioning of cultural studies is also "perhaps" the most "responsible" thing for cultural studies to do, at least in Derrida's sense of the term responsibility, since there can be no responsibility, and no ethics, no politics, and indeed no cultural studies, I would argue (see G. Hall 2002), without the experience of the undecidable; without, in this case, the constant (re)taking of the decision of what cultural studies is.

Will a cultural studies open-access archive really make it possible for us to do this? Obviously I cannot be sure. I have no way of knowing. If there is a transformation in the material supports of knowledge from paper and analogue to digital under way at the moment, the development of the cultural studies open-access archive I am involved with can certainly be seen as (a small) part of this process, experimenting with how this transfiguration in support is going to change the very content and nature of knowledge. Yet at the same time any such cultural studies repository undoubtedly risks failing, visibly if not indeed spectacularly—precisely because of the questions it encourages us to address. Still, this risk—of paralysis, of chaos, of the archive being more or less unused or unusable—is just that of the situation, of trying to do something new, something different, something interesting, something ethical.

II. HYPERPOLITICS

Antipolitics and the Internet

For or against the war on terror, or the war in Iraq; for the termina-
tion of an odious tyrant and his crime family, for the ultimate weapons inspection, the opening of the torture prisons, locating the mass
graves, the chance of liberty and prosperity, and a warning to other
despots; or against the bombing of civilians, the inevitable refugees
and famine, illegal international action, the wrath of Arab nations
and the swelling of Al-Qaeda's ranks. Either way, it amounts to a
consensus of a kind, an orthodoxy of attention, a mild subjugation
in itself. Does he think that his ambivalence—if that's what it really
is—excuses him from general conformity?
                                              —*Ian McEwan*, Saturday, 2006

Stories We Tell Ourselves about New Media

One of the main arguments in this book—as developed in the last two
chapters—is that the potential challenge to the established modes of
academic legitimation offered by the digital reproduction of scholarly
research literature, and open-access publishing and archiving in particular, raises questions one might place under the heading of "ethics."
(Again, I stress that I am using ethics here not according to its conceptualization by traditional moral philosophy, where ethics consists of a
set of predefined codes and norms, but rather in the sense Jacques Derrida gives to the term. Following the philosopher Emmanuel Levinas,
whose work is becoming increasingly important within cultural studies,[1] Derrida understands ethics as an obligation toward the incalculable alterity of the other who renders me responsible and who calls me
into question.) In this chapter and the chapters that follow I will argue that this potential challenge is not just ethical but also *political*—

although not necessarily, or not always, or at any rate not only in the usually recognized sense of the term.

For instance, as I explained in my first set of metadata, "Notes on Creating Critical Computer Media," I am not suggesting that open access in general, and the cultural studies archive I founded in particular, are political in the sense that they provide a means of moving the "deconstructive" philosophy of Samuel Weber or Jacques Derrida, or even my own work, away from a concern with producing a negative theoretical critique of texts, and toward an affirmative, practical, material intervention by means of the creation of an actual institution using the Internet, the Web, e-mail, and so on. That would imply that other instances and performances of deconstruction, those that *do not* involve the production of a material/virtual institution, *are* just negative forms of critique: that they are interested merely in pointing out textual aporias, ambiguities, ambivalences, contradictions, paradoxes, and so on, rather than using them as a basis for inventing something different and new. There is also a related risk of intimating that, in contrast to what I am doing here, other forms of deconstruction are *not* concerned with the institution, whereas for Derrida, at any rate, deconstruction involves a constant position-taking with regard to the institution (1992a). In this respect I would disagree with Weber when, in *Institution and Interpretation*, he writes that deconstruction has not concerned itself too much "with the institutional conditions of its own practice," and has "tended to downplay the forces and factors that always operate to institute and to maintain certain sets of paradigms, notwithstanding (or even because of) their intrinsically aporetic structure" (1987, 19). Deconstruction has often (given its concern with singularity and the event, I am wary of saying *always*) been affirmative, not least because it has been defined as the constant adopting of a position with regard to politics and the institution of the university. The performative staging of Derrida's texts is just one way in which they have challenged traditional academic disciplines and the functioning of the university as it has been institutionally delineated. Witness, too, Derrida's own involvement in founding and supporting numerous "real-life" counterinstitutions such as the Groupe de recherche sur l'enseignement philosophique (GREPH), the Etats généraux, and the Collège international de philosophie. Nor is this aspect of deconstruction solely a feature of Derrida's later work, that written after Weber had published the first edition of *Institution and Interpretation* in 1987. These performative and counterinstitutional facets of Derrida's thought were already evident in his earlier writings, including *Margins of Philosophy* (1982b) and *Dissemination* (1981), to name but two.[2]

Similarly, I am not maintaining that the open-access repository I am involved with, with its focus on making a tactical use of the "real world," empirical, ethnographic, and experiential context of the contemporary university, is potentially *political* because it appears to respond to the regular calls for cultural studies to move away from the grand theoretical, "textual," "linguistic" approaches that supposedly came to dominate the field in the 1980s and early 1990s, and move back to reality, the material, and the sort of political commitment that is regarded as lying at the roots of cultural studies. As I also made clear in "Notes on Creating Critical Computer Media," a number of questions can be raised against this position. Indeed, it is by no means certain that cultural studies *can* return to earlier forms of political engagement, even if it did aspire to go down this route. To attempt to do so would be to ignore the very economic and political realities that the desired move toward politics is supposed to enable cultural studies to take into account. Charting the fate of the university in a world increasingly dominated by an economic and managerial logic of profit and loss, Bill Readings demonstrated in his 1996 book *The University in Ruins* how the "human sciences can do what they like with culture, can do Cultural Studies, because culture no longer matters as an idea for the institution." The "notion of culture as the legitimating idea of the modern university has reached the end of its usefulness" (Readings 1996, 5), according to Readings, and has been replaced by the concept of "excellence," which has the "singular advantage of being meaningless, or to put it more precisely, non-referential" (1996, 22). This process of "dereferentialization" means that we cannot return to what Readings calls the "University of Culture": this institution is ruined and has lost its historical reason for being. Any attempt to dwell in those ruins with the aid of politics simply amounts to taking "recourse to romantic nostalgia" (1996, 169). Rather than enabling a return to politics, then, the present political situation requires cultural studies to give up this "religious attitude toward political action" and move beyond its melancholia "for a lost idea of culture that needs political renewal" (1996, 191).

The challenge to scholarly legitimation that is posed by digitization and the open-access movement is not necessarily, or not always, or not just political in the sense that it conforms to some already established and easily recognized criteria of what it means *to be political.* This is why I have for the most part resisted presenting digitization and open access in terms of the kind of discourses and narratives into which they have usually been inscribed. Among these more typical and familiar narratives concerning open access we can list three characteristic approaches.

The liberal, democratizing approach sees open access as enabling the production of global information commons.

The transition in the sphere of book production from manual copying to print has been described as exerting a number of political effects on society. Prior to this, access to written texts was primarily the preserve of the wealthy or educated elite. The development of mass industrial printing techniques, however, enabled books to be reproduced cheaply on a large scale. As a result the majority of individuals, including many of those with only limited budgets, were eventually able to purchase books, while even the smallest of towns could afford to build a public library of its own, which made books more accessible still. The Enlightenment fantasy of a universally literate and educated society in which all knowledge is obtainable by everyone, no matter how lowly or impoverished, was thus perceived as having become a real possibility.

By placing more ideas and information, from more sources, within easy reach of a greater number of the world's population than any previous form of media or technology, the Internet, and with it open-access publishing and archiving, is often regarded as having the potential to achieve social and political effects on a similarly profound scale. Like the printing press before it, the process of making books, journals, and databases open access, together with the computing technology required to support and develop them, is positioned as democratizing knowledge. It does so by rendering knowledge and technology available to those who cannot afford to invest in the production of such things themselves, but who nevertheless stand to benefit from their collective sharing. Open access thus enables the emergence of a form of "global information commons," in which all the participants are able to give and receive information for free, or at least for very little cost. As such, it is seen as offering a solution to some of the problems of global democracy, especially what is called the "digital divide": the situation whereby some nations around the world, especially those in the "developing world," do not have the same degree of access to knowledge as those in the West and North because of the prohibitive cost of accessing it, and so are unable to participate in the global marketplace on equal terms or otherwise take full advantage of and contribute to advancements in education, science, medicine, technology, and culture.

We have already encountered one variation on this approach in both my Introduction and chapter 2, with Stevan Harnad's conviction that the self-archiving of the refereed scientific research literature is going to make "the entire full-text refereed corpus online / On every researcher's desktop everywhere / 24 hours a day . . . / For free, for all, forever" (2001/2003, n.p.).[3] This belief—that knowledge should not necessarily be owned, copyrighted, or exchanged by publishers solely for profit and restricted to those connected to affluent institutions, and should instead be made available for free (or at least relatively cheaply) to everyone who wishes to access it—a few years ago led 32,362 research scientists in 183 countries to boycott any scientific journal that refused to make research papers freely available on the Internet six months after publication. When that boycott failed, since younger scholars especially found they still had to publish in those journals in order to embark on their careers, this belief then led them to launch their own free online journals (Meek 2001, 3; MacLeod 2003, 9). Another influential example, again concerned with scientific research and its publication, although this time emanating from the world of policy, is provided by Shuichi Iwata, the president of the Global Information Commons for Science Initiative of the International Council for Science's Committee on Data for Science and Technology (CODATA). Iwata lists the following scientific developments as potentially exerting a major impact on the scientific community in the next five to ten years:

- The digitization and general accessibility of all, past and present, scientific data and information.
- An increase in long-distance scientific collaborations enabled by the Internet, which will rely on access to substantial data collections, large-scale computing resources, and high-performance visualization of data. This will lead to e-science gaining precedence over more "localized" scientific work.

- The development of public data access systems that will facilitate general access to the scientific collections mentioned above. (Iwata 2006)

The renewed public sphere approach perceives open access as having the potential to facilitate the creation of a revitalized form of public sphere of discussion, debate, information networking, and exchange.

Famously, for Jürgen Habermas, the commercial mass media have had a major part to play in the demise of the public sphere. They have done so by turning the general populace into passive consumers of media spectacle. Consequently, the problem with political participation today, it is said, is that most members of democratic societies do not possess sufficient information to be able to make knowledgeable decisions and so play an active role in the democratic process. In breaking down the barriers between the academic community and the rest of society, however, as well as between scholarly research and other kinds of work that occur in places outside the academic institution, it is held that open-access publishing and archiving is facilitating the creation of a revitalized form of the idealized public sphere. It does so by supplying the public with the knowledge and information required to enable them to exercise their powers of critical reason and contribute to democratic debate, thus giving them a chance to actually converse and engage with the media, as opposed to passively consuming messages from them.[4]

Although he mentions neither Habermas nor the public sphere specifically, John Willinsky poses a variation on this theme "of helping citizens take advantage of new information sources to further their democratic participation" that "lies at the heart of the political case . . . for open access to research and scholarship" (Willinsky 2006, 127). Willinsky also subscribes to a number of features of the liberal, democratizing, global information commons approach, as my Introduction suggested. Nor is he alone in this. In fact, the above two liberal democratic perspectives on open access are often so interrelated and intertwined in many people's arguments as to make them difficult to distinguish.[5]

The gift economy approach positions open access as helping to establish a new kind of a radical, digital economy of the gift.

From this point of view, open access offers a radically different means for the communication and exchange of knowledge and ideas from that afforded by capitalism's free-market economies—albeit one that, far from being simply opposed to or situated outside of commodity capitalism, actually arises *out of and co-exists with it*. It thus provides a model for the subversion of the logic of commodification and for the development of new and radically alternative forms of social, political, and economic organization to supplement or rival that of capitalism.

In the latter, ideas and knowledge are commodified, given exchange values or prices, and then distributed by means of the market. The emphasis here is on the right to own and control intellectual property to the exclusion of others in order to recoup the cost of their production and distribution by charging a fee to possess them (in this case, in the form of book cover prices, journal subscriptions, the cost of registering for access to online databases, and so forth). It is therefore a system that depends on an economics of lack and insufficiency in that, if there are not enough instances of a particular commodity to meet the needs and desires of everyone in society, then those who can afford to are motivated to pay for such commodities in order to acquire them. The market sets the value or price of these commodities, taking into account the relation between how many are available, and how many people wish to obtain them. The fewer commodities there are to go around and the more people there are who want to purchase them, the higher the price is likely to be. But this system also depends on an economics of lack and insufficiency in that such commodities are rivalrous. If one person purchases and so owns and possesses a singular commodity, that commodity cannot be owned or possessed by someone else, unless it is traded to them in exchange for money or some other commodity. At that point ownership of the original commodity transfers to that second person: it becomes *their* personal property, with its initial purchaser no longer being in possession of it.

Now, within capitalism, legal laws and rights around copyright have been built into its logic of commodification, exchange, and distribution to ensure and enforce this economics of insufficiency and lack. These same laws and rights have then been used to try to control the production, copying, distribution, and exchange of digital culture. (The Federation Against Copyright Theft [FACT] has apparently even trained sniffer dogs to search for pirated DVDs being smuggled though airports by counterfeiting gangs.) However, these laws have had only very limited success. As the case of the open-access publication of digitally reproduced academic scholarship and research clearly shows, it is much more difficult to make digital objects operate according to the logic of commodification and the market and an economics of insufficiency. This is partly because they are so easy and cheap to produce, copy, store, access, exchange, acquire, and distribute. But it also has to do with the fact that digital objects are nonrivalrous. Someone can own a copy of a digitally reproduced journal article, say, and they can make it freely available to as many people as they like simply by publishing it open access or by uploading it into an open-access repository. Yet they do not themselves possess that article any the less for doing so. They still have their copy, to do with as they please. They have also just made their copy freely available to as many others as wish to read and possess it as a *gift*, something that is not scarce and that therefore does not need to be competed or compensated for in financial terms. This does not mean that those who publish open access do not receive compensation for doing so—only that their gifting is compensated by indirect means: in the case of open access, by the greater levels of feedback and recognition authors receive for their work.[6]

Richard Barbrook is just one of those to have put forward a case along these lines. For Barbrook, the academic gift economy that operates within universities, whereby scientists give away and distribute their research and findings for free, is more or less a modern, "hi-tech version" of the Polynesian tribal potlatch gift economy that anarcho-communists from "May 1968 to the late Nineties" believed "demonstrated that individuals could successfully live together without needing either the state or the market."[7] And, indeed, by taking part in a radical, digital system of gift exchange in which people are able to circulate material as free software, open source and open content, and create new kinds of texts like wikis and blogs, open-access journals and archives are often perceived as helping to construct an online economy that promises to fundamentally alter and subvert notions of private property and systems of commodification. It is an emergent economy that for many represents a challenge to capitalism itself.

But if I have reservations about positioning open access as political in terms of the kinds of discourses and narratives into which it has usually been inscribed, how *do* I propose to conceptualize its "politicality"? To answer this question we need to address the very issue of what it is to be political on the Internet by investigating the dominant forms of online politics and political participation.

Remediating Politics

To date, the majority of critics and researchers have approached new media using preestablished (what I will later refer to as "transcendental") frameworks of knowledge and methods of analysis. For the most part they have presumed that the future is understandable in terms of the past, the new in terms of the old. The opening essay of Mark Tribe and Reena Jana's recent book, *New Media Art*, provides an illustration, supplying a number of examples from art history that new media art is supposedly "like," and that can therefore be used to help us understand and interpret it. These include Dadaist strategies of the photomontage, collage, the readymade, pop art and video art (Tribe and Jana 2006, 8–9).[8] Perhaps the most obvious example of this approach, however, is the way in which, from at least the 1990s onwards, the relationship between new media and politics has been articulated. It is perspectives on, and narratives about, this relationship that will concern me in the next section of this chapter.

Before I go any further, I should point out that I realize presenting the politics of emerging media as being made up of opposing perspectives, as I am about to do here, is by now something of a cliché. Most books on the subject begin by positioning new media technologies as being trapped in just such a set of contrasting and conflictual discourses, so much so that one Internet company actually used (or should that be parodied?) the binary form of debates of this kind in its advertising. AOL's "Discuss" ads invited consumers to address such topics as "Is the Internet a good thing or a bad thing?," laying out some of the pros and cons of each side of the argument:

> Some people think the internet is a bad thing. Somewhere your identity can be stolen. . . . It is one of the most dangerous weapons ever created. A way for the unhinged to spread evil, free of supervision or censorship. A place for mankind to exercise its darkest desires. An open market where you can purchase anything you want. Orwell was right. . . .
>
> Some people think the internet is a good thing. The most powerful educational tool the world has ever known. It's preserving our history, making sure that in the future we never forget the past. . . . The internet is a place that is free of state regulation, censorship and control . . . Orwell was wrong. It is not the state that holds all the power, it is us . . . What do you think?[9]

Nevertheless, I have decided to provide a brief replay of these debates—which occur in both mainstream and academic media—in order to illustrate, by drawing on some contemporary examples, that despite the fact that this dialectical rhetoric *has* become something of a cliché, the politics of new media continues to be conceived and understood very much in such a dualistic manner. At the risk of actually legitimating and solidifying the structure I am taking issue with, I hope that this reiteration of the discourses of "digital dialectics" will act as something of a disabling mechanism, making it just a little bit more difficult for new media politics to continue to be conceptualized and approached in this fashion in the future.

"Some People Think the Internet Is a Good Thing . . ."

One such group of narratives positions new media as generating opportunities for democratic participation, challenge, and even resistance. The emphasis here is placed on the way in which cell phones, computers, laptops, the Internet, e-mail, blogs, wikis and the like have brought about a dramatic change in the workings of the media and culture industries. The top-down, few-to-many information flows associated with the hierarchical, broadcast model of the mass media are regarded as having been supplemented, or even supplanted, by a far more democratic, interactive, heterogeneous, affective, many-to-many network model associated with emerging digital media and often seen as operating outside of "official," centralized state or corporate control.

Blogging in particular has frequently been held up as an example of the way in which, thanks to the Internet, the media is becoming much more popularly participatory and democratic. To be sure, there have been reports in *The New York Times* of corporate giants such as Microsoft and Wal-Mart using blogs and bloggers not just to promote their products but also to help improve their public image (Barbaro 2006). Yet none of this has been enough to prevent any number of critics positioning blogging as heralding the death of "big media"; or at the very least as "transforming the way news and information are disseminated," as the journalist and radio host Ariana Huffington put it on the very day *The Guardian* launched the first rolling comment blog by a United Kingdom newspaper:

Blogging has empowered the little guy—levelling the playing field between the media haves and the media have-only-a-laptop-and-an-internet-connection. It's made the blogosphere an invaluable tool for holding the mainstream media's feet to the fire. As blogger extraordinaire Glenn Reynolds (aka Instapundit) puts it in his new book, *An Army of Davids*, "Where before journalists and pundits could offer illogical analysis or cite 'facts' that were in fact false, now the Sunday morning op-eds have already been dissected on Saturday night, within hours of their appearing on newspapers' websites." (Huffington 2006, 30)[10]

Even Rupert Murdoch, owner of Fox, *The Times*, and *The Sun* (among many other things), has conceded that, with the number of blogs doubling every six months, "power is moving away from the old elite in our industry—the editors, the chief executives and, let's face it, the proprietors," and that "we are at the dawn of a golden age of information—an empire of new knowledge."[11]

Nowhere has this e-empire of new knowledge, this "digital democracy" as it has been called, been held to be more in evidence than with regard to what President George W. Bush described as America's "biggest mistake"—so far—of the second Gulf War: the torture and abuse of prisoners in Abu Ghraib prison (Bush 2006). Indeed, if Gulf War One was the first TV war (in the sense that it was the first to be televised as live spectacle), and the Kosovo war the first Internet war (Keenan 2002), then the latest attack on Iraq can be considered the first digital war, in that it is the first in which the troops themselves acted as significant producers and distributors of media, able to shares images and real-time footage of their wartime experiences with the rest of the world. The existence of digital media and culture in general, and blogs in particular, certainly made it extremely difficult for the forces of the "coalition of the willing" to keep the abuses committed at Abu Ghraib under wraps. Which of course is not to say that those who took the pictures and videos of these atrocities were necessarily politically mobilized against the war. According to one government consultant, in many cases images of sexual humiliation were used to "create an army of informants, people you could insert back in the population" and who "would do anything—including spying on their associates—to avoid dissemination of the shameful photos to family and friends" (quoted in

Hersch 2004). This would certainly explain why so many of these images go to the rather unusual lengths of presenting for inspection the actual perpetrators of these crimes and not just their victims. Yet whether they were taken for this reason, or simply as perverse trophies or souvenirs, the ease and speed with which the pictures from Abu Ghraib could be downloaded and e-mailed, made into DVDs, circulated and published in mainstream broadcasting and print media, and posted, archived, and publicized on a rhizomatic network of Web sites and blogs, thus generating further and sustained media and public interest over the long term, made both the images themselves and the ensuing political scandal hard, if not indeed impossible for the U.S. government to contain, control, and manage according to its own political agenda.[12]

From this angle, new media is presented very much as providing a means of overcoming many of the limitations and problems associated with the old, "elite," global mass media, especially their disempowering and homogenizing nature, and the way they are concentrated in increasingly fewer—and richer—hands. Nowadays, the argument goes, people do not just listen to or watch media messages; thanks to the Internet and World Wide Web they are also able to create, broadcast, circulate, and exchange their own ideas and cultural creations. As such, new media is positioned as supplying the necessary knowledge and equipment for just about anyone, even children and those serving in the military, to not only consume media but produce it as well, thus aiding and promoting greater social dialogue, which in turn helps to build and sustain active participation and engagement in democratic forms of politics and social life.

When adopted by media and cultural studies critics, this positive and optimistic championing of the democratic potential of emerging media often constitutes something of a response to earlier, more pessimistic, Frankfurt School–type criticisms of the role of the old, elite culture industries. It therefore comes as no surprise to find Douglas Kellner, a renowned commentator on the Frankfurt School and Web master of the "Illuminations" critical theory Web site,[13] adhering to this view of Internet politics in what is one of the most widely referred to articles on the subject: "Techno-Politics, New Technologies, and the New Public Spheres" (1997). Whereas the mass media—the press, TV, radio stations, film companies, and so on—is for the most part controlled by the same centralized government bodies, institutions, multinational businesses, and media conglomerates that dominate the rest of society, the Internet, for Kellner, along with public-access television and community and guerrilla radio, opens media technologies to "intervention and use by critical-oppositional intellectuals," and thus to the creation of new public spheres of democratic discussion, analysis, and debate. Writing in the mid-1990s, Kellner is able to cite a number of insurgent intellectuals who are already making use of the new public spheres enabled by media technology in their political projects. These include the Tiananmen Square democracy movement in China, the McLibel campaign with its McSpotlight Web site, as well as the EZLN Zapatista movement in Chiapas, Mexico. Using "computer data bases, guerrilla radio, and other forms of media to circulate their struggles and ideas" throughout the world from the beginning of their activity (1997), the Zapatista movement has variously been designated the first social movement of the Internet age, the first informational guerrilla movement (Castells 1996), and the "first instance of Net warfare" (Garrido and Halavais 2003, 166).

In an article from 2005 written with Richard Kahn, Kellner updates his analysis of techno-politics to the twenty-first century. Needless to say, in an era when the rhetoric of the "war on terror" is being utilized "to limit the public sphere, curtail information and communication, legitimate government surveillance of electronic exchange, and to cut back on civil liberties," the ability of digital media technologies to help build and sustain active engagement in democratic forms of politics and social life has assumed added importance (Kahn and Kellner 2005, 77). In fact Kahn and Kellner are now able to identify what they believe to be a "new cycle of Internet politics" as having emerged after September 11 and the attacks on Afghanistan and Iraq. This cycle "has consisted of the implosion of the media and politics into popular culture, with the result being unprecedented numbers of people using the Internet and other technologies to produce original instruments and modes of democracy" (2005, 78). Among the many examples they provide is the use of new information communication technologies, including the Internet, cell phones, and text messaging by political groups such as MoveOn, A.N.S.W.E.R., and United for Peace and Justice to "circulate anti-war information, organize demonstrations and promote a wide diversity of anti-war activities" (2005, 78).[14] They also analyze the efforts of Vermont Governor Howard Dean's team of Internet activists to "successfully catalyse his grassroots campaign" in the

2004 U.S. Democratic primaries through the use of new media. For Kahn and Kellner, the Dean campaign showed that Internet politics was not limited to a "self-contained cybersphere"; rather, it was a force that was able to make practical interventions into the political struggles of contemporary media culture (2005, 79).[15] Last but not least among the examples I want to provide, the authors focus on the Spanish people's use of the cell phone and Internet networks during the March 2004 election. These were employed to denounce the "alleged lies" of the then Conservative Party government regarding the Madrid terrorist bombings of that month (the government had blamed these bombings on ETA in what many saw as an attempt to distance itself from any possible connection to the "war on terror"), and call for an end to Spain's involvement in the occupation of Iraq as part of Bush's "coalition of the willing." According to Kahn and Kellner, the exploitation of alternative models of information and communication mobilized the already discontented public and resulted in an unexpected victory for the opposition candidate.

". . . Some People Think the Internet Is a Bad Thing . . ."

Narratives of this kind concerning the liberatory and thus intrinsically political character of new media are accompanied by, and contrasted to, various stories that instead portray new media as a means for the continuation, reinforcement, intensification, and extension of the powers of both government and the market within late capitalism.

At its most basic, new media is positioned from the latter standpoint as enabling global organizations and corporations to generate greater commercial revenue: both by allowing them to sell their existing products and services to more customers on a worldwide scale, and by allowing them to develop, market, and sell new products and services that have only been made possible by the emergence of specific new media technologies. So not only can consumers purchase CDs online from Amazon and eBay, but also they can now pay to download music via iTunes.[16] While the late 1990s is regarded as the high point of this commercialization of the Internet, the process is very much continuing today, albeit in a less feverish manner following the dot.com crash that occurred between mid-1998 and March/April 2000.

A particularly characteristic feature of this take on new media is the large degree of power that is assigned to late capitalism's economic system. This has led quite a few critics to question the extent to which

Internet subcultures (if "subculture" is the right word), such as those associated with peer-to-peer file sharing, do indeed represent a break with, or a subversive challenge to, the commodifying logic of the free market, as is frequently claimed. It may be tempting to depict file-sharing networks such as Kazaa, Gnutella, and Freenet as an attack on copyright and the very regime of private property itself, one that has the potential to transform and even possibly destroy capitalism as we know it. Nevertheless, the fact remains, no matter how freely MP3 music files are distributed and exchanged, and how much the likes of the RIAA perceive this as a threat, most of those involved in file sharing are not technically competent enough to be able to construct their own computers. So they still have to buy the equipment to do the actual up- and downloading of files, not to mention the Creative Zens and Apple iPods they need to play them on. In this respect, Apple/iPod/iTunes (and now iPhone) can be said to form a mutually supportive nexus for promoting further consumption. Far from facilitating resistance to the logic of capitalism per se, Apple's iconic iPod provides merely a degree of freedom from materials—because it is neater and less bulky than Walkmans or CD players, and simpler to use, organize, and carry. Apple is striving to associate this feeling of "freedom" with the "idea of social/political/cultural liberation," which the company has traditionally used to position itself and its products in the market with an emphasis on the Apple brand being more alternative, individualistic, nonconformist, and countercultural (Heckman 2006). (Witness their "Think Different" campaign and of course the way in which whenever someone arty or liberal uses a computer in a Hollywood film it is almost invariably an Apple Mac.)

Even when it is conceded that an aspect of digital culture *may* operate according to a different logic to much of that of late capitalism, a great deal of time and energy tends to be spent on demonstrating just how difficult it is for that aspect of digital culture to escape the neoliberal economy's processes of co-option and commercialization to any significant degree or length of time. The free software and open-source movements, as championed in such books as Richard Stallman's *Free Software, Free Society* (2002) and Eric Raymond's *The Cathedral and the Bazaar: Musings on Linux and Open Source by an Accidental Revolutionary* (2001), are frequently offered as a case in point. Within these movements themselves, free and open-source software is depicted as providing evidence that distributed groups of people can collaborate in online situations, without the need of formalized relationships, to co-operatively develop, share, and distribute source code to an extremely high standard without having profit as their main motivation. While some have seen in this a model for new kinds of institutions and even for the future organization of society, critics have repeatedly stressed how quickly the forces of capitalist corporate culture have come to embrace and trade upon many of the products, as well as the philosophy, of the free software and open-source movements (sometimes known collectively as FLOSS: Free/Libre/Open Source Software). With the open-source Linux operating system generally being regarded as a low-cost alternative to the available proprietary offerings, and with the open-source Apache system having the largest market share of all the available Web servers, the work of free software and open-source coders is often utilized by commercial organizations to help generate financial profits, for instance. They tend to see FLOSS as a means of acquiring both software and the associated research and development (debugging, upgrading, etc.) at very little expense; and they frequently do so without offering anything much in return themselves—thus going against the ethos of commons-based peer production and open sharing or gifting that characterizes these movements—justifying their actions on the grounds that they have to use free and open-source software if they wish to remain competitive, since their business rivals are doubtless doing likewise. At the same time, it is stressed that a lot of software companies, and the venture capitalists behind them, have been able to turn a handsome profit from open source by operating on the basis that, although the source code they distribute may be free, the hardware and technical support they are able to supply to go with it certainly is not. Similarly, the point is made that many of those involved in the production of free and open-source coding are only in a position to do so because their level of technical expertise means they can often acquire relatively well-paid flexible work in the high-skill knowledge economy. While this enables these "precarious" creative workers to take time away from regular employment to devote to the production of source code, it also means they are no more able to operate outside or in direct opposition to neoliberal capitalism than peer-to-peer file sharers.

When it comes to media and cultural studies specifically, there are any number of variations on this approach. Some critics have argued that the Internet and the discourses surrounding it function very much as "a full consensus-creating machine, which socializes the mass of proletarianized knowledge workers into the economy of continuous innovation," where their labor can be further exploited. "After all if we do not get online soon, the hype suggests, we will become obsolete, unnecessary, disposable" (Terranova 2000, n.p.). This process of consensus creation and exploitation has become particularly apparent in recent years with regard to what has variously been called "Web 2.0," "Live Web," "Social Web" or "social networking"—and not *only* in the sense that if you don't have a presence on MySpace or Facebook nowadays, it's easy to feel you're virtually no one, in at least two senses of the term "virtual." By harnessing the "collective intelligence" of their users to provide "user-generated content" for free, and by having the same community of users moderate that content, and even order and structure it themselves via user tagging, examples of the "Live Web" such as MySpace, YouTube, Flickr, Facebook, and Bebo (or whichever happens to be flavor of the month at the moment) are portrayed as having the potential to generate a second dot.com boom to rival that of the 1990s, as they provide Internet companies with content and organization for free, with minimal staff costs needed for maintenance of the sites.[17] No doubt this ability to retain ownership and control while at the same time externalizing most of their costs is partly what persuaded Rupert Murdoch to buy MySpace, with its reported 98 million members worldwide, for $580 million in 2005; Yahoo! to pay an estimated $35 million for Flickr; and Google to spend $1.65 billion dollars on taking over YouTube in October 2006. But it is also possible to observe in this evidence of the way in which, these days, even the most apparently democratic, distributed, self-organizing, and popularly participatory of communities can also be a commodity that can be bought and sold.[18]

Others meanwhile have positioned such "social computing" as leading to forms of electronic balkanization. The reasoning here is that, yes, people may be empowered to become actively involved in building communities by these social networks—or antisocial networks in the case of Snubster, which brings people together around shared dislikes and the creation of "hate lists," rather like a negative MySpace.[19] However, the Internet's eradication of physical or geographic constraints does not lead to the construction of a form of "global village," as so many, building on the work of Marshall McLuhan (1964; McLuhan and Powers 1989), had earlier predicted with regard to the media of the twenty-first century (although McLuhan was, of course, thinking primarily in terms of the effects of television). Instead, these communities tend to be rather self-selecting, with those with similar social, intellectual, and economic interests and viewpoints gravitating to the same sites and spaces, and then interactively customizing those sites to suit their own interests still further once they get there. The result is a number of self-contained and quite homogenous special-interest groups of like-minded individuals being formed at various locations on the Internet, with relatively little travel or cross-pollination—of ideas, philosophies, or social and political points of view—occurring across and between them.

In a critique of the political impact of the Internet that appeared in the same 2005 issue of *Cultural Politics* as Kahn and Kellner's "Oppositional Politics and the Internet," Jodi Dean takes this kind of analysis of the Internet's "segmentation and isolation of users within bubbles of opinion with which they already agree" still further (Dean 2005, 69). Characterizing the current political-economic formation in terms of "communicative capitalism," Dean portrays the role of networked communication technologies within the current conjuncture as "profoundly depoliticizing." One of the main examples she uses to illustrate her case is that of the numerous critiques of George Bush, the war on terror, the evidence of weapons of mass destruction, and the impending attack on Iraq that were offered by myriad alternative, independent, progressive, and critical media outlets. The antiwar message conveyed by these criticisms "was not received," she claims. Instead, the message merely:

> circulated, reduced to the medium. Even when the White House acknowledged the massive worldwide demonstrations of February 15, 2003, Bush simply reiterated the fact that a message was out there, circulating—the protestors had the right to express their opinions. He didn't actually respond to their message. . . . So, despite the terabytes of commentary and information, there wasn't exactly a debate over the war. On the contrary, in the days and weeks prior to the US invasion of Iraq, the anti-war messages morphed into so much circulating content, just like all the other cultural effluvia wafting through cyberia. (Dean 2005, 52)

Dean analyzes this situation in terms of a distinction and a "significant disconnect" between "politics as the circulation of content" in the public sphere and "politics as the activity of officials" (2005, 53). It is precisely this lack of connection that challenges the very "premise of liberal democracy," in that the "communicative interactions of the public sphere" are meant to have an impact on "official politics" (2005, 53). Such an impact for her no longer happens in the United States today, as debate and a need to respond to the issues raised have been replaced by a constant circulation of communicative flows and the overproduction of information.

Furthermore, Dean positions the kind of argument we have seen Kahn and Kellner develop around Internet politics as an example of "technological fetishism." The latter she regards as both depoliticizing and as helping to maintain the lack of connection between what takes place on the Internet and what occurs in the realm of policy. It is depoliticizing because our involvement ultimately empowers those it is supposed to resist. Struggles on the net reiterate struggles in real life, but "insofar as they reiterate these struggles, they displace them. And this displacement, in turn, secures and protects the space of 'official' politics. This suggests another reason communication functions fetishistically today: as a disavowal of a more fundamental political disempowerment or castration" (2005, 61). In short, the Internet for Dean is a technological fetish in that it acts as a screen onto which ideas of political action can be projected. It provides merely *the fantasy* of political activity and participation. Significantly (especially for some of the things I am going to say in a moment), Dean is able to use many of the same examples Kahn and Kellner draw on—including both Howard Dean and MoveOn—to make her point.

Yet for others, new media may have played an even more fundamental political role within the development of late capitalist societies than that ascribed to it by Dean. As we saw in my Introduction, new or emerging media technology is positioned as having been vital to the development of the "information" or "knowledge economy," helping to transform traditional modes of production, consumption, and distribution, and creating in their place new types of firms, products, and markets based around the commodification and communication of knowledge and information. New media's role might have been even more important than this, however. It may not only have helped with the development of the new economy, but also have had a large part to play in the creation of globalization (although as Lawrence Grossberg points out, since capitalism has always been bound up with globalization, "globalization as a neo-liberal ideology" would be a more accurate way of putting it [2005a, 125]). For the production of a global neoliberal free-market economy could only be achieved as a result of the "deregulation of the international financial markets, characterised in the UK as the Stock Exchange Big Bang of 1988," and the "ending of protectionism under the aegis of the World Trade Organisation (WTO)." This in turn could only take place once sufficient computing technology and networks had been developed and put in place to handle the complex data and information needed to deal with a deregulated, privatized financial market. In this respect, the Internet is not just a product of free-market, neoliberal capitalism, reproducing its belief that the market knows best across the face of the planet, and thus acting as a powerful tool for extending the hegemony of "globalization as a neo-liberal ideology" (Lister et al. 2003, 198, 201). The Internet has in fact helped to *create* capitalism, at least in its contemporary, free-market, neoliberal form.[20]

". . . What Do You Think?"

So far so familiar perhaps. Still, as an account of the relationship between politics and new media this bipartite narrative is too cursory to function as anything more than a signpost for further analysis. While I am convinced it is important to track the development of narrative trends of this kind, and even on occasion to engage with them, I nevertheless have strong reservations about debates on new media being predominantly articulated through, and thus stopping at, an attempt to determine the radical political potential (or lack of potential) of blogging, Howard Dean, file sharing, Apple's iPod, open source, MySpace, Web 2.0, "cyberbalkanization," "communicative capitalism," technological fetishism, Howard Dean again. . . . Or, for that matter, any of those other related issues I have not touched upon but quite easily could have, such as hacking, hacktervism, "wardriving," "culture jamming," viral video, Internet porn, censorship, surveillance, identity theft, the Creative Commons, intellectual property, mash-ups, free content, open publishing, and so forth.

I say this for a number of reasons. First, because arguments of the kind sketched above—where digital technology is presented as either generating opportunities for democratic participation, challenge, and resistance, or as a means for the continuation, reinforcement, and intensification of late capitalism—have already been well-rehearsed and widely debated elsewhere: in the majority of accounts of Internet politics, in fact. Second, because it seems to me that, in setting the issue up in such a way, as a conflict between two contrasting approaches, there is a danger of reducing the politics of new media to a series of more-or-less homologous positions: technophilia or technophobia, optimism or pessimism, radicalism or conservativism, progressivism or corporatism, immanence or transcendence, production or consumption, professionalism or amateurism, theory or practice, utopia or dystopia, inside or outside, authentic or inauthentic, potlatch or the consumer economy, and so on. (Which, as I argue throughout this chapter, is indeed the dominant way in which the politics of digital media *has* been positioned to date.)[21]

A third reason I am reluctant to continue positioning new media debates like this is because it means, paradoxically enough, adopting and perpetuating a very old and, I would argue, rather dated narrative strategy. Certainly, the predisposition to see disputes over new media per se in terms of a dialectic (and often a "stalled" one at that) between techophiliacs and technophobes, optimists and pessimists, and so forth, is not confined to the period stretching from the 1990s to the present, nor even to treatments of digital politics. This narrative tendency has a long history in the analysis of the political effects of media technologies, one that stretches back through the work of Fredric Jameson, Jürgen Habermas, Marshall McLuhan, Raymond Williams, Herbert Marcuse, Theodor Adorno, Walter Benjamin, Bertolt Brecht, and beyond.

Fourth, charting the history of these discussions over the politics of emerging media by outlining the methodologies of one approach in relation to the other would overlook the extent to which—although they may *appear* to be dialectically opposed—both "sides" in this dispute are in fact equally important to the continuation of cultural criticism, including Internet criticism, in its present form, as is the antagonism between them. In short, it would take too little account of the way in which both of these "sides" are implicated in each other as their conditions of possibility.[22] As a result, such a "digital dialectics" approach would merely repeat and reinforce the "radical logic of incompatibility between centrifugal and centripetal forces, simultaneously forcing cultures and peoples together as it pulls others apart," which both Stuart Hall and Robert Young have identified as operating "as the cultural and economic dynamic of late capitalist society" itself (see G. Hall 2002, 44; R. Young 1996b, 8).

New Media Tactics

I am aware that for some people *the very act* of rehearsing these dichoto-mous approaches to new media—although conducted in a critical spirit —is somewhat out-of-date. From this perspective, I am being rather unfair in doing so, since even if at one stage in their history—in the 1990s, say—discussions over the politics of new media did take the dia-lectical form I have attributed to them, things have moved on since then, not least under the influence of the thought of Gilles Deleuze and Félix Guattari. Part of what I am trying to emphasize, however, with my references to recent writings by Richard Kahn and Douglas Kellner, Jodi Dean, even Peter Lunenfeld and Geert Lovink, is the dialectical ghost that still hangs over such debates. To quickly provide just one more example, witness the way in which the chair of the Creative Com-mons project,[23] Lawrence Lessig, positions his contribution to the de-bate over free culture as "a balance between anarchy and control" (2004, xvi): "the debate so far has been framed at the extremes—as a grand either/or: either property or anarchy, either total control or art-ists won't be paid. . . . What's needed is a way to say something in the middle—neither 'all rights reserved' nor 'no rights reserved' but 'some rights reserved'—and thus a way to respect copyrights but enable crea-tors to free content as they see fit" (2004, 276–77). It seems to me that the majority of narratives through which new media and its politics are today conceived and understood have not changed quite so much as some people would like to think and have us believe. Moreover, this can be seen to be the case even with regard to those who *have* attempted to "move on" from positions of the kind I have described above by explic-itly challenging the dialectical terms within which the politics of new media has otherwise been perceived. Elsewhere I have shown how, in order to produce a methodology for their analysis of the multitude of "immaterial laborers" in the new economy that is explicitly nondialecti-cal, Michael Hardt and Antonio Negri unwittingly repeat in their book *Empire* the very dialectics of cultural criticism they are explicitly trying to elude (G. Hall 2006). So let me illustrate this point here with a dif-ferent example: that of "tactical media."

One of the things I am trying to do with this book is to show how new media can be used to create "practical," performative, affective projects that make an institutionally pragmatic "tactical use of the space of the university." I am interested in employing new media tactically to take the opportunity presented to us by digital technology in the form of open-access archiving to *act now*. For once the established institutions and funding bodies become more involved (for example, the Economic and Social Research Council [ESRC], Arts and Humanities Research Council [AHRC], and so forth in the United Kingdom), the opportunities I am outlining here for a more interesting ethically and politically responsible form of open-access archiving may be lost. The "tactical" use of digital media can also serve as a guard against some of the political mechanisms that are inevitably linked with institutionalization. Even if open-access publishing and archiving is "successful" (whatever that might mean) in helping us address the politico-ethical issues and questions I am identifying throughout this book, we might eventually have to move on at some point to other, as yet unmapped, politico-ethical terrains and tasks. Success may well result in a repository such as the CSeARCH cultural studies open-access archive reproducing and acting out, rather than taking on and thinking otherwise, the kind of problems we have identified as being associated with institutions (not least the irreducibly violent and inevitably paradoxical nature of the authority on which they are based).

Having said that, I am not trying to position either open-access archiving or CSeARCH as an example of "tactical media" strictly speaking, at least as the latter has been defined by David Garcia and Geert Lovink together and separately in a range of texts. I want to focus on Garcia and Lovink's definition of tactical media here: partly because it is one of the more detailed and interesting, and partly because it is the most frequently cited (indeed, it is often regarded as "seminal"). But the main reason I want to concentrate on their definition of tactical media is because it has been positioned as an attempt to follow Deleuze's dictum "Experiment, never interpret" (Deleuze and Parnet 2002, 48; cited by Wark 2006b, 274)—an attempt that might, in the words of McKenzie Wark, "free itself from the dialectic of being an alternative or opposition, which merely reproduces the sterile sense of a Wedom versus a Theydom in the media sphere" (2006b, 273).

In "The ABC of Tactical Media," Garcia and Lovink portray tactical media very much in these terms: as an attempt to *not* repeat and reproduce the dialectics of oppositional or alternative approaches to the media. They are quite prepared to acknowledge that adhering to "the classic rituals of the underground and alternative scene" would be by far the easier and safer option (Garcia and Lovink 1997, n.p.). The problem with proposing *alternative* media, actions, policies, or movements, from their tactical media–oriented perspective, is that opposition of this kind is too easily co-opted: it is too easily turned into just another lifestyle statement or branding and marketing opportunity. One need only think of Live 8 and the Make Poverty History campaign, as well as all the Che Guevara t-shirts that are for sale, alongside those bearing the words "Calvin Klein," "fcuk" and "pornstar," to realize that nowadays being overtly "oppositional," "alternative," even "revolutionary" often amounts to little more than a fashion choice. What is more, as Garcia and Lovink make clear, attempts at taking such an oppositional stand too often repeat earlier unsuccessful attempts at being "alternative," as you proceed from a period of initial enthusiasm and excitement to one of frustration that things are not happening fast enough, until that in turn gives way to, and is replaced by, eventual exhaustion and disillusionment. One of the main ways in which tactical media differs from other forms of alternative media, for Garcia and Lovink, is that it is consciously and deliberately endeavoring to break out of this cycle of enthusiasm, disappointment, and failure. It is not trying to construct direct alternatives to the dominant mainstream: a more politically radical newspaper, or a more ethically responsible Internet search engine (a right-on version of Google, say, or a more caring and sharing alternative to Microsoft). "Although tactical media include alternative media," Garcia and Lovink stress that these media forms are "not restricted to that category. In fact we introduced the term tactical," they write, very much with a view to disrupting and taking us "beyond the rigid dichotomies that have restricted thinking in this area, for so long, dichotomies such as amateur Vs professional, alternative Vs mainstream. Even private Vs public" (Garcia and Lovink 1997, n.p.). As they put it in an interview with Andreas Broeckmann: "From Paper Tiger to the BBC's video diaries we discovered that the tactical cuts straight across the marginal vs mainstream dichotomy" (Garcia and Lovink 2001, n.p.).

Tactical media is in this respect presented as being very much a "post-1989" phenomenon (the term *tactical media* was itself first proposed in 1992, according to Lovink [see Meikle 2000]). It is seen as taking up the "legacy of 'alternative' media without the counterculture label and ideological certainties of previous decades" (Lovink 2001, 254). This means that those involved in tactical media do not share the grand narratives or teleological dreams of future revolution and liberation; nor do they identify with the "leftist dogmatism and ghetto group psychology" that are characteristic of many earlier and other forms of radical opposition and resistance (Lovink 2001, 259). Tactical media do not operate by means of large-scale oppositional movements, representative political parties, collective unions, organized social groups, or established institutions. Instead, taking their cue from Deleuze and Guattari, they are about becoming "minor." Their approach is therefore more fluid, viral, hit-and-run. Tactical media are about latching on to those opportunities that are created "because of the pace of technological change and regulatory uncertainty," using whatever medium is appropriate to that particular situation and locale: it could be Web sites, zines, pirate radios, street demonstrations, raves, local TV, or whatever. They are about gaining "access (to buildings, networks, resources), hacking the power," and then, once that has been achieved, knowing the right time to disband and disappear (Lovink 2001, 260). Yes, there are connections to be made between old and new media, theory and practice, underground and mainstream, amateur and professional, creative and uncreative. Yes, often very unusual alliances are forged between the different groups and individuals that are involved in such activities: activists, artists, academics, critics, hackers, programmers, journalists, and so on, who come to the party from a variety of backgrounds, all with their own different specialties, hopes, and expectations. Yet such connections and alliances are always comparatively loose, mobile, and temporary, not least to ensure that particular tactical media actions and events cannot themselves be assigned a fixed identity—not even as "tactical media"—or co-opted in turn into another lifestyle or fashion choice (Lovink 2001, 260). This is why tactical media can be described as "never perfect, always in becoming, performative and pragmatic, involved in a continual process of questioning the premises of the channels they work with" (Garcia and Lovink 1997, n.p.). This is also why the typical champions of tactical media are "the activist, Nomadic media warriors, the pranxter, the hacker, the street rapper, the camcorder kamikaze" (Garcia and Lovink 1997, n.p.); and why "tactical media" itself is something of an ambivalent, problematic, and contentious term to use in relation to such activities.

Now, in this book I am not trying to have an effect on the mainstream media, or at least its news agenda, in the way tactical media often does. Nor am I against large-scale oppositional movements or more alternative, strategic forms of politics per se. Still, a number of discourses and practices are associated with tactical media on this account that I find extremely productive when it comes to thinking about how to exploit new media to produce a pragmatic "tactical use of the space of the university." These include tactical media's awareness that it is often not enough to be just "oppositional" or "alternative," and the willingness of tactical media practitioners to move on from the kind of emphasis on "identity politics, media critiques and theories of representation" that underpin most oppositional or alternative approaches to the media, and that Garcia and Lovink present as being "in crisis" as the "carping and repressive remnants of an outmoded humanism" (Garcia and Lovink 1997, n.p.).[24] Also interesting are tactical media's exploration of forms of organization and resistance other than those associated with representational party politics, organized social and collective movements, the dogmatic left, the unions, even nongovernmental organizations (NGOs); its flexible, mobile, experimental, disorganized, pragmatic, provisional, performative nature; and its ability to exploit what Graham Meikle calls "the small cracks that appear in the mediascape through the rapid evolution of technology and the catch-up process of regulatory policy" (Meikle 2002, 120)—all of which resonates "pragmatically" with my own work around open-access publishing and archiving, to a certain extent.

One of the things that remains problematic in this otherwise often-promising discourse around new media, however, is the manner in which, for all its attempts to explore and experiment with the development of new forms of political and social organization, mobilization, and activism, tactical media reproduces the very approach of "being alternative or oppositional" it presents as having "restricted thinking in this area for so long," and that it is supposedly trying to free itself from.[25] The easiest way to illustrate this is with Garcia and Lovink's positioning of those involved in tactical media as being excluded from the wider culture. "Tactical Media are what happens," they insist, "when the cheap 'do it yourself' media, made possible by the revolution in consumer electronics and expanded forms of distribution (from public access cable to the internet) are exploited by groups and individuals who feel aggrieved by or excluded from the wider culture. Tactical media do not just report events, as they are never impartial they always participate and it is this that more than anything separates them from mainstream media" (Garcia and Lovink 1997, n.p.). Yet, for all their claims that tactical media activists want to go beyond rigid dichotomies such as those between mainstream and underground, amateur and professional, creative and uncreative (and presumably also aggrieved and non-aggrieved, included and excluded), are Garcia and Lovink not setting those involved in tactical media up in something of a dichotomous relation of their own? It is a dialectical structure Lovink repeats when he writes that "tactical media emerge out of the margins, yet never fully make it into the mainstream" (Lovink 2001, 257); or when he positions it as a post-1989 phenomenon, and contrasts its emphasis on limited tactical events to the teleology and grand narratives of previous forms of opposition. In fact, is the whole idea of tactical media as Garcia and Lovink outline it not based precisely on a dichotomy found in the writings of Michel de Certeau: that between tactics and strategy, the weak and the strong? In "The ABC of Tactical Media" the two tactical media theorists put it like this:

> In *The Practice of Every Day Life* De Certeau [*sic*] analyzed popular culture not as a "domain of texts or artifacts but rather as a set of practices or operations performed on textual or text like structures." He shifted the emphasis from representations in their own right to the "uses" of representations. In other words how do we as consumers use the texts and artifacts that surround us. And the answer, he suggested, was "tactically." That is in far more creative and rebellious ways than had previously been imagined. He described the process of consumption as a set of tactics by which the weak make use of the strong. He characterized the rebellious user (a term he preferred to consumer) as tactical and the presumptuous producer (in which he included authors, educators, curators and revolutionaries) as strategic. Setting up this dichotomy allowed him to produce a vocabulary of tactics rich and complex enough to amount to a distinctive and recognizable aesthetic. . . . An aesthetic of poaching, tricking, reading, speaking, strolling, shopping, desiring. . . .
>
> Awareness of this tactical/strategic dichotomy helped us to name a class of producers of who seem uniquely aware of the value of these temporary reversals in the flow of power. . . . We dubbed their (our) work tactical media. (Garcia and Lovink 1997, n.p.)

Caroline Bassett is just one of those to have expressed reservations concerning such "tactical projects" and their justification (although the example she uses is not Garcia and Lovink but Matthew Fuller's *Behind the Blip* [2003]). She argues that, despite establishing its identity in terms of its difference from other approaches to the media, tactical media merely constitutes another form of subculture, developed out of a relation between media artists and activists. Ironically enough, it thus echoes cultural studies' own, much disparaged, romance of the oppositional and resistant "outsider" (Bassett 2006).[26] To be sure, Garcia and Lovink may well believe that it is necessary not to reproduce the dialectics of oppositional or alternative approaches to the media. Nevertheless, in their writings tactical media appears unknowingly and unconsciously trapped in the very discourses it is trying to elude—discourses that, as we have seen, are characteristic of the cultural and economic logic of late capitalism itself. Debates over tactical media, its existence, usefulness, and effectiveness, certainly have a tendency to repeat the dialectical structure of cultural criticism I outlined earlier. This is evident from the way in which Garcia and Lovink's "The ABC of Tactical Media" itself "doesn't entirely succeed in extracting itself from the oppositional language of Wedom versus Theydom," as Wark himself acknowledges, albeit almost in passing (2006b, 273). It is also apparent from the claims some are now making that the kind of experimentation with media to produce creative forms of (romantic) emancipatory political dissent and subversion that often use flexible, networked modes of decentralized (dis)organization and that did indeed come to be caricaturized as "tactical media" is no longer valid in the West and North. It has not been valid since the post–September 11 introduction of a "state of exception" (Agamben 2005) and the associated clampdown on the activities of the likes of Steve Kurtz and Critical Art Ensemble on the one hand,[27] and the co-option of tactical media's do-it-yourself attitude by social networking sites such as Facebook and Flickr on the other.[28]

Politics and the Internet

The preceding sections of this chapter can be accused of being far too quick and schematic as a portrayal of the politics of new media. I therefore want to emphasize that neither "side" in this relation—neither that which I have characterized as perceiving the Internet as a "good" thing, nor that which portrays it as "bad"—is a homogeneous, self-identical entity. The same is also true of the dialectically nondialectical approach of Garcia and Lovink and "tactical media." All these respective takes on new media and its relation to politics differ within themselves as well as between themselves; and if it is important to be attentive to, and even participate in, these debates over media technology, it is just as important not to conflate what are largely heterogeneous, unequal, and differentiated discourses and narratives.

This is one of the main reasons I have not gone into any particularly rigorous detail regarding any of the arguments I have discussed so far (and why I have tried not to cite too many texts by thinkers who have produced theories of digital politics—other than those I am prepared to discuss in a little more depth). To show, in a responsible, ethical, hospitable manner, how dialectics is enacted in discourses on and of digital politics would require me to respond to such texts in a careful, patient, singular fashion. (Not least, it would require me to show how, perhaps in spite of themselves—and depending on the text and the particular strategy to be adopted—such texts in their different and singular ways challenge, resist, and transform the "digital dialectics" narrative, at the same time that such texts, in their different and singular ways, and also perhaps in spite of themselves—again depending on the text and the particular strategy to be adopted—reproduce, maintain, and uphold it.)

Now I could certainly have demonstrated how this is the case by offering singular analyses of the texts of Lunenfeld, Kahn and Kellner, Dean, Garcia and Lovink (or, indeed, Lessig and Creative Commons); or of artistic practices and "tactical media" events and activities such as the Act Up campaign around AIDS policy, the B92 radio station in Serbia in the early 1990s during the Kosovo conflict, the Sarai New Media Centre in Delhi, the guerrilla activities of *Adbusters*, ®™ark, and The Yes Men or the "contestational robots" described by Critical Art Ensemble (2001).[29] However, I am going to leave the performance of at least the beginnings of a more detailed, hospitable, rigorous analysis of this kind for the chapter that follows and a text I believe has the potential to be even more radical and productive. At this stage in my argument, I merely want to draw attention to the way the politics of new media has too often been understood primarily in terms of the past, in terms of old, preestablished ideas of politics and political action and resistance. As I pointed out at the end of my first set of metadata, the problem with such interpretations of the politics of new media for me is that they imply that what politics is, what it means to be political, is already more or less known. Rather than attempting to respond responsibly to each particular instance and conjunction of new media and politics, most of the available narratives are limited to measuring certain new media forms and practices against already established and legitimated ideas of "politics." Since the decision as to the political thing to do is taken in advance, once and for all, it is extremely difficult for such conceptions of digital politics to recognize and remain open to the singularity of specific performances of new media—especially those elements that do not fit the predecided theories, elements that are precisely that which *cannot* be predicted, in other words. As a result, little attention tends to be paid to the possibility that, not only could the politics of digital media (like digitized texts themselves—at least as I described them in chapter 2) be different and new, but also, in order to be capable of understanding how the politics of digital media *could be* different and new, that we might need to be open to the idea of changing, perhaps radically, our current political theories, agendas, vocabularies, and conceptual frameworks. This includes being prepared to reconceive and reimagine their current basis in notions of theory and practice, the dialectic and, as we shall see in the next chapter, citizenship, the public sphere, even democracy itself.

Such a reliance on, and indeed safeguarding of, predecided conceptions of politics is clearly evident in the argument of Richard Barbrook I referred to briefly at the beginning of this chapter. As we saw there, Barbrook positions the academic hi-tech gift economy as political because it offers a radically different model for the communication and exchange of knowledge and ideas from that afforded by capitalism's market economies—albeit one in which "money-commodity and gift relations are not just in conflict with each other, but also co-exist in symbiosis" (Barbrook 1998, n.p.). Barbrook is careful to stress that, although this system played a crucial role in the history and development of the Internet, and as such "has expanded far beyond the university":

> the hi-tech gift economy was not an immanent possibility in every age. On the contrary, the market and the state could only be surpassed in this specific sector at this particular historical moment. Crucially, people need sophisticated media, computing and telecommunications technologies to participate within the hi-tech gift economy. . . . In addition, individuals need both time and money to participate within the hi-tech gift economy. While a large number of the world's population still lives in poverty, people within the industrialised countries have steadily reduced their hours of employment

and increased their wealth over a long period of social struggles and economic reorganizations. By working for money during the week, people can now enjoy the delights of giving gifts at other times. Only at this particular historical moment have the technical and so-cial conditions of the metropolitan countries developed sufficiently for the emergence of digital anarcho-communism. (Barbrook 1998, n.p.)

For all its historical specificity, however, far from attempting to develop a theory of politics that is itself specific to the era of digital reproduc-tion, Barbrook approaches this gift economy for the most part as merely a hi-tech—if less "purist," more compromised, indeed often corporate and state-sponsored—version of the utopian anarcho-communism that was advocated by the Situationists, New Left militants, and similar groups in the 1960s (Barbrook 1998, n.p.).[30]

This protectionism toward "old," "authorized" notions of political action and resistance is also apparent in the more recent analysis of the "new cycle" of Internet politics provided by Kahn and Kellner. For them, it is "not that today's Internet is either wholly emancipatory or oppres-sive technology, but rather that it is an ongoing struggle that contains contradictory forces" (Kahn and Kellner 2005, 80). From this position they are able to acknowledge the relevance of Jodi Dean's argument regarding the potential techno-fetishism of Internet politics, while si-multaneously insisting that she has "inappropriately" identified "Inter-net cultural politics with fetishism" (2005, 97 n. 23). Opposing what they characterize as "totalizing, overly dismissive rejections of the Inter-net and technopolitics" (2005, 93), Kahn and Kellner argue instead "for a more dialectical vision"; one that, while recognizing the "limita-tions of Internet politics," nevertheless permits them to engage "in dia-lectical critique of how emergent information and communication technologies (ICTs) have facilitated oppositional cultural and political movements and provided possibilities for the sort of progressive socio-political change and struggle that is an important dimension of con-temporary cultural politics" (2005, 76). Significantly, in doing so Kahn and Kellner claim that "against the capitalist organization of neo-liberal capitalism" a "Fifth International . . . of computer-mediated ac-tivism is emerging that is qualitatively different from the party-based socialist and communist Internationals of the past" (2005, 84). This leads them to speculate that a number of emergent online political and cultural projects today are involved in reconfiguring the shape of participatory and democratic global citizenship for both the global and local future (2005, 81).

Can we therefore detect in Kahn and Kellner at least the beginnings of a hospitable opening to the idea that Internet politics may take some new, different, surprising, and unforeseen forms? Quite possibly. But if this *is* the case, it is an opening that is not explored rigorously. On the contrary, Kahn and Kellner (like Kellner in his earlier article [1997]) clearly already know what politics, democracy, social justice, oppositional intellectuals, and the public sphere are in this essay; and consequently they know what net politics has to do in order to act politically. Their argument is simply that the "effective use of communication networks" is helping to "define, coalesce and extend" already existing notions of oppositional politics, democracy, social justice, and so forth "across the world" (2005, 78). Far from considering, seriously, the possibility that the Internet and digital culture may require us to conceive our ideas of struggle and the political differently, their main aim is to "articulate Internet politics with actually [already] existing political struggles" (2005, 80), and in so doing "make technopolitics a major instrument of [an already understood and decided upon conception of oppositional] political action" (2005, 80). There is thus relatively little that is particularly new about the politics Kahn and Kellner describe and hardly anything that could not have been said about politics *before* the invention of the Internet. Indeed, given that their essay is concerned with the relation between "oppositional politics and the internet," the Internet seems to have had remarkably little impact on their understanding of oppositional politics. Like Barbrook, they situate politics on the Internet as a continuation of a history of already established alternative and radical media activism. This history includes the "community media movement that from the 1960s through the present has promoted alternative media" (2005, 77–78), and the invention of the Internet in their account has done surprisingly little to transform or to change that.

Post-politics
Turning to the other side in this stalled dialectic (at least as I have set it up here, following Kahn and Kellner and others), this tendency when it comes to thinking about the politics of new media to roll out a politi-

cal project or program that is already known and decided upon *in ad-vance* can be detected even in Jodi Dean's argument in "Communicative Capitalism." Like that of Kahn and Kellner, Dean's take on the politics of new media is far from "all or nothing." She is careful to stress that she is *not* suggesting that "networked communications never facilitate political resistance," and that, for her, the "political efficacy of networked media depends" very much "on its context" (Dean 2005, 52). It is just that, "under the conditions of intensive and extensive proliferation of media" that characterize communicative capitalism, "messages are more likely to get lost as mere contributions to the circulation of content. What enhances democracy in one context becomes a new form of hegemony in another. Or, the intense circulation of content in communicative capitalism forecloses the antagonism necessary for politics" (2005, 53–54). Whereas Kahn and Kellner emphasize the "positive political potentials of the Internet," then, Dean is far less optimistic in this essay (Kahn and Kellner 2005, 97 n. 23). Despite her more critical approach to the understanding of the Internet, however, Dean's idea of Internet politics is no more open to any new, innovative, exceptional, or heterogeneous excess than that of Kahn and Kellner.

Take her characterization of the nature of communicative capitalism in terms of "post-politics" (Dean 2005, 56), a concept she adapts from Žižek:

> [P]ost-politics "emphasizes the need to leave old ideological divisions behind and confront new issues, armed with the necessary expert knowledge and free deliberation that takes people's concrete needs and demands into account" (Žižek 1999, 198). Post-politics thus begins from the premise of consensus and cooperation. Real antagonism or dissent is foreclosed. Matters previously thought to require debate and struggle are now addressed as personal issues or technical concerns. ... The problem is that all this tolerance and attunement to difference and emphasis on hearing another's pain prevents politicization. Matters aren't represented—they don't stand for something beyond themselves. They are simply treated in all their particularity, as specific issues to be addressed therapeutically, juridically, spectacularly, or disciplinarily rather than being treated as elements of larger signifying chains or political formations. Indeed, this is how third way societies support global capital:

they prevent politicization. They focus on administration, again, foreclosing the very possibility that things might be otherwise. (Dean 2005, 56–57)

The situation of communicative capitalism, for Dean, is precisely not political—or, rather, it is precisely post-political. She contrasts it unfavorably with what she refers to as "politicization proper" (2005, 65), the "dangerous terrain of politicization" (2005, 70), which for her has to do with "real" struggle, conflict, antagonism, and the "formation of strong counterhegemonies" (2005, 53). Dean is thus typical of many of those associated with cultural studies in that she conceives politics primarily in terms of hegemonic and counterhegemonic struggle—although, admittedly, her conception of politics is explicitly based on a version of Laclau and Mouffe's neo-Gramscian theory of hegemony rather than a reading of Gramsci himself, as has more usually been the case over the history of cultural studies.[31]

Although it may be less apparent than in the other two examples I have just given, once again we can see that there is a propensity when it comes to thinking about the politics of new media to resort to a political project or program that is already known and decided upon (in this case a conception of the political derived in part from the post-Marxist neo-Gramscianism of Laclau and Mouffe). That said, Dean's essay is somewhat unusual in this respect, since it shows not only that the dialectical structure of debates over digital politics continues into the present, but also that the closing down of the question of politics in relation to new media is itself *not political*, and is actually *antipolitical*.

Antipolitics

To be sure, close inspection reveals that even according to her own criteria Dean's depiction of politics in this essay runs into problems. For if "conflict and opposition" are truly "necessary for politics" (Dean 2005, 54), if politics is only possible in a situation where the "real antagonism or dissent" that is required for politics is not "foreclosed" (2005, 56), then is she not herself acting nonpolitically (and perhaps even post-politically, at least in the sense that post-politics is itself a foreclosure of politics?) in going along with, and repeating, the hegemonic position that the theory of hegemony currently occupies within cultural studies? With regard to the closure of the technological fetish, for example, Dean writes that its political purchase "is given in advance;

it is immediate, presumed, understood. File sharing *is* political. A Web site *is* political. Blogging *is* political. But this very immediacy rests on something else, on a prior exclusion. And, what is excluded, is the possibility of politicization proper" (2005, 65). Yet one is tempted to ask: what about Dean's own belief that (only) hegemonic/counterhegemonic struggle counts as political? Could this assertion not be added to Dean's list? Does hegemonic politics—the "difficult challenge of representing specific claims or acts as universal" and the articulation of struggles together with other struggles in opposition to a shared opponent—not likewise assume the form of a foreclosed political fetish in her work (2005, 57)?[32] Is this decision—as to what can and cannot be considered political—not being taken in advance, too? As Dean herself says, "[b]luntly put, a condition of possibility for asserting the immediately political character of something . . . is not simply the disavowal of other political struggles"—including in her case many of those associated with the Internet, dismissed by Dean as examples of technological fetishism that, in reiterating and displacing real-life struggles, are profoundly depoliticizing. Instead, "it relies on the prior exclusion of the antagonistic conditions of emergence" of that something (2005, 66). But does not Dean's own foreclosure of the question of politics, and the sense that what (for her) it is to be political is already decided and "given in advance" and thus "immediate, presumed, understood," rest on "something else, a prior exclusion," too (2005, 65)? In this case, the "antagonistic conditions of emergence" (within cultural studies) of her own (transcendental) understanding of politics as always taking the form of a hegemonic struggle, and refusal of the "possibility that things might be otherwise" in that respect, as well (2005, 57); that there may be other, rival, conflicting, opposing ways and means of understanding politics and being political, including some that may be associated with digital culture and the Internet. Indeed, is this antagonistic dimension, this conflict and uncertainty over politics, over what politics on the net is, which we can see being kept within particular limits within Dean's work, not precisely part of what politics is for Laclau and Mouffe, especially in a pluralistic, liberal democracy? Given its importance to my argument, it is perhaps worth quoting from (one of) them at some length on this point:

> the specificity of liberal democracy as a new political form of society
> consists in the legitimation of conflict and the refusal to eliminate it

through the imposition of an authoritarian order. A liberal democracy is above all a *pluralist* democracy. Its novelty resides in its en-
visaging the diversity of conceptions of the good, not as something
negative that should be suppressed, but as something to be valued
and celebrated. . . . To believe that a final resolution of conflict is
eventually possible . . . is to put the pluralist democratic project at
risk. . . .

Politics, especially democratic politics, can never overcome
conflict and division. . . . This is why grasping the nature of
democratic politics requires a coming to terms with the dimension
of antagonism that is present in social relations. . . .

. . . This is why an approach like deconstruction, which reveals
the impossibility of establishing a consensus without exclusion is of
fundamental importance for grasping what is at stake in democratic
politics. Because it warns us against the illusion that Justice could
ever be instantiated in the institutions of any society, deconstruction
forces us to keep the democratic contestation alive. By pointing to
the ineradicability of antagonism, notions like undecidability and
decision are not only fundamental for politics . . . they also provide
the very terrain in which a democratic pluralist politics can be for-
mulated. (Mouffe 1996, 8–9)

Mouffe's emphasis on the importance of deconstruction when it
comes to understanding politics is worth paying further attention to.
For what deconstruction tells us about the relation between politics and
undecidability is that the decision as to what politics is and what it
means to act politically *cannot* be left completely open and incalculable.
If it is not going to be subject to the specific demands of the particular
context, the decision regarding politics cannot be taken afresh each
time. It has to be based on rationally calculated *universal* values of infinite justice and responsibility. This is why a decision "has to be prepared by reflection and knowledge," for Derrida (2001a, 61); why "it is
necessary to know the most and the best possible" (2001b, 54). At the
same time (and as I have been emphasizing here, for both tactical and
strategic reasons), any such decision cannot be made solely on the basis
of knowledge known and decided upon a priori, such as a preconceived
political agenda or theory (e.g., that of hegemonic struggle and resistance), which is both beyond question and unconditionally and universally applicable. As I said before, that would be to risk failing to recog-

nize the singularity of the object of knowledge—in this case, Internet politics and the politics of new media—its possible novelty and difference. In order to determine what it means for a specific instance and performance of new media to be political, a decision has to be made based on a calculation that is open to that which *cannot* be known or calculated in advance. This is what Derrida means when he insists that "between the widest, most refined, the most necessary knowledge, and the responsible decision, an abyss remains, and must remain" (2001b, 54).

A responsible political decision, for Derrida, requires respect for *both* poles of the nonoppositional relation between closure and openness, the conditional and unconditional, the universal and the singular, the ideal and the empirical, the calculable and incalculable, decidable and undecidable. "It is between these two poles, *irreconcilable but indissociable*, that decisions and responsibilities are to be taken," he writes (2001b, 45). Indeed, far from the difficult, uncertain nature of this situation having a depoliticizing effect, a just and responsible political act, for Derrida, *has* to go through the ordeal of taking a decision in just such an incalculable and undecidable space. Even then "[o]ne is never sure of making the just choice; one never knows . . . It is here that responsibilities are to be re-evaluated at each moment, according to concrete situations. . . . But to recognise these 'contextual' differences is an entirely different thing from an empiricist, relativist, or pragmatist resignation" (2001b, 56–57).

Returning to Dean's analysis in "Communicative Capitalism," it therefore seems somewhat ironic, especially given her own concerns about the foreclosure of the political and adherence to a conception of the political that portrays it as referring to the "ineradicability of antagonism" Laclau and Mouffe derive from deconstruction, that it is precisely this antagonistic dimension, this conflict, uncertainty, and undecidability regarding politics—which is what politics is, for Dean—that we see being foreclosed in her own essay. This state of affairs leads her to repeat throughout "Communicative Capitalism" what I would argue is the *nonpolitical* gesture of placing her notion of politics very much in a transcendental position with respect to other discourses.

To provide an example: one possibility Dean *is not* open to in "Communicative Capitalism"—and this is the case despite her own repeated emphasis on the importance of context (2005, 52, 66)—is that the historical and social situation may actually have changed so much that hegemonic struggle is no longer an appropriate concept to use when it comes to understanding, analyzing, and resisting the contemporary political conjuncture. Instead, as we have seen, she is willing to recognize something as political only if it continues to conform to the political vocabularies and frameworks of interpretation that are already transcendentally decided in advance—of both the emergence of communicative capitalism and her examination of the Internet—and that were initially developed in a context that, on her own account, was very different from that of contemporary capitalism. It is a context she continues to contrast unfavorably to the "current political-economic formation," and that presumably existed before the proliferation of media she associates with communicative capitalism. (Otherwise how can that proliferation have been depoliticizing and have lead to post-politics [2005, 51]? For that to happen, things must have been politicized and political at some stage first. But when? In what Dean calls, after Agamben, "the old regime" [2005, 56]?) So these political vocabularies and frameworks of interpretation stem from a previous era: before "democratic deliberation and, indeed, struggle" had "collapsed" (2005, 54); when the "political energy" needed for "the hard work of organizing and struggle" (2005, 64)—which is what politics is really about, according to Dean—had not been displaced as it apparently has in the United States today (2005, 53); when an "essential communicativity of human beings" *was* possible (2005, 56); and when politics was still about "actively organized parties and unions" rather than the "domain of financially mediated and professionalized practices centered on advertising, public relations and the means of mass communication," as it is now (2005, 55).

To a certain extent one can understand why she positions her argument in this manner. For as we are told by Dean herself, the paradox of this situation is that the fetish (which in this case is hegemonic politics) "actually enables us to remain politically passive. We don't have to assume political responsibility" for the simple reason that the fetish "is doing it for us" (2005, 63). The only way of opening herself up to any potentially different forms of politics would be, as she points out in a slightly different context, by means of "the Real that ruptures my world, that is to say the evil other [in this case, of different forms of politics to that of the struggle over hegemony] I cannot imagine sharing a world with" (2005, 69). If she did access or admit what is foreclosed and eliminated in advance in this way, the problem Dean would then have is that any such ethical, responsible, hospitable, opening to the (political) other would challenge the very (hegemonic, transcendental, and, as we will see, moralistic) ideas she depends on for her sense of the political. As Dean acknowledges: "if everything is out there on the Internet, anything I fail to encounter—or can't imagine encountering—isn't simply excluded (everything is already there), it is foreclosed. Admitting or accessing what is foreclosed destroys the very order produced through foreclosure" (2005, 69). Yet for me this indeterminacy and temporary suspension of knowledge is precisely the point. And unless we are prepared to accept this, we are resorting to what Wendy Brown has called an "anti-political moralism."

As Clare Birchall and I have shown in a different but related analysis of the politics of cultural studies (2006a), Brown uses this term to refer to a certain "resistance" to thinking and intellectual inquiry on the part of many leftists who either refuse or are unable to give up their devotion to previously held notions of politics. Consequently, while many on the left have:

> lost confidence in a historiography bound to a notion of progress or to any other purpose, we have coined no political substitute for progressive understandings of where we have come from and where we are going. Similarly, while both sovereignty and right have suffered severe erosions of their naturalistic epistemological and ontological bases in modernity, we have not replaced them as sources of political agency and sites of justice claims. Personal conviction and political truth have lost their moorings in firm and level epistemological ground, but we have not jettisoned them as sources of political motivation or as sites of collective fealty. So we have ceased to believe in many of the constitutive premises undergirding modern personhood, statehood, and constitutions, yet we continue to operate politically as if these premises still held, and as if the political-cultural narratives based on them were intact. (Brown 2001, 3–4)

In point of fact, moralism "so loathes overt manifestations of power," Brown maintains, "that the moralist inevitably feels antipathy toward politics as a domain of open contestation for power and hegemony"; and "the identity of the moralist is" actually "staked against intellectual questioning that might dismantle the foundations of its own premises; its survival is imperilled by the very practice of open-ended intellectual inquiry" (2001, 30). Which is why it is perceived as being "antipolitical." The problem is that such moralizing occupies the place of and in fact replaces genuine critical interrogation. Indeed, Brown goes so far as to argue that, "despite its righteous insistence on knowing what is True, Valuable, or Important, moralism as a hegemonic form of political expression, a dominant political sensibility, actually marks both analytic impotence and political aimlessness—a misrecognition of the political logics now organizing the world, a concomitant failure to discern any direction for action, and the loss of a clear object of political desire" (2001, 29).

Post-hegemonic Politics?

It is no doubt worth emphasizing that I am not trying to suggest with any of this that we *have* actually entered a "post-political" era, as Dean, following Žižek, asserts. Nor am I claiming that the politics of another context Dean refers to is today completely outmoded and out of date; and that, consequently, what we really need to do is come to terms with this fact, rather than continuing to struggle futilely against it. Instead of claiming we are in a post-political era, I want to ask: Can the current political terrain not be better understood somewhat differently, as *post-hegemonic*—at least to the extent that it cannot simply be assumed and taken for granted that our political situation *can always and everywhere be analyzed in terms of either hegemonic or counterhegemonic struggle* (as both cultural studies and the left frequently have suggested)?[33]

My response to the question raised by Dean—"Why has the expansion and intensification of communication networks, the proliferation of the very tools of democracy, coincided with the collapse of democratic deliberation and, indeed, struggle?" (Dean 2005, 54)—is therefore somewhat different from hers. For me, the answer to this question lies not so much with the particular conditions and extensive proliferation of networked communication technologies and their "profoundly depoliticizing" effect, as Dean claims. Instead, I wonder if the causes of any such "significant disconnect" do not actually rest, at least in part, simply—yet at the same time more profoundly and radically—with a change to what Dean refers to as "official politics" in the societies of the North Atlantic capitalist industrial nation-states (2005, 53). Let me attempt to pursue this speculative hypothesis a little further, by taking as a specific example that of Britain and New Labour.

As Stuart Hall points out, the New Labour party in the United

Kingdom is a hybrid regime. For Hall, this regime is composed of two interconnected strands: a dominant neoliberal strand and a subordinate social democratic strand. Significantly, the relation between these two strands is not a "static formation"; it is a "transformist" process (S. Hall 2003, 19). New Labour's project, its long-term strategy, is to transform the subordinate social democratic strand "into a *particular variant* of free-market neo-liberalism. . . . (in exactly the same way that Thatcherism delivered a 'neo-liberal variant' of classic Conservativism)" (2003, 12, 22). To the two strands identified by Hall I now want to add a third: a neoconservative one. I am thinking here of the move taken by the New Right (in which I would include the Bush administration in the United States and that of Blair and New Labour in the United Kingdom) over the last decade from the neoliberalism of Thatcher and Reagan to the neoconservativism of much of Bush and Blair's later politics. Now, for Hall, New Labour's strategy is "authentically" a hegemonic one, "even though it may not be capable of producing a stable hegemonic outcome. It aims to win enough consent as it goes, and build subordinate demands back into its logic" (2003, 20). However, adding the neoconservative strand into this already complex hybrid mix means that, as Lawrence Grossberg has insisted, we cannot assume that the contemporary conjuncture *can* be understood as a hegemonic struggle—or not simply as a hegemonic struggle (Grossberg 2005b, 357). Stressing that the "presence of a hegemonic struggle is not guaranteed," and that the theory of hegemony is a "particular kind of political struggle, not a universal one" (2005b, 357), Grossberg perceives the current historical and social context more in terms of "a struggle between those (liberals and to some extent, leftists) who think they are waging a hegemonic struggle, and those (significant fractions of the new right) who are trying to invent not only a new social formation, but a new political culture as well, one built not on compromise but on fanaticism," and in which the settlement is often "accomplished behind the back of those struggling over the field of the social formation" (2005b, 358). This is especially true, I would maintain, with regard to the neoconservatives on both sides of the Atlantic, with their extreme religiousness. For John Gray, for example, "the armed missionaries in the White House . . . reflect the growing power of American fundamentalism." Similarly, he argues that while Blair took up the "neoliberal economic programme" almost by "default," he was very much a neocon "from conviction." It was the neoconservative blend of

"Leninism and religion" that most accurately represented his "personal outlook" (Gray 2005, 18). So while Thatcher sought to win consent in order to lead through a hegemonic strategy of constant (re)negotiation, the "modernization" program implemented by New Labour can often be seen to have operated rather differently. Take the example of the 15 February 2003 antiwar protests. Close to two million people marched on the streets of London to demonstrate against attacking Iraq. Nevertheless, Tony Blair was still prepared to "ignore the public will" and take his country to war on the grounds that he and George W. Bush considered the use of such force and power to impose "freedom" and "democracy" on another nation *the right thing to do*—and what is more he didn't need to hide it (see G. Hall 2006).

Interestingly, Dean uses the same example in her conclusion, claiming it consisted of "ten million people worldwide." While she regards the Internet as being of vital importance to the political activists involved in bringing about such events, enabling them as it does to "establish social connections to one another," for her, this does not automatically link to the formation of "political solidarities with more duration." In truth, she remains convinced that nowadays the "political impact of new technologies proceeds in precisely the opposite direction, that is to say in the direction of post-politics" (Dean 2005, 71). This is due to the fundamental disconnection she identifies between politics as official policy and politics as the communicative interactions of the public sphere. She regards technological fetishism as functioning to disavow and conceal this political "disempowerment or castration" (2005, 61). All of which leads her to characterize Internet politics as "a politics of and through new media, and that's all" (2005, 65), and to contrast it unfavorably, as we have seen, to larger, stronger, and longer-lasting counterhegemonic forms of political struggle and resistance that take place in "real life," "on the ground" (2005, 61, 65). At the same time, she positions the opportunities for such forms of struggle and resistance, somewhat melancholicly, as having now mostly been lost. Regaining them "may well require breaking with and through the fantasies attaching us to communicative capitalism," she concludes (2005, 71).

Yet such an analysis can only be made once Dean herself has foreclosed the question of politics. This elimination of the antagonistic and undecidable dimension of politics allows Dean to continue to assume, and to take it for granted, that the contemporary political context can, like that of the past, *be best analyzed, understood, combated, and resisted in terms of hegemony*; and that the problem rests with those troublesome communicative technologies and their supposed depoliticizing effect, rather than with any changes in the actual nature of politics. For Grossberg, by contrast, the attempt on the part of the new right to invent a new political culture means that the problem lies not only with the apparent collapse, disappearance, or displacement of many opportunities for larger, stronger, and longer-lasting forms of (counter)hegemonic political organization, struggle, and resistance; but also with the more fundamental issue that hegemony per se is often "inadequate," as he puts it, "to either analyze or respond to the complexly changing balance in the field of forces or, more conventionally, to the vectors and restructurings that are potentially changing the very fabric of power and experience" (2005b, 358).

Still, it is not my intention with any of this to side with Grossberg against Dean, and argue that politics *is now necessarily post-hegemonic* and that we have therefore entered what might be considered a "post-hegemonic" political era. Nor am I maintaining that a responsible decision *cannot* ever be taken to the effect that hegemony *is* an appropriate concept to use when attempting to understand, analyze, and respond to a particular situation. The point I am trying to make is not so much about whether hegemony *is* or *is not* still appropriate at all. I am rather using this speculative hypothesis to show that the situation is far more difficult, complex, multiplicitous, and uncertain than Dean allows (although I acknowledge there is something attractive about the will to power-knowledge that goes to produce such a convincing large-scale interpretation of Internet politics). In particular, I am using it as a means of drawing attention to the fact that Dean is not willing to make a decision that is open to the actual complexities of a social or cultural situation, to the incalculable, the other, the undecidable, the unpredictable; and especially to the possibility that politics on the Internet may not always look like politics as it is most easily recognized and usually known and understood, certainly within cultural studies.

As a result, Dean's analysis of politics in "Communicative Capitalism" is not political even according to her own definition of politics. We can see this to a certain extent from the way in which, for all her emphasis on both the importance of context, and the work of Laclau and Mouffe, Dean does not actually take into account the context of her politics, especially the possibility that the "context" may have changed, and that consequently her conception of politics may need to change, too. Dean prefers instead to rely on notions of politics (specifically heg-emonic struggle and resistance) developed in a previous and what she herself describes as a very different historical conjuncture to make mor-alistic condemnations of other forms of politics for *not being political enough*, for being in fact "post-political," as judged by the standards and criteria of that earlier historical context.[34] But Dean's analysis of politics in this essay is also not political because it does not open itself to the "real antagonism and dissent"—including that over ideas of what poli-tics is and what it means to be political—that according to her are nec-essary for politics. If the political for Laclau and Mouffe is a decision taken in an undecidable terrain (see, for example, Mouffe 2000, 130), the terrain in which Dean makes decisions over the political in this es-say is for her very much a decidable one. The upshot is that she uncriti-cally adheres to and repeats the transcendental hegemonic position that the theory of hegemony itself occupies within cultural studies.

What this analysis of Dean (as well as Barbrook, Kahn and Kellner, and the tactical media of Garcia and Lovink) makes clear, then, is that not only does presuming that new media can be understood in terms of pre-decided categories and concepts—including those of the gift econ-omy, hegemony, and the dialectic—lead politics on the Internet to re-main to all intents and purposes trapped in the dialectic of cultural criticism, unable to think a way out (thus failing to challenge the cul-tural and economic dynamic of capitalism and merely repeating its dia-lectical structure instead); but it also ignores or forecloses any possibili-ties for a politics that is new, different, innovative, or exceptional, as well as for any heterogeneous excess that cannot be recuperated within politics as it is already known and understood to emerge. Along with not responding responsibly to the ethical challenge presented by the other, by what cannot be predicted or foreseen, it also turns out to be antipolitical (despite its proclamations to the contrary).

What's more, the tendency to approach new media using old, prees-tablished frameworks of knowledge and methods of analysis like this (including an already established and easily recognized concept of *poli-tics*) may also be one reason why, to date, the literature on new technol-ogy and digital media has yet to produce any indisputable true "exem-plars," to borrow a term from Jeffrey Sconce. Sconce sees the field of digital culture as having generated many "synthesizers"—those who of-ten set the "overall terms of debate for a field and brokers what is and what is not 'hot'"—all of them "vying to generate the visionary exemplar" (Sconce 2003, 190).[35] Yet it has generated few actual visionary "exemplars," in the sense of people who have produced an "influential, groundbreaking work . . . that serves as the foundation for subsequent debate in the field" (2003, 189). The academic spin on new media instead "seems more a competition among former critical exemplars" (2003, 190)—among whom can be included Spinoza, Bergson, Marx, Heidegger, Benjamin, Adorno, Williams, Debord, McLuhan, Habermas, Foucault, de Certeau, Derrida, Deleuze, and Guattari.[36] Instead of developing new, singular, or at least specific theories of the politics of new media, critics have for the most part tended to understand digital politics in terms of already decided and legitimated theories and ideas. (Again, one could speculate that this may be because theories of digital media, like digital publications themselves, also have to derive their authority from elsewhere—from the nondigital "paper" world. And that it is only those figures deemed important in the paper world who are regarded as having the authority and legitimacy to pronounce on the world of the digital.)

One notable (albeit possibly only partial) exception to this "theoretical reiteration of the old" is provided by Mark Poster in his 1997 essay "Cyberdemocracy: Internet and the Public Sphere." What is so innovative about this essay, as I read it, is the way it shows that to address the question of the impact and effect of the Internet's "costless reproduction, instantaneous dissemination and radical decentralization . . . upon the society, the culture and the political institutions" is to "ask the wrong question" (Poster 1997, 205). It is the wrong question for at least three interconnected reasons. First, because far from being different and opposed, both of the above interpretations of politics on the Internet (i.e., that which sees the Internet either as a reinforcement of free-market neoliberalism or as a means of resisting capitalist systems of domination—as well as the dialectic between the two) adhere to what Poster identifies as a "modern"—as opposed to a "postmodern"—understanding of politics. Second, because this "modern" understanding of politics may be precisely what the Internet challenges. As Poster says early on in "Cyberdemocracy," "[w]hile there is no doubt that the internet folds into existing social functions and extends them in new ways . . . what are far more cogent as possible long-term political effects of the Internet are the ways in which it institutes new social functions, ones that do not fit easily within those of characteristically modern organisations" (1997, 202). And, third, because any such new functions may "only become intelligible if a framework is adopted that does not limit the discussions from the outset to modern patterns of interpretation" (1997, 202).

Now it is not my intention to put Poster's essay forward as a candidate for an exemplar in new media studies to rival Sconce's championing of Sherry Turkle's *Life on the Screen* (1996): not least because (as chapters 2 and 3 demonstrated, and as the chapter that follows will proceed to show) it is the *process* of how institutions and fields are *founded* that I am trying to interrogate here (rather than attempting to repeat such foundational and institutionalizing moments myself). Nevertheless, I do want to make a claim for the importance of Poster's essay in the context of this chapter's particular concern for understanding the politics of digitization. I want to do so because "Cyberdemocracy" is (still) one of the places that has perhaps gone furthest toward exploring the question of how to understand politics on the Internet, raising "the issue of a new understanding of technology [that] finally leads to a reassessment of the political aspects of the Internet" (Poster 1997, 210). Although I will argue that "Cyberdemocracy" does not go far enough in many respects, and although it is now relatively old in new media terms, this essay remains for me far more powerful than a lot of more recent texts on digital media. And, interestingly, especially as far as a book on open access is concerned, Poster achieves this by focusing on the Internet's ability (or otherwise) to act as a form of public sphere. He takes this particular focus because for many people politics is often already reduced to the notion of a public sphere (Poster cites the work of Rita Felski by way of illustration [1997, 208]); and because for him the "issue of the public sphere is at the heart of any reconceptualization of democracy" (1997, 206), and thus politics. But I also want to make a claim for the importance of "Cyberdemocracy," because it is perhaps the nearest we have to a classic text on the subject of Internet politics and the Internet as a new form of public sphere, at least if "judged in terms of course assignments and number of citations" (Sconce 2003, 190). Therefore, I turn in the next chapter to Poster's account of politics on the Internet for help with answering the question regarding how digitization and the archive may be political as well as ethical.

The Specificity of New Media

> The archive is first the law of what can be said, the system that governs the appearance of statements as unique events. But the archive is also that which determines that all these things said do not accumulate endlessly in an amorphous mass, nor are they inscribed in an unbroken linearity, nor do they disappear at the mercy of chance external accidents; but they are grouped together in distinct figures, composed together in accordance with multiple relations, maintained or blurred in accordance with specific regularities. . . . Far from being that which unifies everything that has been said in the great confused murmur of a discourse, far from being only that which ensures that we exist in the midst of preserved discourse, it is that which differentiates discourses in their multiple existence and specifies them in their own duration.
> —*Michel Foucault*, The Archaeology of Knowledge, *1972*

Tactical Media Theory

The emphasis placed in the last chapter on acting tactically goes some way toward explaining why it is so important for me not to generalize about new media in this book. What I am primarily focusing on is one actual, specific form and use of new media: that associated with open-access electronic publishing and archiving, and my own "practical" work in this area in particular. I am doing so, as I made clear in my first set of metadata, partly as a way of responding to concerns around research on new media raised by Jeffrey Sconce and Mark Poster, among others. Sconce and Poster see new media research as preoccupied more with other writing on new media than with new media itself (Sconce 2003, 198), too often manifesting a fondness for the general over the particular, and providing strings of catchy but nonetheless vague terms that fail to guide "the virtual traveller in any particular direction" (Poster 2001, 141). At the same time, my focus on the specific is intended to help me argue that the transformation in the publication of academic research literature that is being brought about by the shift from print to digital offers us a chance to raise important questions regarding how scholarship is conducted and how the university works as an institution (and, from there, the politics—and ethics—of cultural studies). As Eva Hemmungs Wirtén writes, "the most basic of presuppositions regarding long-standing cultural relationships are questioned when we are forced to contend with the definitions of what a book really is, and what it means to be an author, a reader, or a publisher. Such questions are always present within print culture, but they insist on being addressed more directly at a time of drastic technological changes" (Hemmungs Wirtén 2004, 67).[1]

I want to stress that this shift or transformation in the mode of reproduction from print to digital media, rather than determining our techno-future in a particular way, *offers us* nothing more than *an opportunity, a chance*. I also want to insist that this opportunity, this chance, *has* to be taken. Hence my emphasis in chapter 4 and throughout this book on the need to act tactically. Witness also my efforts in chapter 2 to show that, to date, the majority of academic online journals and digital repositories—including open-access journals and archives—*do* tend to function in a relatively closed, papercentric manner, not least by attempting to deliver an unchanged and preexisting ink-on-paper content, albeit in a "new," re-mediated form. This is the case, as we have seen, with regard to Stevan Harnad's influential account of how the system of self-archiving of e-prints in open-access repositories works, as well as with many of the already existing open-access archives, including the arXiv.org E-Print Archive at Cornell. Consequently, I maintain that if we do not make the most of the opportunity to raise such questions regarding the authority and legitimacy of scholarship and the institution of the university that are created by the current transition in the mode of technological reproduction, academic online publishing *will* continue to function for the most part in a relatively closed, papercentric, unethical, and antipolitical fashion.

Moreover, I argue that this is a chance that very much has to be taken *now*. Once this period of technological change settles down and is no longer perceived as quite so new—once bodies such as (in the United Kingdom) the ESRC or AHRC are able to fully establish and develop their own disciplinary and institutional repositories, or companies like AOL, Yahoo, and Google become involved and figure out how to make a substantial profit from doing so—then the opportunity to set the policy and agenda for open-access archiving will very likely be lost. This may indeed already be the case in the sciences, where the requirements involved in a journal subscribing to Thompson Scientific's Web of Science (which journals in many fields need to do, as publications listed at the top of its citation indexes are increasingly being linked to funding, employment prospects, career advancement opportunities, promotion, and so on) impose a papercentric form on electronic publications (see chapter 2, n. 12). In this respect there may be little time to lose: at the time of writing only one of the seven U.K. research councils has yet to establish an open-access mandate, for instance.[2] This is why I believe the argument developed here is rather timely; and why it is important to encourage and promote the taking of this chance to address these issues of knowledge, legitimacy, ethics, politics, and the university, and of the difference the new media themselves make.

That said, it is not my intention to associate the digital realm *in general* with the thematics of the unknowable and the incalculable in this book; nor to argue that new media is intrinsically open or undecidable. Other forms and performances of new media operate differently to open access, and in doing so often provide far less opportunity for taking the kind of politico-ethical and institutional chance I am referring to.

This last point has significant implications for how we understand digital culture. For instance, in an article from 2005 entitled "Who Controls Digital Culture?," Poster hypothesizes that it is very much possible that in the future the sharing or gifting ethos of peer-to-peer networks I detailed in my opening chapter will become a prominent, perhaps even the *dominant* mode of cultural exchange:[3]

> An infrastructure is being set into place for a day when cultural objects will become variable and users will become creators as well. Such an outcome is not just around the corner since for generations the population has been accustomed to fixed cultural objects. But as we pass beyond the limits of modern culture, with its standardized, mass produced consumer culture, we can anticipate more and more individuals and groups taking advantage of the facility with which digital cultural objects are changed, stored, and distributed in the network. A different sort of public space from that of modernity is emerging, a heterotopia in Foucault's term, and peer-to-peer networks constitute an important ingredient in that development,

one worthy of safeguarding and promoting for that reason alone. If copyright laws need to be changed and media corporations need to disappear or transform themselves, this result must be evaluated in relation to a new regime of culture that is now possible. (Poster 2005, n.p.; 2006, 204)

Certainly, the idea that the relations of production and distribution associated with peer-to-peer networks can be scaled up to form a new regime of culture or new kinds of networked institutions, even a plan for the future organization of society in which cultural, political, and economic decisions are made in an open, distributed, participatory, cooperative, networked fashion, is a seductive one.[4] (All the more so if this idea is able to incorporate the new notions of the human, technology, citizenship, the public sphere, democracy, and politics—as well as the relations between them—that we will see Poster's analysis of "Cyberdemocracy" opening us up to in chapter 5.) No doubt grand historical narratives of this sort—in which the relatively fixed and stable imagined communities associated with the classical idea of the nation-state are often regarded as being superseded by more complex, fluid, and mobile networks of people—also have a certain tactical and, indeed, strategic value themselves. To be sure, if peer-to-peer networks are to be considered one important ingredient in the emergence of any such potential new regime, I would want to insist upon open access being another. The two are by no means mutually exclusive. After all, one can easily imagine establishing a system of *peer-to-peer review* to rival the peer-review system that is dominant within academia at the moment.[5] Nevertheless, there are at least two questions I would raise as far as any such hypothesis is concerned.

To begin with, if a new, post-"modern" (as distinct from "postmodern") regime of this kind does emerge, what will it look like? Instead of being a realm in which culture in general takes on the distributed, networked, participative, cooperative character of much new media, I wonder if it is not more likely to assume the form of a mixed and (as Poster's reference to Foucault indeed suggests) heterogeneous economy, with different media, both "new" and "old," digital and analogue, and the related infrastructures, operating in a relation of coexistence and even at times convergence and synergy, yes, perhaps, but also of divergence, competition and antagonism. This in turn connects to a further question.

Even if such a new form of "public space"—different to that of modernity and derived at least in part from the gifting ethos of digital culture's peer-to-peer networks—is possible, would the various ingredients that go to make up this "heterotopia" (in which we could perhaps include peer-to-peer file sharing, free software, open source, open content, the Creative Commons, open-access publishing and archiving, and so on) all contribute to such a distributed, networked, participative regime in more or less the same way? Or, just as there are obvious commonalities and points of connection between them, would there not be areas of friction, conflict, and even incommensurability, too?

Of course I cannot answer these questions here if for no other reason than their future-oriented nature makes that impossible. The point I am trying to make in raising them is that, if we *are* to substitute the "cultural analyst's penchant for the particular" for the "philosopher's taste for the general," it is not enough to take into account the *difference* and specificity of the digital medium of reproduction: its material form and properties. Attention also needs to be paid to the many *distinctions* and *divergences* that exist *between* the various ingredients that go to make up digital culture at any one time. This is something I tried to do in chapter 1 by emphasizing that the situation regarding the digital reproduction of scholarly literature is in many respects very different to that of the peer-to-peer sharing of music files.[6] Open access is capable of working in the way described here because of the specific character of both academia and open access at the moment: that is, because the majority of scholars do not expect, or need, to get paid directly or substantially for their writings (their "reward" comes more from the increase in feedback and recognition and enhancement to their reputation that open access offers); and because the e-print self-archiving system enables academics to retain copyright over their work, or at least avoid infringing most publishers' copyright agreements (which means that texts can be distributed freely, rather than being "stolen" or "pirated," as is often the case with regard to music). In this respect one could say that the open-access publishing and archiving of academic scholarship and research constitutes a strategic use of a specific form of digital culture within particular institutional and sociopolitical contexts (although, as we shall see, it cannot be reduced to those contexts). It is not something that is *necessarily* generalizable or transferable to other forms and practices of digital culture—the peer-to-peer sharing of music and video files, the decentered electronic distribution of films, the digital storage of visual art, the online publication of science-fiction literature, and so on— although it may be.[7]

This does not mean that all these various forms and practices are absolutely different and completely heterogeneous either. As I also observed in chapter 2, the very web-like structure of the Web often makes it difficult to determine where texts begin or end; all the cutting and pasting, internal and external linking that takes place blurs the boundaries not only between the text and its surroundings, its material support, but also between other media and cultural texts, techniques, forms, and genres, making such boundaries almost impossible to determine. To be sure, many instances of digital culture—such as Amazon's peer-reviewing, Wikipedia's open editing, YouTube's video sharing, and Flickr's photosharing—have a number of features in common with open-access publishing and archiving: not least that they make use of digital networks, are dependent on an open, social process of collaboration and cooperation, are made up of user-generated content, and have the potential for the individual user (or "producer") to be able to create and modify that content as well as reproduce, store, and distribute it. Together with their material differences, however (as represented by the particular platform, hardware, software, operating system, programming code, graphical interface, and so on), I would argue that they also operate in different ways, situations, and contexts.[8] They are therefore not *necessarily* capable of having the same or comparable effects. Likewise with regard to computer games, search engines, and virtual environments such as Second Life or Habbo.[9] As with open access (or so I have argued here), these, too, may have the capacity not merely to extend prosthetically existing forms and practices of knowledge and information, but also to reconstitute them differently—thus requiring us to develop new forms of knowledge and new techniques of analysis in order to comprehend *them*, and in so doing, cause us to see *them* again, as if for the first time. Still, I am wary of stating that they do so in a manner similar to open-access archiving. The extent to which instances of new media have the potential to reconstitute forms of knowledge differently is again something that would have to be worked out by paying close attention to the specificity and indeed singularity of each in relation to a particular context.

Obviously, this is not something I can do for all the examples of digital culture mentioned above. Instead, I have taken a (tactical) decision to focus on just one, that which has the potential to be of most concern to the scholarly community (from which I imagine the majority of readers of this book are likely to be drawn): the open-access publication and archiving of research literature. Even here things are not so simple, however, as the open-access movement is itself neither unified nor self-identical. There are significant differences even among the various "flavors" of open access. That is why at times in this book I have focused on the model of open access that is being invented and creatively explored by the digital repository of cultural studies texts I am involved with.

I am interested in the actual, singular points of potentiality and transformation that are provided by specific instances and performances of digital media. Let me reiterate: as far as I am concerned there is no system, set of principles, ethos, or philosophy (that of the academic gift economy, say) that can be necessarily privileged and extrapolated out of open access—or any other example of new media, for that matter—and made to function as generally (and unconditionally) applicable to culture, or even digital culture, as a whole, either now or in the future.[10] The issue is more complex, multiplicitous, and uncertain than that. I am arguing that open-access archiving has the potential to work in the way described here in *particular institutional contexts* and *at particular times*. The same ideas and practices may be translatable to other situations and contexts, other singular points of potentiality and transformation, thus becoming in the process a prominent, even perhaps dominant, feature of culture, and possibly even leading to the emergence of a new *regime of culture*, new kinds of institutions or new forms of social and political organization. (This is because any singularity always has a relation to the general and the common. After all, a singularity must escape recognition as a singularity, as something that relates to the common understanding of what a singularity is, otherwise it is not singular but only an example of a general type: "singularity." The singular is by definition that which resists being described in general categories. Yet a singularity also has to be capable of being recognized as an instance of the general type "singularity," since if it were *absolutely different and singular* no one would ever be able to understand it *as a singularity* [see G. Hall 2006, 45]. The forging of connections between different instances and performances of new media and their articulation with other struggles and resistances to form counterhegemonic groups or networks brought together by their opposition to a shared opponent would thus obviously be, for some, as we have seen in chapter 4, one way of being political in relation to the Internet.) However, the ideas and practices concerning open-access archiving may turn out not to be translatable to other situations and circumstances at all. In which case, if questions of ethics and politics are to be raised and responded to responsibly, the development of different ideas, tactics, and strategies may be required— perhaps those associated with peer-to-peer networks, perhaps not. This, too, is something that would have to be worked out by paying close attention to the specificity and singularity of each in relation to particular contexts.

The Specificity of Open-Access Archiving

Instances of new media, then, need to be thought, analyzed and understood in terms of at least a more specific form of analysis, and in fact a "media-singular analysis," I would argue.[11] Such an approach offers a number of advantages. It reduces the risk of producing vague, futurological generalizations about digital culture. It also helps avoid falling into the trap of privileging one specific instance of digital media and assuming that a whole new cultural regime based on its particular principles and ethos is possible. This is not to say peer-to-peer networks and open access *do not* have the potential to be important ingredients in the emergence of a different sort of "public" space from that of modernity, one in which both can operate together with relatively little friction and hostility. It is only to signal that we also have to remain open to the possibility that they *may* conflict and even be incommensurable, and thus lead to a heterogeneous and divided form of space—or even to multiple different regimes of culture that operate in an antagonistic relation toward one another. (Nor need this possibility necessarily be viewed pessimistically since, as we saw in chapter 4, the specificity of politics is marked by a certain refusal to eliminate conflict and antagonism, in a pluralistic, liberal democracy at least.)

Still further, approaching new media in this way assists with eluding the kind of "technological fetishism" that provides merely the fantasy of political activity and participation Jodi Dean locates around blogging and peer-to-peer file sharing, but that, I have argued, she herself succumbs to a variation of with respect to her own antipolitical fetishization of hegemonic struggle. This approach encourages us not to decide in advance what the political and ethical thing to do is when it comes to understanding and interpreting digital culture, and to instead remain open precisely to the latter's specificity and, indeed, singularity. This openness to that which is novel, innovative, or exceptional and to any heterogeneous excess in turn facilitates the appreciation and analysis of the various opportunities that different instances of new media offer with regard to taking the kind of political and institutional chances I am discussing in this book. In this respect, the choice of which specific instances of new media to focus on is very much a tactical and political one.

All of which explains why, although I began *Digitize This Book!* by asking about the university in the age of a host of different examples of new media (Google, BitTorrent, Wikipedia, MySpace, Kindle, and so forth), and although for the sake of convenience, time, and economy (and also in the hope of engaging as many potential readers as possible) I have on occasion referred to digitization in general, I have not attempted to extend my analysis to apply to new media and digital culture as a whole. Instead, I have for the most part focused on one specific form and use of new media: namely, that associated with open-access publishing and especially open-access archiving.

The specificity of open-access archiving resides in the way in which it enables researchers to circumvent a lot of the restrictions placed on access to research and publications by copyright and licensing agreements, and thus provides a response to many of the issues and dilemmas that have been presented to scholars by an increasingly market-driven and commercial academic publishing industry.

Open-access archiving is able to offer a number of advantages and benefits to authors. As we saw in chapter 1, as far as the cultural studies repository I am involved with is concerned, these include enabling authors to:

- Publish their research immediately upon completion
- Make their work available from (almost) any desktop, twenty-four hours a day, to anyone who has Internet access
- Provide their audience, including fellow writers and researchers, undergraduate and postgraduate students, and the general public, with as many copies of their texts as they need
- Increase the size of their readership
- Potentially increase the reading figures, impact, and even sales of their paper publications

- Publish books and journals that have too small a potential readership to make them cost-effective for a "paper" publisher to take on
- Make their research "permanently" available
- Republish texts that are out of print
- Distribute their texts to an extremely wide (if not necessarily "global") audience
- Link to underlying, background, and related research
- Fulfill their obligations to funding bodies easily and quickly

The specificity of open-access archiving also resides in the way it determines what can be collected, stored, and preserved, and the particular nature of the questions this determination raises.

It is important to realize that an archive is not a neutral institution; rather, as we have seen, it is part of specific intellectual, cultural, technical, and economic/financial networks. An archive's medium, in particular—be it paper, celluloid, or tape—is often perceived as being merely a disinterested carrier for the archived material. Yet the medium of an archive actually helps to determine and shape its content; a content, moreover, that is performed differently each time, in each particular context in which it is accessed or material is retrieved from the archive. An open-access archive is no exception in this respect. Its specific form, medium, and structure shape what it preserves, classifies, and performs as legitimate scholarship, in both time and scope.[12]

Consequently, and as I demonstrated earlier, a digital cultural studies archive is not just a means of reproducing and confirming existing conceptions of cultural studies: of selecting, collecting, gathering, interpreting, filtering, organizing, classifying, and preserving what cultural studies already is or is perceived as having been. It is *partly* that. But it is also a means of *producing* and *performing* cultural studies: *both what it is going to look like in the past; and what there is a chance for cultural studies to have been in the future.* (At its most basic, this means that, just as those who were active in the United Kingdom Workers Education Association and who published in paper form *are* remembered as being among cultural studies' founders, while those who taught at the WEA but did not publish *are not* [Williams 1986], so those cultural studies authors whose work cannot be digitized likewise risk being excluded from any open-access initiatives and thus not appearing as part of cultural studies' future or even its past. This is simply because, no matter how "open" any

open-access repository is or how responsibly and hospitably its protocols are designed and applied, it can only accept texts and materials in
digital form.)

The determination of content by the archive's medium is a feature
digital repositories share with other kinds of archives. One of the issues
that is specific to open-access archiving, however, is the manner in
which, as a result of the profound transformation in the publication of the
academic research literature that is being brought about by the change
in the mode of reproduction from ink-on-paper to digital, questions that
were already present with regard to the print medium and other media,
but that tended to be taken for granted, overlooked, marginalized, excluded, or otherwise repressed, are now insisting "on being addressed
more directly" (Hemmungs Wirtén 2004, 67). As Adrian Johns reminds
us in *The Nature of the Book*, up until the middle of the eighteenth century the printed book was an unstable object; for example, Shakespeare's
first folio included more than six hundred typefaces and numerous incon-
sistencies in its spelling, punctuation, divisions, arrangement, proofing,
and page configurations. As a result, readers had to make critical decisions about particular printed books regarding their identity, consist-
ency, and trustworthiness on the basis of "assessments of the people involved in the making, distribution, and reception of books" (Johns 1998,
31–32). Early in the history of the printed book, then, readers were involved in forming judgments around questions of authority and legitimacy: concerning what a book is and what it means to be an author, a
reader, a publisher, and a distributor. The development and spread of
the concept of the author, along with mass printing techniques, uniform
multiple-copy editions, copyright, established publishing houses, editors,
and so forth meant that many of these ideas subsequently began to appear "fixed." Consequently, readers were no longer "asked" to make
decisions over questions of authority and legitimacy. Such issues were
forgotten (much as we have seen in chapter 2, they were forgotten
around questions of academic and disciplinary authority). The digital
mode of reproduction, however, promises to place us in a position where
readers are again called on to respond and to make judgments and
decisions about the nature and authority of (digitized) texts, and of the
disciplines, fields of knowledge, and registers these texts are supposed
to belong to (or not), precisely through its loosening of much of this fixity.[13] In this respect, open-access archiving has for me a certain tactical
quality. We can now see that the destabilization created by the shift

from print to digital offers us *an opportunity* and *a chance*, if only it can be taken, to approach academic research and scholarship anew, as if for the first time; and thus to raise precisely the kind of responsible questions concerning knowledge, the discipline, the university, and the institution that in many respects we should have been asking anyway. These questions concern two further aspects of what I describe as "the specificity of open-access archiving."

The Ethical Issues Raised by Open Access

What is to be included in the archive and what excluded? What categories of inclusion and exclusion should govern disciplinary protocols as far as the digital publication, transmission, dissemination, exchange, storage, and retrieval of academic research and scholarship is concerned?

The ethical problems concerning the maintenance of an infinite and aporetic responsibility to an unconditional hospitality to the alterity of the other that an open-access repository enables us to bring to attention and emphasize were one of the main reasons I wanted to get involved in setting up an open-access archive (even though with *Culture Machine* I have been publishing an open-access online journal since 1999). I became interested in doing so not just for the usual reasons that are offered to justify taking the "green" road to open access (open-access self-archiving) over the "gold" (publishing in open-access journals): that an archive is cheaper, because it does not require the establishment of expensive gate-keeping and copyediting procedures; that it provides open access to research without restricting authors to particular journals, and without asking them to pay for publication (as is the case with some models of open access); that it enables greater ease of searching and retrieval than a dispersed array of journals and articles; or even that, when it comes to promoting the wider adoption of open access, it will be easier to convince academics to self-archive their research—because of the advantages it offers them in terms of gaining increased feedback on their work and developing their reputation through the enhanced levels of recognition and impact it can bring—than it will be to convert the existing journals to open access—because the publishers of the latter are more likely to feel they have something to lose: namely, income from subscriptions. Actually, I would suggest that, as far as the humanities in general and cultural studies in particular are concerned, the opposite may be true. Publishing in digital repositories is newer and less familiar to most people in these fields than publishing in journals, even electronic ones. Open-access archiving may thus require academics to make a larger shift in their thinking and scholarly practices if it is to be accepted than would open-access journal publishing. (That said, this is something that can be countered to a certain extent by funding agencies and institutions making it mandatory that any research they support be either published in an open-access journal or deposited in an open-access repository.)[14]

I also wanted to get involved in establishing an open-access archive because "archives can be filled with objects and documents of a quirky nature: letters; recordings; a lock of hair; a manuscript; a photograph; or documentation of individuals, groups, families, organizations; manifestos; constitutions; tax records and on it goes," as Elvis Richardson and Sarah Goffman remind us in an editorial in an issue of *Photofile* devoted entirely to the subject of the archive (Richardson and Goffman 2006, 16). Compared to a journal, which is a "serious, scholarly publication" (Wikipedia 2006c), an archive (which can be understood as both the objects and documents assembled and the place where they are located) is by definition far more open—at least potentially—to the "quirky": that is, the different, the foreign, the heterogeneous, the excessive. An archive is therefore capable of placing us in a position where we have to make decisions over what can be included in it, and with what authority and legitimacy, in a way a journal simply is not.

A "serious" academic journal, for instance, will primarily publish peer-reviewed articles that are recognizable as "proper" pieces of scholarly writing or research. Yet along with e-prints of peer-reviewed essays, an academic archive could also contain monographs, edited books, textbooks, book chapters, journal editions, out-of-print books, working papers, discussion papers, theses, bibliographies, conference papers, presentations, teaching material, and lectures. Artifacts of a more unusual nature could also conceivably be collected in the most serious of academic archives. I am thinking of drafts of work in progress, manuscripts, leaflets, posters, "underground literature," photographs, sound recordings, film, video, multimedia resources, software, maps, letters, diaries, and personal correspondence. I also have in mind "laundry notes and scraps" like the one stating " 'I have forgotten my umbrella,' " which was found among Nietzsche's papers after his death and about which Derrida has written at length (1979, 139); or even the content of dreams, such as those of Hélène Cixous, which are detailed in her notebooks and which are now included as part of the Cixous archive at the Bibliothèque nationale de France (see Derrida 2006).[15] And that is to restrict myself solely to examples that, though perhaps "quirky," are already authorized.

What is more, if this is true of archives generally, it is even truer of open-access repositories. As chapter 2 made clear, one of the issues that is specific to open-access archiving (or certain instances of it anyway) is the extent to which the digital technology that enables it also makes it possible to multiply the permeability of its border control, thus bringing the problem of what can and cannot be legitimately included to attention and emphasizing it. Because of the speed of the digitization process; the sheer size, number, and variety of texts that can be produced, published, archived, preserved and stored; the geographic range over which those texts can be distributed; and the relative ease and low cost of the digitization process, together with the lack of stability, fixity, and permanence of the digital texts themselves, the irreducibly violent and aporetic nature of any such authority is made much more apparent. By providing us with an opportunity to raise ethical questions of this kind that are often otherwise kept hidden and concealed, an open-access archive is capable of having a much larger impact than an open-access journal. (And in the process we can be potentially far more open, radical, and experimental in making responsible decisions about the quality and value of a piece of writing or research, and ask: what if Sigmund Freud or Richard Hoggart had had, not just e-mail, but the Web, a blog, a wiki, text messaging, Amazon peer-reviewing, podcasting, social networking, peer-to-peer file sharing?)

The fact that an archive is able to include books in particular (both pre- and post-publication) is especially significant as far as raising questions for ideas of knowledge, the discipline, the university, and the institution is concerned. The desire to broach issues of this nature is also why, when working on developing an open-access archive, it was important for me that it have a cultural studies focus. A number of the queries this project raises regarding institutional legitimacy and authority may be applicable to other fields. And yet, as cultural studies is arguably the means by which the university currently thinks itself, it provides a privileged mode of access to questions of this kind, in a way that physics, or the cognitive sciences, say, or even literary studies and philosophy, do not. There *is*, then, something specific for me about a *cultural studies* open-access archive.

The posing of such questions—and the potential to do so that is created by the digitization of the research literature—has radical consequences for cultural studies in turn. Cultural studies has tended to pride itself on its interdisciplinary approach. However, its interdisciplinarity sustains the identity and limits of disciplines as much as it challenges them (see G. Hall 2002, 2004b). Hence cultural studies may include those branches of knowledge that are conventionally included in its interdisciplinary repertoire, but it nevertheless still excludes (more or less violently) nonlegitimate or not yet legitimate forms and kinds of knowledge, including those that are not recognizable as legitimate if judged by the rules and conventions of the "paper" world, as well as what might be called "non-knowledge": the apparently useless, unimportant, irrelevant, trivial, or mistaken.

This is not to say there should be no limits. This is quite simply not possible. Limitation is inevitable, as chapter 3 showed by means of an analysis of the work on institutions and institutionalization of Samuel Weber. There are always limits. The point is rather to realize and acknowledge this process of limitation (rather than try to avoid it and thus end up repeating it unknowingly) and to think about how to assume these limits, and with what authority and legitimacy. For me, open-access archiving helps to put cultural studies in a position where it becomes more difficult to avoid addressing these questions: not least because of its potential openness to the quirky (the different, foreign, and heterogeneous; that which is not necessarily, or not yet, legitimate; and even the apparently useless, unimportant, obsolete, worthless, and trivial); and also because of its use of digital technology, which serves to accentuate the irreducibly violent and aporetic nature of any such delimiting authority.

Now to have an effect on cultural studies and to raise ethical (and political) questions for its own thinking on the university, it is crucial to be able to direct these queries at one of its main sources and criteria of value. This is where the significance of books comes in. Books (such as this one—hence my title: *Digitize This Book!*) have an important role to play as far as the institutionally pragmatic tactical use of open-access archiving I am detailing here is concerned, since they are the main criterion for employment, tenure, and promotion in the humanities in general, and cultural studies in particular. We can thus see that the ability to include books bestows upon an open-access archive such as CSeARCH (which does include books) the potential to have a far larger impact—

on cultural studies especially, but also the humanities generally, and from there perhaps the institution of the university—than an open-access journal.

The Political Issues Open Access Presents
This brings me back to the question of the politics of open access I began by addressing in the previous chapter, with the analysis of the "digital dialectic" and the oppositional structure of new media criticism in general. I want to explore this issue further in the chapter that follows, by means of a reading of Mark Poster's essay "Cyberdemocracy."

5

HyperCyberDemocracy

hyper: excessive; going beyond or above
— The Penguin English Dictionary

Cyberdemocracy: The Internet and the Public Sphere

In his essay "Cyberdemocracy," Mark Poster identifies a number of ways the Internet may "resist" and reconfigure "modern" conceptions of politics. These include one of the basic assumptions underpinning many of the "older positions" regarding politics on the Internet: namely, that we are sovereign, autonomous, and unified individuals communicating rationally with each other, sometimes face-to-face, as in public meetings (the Greek agora, eighteenth-century coffee shops, New England town halls), but more often nowadays via external technological media of communication (television, radio, the press, and so on). For Poster, the Internet represents a challenge to this idea that "the relation between technology and the human is external." It does so by imposing "a transformation of the subject position of the individual who engages within it" (1997, 205). Poster sees in many "'virtual communities'" on the Internet (such as MOOs and MUDs—he originally wrote this essay in 1995) a "direct solicitation to construct identities in the course of communication practices. Individuals invent themselves and do so repeatedly and differently in the course of conversing or messaging electronically" (1997, 211). In this way they produce a new relation to their bodies as they communicate, one that Poster characterizes in terms of the (then) "new social figure of the cyborg" (1997, 213–14).

I want to say more about the relation between the human and technology, and the cyborg, in a moment. At this stage, the important point to note is that technology is not understood here as just prosthetic: that is, as something that is attached to or used by human beings from "a preconstituted position of subjectivity." Technology, according to Poster —like language and culture for "postmodernists"—also *constructs* subjectivity, thus undermining ideas of unified human identity and autonomous selfhood.

It is worth emphasizing that Poster is not advocating with this argument the kind of optimistic celebration of the Internet that has (often incorrectly) been associated with cultural studies' approach to new technology (and not just new technology, but capitalism, consumerism, popular culture, and so forth): that people are free to construct their own identities through acts of pure consciousness. Poster explicitly distances himself from such an idea on the grounds that it would appear he is "depicting the Internet as the realization of the modern dream universal, 'active' speech"; and because it would rest on the "notion of identity as a fixed essence, pre-social and pre-linguistic" (1997, 211). The new human-machine "assemblages of self-constitution" (1997, 213) that Poster perceives the Internet as making possible do not "refer back to a foundational subject"; neither are they produced by means of "acts of pure consciousness." Instead, Poster argues, "Internet discourse constitutes the subject as the subject fashions him or herself" (1997, 211).

According to Poster, this "new regime of relations between humans and matter" installed by the Internet has serious consequences for at least three key aspects of the way in which politics online has generally been understood: technological determinism, the public sphere, and democracy.

Technological Determinism

In the "grand narrative of modernity, the Internet is an efficient tool of communication, advancing the goals of its users, who are understood as preconstituted instrumental identities" (Poster 1997, 205–6). By transforming the relation between technology and the human and between technology and culture, however, the Internet resists "the basic conditions for asking the question of the effects of technology" on society, culture, and political institutions, thus problematizing the modern positions of the majority of political conceptualizations of the Internet, which are premised on the question of the latter's technological effects (1997, 205).

This is a particularly important point—and even more so in the context of the previous chapter's analysis of the antipolitical nature of most theories of the politics of new media to date. The list of those adopting such modern positions toward Internet politics would certainly include Barbrook, Dean, and Kahn and Kellner. In fact, the latter explicitly state that they want to "make technopolitics a major instrument of political action" (Kahn and Kellner 2005, 80). But it would also apply to what are seen by some as more radical or avant-garde approaches to new media criticism, such as the "qualified form of humanism" of tactical media, which Garcia and Lovink describe as offering a "useful antidote to both . . . 'the unopposed rule of money over human beings'—but also . . . to newly emerging forms of technocratic scientism which under the banner of post-humanism tend to restrict discussions of human *use* and social reception" (Garcia and Lovink 1997, n.p. [my emphasis]). For Lovink—who openly admits to advocating a "'radically modern'" approach to new media (which is opposed to, or, in his words, situated "beyond the melancholy of postmodernism")—"all forms of technological determinism should be condemned. Technology is not inevitability; it is designed, it can be criticised, altered, undermined, mutated and, at times, ignored in order to subvert its limiting, totalitarian tendencies caused by either states or markets" (1997, 37). Technology is thus precisely a tool for Lovink, to be used to produce more effective means of action and resistance. To be sure, we have already seen how tactical media is based very much on a notion of "use" derived from de Certeau. "What makes [o]ur [m]edia [t]actical?" Garcia and Lovink ask rhetorically. "In *The Practice of Every Day Life* De Certueau [sic] analyzed popular culture not as a 'domain of texts or artifacts but rather as a set of practices or operations performed on textual or text like structures.' He shifted the emphasis from representations in their own right to the 'uses' of representations. In other words how do we as consumers use the texts and artifacts that surround us. And the answer, he suggested, was 'tactically'" (1997, n.p.).

Yet this modern concern with the question of effects and with seeing the Internet as a tool is far from confined to the approaches I have discussed so far. As Poster points out, it applies to the bulk of political takes on the Internet. The study of networks and netwar illustrates this point. Eugene Thacker has shown that most academic accounts of political networks such as the EZLN Zapatista movement, the anti–World Trade Organization protests, and al-Qaeda focus on the human aspect of these networks, especially the decision-making process. They do so at the expense of analyzing the "uncanny," "nonhuman" characteristics of such networks: that is, the behavior they exhibit that is more akin to herds, swarms, flocks, or the spread of biological viruses than it is to human-managed, rationally regulated entities. Thacker consequently argues that:

> Approaches to studying networks seem to be caught between the views of *control* and *emergence* with respect to networks as dynamic, living entities. On the one hand, networks are intrinsically of interest because the basic principles of their functioning (e.g. local actions, global patterns) reveals a mode of living organization that is not and cannot be dependent on a top-down, "centralized" mindset. Yet, for all the idealistic, neoliberal visions of "open networks" or "webs without spiders," there is always an instrumental interest that underlies the study of networks, either to better build them, to make them more secure, or to deploy them in confronting other network adversaries or threats. (2005, n.p.)

It is worth emphasizing that when Poster writes about the Internet transforming the relation between technology and the human on the one hand, and technology and culture on the other, he sees it as resisting "the basic conditions for asking the question of the effects of technology" on society, culture, and political institutions, not because we are free from technology's determining effects on the Internet, but because the Internet "is more like a social space than a thing; its effects are more like those of Germany than those of hammers." For Poster, "the effect of Germany upon the people within it is to make them Germans . . . ; the effect of hammers is not to make them hammers . . . but to force metal spikes into wood. As long as we understand the Internet as a hammer we will fail to discern the way it is like Germany" (Poster 1997, 205). This is an extremely important point, the full implications of which are often missed by commentators on Poster's essay. For what this means is that there is no simple distinction between technology and its users. Poster acknowledges that the Internet is complicated enough that it may be regarded to some extent as a hammer. Nevertheless, technology here is not reducible to a set of tools that can be used for human ends. In the words of Marshall McLuhan, "media effects are new environments as imperceptible as water to fish" (1969, 22). So we can never position ourselves sufficiently outside of technology to completely understand its effects. If anything, technology is more like a country or an environment: it just *is* the space or medium we occupy.

Thus, as a recent analysis by Poster of the music industry's relation to the innovation of digital technology suggests, the most important question may not be "Who controls digital culture?" or even "Who ought to control digital culture?" (the forces of neoliberal capitalism or those who are attempting to challenge and resist such forces?), but rather, "is *control* a good term to use in relation to digital culture?" (2005, n.p.).

Clearly, all of this has radical consequences for the way in which politics on the Internet is usually understood, as we saw in the previous chapter: in terms of either generating opportunities for democratic participation, challenge and resistance; or as a means for the continuation, reinforcement, intensification, and extension of the powers of late capitalism.

The Public Sphere

According to Poster in "Cyberdemocracy," the Internet also has radical consequences for the idea of the public sphere, since it raises questions for traditional notions of:

1. *Politics*—for we can now see that the Internet undermines not just the basic conditions for asking the question of the effects of technology on society, culture, and political institutions, but also the very idea of a prelinguistic, "pre-social, foundational, individual identity . . . posited as outside of and prior to history," as well as the vision of society that lies at the base of Enlightenment narratives of political liberation (Poster 1997, 203).

2. *Citizenship*—since the above means that the Internet also creates problems for the belief that we are autonomous unified individuals with the right to criticize the government and contribute to the way society is run. (As we saw in my Introduction, this idea underlies many interpretations of open-access publishing and archiving, which are seen as promoting "democracy by sharing government information as rapidly and widely as possible" [Suber 2007b, n.p.]. From this point of view, in breaking down the barriers between the university and the rest of society, and between academic research and other kinds of research that occur in places outside the institution, open-access publishing and archiving is positioned as supplying citizens with the knowledge and information necessary to take part in democratic debate.)

3. *The public sphere*—since the Internet challenges the distinction

between the domains of the public and private on which the very concept of the public sphere depends. (The former, the public, is perceived as being governed by a desire for human community and group solidarity; the latter, the private, by a desire for freedom, self-realization, and creation.)[1]

The notion of the public sphere is especially under threat at a time when personal means of communication are becoming increasingly ubiquitous, mobile, and easy to use in communal spaces, and when more and more of the public arena is being privatized, and—in the case of motorways, town centers, railway and subway stations, shopping centers, parks, and football stadiums—placed under increased surveillance. (Interestingly, while the United Kingdom has only 1 percent of the world's population, it currently has 20 percent of the world's closed-circuit television [CCTV] cameras—a figure estimated at 5 million.) Similarly, while the most personal and private of spaces is in many ways one's home, nowhere is one linked to the outside world more than at home, when communicating by e-mail, surfing the Web, or taking part in "social networking." How exactly is "public" communication on the Internet in chatrooms and electronic cafés to be distinguished from "'private' letters," Poster asks (1997, 209)? We can see that the distinction between public and private is being rendered unstable on the Internet—and that is before we even begin to consider examples provided by Web sites such as JenniCam (which was one of the first live, not-for-profit webcam sites, allowing anyone to look in on a 20-year-old American student's daily life in a college dorm), TV shows such as *Big Brother* (where contestants are confined to a house and watched 24 hours a day over the Internet and on satellite TV, with the edited highlights being broadcast on terrestrial television), and other, even more extreme Internet phenomena.[2]

Poster goes so far as to present Habermas's model of the public sphere as being "systematically denied in the arenas of electronic politics," not least because, as we saw earlier in this chapter, on the Internet the public and external space of technology is always already a part of the private, internal space of human subjectivity and even the body (1997, 209). This, too, is an important point, as it highlights a common misconception evident in many interpretations of the Internet (and consequently, of open-access publishing and archiving, too), interpretations that perceive the Internet as a new form of public sphere of the kind Habermas outlined in his 1962 book, *The Structural Transformation of the Public Sphere*. This is a misconception, not only because the difference between public and private is being rendered unstable on the Internet; but also because it simultaneously collapses the significant distinction between the idea of the Internet as a new form of public sphere, and the idea that the Internet (and with it open-access publishing and archiving) might help *facilitate* the production of a new form of public sphere. To argue for the former rather than the latter is a common tendency among many theorists of the Internet, who attempt to understand the Internet in terms of Habermas's model.[3] Indeed, this is how Poster himself analyzes the current situation in the recent essay cited above, when he claims that the peer-to-peer landscape of music download sites and file-sharing networks, applications, and protocols such as eDonkey, FastTrack, and BitTorrent "is maintained as a public sphere outside the commodity system" (Poster 2005, n.p.). Yet as Lee Salter has pointed out, the only thing that the public sphere according to Habermas and the Internet have in common is that they both remain formally open to everyone. While the bourgeois public sphere sought to form a common will, the Internet for Salter, by contrast, fragments or at least appears to place in question notions of universality and common interest, leading as a consequence to the pluralism of goals and wills (Salter 2003, 122). If what Habermas calls in *Between Facts and Norms* the periphery or informal public sphere (as opposed to the eighteenth-century bourgeois public sphere) "can best be described as a *network for communicating information and points of view*" (Habermas 1996, 360; quoted by Salter 2003, 124; Salter's emphasis), then the Internet remains closer to being the "facilitating mechanism" required by this *informal* sense of the public sphere. If Habermas's requirement of the informal public sphere is that it should have "'the advantage of a medium of *unrestricted* communication'" whereby it would be more capable of identifying problem situations, expanding the discursive community, and enabling the articulation of collective identities and need interpretations, then certainly a medium to facilitate this must be in place (Salter 2003, 125). In short, if we do want to perceive the Internet in Habermas's terms, rather than declare it a public sphere in itself, it would be more accurate to present it as "a supporting foundation on which public spheres can be built" (Salter 2003, 136) (or new forms and kinds of public spheres, in Poster's case, as we shall see). However, that would still leave the problem of the way in which the Internet, no matter how much it encourages active participation, appears to "question the idea of universality or common interest," as Salter says, "facilitating precisely the opposite—pluralism," and thus making the production of any Habermasian informal public sphere difficult to achieve by means of the net (2003, 122). Not only that, the Internet challenges the very distinction between the public and the private on which the concept of the public sphere rests, in both its informal and bourgeois guises.

Democracy

The above argument obviously raises questions for the idea of the autonomous unified subject who can participate in the public sphere through the public exercise of reason. Yet the Internet does not merely constitute an interference in the ability of the contemporary public sphere to operate as a "homogenous space of embodied subjects in symmetrical relations, pursuing consensus through the critique of arguments," thus facilitating democracy (Poster 1997, 209). According to Habermas in *The Structural Transformation of the Public Sphere* (1962), the commercial mass media have turned people into *consumers* of information and entertainment, rather than *participants* in an interactive democratic process. What Poster shows, however, is that the Internet enables "new forms of decentralized dialogue . . . new combinations of human-machine assemblages, new individual and collective 'voices,' 'specters,' 'interactivities' which are the new building blocks of political formations and groupings" (1997, 210). He cites as an example individuals constructing their identities online in ways that appear to reduce the "prevailing hierarchies of class, race and especially gender." Internet communities thus operate "as places of difference from and resistance to modern society" (1997, 213). The Internet in this manner raises the possibility of the emergence of "new forms of power configurations between communicating individuals" (1997, 206).

In this respect, it looks as though it would not be too difficult to construct an argument to the effect that the Internet answers some of the problems with Habermas's concept of the public sphere that have been identified by Nicholas Garnham and others, such as Habermas's failure to take seriously notions of pleasure, desire, and play, and his overlooking of the development of a working-class "public sphere alongside and in opposition to the bourgeois public sphere," one based on "solidarity rather than competitive individualism" (Garnham 1992, 359); or the fact that, in terms of class, gender, ethnicity, and sexuality especially, Habermas's public sphere excludes far more people than it includes. However, as I made clear above, most accounts of Habermas and the public sphere restrict themselves to his *Structural Transformation*, without referring to the more nuanced notion of the public sphere Habermas puts forward in other books, such as *Between Facts and Norms* (1996) and *The Theory of Communicative Action* (1986/1989).[4] I am consequently reluctant to start building an argument regarding the Internet and Habermas's conception of the public sphere without embarking on a far more careful, patient, and hospitable (re)reading of Habermas's various texts first. So let me just stay with Poster for the time being.

For Poster, one of the consequences of the Internet's ability to "instantiate new forms of interaction and . . . pose the question of new kinds of relations of power between participants" (1997, 206) is the need to discard Habermas's idea of the public sphere, at least as it was laid out in *Structural Transformation*, "in assessing the Internet as a political domain" (1997, 209–10). Instead, we need to ask whether there has emerged a "new politics on the Internet" (1997, 206), a new form of public sphere that would be capable of representing new subjectivities and collectivities.[5]

Now of course a number of criticisms have been raised with regard to what some have seen as Poster's positive, optimistic, even technophiliac account of Internet politics (see Lister et al. 2003, 179–82). For example, it has been pointed out that, even if his is an accurate study of what happens *on the Internet*, the net is just one part of life and society, and cannot, on its own, overcome relations of power and social, political, and economic inequalities elsewhere. It has also been stressed that, on a global scale, Internet access is still relatively limited; and that Poster's analysis in "Cyberdemocracy" is very much based on a pre–World Wide Web model of the Internet, a lot of the post-Web net being much less interactive, operating as it does primarily in terms of clicking on Web pages (as opposed to the writing and reading of text in ASCII-formatted documents). Furthermore, for all the enthusiasm about the public sphere and distributed interactivity that is manifested by Poster, Kellner, and others, nowadays the Web functions for the majority of people according to the broadcast, few-to-many mass media model—and this is the case even in the era of Web 2.0 and the so-called "live Web." Witness the nationally reported findings of Directgov that, while there are 75.8 million Web sites, as of 2006 most British Internet users were still visiting only six: Google, eBay, Amazon, Streetmap,

Lastminute.com and BBC.co.uk, with 51 percent of users returning to one of these "supersites" (Directgov 2006; Sayid 2006, 26).

But it is not just the questions Poster raises for politics on the Internet and the optimism of his idea of the net as a new form of public sphere that make "Cyberdemocracy" so interesting for me; it is also his awareness that the Internet represents a potential challenge to our conventional understanding of politics, disrupting the "basic assumptions of the older positions" (Poster 1997, 204). Consideration of this issue leads Poster to go much further than merely suggesting that chatrooms, bulletin boards, e-mail lists, and the like may "serve the function of a Habermasian public sphere without intentionally being one" by operating as "places not of the presence of validity claims or the actuality of critical reason, but of the inscription of new assemblages of self-constitution," which is how this essay is usually read by both technophiliac and technophobic critics alike (1997, 213). In what is undoubtedly one of the most radical sections of his analysis, but that (perhaps for this very reason) is also one of its most often overlooked, Poster extends his questioning of modern forms of politics to take in even that most dominant of our ("old") political norms and ideals: democracy (1997, 203) (the issue of the public sphere being "at the heart of any reconceptualization of democracy," for Poster, as I say [1997, 206]). From this point of view, "rather than being 'post-' and representing a break of some kind," even Ernesto Laclau's "postmodern," post-Marxist, *radical* democratic politics appears as merely the extension of "existing [modern] political institutions" (1997, 204).

Pause . . .

I want to pause a moment in my reading of "Cyberdemocracy" to consider some of the concepts Poster is working with, not least those of the "modern" and the "postmodern."

To my knowledge, none of the thinkers Poster explicitly associates with postmodernism in "Cyberdemocracy"—Philippe Lacoue-Labarthe, Jean-Luc Nancy, Ernesto Laclau—have overtly identified themselves with the term. They associate themselves more closely, I would suggest, with deconstruction. The only philosopher Poster mentions who does explicitly take on the concept of postmodernism is Jean-François Lyotard. He does so in his celebrated book *The Postmodern Condition* (1984)—although interestingly Poster describes Lyotard as a post-structuralist rather than a postmodernist. (Given that Lyotard, unlike Lacoue-Labarthe, Nancy, and Laclau, is not generally explicitly associated with deconstruction, is this slip an indication that when Poster refers to postmodernism in "Cyberdemocracy" he is really thinking about deconstruction?) But even in *The Postmodern Condition* things are not quite so straightforward. At first, Lyotard does give the impression of simply going along with the idea that the postmodern follows on from the modern in a logical sequence of historical progression, and thus does indeed "represent a break of some kind." From this vantage point, we encounter the postmodern condition, in which grand narratives of scientific advancement and progress have lost their legitimacy, "as we enter so-called post-industrial society"—or, indeed, Poster's "second media age" (1995). Yet at the same time Lyotard's book also provides a rigorous critique of any such "grand narrative" of historical development and progression. For is not the argument that grand narratives are now no longer desirable or even possible itself a grand narrative? Is such a narrative not in fact more modern than postmodern? This is something Lyotard himself acknowledges: both in a later definition of the postmodern (Lyotard 1986, 6); and also in his essay "Answering the Question: What Is Postmodernism?," which forms an appendix to the English translation of *The Postmodern Condition*. Here the postmodern no longer constitutes a grand narrative; nor does it function as a break or boundary line separating the modern from the postmodern. A "work can become modern," for Lyotard, "only if it is first postmodern. Postmodernism thus understood is not modernism at its end, but in the nascent state, and this state is constant" (1984, 79). The postmodern does not just come *after*, then; it also in a paradoxical sense comes *before*, too. This point is again made explicit by Lyotard in a further definition of postmodernism, this time characterized not as a "new age" but as the "rewriting of some of the features claimed by modernity"; a process of rewriting, furthermore, that "has been at work, for a long time now, in modernity itself" (1991).[6]

Now analyses of this kind regarding notions of the postmodern have of course been made a number of times before. The reason I am mentioning this somewhat well-rehearsed point again is because it has serious implications for Poster's argument regarding the Internet's reconfiguration of the political. To return to just the first of the examples provided above (not least because it seems to underpin many of the others): the challenge Poster sees the Internet as presenting to the idea that "the relation between technology and the human is external"

(1997, 205) would, on this basis, not be confined merely to chatrooms, MOOs and MUDs, the Internet, or even the postmodern age seen as a new and distinct historical era. This kind of relation between technology and the human would be a feature of other eras, too, since from this perspective technology is not just part of what makes us "a cyborg in cyberspace," as Poster has it; it is part of what makes us *human* per se (1997, 213).

Interestingly, this is something that *has* been insisted upon by two other philosophers associated with "postmodernism"/deconstruction: Bernard Stiegler, who understands this relation in terms of "originary technicity" (1998); and Jacques Derrida, who refers to it as the "*technological condition*." As far as they are concerned, technology "has not simply added itself, from the outside or after the fact, as a foreign body . . . this foreign or dangerous supplement is 'originarily' at work and in place in the supposedly ideal interiority of the 'body and soul.' It is indeed at the heart of the heart" (Derrida 1994b, 244–45). Seeing the relation between the human and technology in this manner enables us to respond to at least one of the criticisms that is often directed at Poster's analysis of Internet politics in "Cyberdemocracy": namely, that individuals are only able to invent their identities and experiment with new human-machine "assemblages of self-constitution" by conversing or messaging electronically on the Internet. Offline, the body, the meat, is never left behind entirely, which means that the prevailing hierarchies of age, class, race, gender, and sexuality remain relatively intact. After Stiegler and Derrida, we can see that technology is not just constitutive of the human in the course of online communication practices; rather, the human is always already constituted in and by a relation with technology. What is more, this is the case even *before* individual humans engage in such explicitly technological acts as taking part in Internet chatrooms and online virtual communities. The effect is to broaden Poster's analysis out, from being confined to the Internet, and specifically to virtual online textual communities, to encapsulating something of the relation between the human and technology in society in a more general sense. Which is not to say that the "originary" relation between technology and the human is always and everywhere the same. Different technologies—writing, the book, the printing press, the typewriter, photography, radio, cinema, television, the Internet, the Web, P2P, "Web 2.0"—enable different ways of conceiving this relation at different times. What we *can* perhaps say is that the manner in which technology is both fundamental to, and functions as a disturbance of, our sense of the human is something that is highlighted and made more visible by the Internet.

The "novelty" of what Poster calls "postmodern politics" therefore perhaps lies with the fact that it is not different from "modern politics" in any kind of binary, oppositional, or dialectical sense. To be fair, this is something Poster himself appears to acknowledge in "Cyberdemocracy" when he writes that:

> the "postmodern" position need not be taken as a metaphysical assertion of a new age. Theorists are trapped within existing frameworks as much as they may be critical of them and wish not to be. In the absence of a coherent alternative political program the best one can do is to examine phenomenon such as the Internet in relation to new forms of the old democracy, while holding open the possibility that what emerges might be something other than democracy in any shape that we can conceive given our embeddedness in the present. (1997, 204)

. . . Restart

What is important here—and what I have been attempting to draw attention to albeit in a roundabout way—is Poster's awareness that we cannot understand the Internet simply by relying upon the old, preestablished (and legitimated) ideas and criteria—in this case, that of technological determinism, the public sphere, and democracy; that, indeed, to ask "about the relation of the Internet to democracy is to challenge or to risk challenging our existing theoretical approaches to these questions" (1997, 202–3); and thus his *openness* to rethinking politics beyond, in excess of, its traditional, subjective, foundational, democratic, transcendental determinations. As I said earlier, as far as Poster is concerned, even Ernesto Laclau's post-Marxist *radical* democratic hegemonic politics would in this sense appear to be merely an extension of current, modern, political institutions. What Poster is suggesting, by contrast, is that, in order to understand the politics of the Internet we need to remain open to the possibility of a form of politics that is "something other than democracy" as we can currently conceive it (1997, 204). In this way "Cyberdemocracy" can be held as creating a space for the emergence of a conception of democracy, and indeed of politics, that is as yet unthought within, or only thought in relation to the ruptures of, the Western, Northern tradition.

HyperCyberDemocracy

Unfortunately, this latter aspect of Poster's essay is one that is rarely commented upon. Most responses to his work (whether supportive or not) tend to concentrate on those elements that can be accommodated within conventional, modern conceptions of politics and the related debates: his focus on the public sphere; the challenge that is presented by the Internet to hierarchies of race, class, gender, and so forth; and the way in which the Internet provides an alternative space for politics to the rest of society.

What is more, there may be good reason for this. (In fact I would argue that the kind of criticisms I identified earlier as having been raised with regard to Poster's optimistic account of politics in "Cyberdemocracy" are partly answered by the very premises of his thesis in this essay.) Certainly, his argument—that it might be possible to recognize the novelty of politics on the Internet only by being open to new ideas of politics and new frameworks for the analysis of politics—creates problems for more conventional attempts to understand the political potential of the Internet (and for any routine claims we might therefore make as to the political nature of open-access publishing). On the one hand, we can now see that it is impossible to simply invent a new theory of politics in order to arrive at an understanding of what takes place on the Internet. This is partly because any such new theory (and associated new politics) would be perceived to lack a certain legitimacy and authority. Its legitimacy would no doubt have to be shored up in some manner, possibly by references to already established sources and figures—including the aforementioned Benjamin, Heidegger, Debord, McLuhan, Williams, Derrida, Deleuze, and others. But it is also partly because, as Poster shows with his own analysis, "theorists are trapped within existing frameworks" (1997, 204). There is nothing that is absolutely new. Even the idea that things have changed and that we are living in a new era is an old one that has been repeated at various points throughout history. In fact, if politics on the Internet were absolutely new, it would be unrecognizable, since (as we know from chapter 3, and Derrida and Weber's work on iterability) in order to be able to *cognize* something, we already have to be able to *re-cognize* it, that is, *re-peat* it, see or take it *again*, to be able to compare and assimilate this "new" object to that which is already known and understood. (This is also why I have decided to approach the question of politics on the Internet by drawing on an "older" analysis, of new media at least—that of Poster from 1995 and 1997—rather than, say, attempting to provide a completely "new" analysis of my own.)

On the other hand, if we cannot invent a politics that is absolutely new, neither can we merely apply the old, modern, legitimate forms of politics—forms that, as we have seen, apply notions of technological determinism, the sovereign individual, the public sphere, even democracy—to the Internet. As Poster shows, that would be to risk failing to recognize the latter's potential difference, its novelty; and particularly the way in which the digital medium challenges and raises questions for our ideas of the public sphere, democracy, and indeed politics (as well as legitimacy and authority) in general. Once again, then, we are caught in an aporetic tension between openness and closure.

Now most politically committed cultural critics have (in their own terms) good reasons for not wanting to raise such questions regarding their political projects. This is because politics is a fundamental part of what they think they are doing. So they cannot question their politics too much without putting the identity of their projects, and with it their own identities *as politically committed cultural critics*, at risk (see G. Hall 2002). Or, to express it somewhat differently, drawing this time on the analysis I developed in chapter 4 by means of a reading of Jodi Dean's "Communicative Capitalism" essay, the paradox of this situation is that the fetish—which is in this case politics—"actually enables us to remain politically passive. We don't have to assume political responsibility" for the simple reason that the fetish "is doing it for us" (Dean 2005, 63). The only way of opening ourselves up to any potentially different, non-modern, nonhegemonic, non-technologically determinist, nondemocratic forms of politics would be, as we saw Dean point out, via "the Real that ruptures my world, that is to say the evil other I cannot imagine sharing a world with" (2005, 69). Yet if we did access or admit that which is foreclosed and eliminated in advance in this fashion, the problem we would then face would be that any such responsible, hospitable opening to the political other would challenge the very modern, hegemonic, technologically determinist, and democratic ideas we depend on for our sense of the political.

It is therefore perhaps not surprising that the majority of critics have not wanted to "risk challenging our existing theoretical approaches to these questions," and have preferred instead to continue with the conventional, legitimate, transcendental, modern, hegemonic conceptions of politics and frameworks of analysis when it comes to understanding the politics of the Internet, including ideas that view it in terms of technological determinism, çitizenship, the public sphere, and democracy.

Nor, it has to be said, is Poster himself immune to this tendency. Despite the questions he raises for modern approaches to politics in "Cyberdemocracy," he is often still to be found retaining a commitment to politics as it is conventionally (and transcendentally) understood in this essay—thus perhaps making interpretations of "Cyberdemocracy" along these lines understandable to a degree. A hint of this comes early on, with the example he gives of limiting the discussion from the outset to modern forms of interpretation: that "if one understands politics as the restriction or expansion of the existing executive, legislative and judicial branches of government, one will not be able to even broach the question of new types of participation in government" (1997, 202). Yet one is entitled to ask, regardless of whether the forms of doing so are old or new, is politics really to be understood as *only* or even *primarily* in terms of participation in government? Is this not also an example of limiting the discussion from the outset to modern categories and patterns of interpretation? As Samuel Weber asks when speaking on, and during, the events of September 11:

> Is the political necessarily tied to the state? To society? Is it primarily a question of Power? Of the Common Good? The General Will? Community? Is it manifest primarily in "action"? In strategies? In policies? Is it necessarily bound up with "subjects," in either the philosophical, grammatical or social sense of the word? What is its relation to spatial and temporal factors: to the organization of space through the assigning of places, and to the organization of time through the regulation of past, present and future? . . .
>
> The problem in doing "justice" to "the political" is the "cut" required to define the term. "State," "power," "action"—the triad presupposed in most consensual definitions of the term—are notions that operate like "freeze-frame photographs" . . . bringing to a

halt an ongoing and highly complex and dynamic *network of relations* that is constantly evolving and therefore only *provisionally delimitable*. (Weber 2001, n.p., my emphasis)

Jacques Derrida develops a similar argument in *Echographies of Television* (Derrida and Stiegler 2002). Given that politics is produced and carried out by, or in relation to, a nation-state, and given the way in which what he refers to as "teletechnologies" are challenging the sovereignty of the nation-state, the question arises for Derrida as to whether politics in its most easily recognizable (modern) form is still possible.

Witness, too, Poster's claim in this essay that "there is no adequate 'postmodern' theory of politics" (1997, 203). This is also somewhat troubling. For is this *really* the case? Or is it just that Poster fails to recognize an adequate theory of politics in the Heideggerian flavored deconstruction of Philippe Lacoue-Labarthe and Jean-Luc Nancy, as well as the post-Marxist deconstruction of Ernesto Laclau, because their "postmodern politics" *does* represent the kind of "break" with the existing institutions and ways of being political he is looking toward—at least to the extent that it rethinks the concept of politics outside and beyond many of its traditional, subjective, foundational, and democratic determinations. Consequently, it does not necessarily look like a "theory of politics" as this is usually defined and understood, because it does not come in the form of a "coherent alternative [for which we can perhaps read 'modern'] political program" (1997, 204). Just as democracy is "itself a 'modern' category" for Poster, is the idea that a theory of politics is adequate only if it offers a recognizably "coherent alternative political program" and definition of a "new political direction" (1997, 203) not also a rather modern notion? Is Poster's idea of politics not also raised here to a transcendental position, where what it means to be political is already given and agreed upon a priori? Indeed, is it not possible to establish a connection between the above two examples of Poster's continued complicity with modern categories and conceptions of politics? Does his decision, taken in advance, that politics on the Internet is postmodern (whereas politics for Laclau, for example, is rather a decision taken in an undecidable terrain), and at the same time his inability to perceive a "theory of politics" and definition of a "new political direction" (1997, 203) in "postmodern theory," not mean that—despite his "plea for indulgence with the limitations of the postmodern position on politics" (1997, 204)—he himself often has to resort to "political theories that address modern governmental institutions in order to assess the 'postmodern' possibilities suggested by the Internet" (1997, 203), precisely because, to his mind, postmodern theories are not really adequate alternatives for doing so? And does this not go against his own openness elsewhere in this essay to reconfiguring the concept of politics beyond, and in excess of, its traditional, subjective, foundational, democratic, transcendental determinations?

Although Poster shows how the Internet may require us to think beyond and in excess of our usual notions of the public sphere, democracy, and even politics, then, we can see that he himself at times displays a certain reluctance to do so, preferring instead to stay more or less within conventional understandings of cultural criticism and academic legitimacy (largely because of the problems outlined above, as I say). Witness, to provide another brief example, the way in which, at the very end of "Cyberdemocracy," he refers explicitly to the fact that the "nature of authority as we have known it," including "scholarly authority" (1997, 214)—and later, in *What's the Matter with the Internet*, the very idea of the author—is challenged and changed drastically, and indeed, "seriously undermined" (1997, 214) by the shift from print to digital technology. Despite this, Poster appears unwilling to place the legitimacy and authority of his own identity and function as an author at risk: he does not perform a reimagining of his own authority and "scholarly enterprise" (2001b, 60) (in the way that, say, we saw open-access publishing and particularly archiving enabling us to do in chapters 2 and 3 by opening cultural studies to other forms of "non-legitimate knowledge," and thus assuming—rather than repeating—the ambivalence in authority that makes it possible). Instead, Poster likens himself to a "reporter, returning home from a foreign culture"—in this case the land of networked "digital authorship"—to relate exotic discoveries in the old imperial language of print (2001b, 61). Poster makes the decision not to risk the legitimacy and authority of his own work and does not pursue the radical potential outlined in "Cyberdemocracy." Even though he encourages or even pushes us toward taking the risk that is implied by his argument—that the Internet may require us to think beyond current conceptions of the public sphere, democracy, politics, and even scholarly authority—he stops short of taking this risk himself. Instead, he decides to stay within the accepted conventions of academic criticism. Like Harnad, he too remains confined to the print mode of legitimation (2001b, 61).

Nevertheless, Poster's essay—and especially what might be called his *hyper*politicization, his refusal to consider the question of politics as closed or decided in advance, and his consequent willingness to open up a space for thinking about politics and the political (and democracy and the public sphere) "limitlessly and unconditionally," beyond and in excess of the way in which they are traditionally conceived—has profound implications for our understanding of the forms of politics that are made possible by the Internet. By following the logic of his analysis we can see that, in order to be able to address the question of what it means to be political on the Internet, we need to be politically committed. For as we have seen, Poster himself does not abandon his commitment to modern politics. "Theorists are trapped within existing frameworks," as he admits. Indeed, one could say that it is his commitment to politics that leads him to question ideas of politics in this manner. But we also, and at the same time, need to be open to the possibility that we might be able to understand the novelty and difference of these forms of politics only by adopting, or at least being open to, new ideas of politics and new frameworks for the analysis of politics. In short, we need to be committed to both politics *and hyper*politics.

Consequently, if I am at all able to ask the above questions of his work, it is only because he has opened up a path, a space, for me to do so. In other words, Poster has already drawn attention to the problems of "limiting the discussion from the outset to modern [transcendental] patterns of interpretation." Far from being a critique, then, I regard my "provocation" in this chapter as more of a continuation and extension of the critical potential of his project; as a way of using Poster's work on "cyberdemocracy" and the "Internet as a public sphere" to think through and *beyond* him. In short, I see it as a way of following the logic of his analysis to *excess* in order to produce what might be thought of as a *hyper*cyberdemocracy.

Next-Generation Cultural Studies?

> Yes, I also accept the term *hyper-analysis*. For two reasons. First,
> you have to push the analysis as far as you can, limitlessly and
> unconditionally. But secondly, you also have to take yourself
> *beyond* analysis itself . . .
>
> —*Jacques Derrida,* Paper Machine, *2005*

The Politics of Open Access

Having considered some of the multiple discourses and narratives
around the politics of new technologies and new media in the last few
chapters, let us now return to the specific (or perhaps even singular)
question of the politics of open access, weaving together some of the
connections that can be made between a number of the nodal points I
have touched upon in this book on the way.

By following the logic of Poster's argument in "Cyberdemocracy,"
and especially his openness to reconfiguring politics beyond, and in
excess of, its traditional, subjective, foundational, democratic, and
transcendental determinations, we can see that the potential challenge
to the accepted, established modes of scholarly authority and knowledge legitimation that is offered by the digitization of research literature is not just ethical (in the sense that it poses the question of an
aporetic responsibility to Levinasian alterity). This challenge is also
political—although not necessarily in the most usually recognized
sense of the term.

For instance, it would be a relatively easy matter for me to present
open access as a means for the continuation, intensification, and extension of neoliberal capitalism, and thus as going along with capitalist
domination and the maintenance of social and political inequalities.
From this perspective, I could argue that open access is political to the

extent that it helps to maintain and support the ideals of the "knowledge economy," making more knowledge and information available to more people (just as that economy's emphasis on competition and the market has produced the "crisis in scholarly publishing" we saw in chapter 1), and so helping to train the flexible, continually retraining labor force of "knowledge workers" and "precarious" creative workers required by contemporary capitalism. It is certainly important for neoliberal governments that knowledge and information should be readily accessible, given that it is knowledge and its successful commercial exploitation by business that is held as the key to a society's success and future economic competitiveness and prosperity. Therefore, it should not surprise us that open access holds a special attraction for many government bodies. It does so because it is capable of providing an extremely cost-effective means of disseminating knowledge and research, and thus making it widely available—especially when compared to the levels of investment that are necessary to fund institutional research libraries to continually purchase books and subscribe to increasingly expensive academic journals. (Basically, there is comparatively little expense involved in accessing research published in many flavors of open access, or in disseminating it: the resources it takes to publish and distribute a hundred thousand copies of an article or even a book are frequently more or less the same as it takes to do so for just one.) At the same time as introducing more competition into the scholarly publishing market, the open-access approach to academic publishing offers a means for governments to obtain maximum return on their financial investments by making the results of the research they fund "more widely available, more discoverable, more retrievable, and more useful" (Suber 2007b, n.p.).[1] Such "outcomes" are therefore open to greater adoption, development, and exploitation, not just by other academics, but by business, industry, entrepreneurs, journalists, consultants, policy makers, teachers, and the general public, too. This in turn can lead to both increased levels of social learning and understanding, and to new research results and innovation. Moreover, open access provides government agencies with a way of ensuring that publicly funded researchers make visible for public scrutiny exactly what it is they do with any money they are awarded, enabling those agencies to better monitor, assess, and manage such research activities and funding. By enabling them to collect increasingly detailed data and information on what and who is being cited, by whom, and where—and so supposedly track trends, identify hubs, and predict future directions—it thus goes along with the insistence of many neoliberal governments on political accountability and on developing mechanisms for greater "transparency" (such as the RAE, RQF, and bibliometrics—the indexing and ranking of journals and articles in terms of their impact, the number of times they are cited, and so on) as a means of promoting economic efficiency and "value for money."[2]

In this respect open access can be seen to be very much adhering to, and helping to support, the ideology of the knowledge economy and its emphasis on developing structures and processes for the management and promotion of imaginative, creative, innovative knowledge and ideas. (This is why, while the likes of the RIAA are trying to maintain and enforce copyright around music and film, others are arguing that such laws should be relaxed, or that different laws should be applied as far as knowledge and information are concerned, in order to enable and encourage their transfer and communication.) Open access provides officials and institutions with the hope of generating and promoting further research, education, and training opportunities, both nationally and internationally. It also facilitates organizations, institutions, and researchers in cooperating and collaborating quickly and cheaply across traditional boundaries and over large geographical distances, a process that simultaneously spreads the values of neoliberalism and the knowledge economy globally. All of which explains why funding agencies are increasingly insisting that the research they support financially is published in an open-access repository by a specified period of time after the date of its initial publication in paper form (usually somewhere between six months and two years); and why by January 2004 more than thirty nations had already signed on to the Organisation for Economic Co-operation and Development's (OECD) Declaration on Access to Research Data from Public Funding.[3]

By the same token it would be almost as straightforward to portray open access as, alternatively, allowing *more* opportunities for democratic participation, challenge, and even resistance. We have already seen how, just as much new media can be said to help strengthen late capitalism, so many of its practices also come to threaten capitalism's established ideas of property, its business models, and its film and music industries. This argument applies to open access, too. Open access is political on this account because it provides a means of overcoming many of the limitations associated with the old, mass or "big" media, particularly the disempowering and homogenizing nature of the academic publishing industry.[4] Open access allows academics to take the means of (re)production into their own hands (although, as my first set of metadata showed, "production" is a concept that is complicated and rendered problematic in a new media context), and cut out the middlemen and middlewomen of the publishing industries, in order to not only create but also publish, disseminate, broadcast, and exchange their own ideas, messages, and cultural creations.[5]

Variations on this theme of the politics of open access have been offered by a wide range of critics writing from a variety of perspectives. For some, because the digital mode of reproduction means knowledge may be communicated and distributed at very little cost, decisions over the publication and distribution of research can now be made, not on the basis of the market and a given text's value as a commodity together with its related ability to make a financial profit for its author, publisher, producer, or distributor, but on the basis of alternative values and criteria. These include, for the author, the work's capacity to act as a form of self-advertisement that enhances his or her reputation and level of recognition; and, for the publisher (who is also often its author in open access, especially when it comes to the self-archiving of e-prints), the work's intellectual value and quality. With participants now able to give and receive information more or less for free, open access is perceived as enabling the emergence of a "global public information commons" in which access to knowledge and ideas is available to everyone who is connected to the Internet: rich and poor, privileged and underprivileged alike. This enables the breaking down of the barriers between the university and the rest of society, as well as between countries in the "developed" and "undeveloped" worlds; and helps to overcome both the "Westernization" of the research literature and what has been referred to as the "digital divide" through the creation of a far more decentralized and distributed research community.

Others, meanwhile, have emphasized the manner in which open access aids and promotes greater academic and even social dialogue as archives of research and publications are made available to the public. Open access is positioned here as containing the possibility of changing the public presence of academic and intellectual thought in society; something that in turn helps to build and sustain active engagement in democratic forms of politics. It is thus credited with the potential to help create a new democratic, public sphere of debate, discussion, information networking, and exchange. Quite a few people have even gone so far as to present open access as part of a radical, hi-tech, gift economy, one that acts as a model for new or alternative forms of social and political organization. From this viewpoint, open access takes part in, and draws attention to, a very different form of symbolic economy from that afforded by capitalist free-market neoliberalism. It is an emergent economy that promises to alter and fundamentally subvert capitalism's notions of private property and systems of commodification, and that for some even poses a threat to capitalism itself.

Capitalism vs. the Commons

Now, while I would not want to entirely dismiss the arguments and positions delineated above, I am not particularly inclined to argue for the politics of open access along any of these lines. For one thing, as I pointed out in chapter 4, these two sides of the digital debate are not so easily distinguished and opposed. To be sure, the "global information commons" model is often regarded as being very *different* from that of capitalist neoliberalism, with the latter's belief in the idea that "the market knows best." Be that as it may, the idea of a "commons" is not in itself necessarily *oppositional* or *alternative* to capitalism and the market (and it is certainly not situated outside of it)—despite the various objections to open access lodged by the publishing industry and companies such as Reed Elsevier.

In a recent discussion with Paulo Virno on the subject of the relations between capitalism, the public sphere, and the common, Antonio Negri makes precisely this point, arguing that *capitalism in fact creates the common.*[6] Negri defines the common as "abstract labour: i.e. that ensemble of products and energies of work that gets appropriated by capital and thus becomes common." In other words, "it is the result of the law of value." Accordingly, the common is inextricably linked with exploitation:

> It is capitalism that creates the common. In Marx there isn't a conception of the common that is a pre-capitalist common (yes, there are the commons, but they are not productive). If we want to reduce and bring the common within a modern conception we must accept this definition of the common as abstract labour, accumulated, consolidated. . . .

> Evidently, we have to start thinking this abstract, common, as something that is the common of exploitation. (Negri in Virno and Negri 2003, n.p.)

How to separate the two, how to detach the common from exploitation, becomes a key question for Negri, not least with regard to the emergence of his concept of the multitude (Hardt and Negri 2004). Indeed, for Negri, "the concept of the multitude can only emerge when the key foundation of this process (i.e. the exploitation of labour and its maximal abstraction) becomes something else: when labour starts being regarded, by the subjects that are at stake, involved in this process, in this continuous exchange of exploitation, as something that can no longer enter the relation, this relation of exploitation. When labour starts being regarded as something that can no longer be directly exploited" (Negri in Virno and Negri 2003, n.p.).

So the common is closely bound up with capitalism, and is in fact impossible without it. It is not that the common and capitalism are completely opposed, with the common offering an alternative to capitalism and the market. The differentiating factor is rather the relation of exploitation. For Negri, this "unexploited labour is creative labour, immaterial, concrete labour that is expressed as such." Significantly (and this is where we come back to the relation between open access and the production of a "global information commons," as opposed to the "common"), at the end of his contribution to this discussion Negri cites networks and the Web—which I would suggest would also include open-access and peer-to-peer networks—as examples of the kind of cooperative activity that could go to create the "active common of labour," and hence the multitude:

> Cooperation itself is part of that creativity of singular labour. It is no longer something that is imposed from outside. We are no longer in that phase of capitalist accumulation that also has a function of construction of the workers' labour capacity to be put into production. Singularities of and in the multitude have assumed cooperation as quality of their labour. Cooperation—and the common—as activity is anterior to capitalist accumulation. Hence we have a common that is a foundation of the economy, only in so far as it is seen as this element of cohesion of the production of singularity within the

multitude. Examples of this could be networks and all the consequences of a definition of the common as the phenomenology of
the web. (Virno and Negri 2003, n.p.)

What is more, this argument that the activity of cooperation and
the common that is a founding phenomena of the Internet may not
necessarily be intrinsically opposed to capitalism does not just apply
to the relation of open access to a "global information commons."
Tiziana Terranova makes a similar case when arguing against Richard
Barbrook's vision of the hi-tech gift economy as "a process of overcoming capitalism from the inside" that is preparing for the latter's eventual transformation "into a future 'anarcho-communism'" (Terranova
2000, n.p.).[7] No matter how convinced its participants are that they are
drawing on the resources of government and the market to establish
a potlatch economy of free exchange, and so develop an anarcho-
communism on the net that "transcends both the purism of the New
Left do-it-yourself culture and the neo-liberalism of the free market
ideologues," for Terranova the two economic models—the commodity and the gift—do not remain in the end irreconcilable, as they
do for Barbrook. She is thus not quite as optimistic about the capabilities of the Web as Negri, arguing that Barbrook in particular "over-
emphasises the autonomy of the hi-tech gift economy from capitalism."
Indeed, for her, the "free labor" of the digital economy's "immaterial
laborers" is "structural to the late capitalist cultural economy."[8] Moreover, it is a relationship that should by no means be reduced to the
"benign, unproblematic" coexistence of two "equivalent" economic
models. No matter how idealistic many of its adherents may be, the
Open Source movement cannot be seen as principally oppositional
or anarcho-communist, for instance. Rather, like the digital economy
as a whole, for Terranova, Open Source actually sustains and even in-
tensifies capitalism through its overreliance, indeed dependency, on
free labor.

Hyperpolitics

It would be interesting in this respect—and would definitely require
careful analysis—to examine the extent to which Terranova's depiction
of the intensification of capital remains caught in the kind of adherence to "modern" conceptions of the Internet that approach it in in-

strumental terms—asking questions about the impact and effect of technology on society and culture—and also to pre-decided and pre-legitimated political theories, vocabularies, and agendas—including both the digital dialectic and the dialectical relation of the politics of digital culture—I have analyzed earlier. For instance, when she positions her article as looking "at some possible explanation for the coexistence, within the debate about the digital economy, of discourses which sees it as an oppositional movement and others, [taken from the managerial literature, which present] it as a functionalist development to new mechanisms of valorisation"—what we might call the politically optimistic *and* pessimistic positions—and writes, contra Barbrook, that "the Internet is always and simultaneously a gift economy *and* an advanced capitalist economy" (free labor being for Terranova a "concept which embraces the contradictions of these debates without providing a synthesis" [2000, n.p.]), does her attempt to hold the two economic models together repeat this dialectic (as do in their own way Lovink and tactical media)? Or does it actually enable her to think through this relation in a more subtle, Foucault/Deleuze and Guattari–inspired, nondialectical fashion? To put this another way, to what extent is Terranova actually successful when it comes to thinking "beyond the categories that structure much net-debate these days," as when she writes in a version of her text from 2003:

> I have started from the opposition between the Internet as capital and the Internet as the anticapital. This opposition is much more challenging than the easy technophobia/technophilia debate. The question is not so much whether to love or hate technology, but an attempt to understand whether the Internet embodies a continuation of capital or a break with it. As I have argued in this essay, it does neither. It is rather a mutation that is totally immanent to late capitalism, not so much a break as an intensification, and therefore a mutation, of a widespread cultural and economic logic. (2003, n.p.)

Again, answering these questions would require me to make a patient, rigorous, ethical response to Terranova's text along the lines of what I at least began to perform in chapter 5 for Poster's "Cyberdemocracy." Otherwise, I risk merely perpetuating the very irresponsible, inhospitable, dialectical structure I have begun to try to think through and imaginatively reinvent here. Suffice it to say at this stage that I am not disposed to argue for the politics of open access along the lines I detailed above because, as I mentioned earlier, it seems to me that these two "sides" of the digital debate are not so easily distinguished and opposed. I am also not of a mind to do so because, as the previous chapters have shown, to insist that digitization is political per se and thus view a cultural studies open-access archive solely through pre-decided conceptions of the politics of the Internet (whether these be based on Laclau and Mouffe's neo-Gramscian theory of hegemony, the philosophy of Foucault, Deleuze and Guattari—or Derrida, for that matter—or the Italian Autonomist Marxism of Negri, Lazzarato, and Virno), would be precisely *not political*. In fact, the last question that would be raised by any such presentation of the politics of a cultural studies open-access archive as far as I am concerned would be the question of politics. Politics would instead be placed in a transcendental position with respect to all other discourses. To adopt such a stance would thus result in little or no attention being paid to the potential of the net to resist and reconfigure the very nature of politics as we currently understand it, its basis in notions of citizenship, the public sphere, democracy, and so on (and I would include both the digital dialectic and the dialectical relation of the politics of digital culture I analyzed in chapters 4 and 5 in this); as well as the possibility that politics on the Internet (like digital texts themselves, at least as I described their possibilities in chapter 3) may be new, different, surprising, and heterogeneous. In short, there would be no responsible or ethical opening to the future, the unknown, the incalculable, or the other here, at least in terms of any understanding of Internet politics.

This is what is so interesting about Poster's "Cyberdemocracy" essay: the way it shows that to address the question of the politics of open access in the manner of most analyses of the Internet—that is, in terms of the impact and effect of its "costless reproduction, instantaneous dissemination and radical decentralization . . . upon the society, the culture and the political institutions"—is to "ask the wrong question" (1997, 205). As we have seen, it is the wrong question, first, because the vast majority of interpretations of Internet politics adhere to what Poster identifies as a "modern" understanding of politics—and I would include Barbrook's "hi-tech gift economy" (1998), Lunenfeld's "digital dialectic" (2001a), Garcia and Lovink's "tactical media" (1997, 1999, 2001), Kellner's "techno-politics" (1997; Kahn and Kellner 2005) and

Dean's "communicative capitalism" (2005), in this (albeit in different ways), as well as Harnad's and Willinsky's visions of open access as helping, in a democratic manner, to produce a form of global information commons and revitalized public sphere. Second, it is the wrong question to ask because this modern understanding of politics may be what the Internet resists and reinvents. Third, it is the wrong question because any such new functions may "only become intelligible if a framework is adopted that does not limit the discussions from the outset to modern patterns of interpretation." As Poster points out, "we may need to look elsewhere for the means to name the new patterns of force relations emerging in certain parts of the Internet" (1997, 204). And I would argue this includes not just the term "democracy," which is what Poster is referring to with this comment, but the term "politics" as well. Consequently, if the reader has thus far failed to perceive my politics in this book in any terms other than those of incalculability and undecidability and a certain respect for the other, I would suggest this is perhaps because projects such as this almost invariably tend to be recognized as political only to the extent they adhere to the old, "modern patterns of interpretation"—which is of course what I am suggesting may be inadequate when it comes to understanding new media. One could even argue, on the basis of the readings I have provided of Jodi Dean, Ernesto Laclau, and Chantal Mouffe, that this uncertainty, undecidability, and conflict over politics—this antagonistic dimension, in other words—is precisely what politics is.

Part of what I am saying here, then, is that certain forms, practices, and performances of new media—including many of those associated with open-access publishing and archiving—make us aware that we can no longer assume that we unproblematically *know* what the "political" is, or what sorts of interventions count as political. At the same time, I realize it is not enough for me to just conclude with what might be characterized (quite wrongly, in my view) as a typically "Derridean" move of "it's all open/undecidable/an aporia/about respecting the other." That would merely be to leave the space of judgment and decision empty, and therefore liable to being filled in and occupied by the return of the kind of dominant modes of power, judgment, authority, and legitimation I am attempting to interrogate and place in question. As the work of Harnad, Guédon, Suber, Willinsky, and others has shown, we need to have a philosophy of open access if we are going to make it happen and persuade more scholars and academics, not to mention governmental, organizational, and institutional policy makers, to participate in publishing research in this fashion. Again, none of this is to say that all we need to do is operate on some "meta" level and just endlessly think and theorize. I am not arguing against making judgments and decisions about acting this way rather than that, or suggesting that the need to *think* should be used as an excuse for inaction and for *not* making a decision. Neither am I against taking a position or maintaining that one particular cultural, social, political or ethical issue is more urgent at a given moment than another. And I am certainly not claiming that, because of the aporetic nature of any authority and claim to legitimacy I identified in chapter 3, we should no longer attempt to produce forms of commons or community, new public spheres or different modes for the sharing and exchange of knowledge to that provided by capitalist neoliberalism. While what I am offering here may not in itself be a politics, we nevertheless still have to be "political." This remains for me one of the unconditional horizons of both cultural studies and new media work. In fact, I would maintain that the setting up of the Cultural Studies e-Archive is itself very much the taking of an affirmative political (and ethical) position with regard to the production, reproduction, publication, communication, distribution, dissemination, and exchange of academic research and scholarly literature, the institution of the university, and even cultural studies. However, open access cannot *always* be positioned as being politically progressive, in *every* situation and circumstance, for the foreseeable future. Open access may have the potential to be democratic, but, as we have seen, *it is not always and everywhere democratic in every conceivable situation.* Open access also has the potential to be neoliberal, for example. So there is nothing intrinsically or inherently democratic or even political about open access. Moreover, there may not be too much disparity between many of these different notions of open access, as we have already seen by means of my reading of Negri above. As John Willinsky notes, when it comes to open access, it is often hard to distinguish "the human-rights concerns from the human capital perspectives" promoted by the likes of UNESCO (United Nations Educational, Scientific and Cultural Organization) and others (Willinsky 2006, 95; see also n. 3 of this chapter).

As the previous chapter showed, in order to address the question of what it means to be political on the Internet, we need to be committed to both politics *and* what—if the hyperreal is understood as being more real than reality—I want to call a *hyperpolitics.* The latter names a refusal to consider the question of politics as closed or decided in advance, and a concomitant willingness to open up an unconditional space for thinking about politics and the political "beyond" the way in which they have been conventionally conceived—a thinking of politics which is *more than politics*, while still being political.[9] I would even go so far as to argue that the two—politics and hyperpolitics—cannot be easily separated; that in fact we cannot *do* politics without *doing* hyperpolitics.

The challenge to scholarly authority that is represented by digitization and open-access archiving is therefore not necessarily or not only political in the sense that it conforms to some already established and easily recognized (transcendental) criteria of what it means to *be political*: for example, that it helps to facilitate the production of a global information commons, new form of public sphere, or high-tech gift economy. But it may have the potential to be political in that so far as it remains vigilant about the ethical question of the other it also helps us to keep open the question of politics—and thus to be both political and hyperpolitical.

Let me round off my argument by sketching three "political possibilities" that present themselves at this point.

Hyper–Cultural Studies

Elsewhere I have shown how the field of cultural studies is defined, in certain important conceptions at least, as a politically committed analysis of culture and power that at the same time critically reflects back on itself to analyze its own relations to politics and power (G. Hall 2002). The specificity of cultural studies is thus marked by what Stuart Hall refers to as an "irresolvable but permanent tension" between its commitment to politics and its "endless," theoretical self-interrogation of what it means to "do cultural studies" (S. Hall 1992, 284). From the perspective of the latter, cultural studies is unconditional in the sense in which Derrida describes the humanities as being "without condition" in "The Future of the Profession" (2001c). It has the right, the freedom, the ability, to analyze and criticize "everything," including itself and its politics, even the idea that cultural studies is inherently left-wing (Flew 2005, n.p.). In fact, I would go so far as to say that cultural studies is only possible through a certain self-critique, a certain pervertability, by which its various norms, protocols, and conventions are transgressed and rethought *beyond* and *in excess of* the way in which they have traditionally been conceived—to the point where cultural studies may no longer be recognizable *as cultural studies.*

This is not to say cultural studies *does not* entail certain beliefs, values, and commitments, including political commitments, that mark the limits and boundaries of this self-critical, self-reflexive, unconditional attitude. It does. (One current manifestation of these boundaries can be seen in the decision made by the majority of those in cultural studies to date—including academics, teachers, researchers, editors, librarians, publishers, and scholarly associations and societies —not to make too much of the research literature available in open-access form; a decision that, it could be argued, passively renders that literature subject [albeit unconsciously perhaps] to the neoliberal corporatization and marketization of both the university and academic publishing.) It is just that, if cultural studies is to remain consistent with many of its own ideas about itself, at the same time as being politically committed and engaged, it also has to keep the question of politics open and undecided. It has to be simultaneously capable of placing its conceptions of politics at risk, of questioning and critiquing them, and in doing so of taking the chance that its ideas of politics and what it means for cultural studies to *be political*—and with it cultural studies' very identity *as cultural studies*, since cultural studies' political commitment is a fundamental part of its identity—will be transformed and changed. It, too, has to be both political and hyperpolitical, then.

Now in a way cultural studies *just is* this irresolvably difficult relation, this aporia or insoluble impasse between these two equally undecidable positions, which are neither reconcilable nor dissociable from one another. (Here, too, we cannot decide and yet we must decide, as we cannot escape the necessity of making a decision—not least because, as we have seen, deciding not to decide is still a decision.) Cultural studies in this sense has always been "hyper–cultural studies." The problem is that this open and radicalizing aspect of cultural studies, this unconditional right to analyze and criticize everything, including itself and its politics, is something cultural studies has often attempted to marginalize or at least keep within certain limits, in recent years especially. It has done so partly in an attempt to police and reinforce its boundaries so as to not risk the designation "cultural studies" being applied to any old collection of subjects and approaches. The latter is something that appears to be happening fairly often nowadays, not least as a result of the contemporary university's enthusiasm for downsizing. I am thinking of the way in which departments and subjects areas are "restructured" and the survivors grouped together in an interdisciplinary fashion under the name "cultural studies," as if this were enough to somehow give this "rationalization" an intellectual justification, when more often than not it has the reduction of financial costs as its primary motivation. I also have in mind the associated fondness of language departments for using the term to "rebrand" and give themselves a boost in popularity among students and university managers alike, by becoming departments of Italian cultural studies, Spanish cultural studies, South American cultural studies, and so on. Despite how Derrida (somewhat irresponsibly, perhaps) depicts it in "The Future of the Profession," cultural studies is not a "good-for-everything concept" (2001c, 50). In this regard I very much agree with Stuart Hall when he insists that "it does matter whether cultural studies is this or that. It can't be just any old thing which chooses to march under a particular banner. It is a serious enterprise, or project, and that is inscribed in what is sometimes called the 'political' aspect of cultural studies. Not that there's one politics already inscribed within it. But there is something *at stake* in cultural studies in a way that I think, and hope, is not exactly true of many other very important intellectual and critical practices" (S. Hall 1992, 278). Indeed, it is only by delimiting this unconditional right to analyze and criticize everything, including itself and its politics, in this manner, that cultural studies can attempt to stabilize and maintain its (politically committed) identity and difference *as cultural studies*.

But cultural studies has also marginalized or downplayed its unconditional right to analyze and criticize everything out of a desire to become, if not necessarily a "discipline in its own right" (S. Hall 1998, 191), then certainly a "legitimate" academic field of study and research;[10] and to be recognized and accepted within the institution as such (and this in a period of institutional transition and change when many fields *are* being "rationalized" and "restructured"). The reluctance on the part of many in cultural studies to publish their research in e-print archives or open-access journals can be seen as one symptom of this desire. The spate of introductions and readers that have been produced over the last fifteen to twenty years or so, and that are often designed to precisely establish, define, and delimit the cultural studies field and various aspects of it by (re)telling its narratives of origin, can be seen as another. Nor is this desire necessarily always, in every situation and circumstance, unwelcome. People in cultural studies need jobs, funding, and support if they are to continue to teach and to train others and produce research. Establishing and sustaining cultural studies as a legitimate area of teaching and research within the academy is an important part of making this possible.

Still, all this may provide one explanation as to why cultural studies is for some currently experiencing something of a crisis over its politics: why its attempts to be political according to the most obvious, easy-to-identify, and taken-for-granted signs and labels no longer appear particularly effective; why it is hard to see much engagement between "theory" and "politics" in cultural studies today.[11] Which is not to say that the politics associated with the New Left, Stuart Hall, the Birmingham School, Lawrence Grossberg, Angela McRobbie, David Morley, Meaghan Morris, Henry Giroux, Paul Gilroy, John Clarke, Kuan-Hsing Chen, Tony Bennett, bell hooks, Tricia Rose, Douglas Kellner, Jodi Dean, and others must now in every situation and circumstance be abandoned; just that we cannot take the "politicality" of their politics for granted. As we have seen, to have certain political "convictions" fixed and defined a priori, to foreclose the space of the political, is precisely what it means for cultural studies *not to be political*. If we want to be capable of understanding how cultural studies can think through its relation to contemporary forms of politics, including those associated with anticapitalism, anti-neoliberalism, and the Internet, and thus enact a responsible analysis and critique of politics, we need to be capable of at least raising this question of what it means to be political in *this particular context*. We cannot simply apply the established, legitimate, traditional cultural studies methods and politics derived from the New Left, Hall, the Birmingham School and so on—nor the neo-Gramscianism of Laclau and Mouffe for that matter—to this situation. That would be to take little if any account of the specificity of either their historical and political conjuncture or ours, and in fact would be to succumb to the kind of moralism or melancholia Wendy Brown sees as symptomatic of so much of the left. In order to be political we need to remain open to the pragmatic demands of each particular, finite conjunction of the "here" and "now," whatever and wherever it may be. Indeed, and as I have argued elsewhere (G. Hall 2008; Hall and Birchall 2006a), if today we really want to produce something equivalent to what, say, Stuart Hall and the Birmingham School were able to achieve using Gramsci and the theory of hegemony, and in this way maintain cultural studies' politically committed identity, we need to repeat neither the content of their analyses (the focus on working-class/ youth/black culture/ the culture of young women . . .), nor their disciplinary objects (English literature, popular culture, the mass media . . .), nor their approaches and methodologies (as derived from sociology, ethnography, political economy . . .), nor even their theory (Marxism, semiotics, structuralism, structuralist Marxism, feminism, psychoanalysis, post-colonialism . . .), but rather their openness to alterity, to the "singularity of the other," including that of the contemporary political conjuncture, and thus the *difference*, the disruptive force and performative affect of their analyses, not least within the institution of the university. As part of this, we have to face the possibility that the "here" and "now" may change us and our politics; that we may indeed have to change if we are to be capable of recognizing each such singular conjunction or conjuncture and responding responsibly and doing justice to it. In short, we have to be able to imagine and invent new forms of politics—and with it, new forms of cultural studies, beyond moralism or melancholia.

In this light, digitization, open-access publishing, and the archive *are* also potentially political, I want to argue, in that they encourage us to ask those questions—of politics, but also of ethics and of legitimacy—that are otherwise often kept concealed and ignored but that cultural studies should be posing if it wants to remain consistent with its own definitions of itself and its ideas of what it means to be political and to "do politics." How does open-access archiving achieve this? It does so by positioning the normal and the usual—in this case, cultural studies and the more conventional modes of "doing cultural studies"— in a "strange and disorientating new context," thus helping us to see cultural studies again "in a new way," as if for the first time, and so account for it and judge it anew. Included in this is the chance to raise the question of cultural studies' politics. The open-access archiving of cultural studies, in other words, places us in a position where we have to make the decision over cultural studies—and with it what its politics is, what it means for cultural studies to be political—again, as if for the first time (and to keep on doing so, as we continue to be confronted with new texts, which are different in both form and content, and which require us to make new judgments, interpretations, and selections).[12] In this way, open-access archiving offers us a chance, if only we can take it, to take the decision over cultural studies' politics in an undecidable terrain *without* ultimate recourse to any determinate transcendental gestures or preestablished canonical definitions. Or, to put it another way, it calls on us to respond and to make (responsible) judgments in a relation of singularity to each particular conjunction of the "here" and "now." In doing so it opens cultural studies to as yet unheard of concepts of politics—concepts perhaps "beyond" its traditional, individual, subjective, foundational, democratic determinations with their basis in ideas of sovereignty, citizenship, the public sphere, and so forth—to the extent that we may indeed need a new word to refer to the politics that new media and open access (eventually) make possible.

As such, digitization and open access represent an opportunity, a chance, a risk, for the (re)politicization—or, better, hyperpoliticization—of cultural studies; a reactivization of the antagonistic dimension that is precisely what cultural studies' politics is. For as I said at the beginning of this section's discussion of cultural studies, this questioning of politics and the political has long been an important part of what it means to do cultural studies. Although this kind of responsible questioning of the cultural studies tradition may be in excess of that tradition and may take us beyond it, thus producing what we might call "hyper–cultural studies," it is a fundamental part of it, too.[13]

Another University Is Possible . . . Perhaps

As I observed in my Introduction, following the increasing corporatization of the academy that has taken place over the course of the 1990s and early 2000s, a number of people associated with cultural studies *have* turned their attention to the university in recent years. Nevertheless, the tendency within cultural studies to fetishize the politics associated with its "founding" thinkers, their followers, and interpreters (Stuart Hall, the Birmingham School, and so forth) that I analyzed earlier has meant that cultural studies has continued to place at least two significant (and interconnected) limits on its own otherwise important thinking on the university. On the one hand, cultural studies has largely insisted on adhering to already established and legitimated conceptions of politics and the political. On the other hand, it has at best tended to downplay, and at worst marginalized and even remained blind to, other means and spaces for politics and for being political. Included in this are many resources for being political that are associated with the university, such as the kind of analysis of the institutional structures of academic discourse that has been provided by thinkers associated with deconstruction over the last twenty years or so. This is why (as I made clear in my Introduction) I have supplemented my cultural studies approach to the electronic reproduction and publication of knowledge and research in open-access archives here with the thought of a number of writers who have been influenced by the philosophy of Jacques Derrida, including Samuel Weber, Bernard Stiegler, Ernesto Laclau, and Chantal Mouffe: in order to help me shift cultural studies beyond some of the limits it has set to its own important engagement with the university.

That said, I want to emphasize that, as I pointed out in chapter 4, I am not suggesting that the digital reproduction, publication, and archivization of knowledge and research, and with it the cultural studies open-access archive I am involved with, CSeARCH, are political to the extent they provide a way of turning the supposed negative theoretical critique (or even theoretical "critique of a critique") of deconstruction into affirmative, practical, creative, and constructive material production. Nor am I maintaining that, by making a pragmatic intervention in the "real world" context of the contemporary university, open-access archiving has the potential to be *political* in the sense that there has been a call in recent years for cultural studies to move away from the theoretical, "textual," linguistic, and language-based approaches that are portrayed as dominating the field in the 1980s and early 1990s, and back to the material and to concrete reality. The challenge to scholarly legitimization that is represented by open-access archiving is for me not necessarily (or not just, or not only) political in the sense that it conforms to some already established and easily recognized criteria of what it is to *be political* (i.e., that it helps to facilitate some form of renewed public sphere, helping nearly everyone in democratic society to make knowledgeable decisions by giving "the public free access to the memory and databanks"—the political path Lyotard suggests we follow at the end of *The Postmodern Condition* [1984]).[14] However, open-access archiving may be potentially political in the sense that one way in which cultural studies *can* think the contemporary university without resorting to either nostalgia for a national culture or the discourse of business and consumerism that is increasingly taking over the institution (not least by means of the sort of process and procedures by which intellectual work is turned into a form of property and source of profit, something that can be primarily bought, sold, and accounted for, and for which property rights are therefore needed) is by keeping the question of thought—including that of politics and ethics—open and unde-cidable (see G. Hall 2002). The digitization of academic texts and re-lated materials, and the depositing of them in open-access archives seems to me to provide an opportunity to do just this; and, by creatively experimenting with the invention of new institutional forms in this way, to think the university (and ethics, and politics, and the Internet) af-firmatively and otherwise, in excess of both the neoliberal corporatism of what Readings referred to as the "University of Excellence" and the traditional elitism of the "University of Culture." In fact, what is so ap-pealing about open-access archiving for me (as I made clear at the end of chapter 2) is precisely the extent to which it enables us to begin *con-ceiving a different future for the university*: beyond regarding it as trapped by the forces of capitalist neoliberal economics that are increasingly transforming higher education into an extension of business; but also beyond advocating a return to the kind of paternalistic and class-bound ideas associated with F.R. Leavis, Matthew Arnold, and John Henry Cardinal Newman that previously dominated the university—ideas that view it in terms of an elite cultural training and reproduction of a national culture, with all the hierarchies and exclusions around differ-ences of class, race, gender, and ethnicity that that implies.

Another university *is* possible, then, it seems.

What is more, the situation for taking this chance, this risk, may if anything be even more opportune now than it was when Readings was writing about the "University of Excellence" in the 1990s. Can certain weaknesses and vulnerabilities not be detected in the current discourses of managerialism, economism, and the market that are dominating the university? To be sure, as Jacques Derrida contends in both *Specters of Marx* (Derrida 1994a) and *Echographies of Television* (Derrida and Stieg-ler 2002), we may not be able to rid ourselves of the idea of the market entirely; nor would this necessarily be desirable. The idea of the com-mon, as Antonio Negri has shown, is not *opposed or alternative* to capital-ism. "There is no common before capital. There is no common before capitalist history imposed it." The question for Negri is rather "how to take the common away from exploitation?" (Negri in Virno and Negri 2003, n.p.). Derrida similarly distinguishes between "a certain commer-cialist determination of the market" (Derrida and Stiegler 2002, 47), with its emphasis on "immediate monetaristic profitability" (2002, 83), and a sense of the market as a "public space," which is a "condition of what is called democracy" (2002, 44). Nevertheless, the financial crisis in Asia; the decline of the dotcoms; the events of September 11; the impending defeat of the coalition forces in Iraq; the "credit crunch"; together with the increase in popular support for anti-neoliberal globalization and pro-environmental movements and issues; the election victories for left-wing parties in Latin America and elsewhere; the further development of the Internet and the World Wide Web; and the general movement toward "free cooperation" or "give-away culture" in which open-source operating systems such as GNU/Linux are being created and distributed free of charge for others to use and cooperatively build upon and develop; peer-to-peer music file sharing networks such as eDonkey that are hosting "on average approximately two to three million users sharing 500 million to two billion files via 100 to 200 servers" (Wikipedia 2006b); and an unpaid, collaborative community of anonymous amateur editors who have participated in constructing the largest and most consistently up-to-date encyclopedia in history—these all seem to have placed a question mark for many against something that for the preceding decade seemed so unquestionable. Namely, the merits of the "free market," and the idea that the market and the associated vision of the "knowledge economy" offer the best of all possible worlds. Might this not, then, be an opportune moment for academics and intellectuals to productively counter and challenge the discourse of global neoliberalism, managerialism, economism, and consumerism that is currently taking over the university—not least by experimenting with new kinds of institutions and different modes of exchange, including some of those associated with digital culture?

Perhaps, perhaps . . .

A New, Innovative, Creative, Experimental Militancy?

More immediately, it might even be possible (although this is very much a speculative conjecture at this stage) to link my argument concerning the implications of new media for academic research and scholarship in this book, and cultural studies research and scholarship in particular, to certain "political" developments and events, including some of those associated with political and environmental activism, "autonomous" politics, and the "anticapitalist," anticorporate, anti-neoliberal, and global justice, world, and European social forum movements. I am thinking here not just of the way in which, for Negri, networks and the Web—including open-access publishing and archiving and peer-to-peer networks—are examples of the cooperation that goes into to creating the common, and hence the multitude. The questions I am raising around this subject also concern the connections, if any, that are to be made between cultural studies and such progressive social movements. What role are cultural studies writers and practitioners to adopt toward them? Are they to assume the traditional cultural studies role of the Gramscian organic intellectual? Is this still desirable or even possible today? Are these "older" ways of being political still relevant? Does the world in which we currently live continue to be best analyzed and understood in terms of hegemonic struggle and resistance? Or are they to adopt a new role, something perhaps more akin to what Hardt and Negri ascribe to the figure of the militant today, as compared to militant intellectuals of the past, when at the very end of *Empire* they write that:

> *Today the militant cannot even pretend to be* a representative, *even of the fundamental human needs of the exploited. Revolutionary political militancy today, on the contrary, must rediscover what has always been its proper form:* not representational but constituent activity. *Militancy today is a positive, constructive, and innovative activity. This is the form in which we and all those who revolt against the rule of capital recognize ourselves as militants today. Militants resist imperial command in a creative way.* (Hardt and Negri 2000, 413)

In short, besides attempting to represent some larger social or historical movement, be this the proletariat, the anticapitalist, or "alterglobalization" "movement of movements," or what Hardt and Negri refer to as the multitude, do cultural studies writers, thinkers, and practitioners not also need to experiment with ways of being "militant" in a positive, innovative, creative, and constructive fashion in their own situations, institutions, and places of work?

In which case, can open-access journals and archives such as *Culture Machine* and CSeARCH be seen as specific and indeed singular instances of this kind of inventive, creative, affirmative, experimental militantism—singular instances that are nevertheless always linked to a certain generality and cooperative commonality?

The Singularity of New Media

Experiment, never interpret.
— *Gilles Deleuze, Dialogues II, 2002*

Can open-access journals and archives such as *Culture Machine* and CSeARCH be seen as singular instances of the kind of inventive, creative, experimental militantism Hardt and Negri talk about? Due to the (by now understandable, I hope) reluctance on my part to subscribe to a "ready-made" version of politics, I want to leave this question in abeyance for the time being. I only want to stress that, while a cultural studies open-access archive would not be simply or even most interestingly political to the extent that it adheres to preconceived ideas of politics, it *may have the potential to be so* in at least two ways:

- by encouraging us to take a decision over cultural studies without recourse to determinate transcendental justifications as to what cultural studies is, and where its politics and ethics lie
- in its potentiality to keep the question of thought open and undecidable in the context of the contemporary university

Furthermore, if we are to take this chance, this hyperpolitical keeping open of the question of politics also needs to include the keeping open of politics "itself." The decision as to what it would mean for open access and the archive to be political cannot be made once and for all. As Chantal Mouffe explains, with regard to what is for her also a hyperpoliticization:

Undecidability is not a moment to be traversed or overcome and conflicts of duty are interminable. I can never be completely satisfied that I have made a good choice since a decision in favour of one alternative is always to the detriment of another one. It is in that sense that deconstruction can be said to be "hyperpoliticizing." Politicization never ceases because undecidability continues to inhabit the decision. Every consensus appears as a stabilization of something essentially unstable and chaotic. Chaos and instability are irreducible, but as Derrida indicates, this is at once a risk and a chance, since continual stability would mean the end of politics and ethics. (Mouffe 1996, 9; 2000, 136)[1]

We cannot therefore state that the manner in which open access enables us to keep questions of ethics, politics, cultural studies, disciplinarity, and the university open is political always and forever. This decision is one we constantly need to (re)take anew: both because we can never be sure that our previous decisions were the correct, or the best, or at any rate the least worst ones we could have taken; and because any such open-access archive will keep on being confronted with texts that are different in both form and content, and thus in effect new potential parasites, viruses, and unwelcome guests.

Hyperanalysis (More Than Just Another New Theory of New Media)

At this point a question concerning the relation between politics and ethics arises. What exactly is this relation if both the political and ethical dimensions of the archive appear to depend on keeping open the question of cultural studies' identity and role? (This is certainly a decision that anyone involved with a cultural studies open-access archive is going to have to make—and more than once.)

We have already seen how ethics, for Derrida, following Levinas, is an infinite and aporetic responsibility to an "unconditional hospitality" (Derrida 1999; 2000, 147); and how politics is, as Laclau and Mouffe put it, a decision taken in an undecidable terrain (see, for example, Mouffe 2000, 130). But can an ethics of hospitality such as that I have outlined regarding digitization and the archive *found* a politics, or be used to work out a program or plan as to how this might be achieved? In *Adieu to Emmanuel Levinas*, Derrida would appear to suggest that it cannot; or at least that there can be "no assured passage, following the order of a foundation . . . between an ethics or a first philosophy of hospitality, on the one hand, and a law or politics of hospitality, on the other" (1999, 20).[2] In marked contrast to Poster's claim that such a "postmodern" position does not offer us an "adequate" theory of politics, because it does not offer a "coherent alternative political programme" (Poster 1997, 203, 204), Derrida does not interpret this lacuna between ethics and politics negatively, as a failing. Instead, he sees it as putting us to the test, as in effect requiring us "to think law and politics otherwise" (Derrida 1999, 20–21), and thus as being both ethically and politically welcome:

> Would it not in fact open—like a hiatus— . . . a decision and a responsibility (juridical and political, if you will), where decisions must be made and responsibility, as we say, *taken*, without the assurance of an ontological foundation? According to this hypothesis, the absence of a law or a politics . . . would be just an illusion. Beyond this appearance or convenience, a return to the conditions of responsibility and of the decision would impose itself, between ethics, law, and politics. (Derrida 1999, 21)

The lacuna between ethics and politics does not amount to the absence of rules, then. It involves the inevitability of having to make a leap of faith at the moment of the ethical and political decision, as if beyond this decision. Unless we do this, we will simply be following a previously outlined project, plan, or course of action where no decision and no leap needs to be taken. "Nothing could make us more irresponsible; nothing could be more totalitarian," Derrida warns (1999, 117).

At the same time Derrida is careful to emphasize that if politics is not founded once and for all—because that would limit the freedom to make the leap that is necessary for a decision to be taken—neither is it entirely arbitrary. As we saw in chapter 4, the decision as to what politics is and what it means to act politically cannot be left completely open and incalculable. In fact, if we were to agree that politics is arbitrary, we would be returning to a conception of the sovereign who is always instituted in an inherently unstable and irreducibly violent and arbitrary manner, but whose conditions of institution are usually forgotten or obscured. We would also be reinstating the autonomous and unified sovereign subject as the originator of any such decision and ethics. A decision that remained "purely and simply 'mine,'" that "would proceed only from me, by me, and would simply deploy the possibilities of a subjectivity that is mine" would not be a decision, according to Derrida (1999, 23, 24). It would be the "unfolding of an egological immanence, the autonomic and automatic deployment of predicates or possibilities proper to a sub-ject, without the tearing rupture that should occur in every decision we call free" (1999, 24). For Derrida, "decision and responsibility are al-ways *of the other*. They always come back or come down to the other, from the other, even if it is the other in me" (1999, 23). Indeed, it is pre-cisely from this demand for an ethical response on my part "to the other, from the other," and from the "alterity" of a decision made by the other in me, as if for me, that political invention, understood as the working out of rules, norms, conventions, principles, and procedures, occurs.[3]

So, we cannot devise a "coherent alternative" preconceived pro-gram or plan for founding a politics on ethics that is going to be uncon-ditionally and universally applicable to every circumstance and situa-tion. But, if we are not going to simply reinstate the autonomous and self-contained subject, or be determined purely by the pragmatic de-mands of the particular context, neither can the decision regarding poli-tics be entirely arbitrary. We have to base it on *universal* values of infi-nite justice and responsibility; there has to be *some* link between ethics and politics. Once again, we find that making a just and responsible decision for Derrida requires respect for *both* poles; we just have to go through the trial of taking a decision in such an undecidable terrain. And it is here, too, "that responsibilities are to be re-evaluated at each mo-ment, according to concrete situations" (Derrida 2001b, 56); because each time a decision is taken is different, each situation and context in which a decision is taken is different. So on each occasion we take a decision we have to invent a new rule, norm, or convention for taking it that exists in a relation of singularity to both the infinite demand for *uni-versal* values of justice and responsibility placed on us by the other (by the other in us), and each particular, finite, "concrete" conjunction of the "here" and "now" in which this demand occurs.[4]

Coming back to digitization and the archive, we can now see that the link between ethics and politics cannot be decided responsibly once and for all a priori; rather this is something that has to be worked out, invented, and creatively explored in a relation of singularity to the par-ticular situation and context of a specific archive. I therefore want to offer at least one more speculative hypothesis as to how digitization and the archive may be ethical *and* political: this is that it may be so to the extent that it takes us "*beyond* analysis itself" (Derrida 2005, 138); or at least beyond what can be discerned, discovered, and predicted by means of analysis. For what is important about a cultural studies open-access archive specifically now is not merely the intended consequences and effects I can predict, foresee, and articulate here on an individual level, consequences that are informed by my own theory and philosophy of new media and open-access archiving. To paraphrase Poster, the way to understand the ethical and political effects of a cultural studies archive is not *just* to analyze and critique it, but *to build the archive* (Poster 1997, 205). And by building it I mean devising, developing, constructing, and programming it (in the sense Steve Green and I have constructed and programmed CSeARCH); but I also mean inventing it by using it, uploading and downloading texts and material into and from it, making the associated ethical and political decisions, creating an environment, setting "in place a series of relations" (1997, 205), and otherwise "doing things with the archive" that may be unanticipated and unpredictable. For there is always something that resists theory, something that is engaged only in the archive's performance, and that therefore escapes or is in excess of any attempt to analyze it merely in terms of its specificity.

This is why I would argue that, although I have initiated and developed the CSeARCH open-access archive for cultural studies along with Steve Green, it does not necessarily represent anything especially attached to *me*. Admittedly, I am writing *Digitize This Book!* in my own name, as one of the people who devised and worked on this project. But this archive does not represent Gary Hall, *Culture Machine*, or cultural studies for that matter. It is not my intention to use CSeARCH as a means of illustrating or embodying any ideas, theories, groups, fields, or modes of thought to which I am attached or with which I am involved. The Cultural Studies e-Archive is rather an emergent project, constantly in the process of becoming. It remains open to use, critique, transformation, and perversion by others, whose purposes and intentions may be very different or even antagonistic. If it does constitute an ingredient in the possible emergence of what Poster refers to as "a different sort of public space from that of modernity . . . a heterotopia in Foucault's term," it would be in this sense—at least to the extent that it does not have a fixed or central idea, or one person or group of people controlling it. Instead, CSeARCH endeavors to allow for multiple uses and functions.

This is also why, for all my talk of specificity, I have not attempted to lay out a set of sharply defined rules or protocols governing the functioning of CSeARCH, either here or elsewhere, other than those outlined in chapter 1 regarding the benefits it brings to cultural studies authors: that it is free to download from and upload to and so forth. For example, CSeARCH does not contain a "controlled vocabulary" of metadata or a preset list of terms and categories under which articles can be submitted, classified, and indexed: that is something for authors to decide upon and develop.[5] Likewise with regard to the archive's system of peer review: it would be quite possible for "users" to make a decision not to have a system for the judgment and assessment of contributions at all. We could simply leave the archive in the condition it is in at the time of writing, where it is relatively open, and authors are just asked to indicate the "status" of their work (that is, whether it is published, in press, undergoing peer-review, unpublished, and so on), and let value and quality be determined by what is picked up on and used and what is not. Alternatively, users could decide to generate for CSeARCH a system of peer review; of peer review and open peer commentary (of the kind Stevan Harnad runs at the journal he edits, *Psycoloquy*, and that the journal *Nature* recently experimented with); or of peer-to-peer review (such as that advocated by Kathleen Fitzpatrick and The Institute for the Future of the Book).[6] We could even invent something altogether different regarding peer review, a system as yet unknown and that I cannot predict. For, as I said earlier, the Cultural Studies e-Archive should not be regarded as "finished"; it is "experimenting" in the sense Samuel Weber has given to this term when he refers to it as meaning "repetitive," "never conclusive or contained," "on-going and futural" and so forth.[7]

In view of this, part of *my* own political and ethical project with this book has not been merely to work out as rigorously as possible a new theory or philosophy of open-access publishing and archiving based on my own experience that others can then discuss, analyze, criticize, and engage with. Without question I have done this with my comments on the relation between politics and hyperpolitics, academic publishing, or reinventing both cultural studies and the university. Moreover, it has been crucial for me to have done so: both with regard to attempting to perform this philosophy in the construction and functioning of a specific instance of open-access archiving, and the making of just and responsible decisions in relation to it; but also with respect to using this as an opportunity to keep the question of thought—including that of the politics and ethics of open-access publishing and archiving and how to make an ethical and political response to the increasing corporatization of the contemporary university—open. *Digitize This Book!* will thus itself perhaps be capable of making affirmative, performative, affective interventions into the field of open-access publishing, cultural studies, and the idea of the university in its own way.

To leave it at this, however, would be to very much go against what I have said about politics not being defined in advance and not being raised to a transcendental position. It would imply that I already have my (new) theory or philosophy of new media thoroughly worked out and in place, and that I am merely using open-access publishing and archiving and *Digitize This Book!* as a means of *illustrating* it. It would therefore be to fail, conspicuously, to remain open to the singularity of either CSeARCH or *Digitize This Book!*, as well as to their possible unintended and unforeseeable consequences and effects. In particular, it would be to fail to remain open to the temporal and affective performativity of their functioning: the way in which the politics and ethics of open-access archiving cannot simply be decided in advance but have to be created and invented by its users in a relation of singularity to finite, "concrete" conjunctions of the "here" and "now," too. Along with developing a theory and analysis of ethics and politics in relation to open-access publishing and archiving in this book, then, I have also attempted to go beyond theory and analysis and produce a "hyper-analysis," as it were (Derrida 2005, 138). Or, to think this another way, one of the ideas behind CSeARCH has been to place the academic institution or community, or at least that part of it which includes cultural studies scholars, writers, researchers, practitioners, librarians, editors, and journal and book publishers, in a position where they are called on to respond and to make ethical and political decisions in this respect, rather than passing the responsibility for such decision making over to others (to archive directors such as myself and Steve Green, for example).

This is another aspect of the specificity of open-access archiving that can be added to those I detailed in my third set of metadata, "The Specificity of New Media." Since authors are largely in charge of self-archiving their own work (even in institutional repositories), an open-access archive—in marked contrast to a journal, where the responsibility for publication falls primarily on the editors and selected peer reviewers—distributes the responsibility for doing justice to the situation among everyone in the field, even if many decide to forfeit or ignore this responsibility. (What is more, this responsibility includes those in the field making decisions, not just with regard to archives such as the one I am involved with, but also about whether they should experiment with thinking the university differently and otherwise, perhaps by creating open-access repositories or journals of their own, using the software that is freely available on the net for doing so, as I suggested at the beginning of chapter 3.)

Digital "counter-institutions" such as CSeARCH can in this way act as actual, "concrete" institutional points of potentiality and transformation, by creating specific and, indeed, singular institutional situations in which academics and other members of society are required to take these kinds of responsible ethical and political decisions and where, at the very least, it becomes that little bit harder for them to avoid doing so. This is not to say that I can somehow, by means of the Cultural Studies e-Archive or even books on open access, institute ethical or political decision making. There can be no guarantee that others *will* perform the ethical and political roles and tasks I have suggested here in relation to the archive (not in relation to CSeARCH; not even if they *do* get involved in creating open-access repositories of their own). Nor is there a guarantee that open-access publishing and archiving in general, and CSeARCH in particular, will not be taken up and utilized by neoliberal political processes and organizations involved in the current move toward the corporatization of the university and the creation of a climate of accountability. To attempt to invent a cultural studies institution or open-access archive that could not be co-opted in this way, however, would not only be a rather uninteresting and sanctimonious thing to do, it would also be impossible.[8] A fixed, pure and incorruptible institution could only be a violent, transcendental, totalizing, and totalitarian fantasy. One could even argue, *after* Derrida, that it is precisely the structurally open and undecidable nature of the situation—the fact that an institution or archive *can* be used to facilitate the forces of capitalism and globalization—that gives it ethical and political force.

NOTES

Introduction. Another University Is Possible

1. The title of this chapter is a play on a slogan of the World Social Forum movement: "Another World Is Possible."

2. Of course, not all of the changes I detail here apply to every institution internationally. Does this mean we should refer to "universities" rather than to "the university"? Perhaps. But at the same time would there not be a risk in doing so of going along with a neoliberal agenda that wishes to position "universities" in both the national and international marketplace as being extremely diverse in their missions, capabilities, and profiles, with some being more "research-intensive" and others more "teaching and learning"–centered? (The implications of this shift from the idea of "the university" to "universities" are apparent in the attempts being made in various countries to move away from national collective bargaining around academic salary levels and toward more local forms of nego-tiation based partly on differences in institutional missions, profiles, and status.) This is one of the reasons why I continue to refer to "the university" throughout *Digitize This Book!* Still, I agree with the edu-factory collective to a certain extent when they write: "The university is a key site for intervention because it is now a global site. Indeed, there is no such thing as 'the university' but only universi-ties, in their specific geographical, economic, and cultural locations. Even within universities there exists a range of labour practices and conditions as well as dif-ferent cultures of organisation. If, in analogy to the factory of yesteryear, we are to understand the university as a paradigmatic site of struggle, we must map and understand these differences (even as they are taking shape)" (2007, n.p.).

For the purposes of this book, most of my specific examples are taken from the United States, United Kingdom, and Australia, both because these are the main centers of neoliberalism and because the university systems in these coun-tries are often held up as models for the transformation of educational systems elsewhere. These examples may be translatable to the situation of universities in other geographical, economic, and cultural locations, or they may not. This is something that would have to be worked out by paying close attention to the specificity and singularity of each in relation to particular contexts.

To get more of a flavor of the current state of "the university" internationally, see the various discussions and articles posted on the edu-factory discussion list and Web site at http://www.edu-factory.org. For a discussion of the relation be-tween the specific, the singular, the general, and the common in the context of the university, see my third and fourth sets of metadata.

3. In the United Kingdom and Australia this process has been under way for

some time via the introduction of the Research Assessment Exercise (RAE), Research Quality Framework (RQF) and other mechanisms for the distribution of funding. The RAE and the RQF are exercises designed to measure the quality of academic research in the United Kingdom and Australia respectively. Similar exercises have also been carried out in New Zealand, Hong Kong, and elsewhere. The Web site for the last United Kingdom research assessment exercise (RAE 2001) describes the main purpose of the RAE as being to "enable the higher education funding bodies to distribute public funds for research selectively on the basis of quality. Institutions conducting the best research receive a larger proportion of the available grant so that the infrastructure for the top level of research in the UK is protected and developed. The RAE assesses the quality of research in universities and colleges in the UK. It takes place every four to five years" (RAE 2001).

4. As part of the neoliberal "audit culture" in which everything is deemed measurable, league tables ranking the performance of universities according to various criteria have been published in the United Kingdom by a number of newspapers since the early 1990s. The practice of ranking universities using league tables is far from confined to the United Kingdom, however. There are also league tables that rank universities internationally, such as the Shanghai Jiao Tong University Ranking, available at: http://ed.sjtu.edu.cn/ranking.htm.

Stuart Hall characterizes the "rich panoply of 'audit culture'" as follows: "[t]he exponential expansion of public service managers over professionals at the coal face; unachievable targets; socially uninformative league tables; perpetual monitoring; the merciless proliferation of pointless bureaucratic detail; the introduction of selectivity under the guise of 'diversity'" (2003, 21). Although Hall is referring to the effect of the "top down managerialist approach" of the New Labour government in Britain on society in general, his description will be only too familiar to a lot of those who are working within the context of the contemporary university.

5. Many of the processes I am describing are of course far from confined to higher education. For instance, it would be interesting to provide an equivalent analysis of the corporatization and marketization of secondary and even primary school education. See Klein (2000) and Rikowski (2003) for the beginnings of such an analysis. I have restricted my account here to the university for tactical reasons that I hope will become clear.

6. The term neoliberalism is often used nowadays but rarely or only vaguely defined. For two interesting recent exceptions, see Lawrence Grossberg's *Caught in the Crossfire* (2005a) and Stuart Hall's "New Labour's Double-Shuffle" (2003).

Grossberg begins his chapter on the subject by emphasizing that "[n]eoliberalism is not a unified movement. . . . It describes a political economic project." He then proceeds to characterize it as follows: "[First,] [i]ts supporters are bound together by their fundamental opposition to Keynesian demandside fiscal policy and to government regulation of business. . . . Many neoliberals support laissez-faire and define the free economy as the absence of any regulation or control. Second, neoliberals tend to believe that, since the free market is the most rational and democratic system of choice, every domain of human life should be open to the forces of the marketplace. . . . Third, neoliberals believe that economic freedom is the necessary precondition for political freedom (democracy); they often act as if democracy were nothing but economic freedom or the freedom to choose. Finally, neoliberals are radical individualists. Any appeal to larger groups (e.g., gender, racial, ethnic, or class groups) as if they functioned as agents or had rights, or to society itself, is not only meaningless but also a step toward socialism and totalitarianism" (2005a, 112).

Stuart Hall, meanwhile, writing in a British context, characterizes New Labour's particular variant of free-market neo-liberalism—their "*social democratic variant*" as opposed to Thatcherism's "neo-liberal variant of classic Conservatism" (2003, 22)—like this: "New labour has worked—both domestically and globally (through the institutions of 'global governance' such as the IMF, the WTO, the World Bank etc.)—to set the corporate economy free, securing the conditions necessary for its effective operation at home and globally. It has renounced the attempts to graft wider social goals on to the corporate world . . . It has deregulated labour and other markets, maintained restrictive trade union legislation, and established relatively weak and compliant regulatory regimes. . . .

"New Labour has spread the gospel of 'market fundamentalism'—markets and market criteria as the true measure of value—far and wide. It has 'cosied up to business,' favouring its interests in multiple public and private ways . . .

"However, New Labour has adapted the fundamental neo-liberal programme to suit its conditions of governance—that of a social democratic government trying to govern in a neo-liberal direction while maintaining its traditional working-class and public-sector middle-class support, with all the compromises and confusions that entails. . . .

"'Entrepreneurial governance' . . . promotes competition between service providers, favours the shift from bureaucracy to 'community,' focuses not on inputs but on outcomes (delivery), redefines clients as consumers, de-centralises authority through 'participatory management,' and prefers market mechanisms to administrative ones" (S. Hall 2003, 13–15).

I will be returning to say more about Hall's analysis of New Labour in relation to neoliberalism in chapter 4.

7. See Gary Hall (2002, 112–15), where I argue any attempt to move outside the university is already a university move; the idea that there is an outside to the university itself being a university idea.

8. Readings is here adapting Samuel Weber's term "deconstructive pragmatics" from his book *Institution and Interpretation* (1987). For Weber, a "deconstructive pragmatics" would "work from the 'inside' of the various disciplines, in order to demonstrate concretely, in each case, how the exclusion of limits from the field organizes the practice it makes possible" (1987, 32; cited by Readings 1996, 225 n. 8). For more on the central thesis of Readings' book, see my "www.culturalstudies.ac.uk" (in G. Hall 2002).

9. See w.ww.culturemachine.net. It also includes the non–open-access *Culture Machine* book series, published by Berg.

10. See www.culturemachine.net/csearch. I may be wrong in making this claim. In many ways I would like to think so. Still, while the DSpace archive

established at Flinders University in Australia (http://dspace.flinders.edu.au/
dspace/) has focused on the humanities, CSeARCH is the only archive I am
aware of (at the time of writing) that focuses on cultural studies and cultural
theory.

11. I will give a more detailed and nuanced account of open access later in
this Introduction as well as in the chapters that follow. For other definitions of
open access, see the Budapest Open Access Initiative (2002) at http://www.soros
.org/openaccess/; the Bethesda Statement on Open Access Publishing (2003) at
http://www.earlham.edu/~peters/fos/bethesda.htm#summary; the Berlin Dec-
laration on Open Access to Knowledge in the Sciences and Humanities (2003)
at http://oa.mpg.de/openaccess-berlin/berlindeclaration.html; and Peter Suber's Open Access News blog at http://www.earlham.edu/~peters/fos/fosblog
.html.

12. See http://www.arXiv.org.

13. Certain parts of my argument in *Digitize This Book!* first appeared in earlier forms as articles, conference papers, seminar presentations, e-mails and listserv postings designed to at once found, announce, and introduce the cultural
studies open-access archive CSeARCH (see, e.g., G. Hall 2003, 2004a, 2004b,
2007a). That said, this book should not be regarded as a description of a finished product or institution. Nor is it a text that claims to already know the
answers to the many questions it poses. Rather, like CSeARCH itself, *Digitize This
Book!* is "experimenting" in the sense Samuel Weber has given to this term: "The
present participle involves a movement that is first of all, repetitive, second of
all, never conclusive or contained, third, on-going and futural, and fourth and
finally, actual and immediate" (Weber 2000, n.p.). Elsewhere in his exploration
of this concept Weber refers to Kierkegaard: "I am thinking here . . . of the kind
of experimenting practised by Kierkegaard, for instance in his study of *Repetition*,
which bears the subtitle: *A Venture in Experimenting Psychology*. . . . Kierkegaard
invokes this notion [of a different kind of experiment] as a necessary corollary
of a temporality of repetition that excludes all immanence and cognitive control,
in which reflexivity does not come full circle to produce a concept of itself, but
instead doubles up into a language that can no longer be assigned to a single,
authoritative speaker or to a reliable, truthful voice. . . . For Kierkegaard, experimenting has to do with the way concepts emerge and operate in a singular situation: 'I wanted to let the concept come into existence in the individuality and
the situation,' he wrote. The situation he here describes could be described as
a virtual situation; it is that of a text whose import only is accessible to a reading
that moves it elsewhere; and it is that of a theatre, in which the spectacle moves
the spectator somewhere else" (Weber 1999, n.p.).

14. For a definition of "immaterial labor," see my first set of metadata. See
also the distinction between "knowledge worker" and "immaterial laborer" provided in my Conclusion (n. 8).

15. Is this perhaps another reason many modern governments are currently
advocating open access?

Questions as to what should be archived and remembered and what forgotten certainly have far-reaching consequences; one need only consider the rela-

tion between new media and collective memory to see that. As Geert Lovink has pointed out with reference to the work of James Young: ". . . the Holocaust still is the primary test case about how media and memory should relate to each other. . . . James Young, in his book on the history and meaning of holocaust memorials, *The Texture of Memory* (1993) . . . says that 'the society's memory might be regarded as an aggregate collection of its members' many often competing memories. If societies remember, it is only insofar as their institutions and rituals organize, shape, even inspire their constituents' memories. For a society's memory cannot exist outside of those people who do the remembering—even if such memory happens to be at the society's bidding, in its name.

"Media memory, in this context, could be the way in which society actively uses the stored information about the past. With Young, we could speak of an 'art of public memory,' in which large interactive archives play an important role in the future, as extensions of the existing sites of memory. Media memory is embedded in the way people are using machines, it is an active process of constructing the past, not merely [a] technical one, which can be reduced to 'storage' and 'retrieval' " (Lovink 1999a, 162–63).

This connection between "new media" and the Holocaust is not a new one; nor does it only concern contemporary new media's treatment of the past. As Edwin Black shows in *IBM and the Holocaust* (2001), "new" Hollerith punch-card technology was part of what made the identification of the Jewish population possible for the Nazis. So the connection between new media, archiving, and power is perfectly clear, even if it was not before.

16. For more on Google Book Search, see Kelly (2006) and Jeanneney (2007). Jeanneney offers an interesting book-length critique of Google Book Search in terms of its Anglo- and American-centrism.

17. See http://cogprints.soton.ac.uk/.

18. Indeed, the open-access archiving of research has been built into Australia's Research Quality Framework (RQF). It is therefore mandatory, as far as the RQF is concerned, that all Research Output generated by Research Groups within Australian universities is deposited in Institutional Repositories (IR) for the 2008 RQF. Consequently, as Arthur Sale reported in November 2006, "every university will have to have an IR to hold the full-text of Research Outputs. About half already do, with EPrints and DSpace being the most popular software with a few Fedora-based repositories and outsourced ProQuest hosts" (Sale 2006). Even more recently, Danny Kingsley noted that: "Of the 38 universities in Australia, approximately half have active, online, repositories that carry current research documents. . . . The OpenDOAR website . . . [lists] 52 repositories for Australia. Of these, 24 are digital theses repositories, four institutions have more than one repository listed, one was a pilot and two were for public libraries, leaving 21 institutional repositories at Australian universities" (Kingsley 2007).

19. See http://www.openarchives.org and http://www.arl.org/sparc. A registry of those universities that have adopted a self-archiving mandate that requires staff members to deposit their research and publications in an institutional OA repository is available at ROARMAP (Registry of Open Access Repository Material Archiving Policies): http://www.eprints.org/openaccess/policysignup/.

20. A Directory of Open Access Journals (DOAJ) in Lund, Sweden, is available at http://www.doaj.org/. In April 2008 this contained details of 3,338 journals.

21. See, for example, http://www.nature.com/nature/debates/e-access/index.html; http://www.sciencemag.org/cgi/eletters/291/5512/2318b; http://amsci-forum.amsci.org/archives/september98-forum.html; *The Times Higher Education Supplement*, 6 June 2003, 16, and 8 November 2002, 18–19; *The Guardian, Education*, 17 June 2003, 1.

22. See the Alliance for Taxpayers Access in the United States, which bills itself as "a diverse and growing alliance of organizations representing taxpayers, patients, physicians, researchers, and institutions that support open public access to taxpayer-funded research" at http://www.taxpayeraccess.org. Accessed 26 October 2006.

23. For some of the problems inherent in this idea of having a fully integrated, indexed, and linked global archive of academic work that can be centrally harvested and searched, see my third set of metadata. For a variation on this theme, see also Jeanneney on Google and "the myth of universal knowledge" (2007).

24. As John MacColl, Head of the Digital Library Division at Edinburgh University Library, neatly explains: "It makes little sense for academic libraries to be purchasing journals which no one actually reads, and whose main value to the community is their 'citability.' The logical resolution to this absurdity, as Harnad has advanced in his work, is for the journal titles to continue to exist but primarily to provide the function of quality control, the organisation of peer review. The titles should continue, almost certainly in electronic-only form, and will continue to pick up subscriptions—perhaps from individual subscribers, or members of the learned societies who publish them in many cases, rather than from academic libraries—but will not depend upon library subscriptions for their existence. Their economic basis will change as they disinvest in the machinery of print and electronic distribution, scaling down their production to a much reduced level (and abandoning print distribution entirely), and will be funded through charges levied on academic and research institutions for the provision of peer-review services" (MacColl 2002).

Meanwhile John Willinsky provides an alternative economic model for open access based on the concept of a publishing and archiving cooperative (2006, 86–87).

25. By comparison (and for reasons that will become even clearer with chapter 1), the adoption of open-access publishing in the humanities has been much slower. A number of explanations can be offered to account for this discrepancy. They include the fact that the crisis in publishing has not yet reached the same level in the humanities as it has in the sciences: in the latter, academic journals are not only already very expensive; they are rapidly increasing in cost all the time. Things are changing in this respect, however. There is now something of a crisis in publishing in the humanities, too (see Greenblatt 2002; and chapter 1). This is in large part owing to the rising costs of books and journals in the humanities; the growing reluctance of publishers in the humanities to commission research-led books that will not generate significant financial profits (although there are of course still exceptions, including many American university presses,

that are not quite so profit oriented); and the preference of such publishers for publishing introductions and readers instead.

Nevertheless, open-access publishing in the humanities continues to be dogged by the perception that online publication is somehow less "credible" (that is, less rigorously managed editorially and in terms of quality control and peer review) than print. Although such concerns are also a feature of open-access publishing in the STMs, they are in many ways easier to counteract there. That is because the main mode of publication in the sciences is the academic journal, with peer review being the main system of validation, and academics run both of those. As Vitek Tracz of BioMed Central put it when testifying before the United Kingdom's House of Commons Science and Technology Committee in 2004, "it is the scientists who do the research, who publish, who referee, who decide. Most of the referees are chosen by another scientist. This is a process run by scientists and for us publishers to presume that we have some major scientific role or influence is wrong" (cited in Willinsky 2006, 8). So if academics in the sciences have wanted to change the journals they run to publishing online and open access, with validation being maintained through peer review, it has been comparatively easy for them to do so; or at least it has been compared to the humanities, where the situation is a little more difficult.

In the humanities (although it differs from discipline to discipline and language group to language group) the most valued unit of institutional and professional currency tends to be the book and the system of validation dependent on the prestige of the press that publishes it. Peer reviewing still takes place, but it is taken for granted and is in a way less of an issue, or at least less of a source of anxiety, as it is regarded as something that is provided more or less automatically by virtue of being attached to a quality press. It is here that the difference, and the difficulty, lies. For though they may be involved in doing the research and also in peer-reviewing it, academics do not run the majority of publishing companies—not even the university presses (although there are again exceptions, most notably Polity Press in the United Kingdom). So in marked contrast to the situation described by Tracz in the sciences, it is not academics who in the main are deciding in the humanities, it is publishers. This is one reason it has been harder for scholars in the humanities to bring about a shift to online open-access publication.

The problem has been compounded by the fact that there has been less interest in doing so in the humanities, since for publishers open access does not appear to generate profits, and for academics electronically reproduced books do not carry the same prestige, even if they have been peer-reviewed every bit as rigorously as a book published by, say, Duke, Harvard, MIT, or Minnesota.

Other reasons for the comparatively slow acceptance of open access in the humanities, despite the fact that it has been very successful in the sciences for more than fifteen years now, include:

- What is arguably the main open-access funding model in the sciences, "author-pays," is not easily transferable to the humanities. Authors in the humanities are not used to paying to have their work published, even if this is just a matter of covering the cost of its production and processing. They tend to associate doing so with vanity publishing. At present they are also less likely to obtain the grants from either funding bodies or their institutions that are necessary to cover the cost of paying the equivalent of often $300 or more to do so (despite the name, authors do not usually pay for publication out of their own pocket in the author-pays model).

- Scientists have a longer history of working with computers, since the very nature of research in the sciences—which often involves accessing and compiling complex datasets, empirical data, statistical modeling and running simulations—means it is better suited to being supported by computing than the more "fuzzy" kinds of knowledge and information that is being dealt with in the humanities.
- There is greater emphasis on collaboration (those in the scientific, technical, and medical fields more often work in groups and research teams), and on the dissemination of findings as fast as possible in the sciences than in the humanities generally. After all, if you find a cure for cancer, there is a sense in which it is important to let people know about it and have them test and verify your research as soon as possible—a sense that is not quite present with regard to a philosophical reading of Deleuze or Whitehead, no matter how interesting or original it may be. There is also prestige to be gained from being the first to publish particular findings.
- There is more emphasis on the idea rather than its expression in the sciences. By contrast, scholars in the humanities can spend a long time carefully crafting their texts, not just as the vehicle for the expression of their ideas, but as pieces of writing. They are therefore less inclined to distribute drafts or works-in-progress.
- The sharing of material has a long history in the sciences. As Tschider notes, "before the Internet, scientists often sent papers to competing scientists in pre-published formats, perhaps simultaneously to share their worth and claim ownership over ideas they presented" (Tschider 2006, n.p.).
- As Jöttkandt points out, "humanities disciplines have certain established bibliographic conventions that are slow to change. Many still only recognize the publisher version of an article as the 'official publication of record' and do not yet accept pre- or postprints as acceptable citation alternatives" (Jöttkandt 2007, n.p.).

It would therefore be a mistake to present the development of open access in the sciences as *solely* a response to the corporatization of the university and the academic publishing industry. Although when glossing this history I have concentrated (for tactical and political reasons, one could say) on the open-access movement's relation with neoliberalism and the rise in the price of journals, it is clearly also a part of this longer history of "gifting" within the sciences.

26. This seems like an appropriate point to comment on the length of many of my endnotes (such as n. 25 above). These are often longer than might ordinarily be expected in a book of this kind. This is because endnotes are one of the devices I am employing to explore and experiment with some of the differences

and similarities between ink-on-paper and digital publishing. For instance, if I *were* to digitize *Digitize This Book!*, many of my endnotes would no doubt take a very different form. Most obviously and straightforwardly, one can speculate that they would appear as links to separate pages or files where they could constitute short extracts, sections, or micro-chapters in their own right. (If it helps, this might be one useful way to think about them. This endnote is itself no exception in this respect.) As it is, the specificity of the medium of the printed codex book along with the codes and conventions of academic publishing mean that I am often (but not always, as we shall see) restricted to relying on endnotes to provide such material.

Another way I am attempting to creatively explore and experiment with some of the differences between print-on-paper and digital media in *Digitize This Book!* is with the four sets of "metadata" that are interspersed throughout the book. As the epigraph to the first of these sets indicates, metadata is "data about data." It is "information that describes another set of data"—say, the contents of a book—and helps one to locate and access it. In the context of new media, metadata (such as the author's name, title of publication, date and place of publication, and so on) enables computers to access the content of files and documents, potentially across a range of different sites and databases. In one particularly interesting definition, "metadata" is positioned as being "everything that does not belong to the document itself as it is consulted in its original form but that is added to the document when it is put online" (Jeanneney 2007, 55).

I have included these sets of metadata partly because, as I say, they offer yet another means of highlighting and experimenting with some of the differences between ink-on-paper and digital publishing (see my second set of metadata especially); and partly because they allow me to further describe *Digitize This Book!*, and so help the reader access and understand both the book itself and some of the thinking that lies behind it. (No doubt these sections of *Digitize This Book!* will appear to some to be too self-reflexive—or, indeed, *meta.*) But I have also included these sets of metadata because they provide me with a space to speculatively comment upon and explore some of the underlying processes, protocols, and systems that go to organize and shape knowledge and information about new media. In doing so I have focused especially on the kind of "data about data" or ways of selecting, ordering, structuring, and presenting knowledge and information about new media that would most likely come into play if a decision *were* to be taken to put this book online. This includes ideas of activity, action, creativity, practice, production, and so forth. Of course, given that "metadata is also data," analysis of this sort is a feature of some of the more apparently straightforward, supposedly non-meta chapters of *Digitize This Book!*, too. If this only serves to disrupt and render ambiguous and uncertain the precise relation between what is to be considered data and what is to be considered metadata here (or embedded metadata, or even "meta-metadata"), then that is all to the good, at least as far as the argument regarding ethics and politics I go on to develop in this book is concerned.

27. For motives that I expound upon in my first set of metadata, a lot of the time I am focusing on one specific archive in *Digitize This Book!*: CSeARCH. This

is a subject archive, at least in the sense that it is designated as a cultural studies repository, although like some institutional archives it also accepts books.

This is one reason I often refer to "open-access archives" rather than, for example, continually distinguishing between e-print or subject archives (which as a general rule are made up of the pre- and post-prints of scholarly articles of a particular field or fields) and local institutional repositories (which are composed of the scholarly publications of a particular institution and are more likely to include books as well as articles): because alongside e-prints of journal articles, the kind of open-access archiving I am specifically interested in in *Digitize This Book!* is that which can also include books. For more on this, see my third set of metadata on "The Specificity of New Media."

28. See, for example, Robert Young (1992), Bill Readings (1996), and Diane Elam (2000).

29. This is why CSeARCH has been designated a cultural studies archive, rather than, say, a literary theory or philosophy archive—although it is open to submissions from both of the latter fields, too, as well as a number of others, including critical and cultural theory, new media, visual culture, communication and media studies, philosophy, psychoanalysis, and postcolonial theory.

30. In the deconstructive tradition, for example (assuming for the moment that there is such a thing), "politics" and "the political" are not the same. Chantal Mouffe provides one way of distinguishing between them: "By 'the political' I refer to the dimension of antagonism that is inherent in human relations, antagonism that can take many forms and emerge in different types of social relations. 'Politics,' on the other side, indicates the ensemble of practices, discourses and institutions which seek to establish a certain order and organize human coexistence in conditions that are always potentially conflictual because they are affected by the dimension of 'the political'" (2000, 101).

If I have not always rigorously adhered to such a distinction in *Digitize This Book!* it is partly because, for me, the relation between politics and the political is at the same time also somewhat conflictual, difficult, multiplicitous, unstable, and uncertain (as the above quotation from Mouffe indeed suggests). For more, see in particular my Conclusion. For more on Mouffe's conception of politics and the political in relation to antagonism, see my "Hyper-Cyprus" (G. Hall 2007b).

31. Books focusing on the institution of the university, such as E.P. Thompson's *Warwick University Ltd* (1970), are actually relatively rare within the history of cultural studies; even Thompson's book is out of print and hard to get hold of these days.

Sometimes when I make this argument regarding the politics of cultural studies I worry that people may think I am setting cultural studies up as something of a straw man: that I am merely repeating what so many people do around it, which is to write and talk about cultural studies without referring to specific examples, which in turn means that I often do not recognize the cultural studies they are referring to. Instead, such analyses seem to be more a product of projection and stereotype and certainly bear little relation to anything I might understand or identify as cultural studies. This is why I have previously taken great care to locate versions of the argument I am making here in specific texts at specific points in cultural studies' history (see G. Hall 2002). But just to show that all this is not a thing of cultural studies' past, let me briefly cite, as an example of what I mean, one of the more recent instances of it I have come across. This is Marcus Breen's urging—in a contribution to the September 2006 Association for Cultural Studies newsletter, written in response to a request from the editors for comments on the current "state of cultural studies"—for cultural studies to be less concerned with discussing its current state, and more concerned with engaging "the current world crisis." Included in the latter, according to Breen, are: "the rumblings that seem to grow louder and louder about the end of sustainable life on our fragile planet; the fact that 120F degree heat is killing the poor and elderly in France and Germany, the United States and elsewhere; Israel is given the go-ahead to wage a proxy war in its and the US's efforts to prove a pointless point; jihadists are prompted to greater heights of negativism through the provocations of 'entitled' westerners; the rate of global poverty increases daily" (2006).

32. There are other exceptions one could provide here besides Striphas. These include, in their different ways, Neilson and Mitropoulos (2005) and Gregg (2006), to cite just two of the most recent and interesting.

33. See, for example, Aronowitz (2000); Giroux and Myrsiades (2001); Robins and Webster (1999, 2003); Ross (2000); Rutherford (2003, 2005); Webster (2004)—although the argument I go on to expand upon in chapter 4—about wanting to develop an ethics that retains a relation of infinite responsibility to an unconditional hospitality even when it comes to the reading of other texts, and about my concern over citing too many texts I am not prepared to respond to here in a careful, patient, singular fashion—would also apply to these and other examples, too.

34. See, for example, Aldred and Ryle (1999); Giroux (1988); and Steele (1997).

35. See, for example, Clark (1999); Fynsk (2004); Kamuf (1997, 2004); Miller and Asensi (1999); Readings (1996); Royle (1995); Stiegler (2003); Weber (1987, 1999, 2000); and Young (1996a).

Metadata I. Notes on Creating Critical Computer Media

1. Most books on new media include in their opening pages an attempt to define the term (i.e., that although it means different things in different contexts, what is commonly meant by new media is digital or electronic media; and that this is frequently, but not always, associated with the computer: the Web, the Internet, e-mail, blogging, podcasting, and so forth), along with an acknowledgment of the difficulty of doing so. More often than not this definition is then accompanied by an account of the various debates over the merits of using the particular expression "new media" over other possible rivals, including "emerging" or "emergent media," "digital media," "computer media," "networked media" and "new technology." I must confess that, if anything, I have a slight preference for "emerging media," as derived from Raymond Williams notion of the "dominant, residual, and emergent" (1997). It seems to me that "emerg-

ing media" has more of the sense of "becoming," of things in process, that I am trying to articulate in *Digitize This Book!*. It is also somewhat broader in scope than, say, "computer media," "networked media," or even "digital media," with their privileging of the formal and the technical. At the same time, however, I find "emerging media" a rather awkward expression to use regularly over the course of a book-length project. Plus, as Wendy Chun observes, "new media has traction because of jobs and programs perpetuated in its name—it is a field with its own emerging canon and institutional space" (Chun 2006, 2). I have therefore resorted in the main to the term "new media" in *Digitize This Book!*, although I have also on occasion made use of other terms, including "computer media," partly to indicate something of the fluid, ambivalent, conflictual, undecided nature of the relations between them.

Since this debate over "new media" and its relation to "old," "residual," or obsolete media is now itself rather old, I do not intend to retrace it here, nor account for the various differences between "emerging media," "digital media," "computer media," "new technology," and so on (not least because the difficulty of defining "new media" in any final or complete sense tells us rather a lot about it). Instead, I refer the interested reader to some of the places where these issues have been dealt with in detail. These include Marvin (1988), Gitelman and Pingree (2003), Lister et al. (2003), Manovich (2001), Chun (2006), and Acland (2007). For an interrogation of the term "new" in a slightly different context, see Hall and Birchall (2006a).

2. See my third and fourth sets of metadata: "The Specificity of New Media" and "The Singularity of New Media."

3. For Derrida, for instance, writing is very much a material practice. In order to understand a written mark, a sense of its permanence is necessary, which means it must have the possibility of a material or empirical inscription. "Materiality" is thus the condition of writing's very possibility. This is why the transcendental is always impure, for Derrida: textuality and materiality cannot be simply opposed, as language and writing are already material.

I thank Federica Frabetti for reemphasizing the importance of this point to me in relation to the tendency within much contemporary new media theory to position Derrida's thought as being too concerned with the transcendental as opposed to the material. See Frabetti (2007).

4. For more on the relation between cultural studies and deconstruction, see Hall (2006).

5. The use of proprietary technologies—when a range of free software and open-source technology for the construction and operation of open-access archives is also now available—could be said to be just one of the tactically pragmatic decisions made in relation to CSeARCH.

6. See the call for papers for "Counter-Movements: Institutions of Difference," a two-day conference held at the University of Portsmouth, 24–25 July 2006.

7. Matthew Fuller describes "critical software" as being "designed explicitly to pull the rug from underneath normalised understandings of software": either by "using the evidence presented by normalised software to construct an arrange-

ment of the objects, protocols, statements, dynamics, and sequences of interaction that allow its conditions of truth to become manifest"; by running "just like a normal application," but one which "has been fundamentally twisted to reveal the underlying construction of the user, the way the program treats data, and the transduction and coding processes of the interface"; or by rewriting the interfaces of standard software packages "in order to gain access to [their] kernel of truth" (2003, 22–23). The impression of an underlying structuralist feel to Fuller's account—something that is in fact quite common to those interested in software due to the influential role Chomskian linguistics has played in the history of software development (Frabetti 2007)—is only compounded by the positioning of a reference to Barthes's *Mythologies* at the beginning of his discussion of critical software in *Behind the Blip*.

8. See, in particular, Hayles's chapter in *Writing Machines* on "Media-Specific Analysis" (2002, 29–33).

9. See my fourth set of metadata, "The Singularity of New Media."

10. A variation on this argument could certainly be made with regard to the wave of new media artists and net critics who are attempting to establish the originality and distinctiveness of their work by opposing their focus on the unfolding "particularities" of software culture to the "grand theory–panoramas," "generic summations" and "pretensions to timelessness" of previous generations. These latter are 1990s cyberpunks and cyberculturalists more often than not, although I notice the "depleted jargons and zombie conferencing of Film Studies" get a mention, too (Fuller 2003, 17, 16–17, 18).

11. Is CSeARCH theory or practice? Is *Digitize This Book!*? Of course, that they occur in different mediums with different kinds of material support—the book and the archive, the "textual" and the "real"—makes it a relatively easy matter to quickly and unthinkingly divide them into the "theoretical" and the "practical." But is that really enough to ensure the two can be so simply contrasted in this way?

12. For more on the fetish in relation to new technology, see chapter 4.

13. Andrew Ross, for instance, goes so far as to argue that "the traffic goes in both directions," and that along with the corporatization of the university, "the mentality and customs of academic life are being transplanted into knowledge firms, whose research is increasingly conducted along similar lines" (Lovink 2007, n.p.).

14. Kamuf provides as one exemplary example: "the Human Rights Project at Bard College, directed by Thomas Keenan (a professor of Comparative Literature), [which] coordinates numerous human rights actions into an undergraduate curriculum: "'The project is interdisciplinary and humanities-based, with a focus on the philosophical foundations and the political mechanisms of human rights, and a special interest in freedom of expression, the public sphere, and media. The Project's main emphasis is on forging links between the human rights movement and the academic world, including activists, faculty, and the undergraduates who might otherwise not find ways to develop and apply their interest in human rights'" (Kamuf 2004, n.p.).

For another example of using media tactically within a university context, see "From the Top Down: A Film About the University of Sussex Management" (2006), available at http://www.ussu.net/sortUSout/documentary/index.html. Accessed 8 October 2006.

15. Caroline Bassett has also expressed this doubt in relation to the tactical media approach with which CAE and Lovink are both associated, although the specific example Bassett is referring to is Matthew Fuller's *Behind the Blip* (2003). Bassett's concern is with "the degree to which a focus on tactical media obscures a strength of cultural studies, which is its capacity to consider forms of practice that do not register as explicitly political, and that do not require the kinds of active skills or expert knowledge that the free software movement valorises and that tactical media employs, but which nonetheless do not conform" (2006, 234).

16. It is interesting in light of this that Lovink associates his tactical media activism with a "qualified form of humanism" (Garcia and Lovink 1997). For more, see my discussion of humanism and tactical media in chapters 4 and 5.

For a critique of the term "creative" in this context, see Donald (2004, 235–46).

17. For more, see Hall and Birchall (2006a), from which this part of my analysis has been taken.

18. The term "Queensland Ideology" is itself a play on Richard Barbrook and Andy Cameron's "Californian ideology" (1995).

19. The problems with the production/consumption, and especially theory/practice relations outlined above, go some way toward explaining why, in the past, I have turned to theory and the thought of Jacques Derrida when attempting to think through such relations. Far from being capable of being positioned as one pole in the dialectical relation between theory and practice, deconstruction offers a means of thinking through oppositions of this kind and, in particular, the problem of the incommensurability of the relation between theory and practice (the way, as we have seen, theory and practice *cannot* be combined because theory creates difficulties for such simplistic notions of theory and practice as well as any dialectical relation between them). Deconstruction does so by enabling us to hold theory and practice together in a productive economy in which their irreconcilable differences are neither dialectically subsumed into some all-encompassing synthesis or unity, nor left in some negative dialectic of debilitating disunity.

Saying that, it has been important for me not to position deconstruction (or theory) as something that could be applied to practice from the outside, as a form of corrective. Instead, I have tried to show, by means of close and singular readings, that a more interesting understanding of this issue is already available from "political," "practical," "creative" texts. And I want to do something similar as far as deconstruction's relation to the digital dialectic between new media theory and practice is concerned. I would not want to say too much more about the work of Lunenfeld, Lovink, and some of the other people I mention here without tackling it in a similar depth and degree of singularity.

1. Why All Academic Research and Scholarship Should Be Made Available in Online Open-Access Archives—Now!

1. Interestingly, the sale of vinyl was at the time reported elsewhere to have increased by a corresponding amount, driven largely by the enthusiasm for DJ-ing, which uses vinyl for mixing tracks.

2. The decline is reported to have continued with a worldwide decrease in sales of 4 percent to $US8.4 billion (£4.5 billion) being recorded for the first half of 2006 as compared to the previous year (Allen 2006a, 35).

3. See http://www.napster.com.

4. Mark Poster goes even further, suggesting that "most discussions of the current condition of . . . file-sharing begin *and end* with Napster" (Poster 2005, emphasis mine). Poster gives as an example Lawrence Lessig's book *Code: And Other Laws of Cyberspace* (1999).

5. See http://www.kazaa.com; http://www.gnutella.com; http://www.edonkey2000.com; http://developer.berlios.de/projects/gift-fasttrack; http://www.emule-project.net/home/perl/general.cgi?l=1; and http://www.bittorrent.com.

Strictly speaking, Napster, Gnutella, and Kazaa are peer-to-peer (P2P) networks; eMule is a peer-to-peer file-sharing application, working with the eDonkey network; FastTrack is a peer-to-peer protocol, used by the Kazaa (and other) file-sharing programs; while BitTorrent is also a peer-to-peer file-distribution protocol, as well as the name of a free software implementation of that protocol.

At the time of writing, the three main networks for file sharing are eDonkey, FastTrack, and Gnutella. In mid-2005, the most popular, eDonkey (also called eDonkey2000 network or ed2k) was reported as hosting "on average approximately two to three million users sharing 500 million to two billion files via 100 to 200 servers" (Wikipedia 2006b).

For more information about the various kinds of file-sharing programs, see http://en.wikipedia.org/wiki/Peer-to-peer and http://www.slyck.com.

It is not my ambition here to provide an accurate record of all programs, clients, and Web sites currently in operation. Ink-on-paper books are notoriously bad at this sort of thing quite simply because of the time it takes to write, publish, and distribute them. By the time you are reading this some of the examples of P2P I have provided here may well have changed or even ceased operation. I am only endeavoring to capture a certain slice of what is happening at the time of writing.

6. See http://www.apple.com/itunes; http://www.hmv.co.uk/hmvweb/navigate.do?ctx=1530;8;-1;-1&pPageID=1530&pGroupID=8; and http://virgindigital.co.uk/download.php.

Even with the emergence of the legal music download sites, young people are still reported to be spending very little on music. As Steve Redmond of the BPI points out, "the biggest sites require you to have a credit card and kids tend not to have credit cards. . . . Fundamentally, it's been quite difficult for kids to engage in the legal purchase of music. . . . Undoubtedly a lot of kids have been file-sharing" (quoted in Allen 2006b, 29).

7. See http://www.myspace.com and http://www.facebook.com. Other social networking sites currently popular in different places around the world include: Cyworld (South Korea), http://www.cyworld.com; Fotolog (South America), http://www.fotolog.com; hi5 (Central America), http://www.hi5.com; LiveJournal (United States and Russia), http://www.livejournal.com; and Orkut (Brazil and India), http://www.orkut.com.

8. Interestingly, at least one study has suggested that "there is little evidence" that music sales have been affected by file sharing, or that it "is the main culprit behind the recent decline in CD album sales" (Oberholzer-Gee and Strumpf 2005, n.p.).

9. Finkelstein and McCleery provide the following example: "When the Bertelsmann conglomerate took over the Random House conglomerate in 1998 [whose Vintage Classics list includes works by Barthes, de Beauvoir, and Freud], the new owners expected Random House to make a 15 per cent profit and to increase turnover by 10 per cent annually. This would have entailed a leap in profits from $1 million to $150 million on annual sales of roughly $1 billion; it would also have involved concurrent growth in those sales of $100 million" (2005, 124).

10. What is more, this is the case despite what some have identified as a substantial "shift in library acquisitions, from purchased ownership to licensed access" (Covey 2005, 5), and the fact that various package deals and licensing agreements mean that many journals are now also available online. As Willinsky notes, ironically enough: "the inevitable cancellation of journal subscriptions and reduced circulation resulting from higher prices is still leading to greater publisher profits. The publishing goal is not necessarily increased circulation for the journals. Profits are coming not only from increased prices and publishing efficiencies, but from taking greater advantage of the growing number of titles publishers hold, through such strategies as 'bundling' titles in licensing arrangements with libraries that carry no-cancel policies for all of the titles in the bundles. The effect is to increase the publisher's share of subscribing libraries' budgets beyond the number of titles that libraries might otherwise have ordered (leading to cuts in other titles).

"Elsevier has a higher profit margin on its lower-quality journals (with fewer submissions), which is one of the reasons for a bundling strategy that does not allow libraries to cancel these lower-quality journals without cancelling the higher quality ones in the same bundle" (Willinsky 2006, 17, 17 n. 5).

11. The average price of a 200-page hardback paper published book is £50 or $US99 (this figure is for 2006). Lightning Source is able to produce a 168-page print-on-demand book for as little as $3.09 (Rosenthal 2006). Given that software and open-source code for creating e-print archives is available on the Web for free (see http://www.eprints.org/software and http://dspace.org), it is possible for many models of open-access publishing to be far cheaper even than this.

12. See http://www.arXiv.org. Far from being a case of academics belatedly following the Napster model, it could be argued that Napster was only a version of a gift economy that has long existed within academia, and which has had a profound influence on the shaping of the net. As Richard Barbrook

has maintained: "From its earliest days, the free exchange of information has therefore been firmly embedded within the technologies and social mores of cyberspace. When New Left militants proclaimed that 'information wants to be free' back in the Sixties, they were preaching to computer scientists who were already living within the academic gift economy. Above all, the founders of the Net never bothered to protect intellectual property within computer-mediated communications. On the contrary, they were developing these new technologies to advance their careers inside the academic gift economy. Far from wanting to enforce copyright, the pioneers of the Net tried to eliminate all barriers to the distribution of scientific research" (Barbrook 1998, n.p.).

13. An archive of the ongoing (1998) discussion on the American Scientist Open Access forum regarding the provision of open access to the peer-reviewed scholarly research literature is available at http://www.ecs.soton.ac.uk/~harnad/Hypermail/Amsci/. Accessed 18 May 2007.

14. This is of course not the only important difference between them. Another concerns the way in which the open-access e-print self-archiving system, at least as it is characterized by the arXiv.org E-print Archive, is based on a database, hosted on a central server, which collects, publishes, and stores written academic texts. Napster, by contrast, is (or was in its original incarnation) a music file-sharing tool based around a central directory that lists the data that is being offered for exchange by other registered participants. Neither arXiv.org nor Napster are therefore what is called a peer-to-peer (P2P) network, at least not in the proper sense of the term. "Pure" P2P file-sharing networks such as Gnutella consist of a decentralized network of connected machines that are independent of either a centralized client server or a centralized directory. This allows the responsibility for any breaches of copyright to be transferred to the much harder to prosecute individual end-user rather than lying with a central server.

None of which was enough to prevent Kazaa—a semi-centralized system, in contrast to Napster's centralized system and Gnutella's fully distributed one—being forced by a lawsuit from the Recording Industry Association of America (RIAA) to agree in July 2006 to "stop facilitating the pirating of copyrighted material . . . to cough up more than $115m to account for past transgressions [and] become a legitimate, Napster-esque service" (Harris 2006). However, in the "recent case in California of Virgin vs. Marson, Mrs. Marson had a claim being made against her on the basis that she owned the computer and paid for the Internet through which the illegal file sharing was taking place" dropped, on the grounds that the RIAA considered that "the use of an IP address as evidence against file sharers is not enough to prove that the person being charged committed copyright infringement." This has led some to now suggest that "the best way to defend yourself against the RIAA is to open up your WiFi network to your neighbours. Essentially, the more people who are using the internet through a shared IP address the weaker the evidence the RIAA can summon against you" (Garside 2006).

15. For a somewhat different take on the music industry's relation to piracy and copyright, written from the point of view of a musician, see "Courtney Love Does the Math" (Love 2000).

16. In March 2002 the Motion Picture Association of America began a legal action against MusicCity.com and others for swapping "pirated" television programs and films online.

17. In *Books in the Digital Age*, John B. Thompson defines electronic publishing as comprising "at least three different forms of computer-based media: diskette, CD-ROM and the internet." However, since it was, as Thompson acknowledges, "above all the rise of the internet in the 1990s which opened the way for a much more radical vision of electronic publishing," it is this version of electronic publishing I am most interested in here (J. Thompson 2005, 316).

As far as open access itself is concerned, there are numerous styles. In his 2006 book *The Access Principle*, John Willinsky identifies as many as ten "flavors" of open access: "Home page open access"; "Open access e-print archive"; "Author fee open access"; "Subsidized open access"; "Dual-mode open access"; "Delayed open access"; "Partial open access"; "Per capita open access"; "Open access indexing"; and "Open access cooperative" (Willinsky 2006, 211–16).

Nevertheless, open access is generally presented as taking one of two main forms. The first is what is called the "golden road" to open access. This is where journals make their contents open access, either immediately upon publication, or after a specified period of time, such as six months after initial publication. David J. Solomon recently summed up some of the different "golden" models in use as follows: "On the one end of the spectrum there are journals that provide freely accessible abstracts but restrict access to full articles to paid subscribers. On the other end of the spectrum is what Willinsky (2006) has called subsidized journals. These journals provide unrestricted access to full texts of articles from the date of publication without having to resort to charging authors for publication. [*Culture Machine* would fall into this category.] In between there are delayed access where open access is restricted to subscribers for a period of time, partial open access, where some content is open and some restricted to subscribers and dual mode where some forms of publication such as printed or PDF versions are restricted to subscribers but other less desirable or less expensive forms of access such as HTML are freely available. There are also models where there is open access to the content of journals but authors are charged to fund publication" (Solomon 2006, n.p.). The purest form of open access in this "golden" sense, however, is when journals charge neither their authors to publish in them nor their readers to access them.

The second form of open access is called the "green road" to open access. This is where authors "self-archive" copies of their research (which may or may not be published elsewhere) in subject repositories (such as arXiv.org and CSeARCH) or personal, departmental, or institutional repositories and Web sites, including individual blogs. (Compared to blogs, open-access journals and open-access archives obviously constitute more organized and systematic ways of publishing, at least in terms of prospective readers being able to search for and find material.)

As far as publication in institutional repositories is concerned, the Harnad/ Oppenheim preprint and corrigenda strategy has been superseded for Harnad as the *optimal* strategy by the Immediate-Deposit/Optional-Access (ID/OA) mandate, as proposed and recommended by the European Research Advisory Board (EURAB). This is as follows:

1. The repository may be a local institutional and/or a subject repository.
2. Authors should deposit post-prints (or publisher's version if permitted) plus metadata of articles accepted for publication in peer-reviewed journals and international conference proceedings.
3. Deposit should be made upon acceptance by the journal/conference. Repositories should release the metadata immediately, with access restrictions to a full-text article to be applied as required. Open access should be made available as soon as practicable after the author-requested embargo, or six months, whichever comes first.
4. Suitable repositories should make provision for long-term preservation of, and free public access to, published research findings. (Harnad 2007a, n.p.)

According to Harnad, this mandate is "specifically designed to immunise the policy from all the permissions problems (imagined and real) and embargoes that have been delaying adoption of Green OA mandates [whereby institutions and research funders have made it mandatory that any research they support financially is made available OA; see my Introduction, n. 19] or have led to the adoption of sub-optimal mandates (that allowed deposit to be delayed or not done at all, depending on publisher policy). . . . The key to the ID/OA mandate's success and power is that it separates the mandatory component (deposit of the final peer-reviewed draft immediately upon acceptance for publication— no delays, no exceptions) from the access-setting component. (Immediate setting of access to the deposit as Open Access is strongly recommended, but not mandatory: provisionally setting access as Closed Access is an allowable option where judged necessary.)" (Harnad 2007b, n.p.).

For more on the "golden" and green" roads to open access, see Guédon (2004) and Harnad, Brody, Vallières et al. (2004), as well as the *Self-archiving FAQ* at http://www.eprints.org/openaccess/self-faq/. For an account of why, although I am in favor of and support both, I am for the most part specifically privileging the "green road" to open access here (that is, publishing self-archived copies of research in digital archives), see my Introduction, the end of the current chapter, and my third set of metadata, "The Specificity of New Media."

18. Research on the impact of open-access publishing has been carried out by, among others, Lawrence (2001), Antelman (2004), Harnad and Brody (2004), and Eysenbach (2006). Eysenbach, for example, found that articles published "as immediate open access in the *PNAS* [*Proceedings of the National Academy of Sciences*] were three times more likely to be cited than non–open access papers, and were also cited more than *PNAS* articles that were only self-archived by their authors" (Wikipedia, 2006a). However, other studies have disputed the degree of the impact of open access. For the very latest figures regarding the impact of open access (figures that are regularly updated), see the Web site of the Open Citation Project at http://opcit.eprints.org/oacitation-biblio.html.

19. In an article written in honor of Stuart Hall and his activities over the

years, Angela McRobbie describes being in the "audience at an academic media and communications conference where a whole array of editors were on the stage and asked to give an update on publishing in their RAE rated journals." To her horror, not one of these editors so much as "flinched when they described their readerships as a paltry 300 or 400 internationally" (McRobbie 2000, 219). Myself, I am surprised she was so surprised. Of course, these figures have to be qualified by the fact that, as most paper journals are purchased by university libraries, they are often read by far more people than actually buy them. The amount such journals may be photocopied, and the way a lot of them appear in multiple formats (digital as well as paper, including aggregate databases of journal contents), also has to be taken into account. Still, the figures McRobbie cites go a long way to explain why so many new journals are being produced. After all, if individual journals only sell in the region of 500 copies or so per edition, one way for publishers to sell more journals is simply to increase the number of titles they publish—especially if they have a captive market in university libraries who are likely to feel obliged to subscribe to most if not all the journals produced in a particular area. Considering that publishers frequently pay for neither the content, the editing, nor the peer-review process that makes these journals possible (and that at the time of writing the yearly subscription to at least one journal in the sciences, *Brain Research*, costs over $US21,000, with others in the humanities and social sciences already operating on a "pay-to-play basis," charging the likes of $US200 reader's fee for reviewing articles and then $US100 per page that is actually published), academic journal publishing can be extremely profitable.

20. See http://www.culturemachine.net.

Of course success stories in open-access publishing abound. Most famously, the Public Library of Science's (PLoS) open-access journal *PLoS Biology* is reported to have had an "initial impact rating of 13.9 and a Thompson Scientific (formerly Institute for Scientific Information) ranking of Number 1 in biology journals" only two years after it was first established (Tschider 2006).

In contrast to *Culture Machine* and CSeARCH and others, the not-for-profit PLoS (http://www.plos.org/), like the for-profit BioMed Central (http://www.biomedcentral.com), the foremost corporate open-access publisher, charges authors a fee to publish, although access to the journals themselves is free. The fee for BioMed Central, which produces more than one hundred journals in the areas of biology and medicine, is £750–£900 or $US1350–1750; while *PLoS Biology* charges author's fees of $US2,500 to publish (these figures are for June 2007). However, BioMed Central and PLoS will grant individual publication fee waiver requests in "genuine" cases of an author's financial hardship (as judged on a case-by-case basis).

21. See http://cogprints.soton.ac.uk/. The United Kingdom Government's Science and Technology Committee, chaired by Ian Gibson, MP, even conducted an inquiry into the "open-access" publication of academic research (Gibson 2004). It concluded in support of depositing publicly funded research in open-access archives, seeing it as a public good. It was more cautious around the possibility of open-access, author-pays journals: both because this would have drastic consequences for the publishing industry as it currently stands, and also because

it was believed that there was likely to be little enthusiasm for it among many academics, especially in arts and humanities fields, where grants and institutional funding to cover the cost of publishing in this way are harder to come by.

22. See http://www.free-culture.org/freecontent. Accessed 12 August 2006.

23. "Permanently" has been placed in quotation marks here to indicate that I am aware that digital media can quickly become obsolete, URLs dead, and so on. We should certainly not assume that the Internet will remain in its present form for the long or even mid-term future. As the technology changes, it is quite possible that "older" forms will become outdated and increasingly inaccessible, just as it is now hard to watch a Betamax video or listen to an eight-track tape. As Nicholson Baker makes clear in *Double Fold: Libraries and the Assault on Paper* (2002), there is even a case to be made that paper will survive as long, if not longer, than many other forms of information storage, including those associated with digital technology.

24. See http://globaltext.org.

25. More details are available at: http://www.rcuk.ac.uk/access and http://www.esrcsocietytoday.ac.uk/ESRCInfoCentre/Support/access.

Similarly, in the United States Congress, The Federal Research Public Access Act of 2006, which was introduced in Senate in May 2006, advocates that all federally funded research be made available open access no later than six months after its initial date of publication. My thanks to Rachel Wilson of RMIT University in Melbourne for bringing this act to my attention. Indeed, such is the momentum of the movement toward open access in the United States that what had previously only the status of a request has now also been made mandatory by the National Institutes of Health (NIH). As of 7 April 2008, most NIH grantees are required to make their research outputs available open access through PubMed Central (http://www.pubmedcentral.nih.gov).

26. I suspect in a lot of cases (and for some of the reasons given below) this particular variation on the Harnad/Oppenheim preprint and corrigenda strategy may well work better in practice for texts published as journal articles than in or as books. Although of course they differ, many publishers' copyright agreements, especially for books, cover derivative works in a manner that would include such revised second editions. As is pointed out on the *Self-Archiving FAQ* on the EPrints Web site: "Where exclusive copyright has been assigned by the author to a journal publisher for a peer-reviewed draft, copy-edited and accepted for publication by that journal, then *that draft* may not be self-archived by the author (without the publisher's permission). The pre-refereeing preprint, however, has already been (legally) self-archived. (No copyright transfer agreement existed at that time, for that draft.)" (*Self-Archiving FAQ*, written for the Budapest Open Access Initiative 2002–2004, n.p.).

But "where exclusive copyright" has been transferred by the author to a publisher in toto—for example, "in a 'work for hire,'" where "the author has been paid (or will be paid royalties) in exchange for the text," as is often the case in book publishing—it may well be that the author is not legally allowed to self-archive it or any future editions derived from it (unless those future editions are *very* extensively revised, that is; and even then that may not be enough). This is because, although "[t]he text is still the author's 'intellectual property,' . . . the exclusive right to sell or give away copies of it has been transfer[r]ed to the publisher" (*Self-Archiving FAQ*, written for the Budapest Open Access Initiative 2002–2004, n.p.).

As Harnad makes clear, however, this particular strategic variation is designed to be employed *only* in those instances where a publisher will *not* explicitly allow the self-archiving of either the edited and published version of the text, or the refereed but unedited post-print. Writing in 2001–2003, Harnad was already able to note that such cases are rarer than one might think. He cites figures to the effect that approximately 10–30 percent of journal publishers will allow the self-archiving of the refereed post-print. By August 2007 this figure had risen to over 60 percent, with more than 90 percent of journals permitting the archiving of either post- or preprints (see http://romeo.eprints.org/stats.php; see also Harnad, Brody, Vallières et al. 2004). Other publishers will allow authors to modify their copyright transfer agreement forms in advance of publication to permit the self-archiving of post-prints with something along the lines of the following clause, "but only if you explicitly propose it yourself (they will not formulate it on their own initiative)": "I hereby transfer to [publisher or journal] all rights to sell or lease the text (on-paper and on-line) of my paper [paper-title]. I retain only the right to distribute it for free for scholarly/scientific purposes, in particular, the right to self-archive it publicly online on the Web" (http://cogprints.soton.ac .uk/copyright.html; Harnad 2001/2003, n.p.).

If you ask, most journal publishers will generally release texts for self-archiving at some stage once the volume in question has been published (not least because after a certain date journal sales often drop and they have no real sale value); and all the more so now that, as I say, funding bodies are increasingly requesting if not requiring researchers to include their research in open-access journals or repositories as a condition of receiving funding.

Harnad's focus is on journal articles because the issue of fees and royalties means that, for him, "books . . . are not, and never will be, author give-aways" (Harnad 2001/2003, n.p.). But this is not necessarily so. As we have seen, while the majority of authors have little to lose in terms of royalty/fee income from publishing open access, they have a lot to gain potentially in terms of increases in readership and so on. Witness the way I have already been able to cite a number of books whose authors and publishers *have both* agreed to make them available open access (e.g., Lessig 2004; Willinsky 2006). So it is always worth it for those royalty/fee book authors who wish to publish open access to ask their publishers to permit the self-archiving of their titles, too. Especially since most academic books do not have much long-term sales value, either. Or these authors could simply refuse to give a publisher exclusive copyright and only sign a contract with a press that will publish their work on a nonexclusive basis. (This is what the Faculty of Arts and Sciences at Harvard University now requires its staff to do, for instance.)

For details of a number of "author addendums"—that is, lawyer-written documents that authors can "sign and staple to a publisher's standard copyright transfer agreement" and that "modif[y] the publisher's contract to allow authors to retain some rights that the default contract would have given to the publisher," and so enable them to publish open access—see the 2 June 2007 issue of the SPARC Open Access Newsletter (http://www.earlham.edu/~peters/fos/newsletter/06-02-07.htm). These include, in chronological order, the author addendums produced by "SPARC (May 2005), MIT (January 2006), Science Commons (June 2006), OhioLINK (August 2006), SURF-JISC (October 2006)" and, most recently, that adopted by a group of universities making up the Committee on Institutional Cooperation (CIC) in May 2007 (Suber 2007a).

For those still unsure about making such a proposal to their publishers for whatever reason, in June 2007 SHERPA's RoMEO service listed three hundred publisher copyright policies on self-archiving, including those publisher policies that comply with funding regulations. SHERPA stands for Securing a Hybrid Environment for Research Preservation and Access, RoMEO for Rights Metadata for Open Archiving; see http://www.sherpa.ac.uk/romeo.php. For details of those journals that explicitly permit author self-archiving, see http://romeo.eprints.org; and for journals that specifically endorse the self-archiving of the publisher's edited PDF, HTML or XML version (as opposed to just the author's refereed version), see: http://www.sherpa.ac.uk/romeo.php. Another option is, of course, to go along with the ID/OA (Immediate-Deposit/Optional-Access) mandate (see n. 17 above).

When it comes to the "past (retrospective) literature," Harnad writes that: "The Harnad/Oppenheim pre-print+corrigenda strategy will not work there [although he insists that the variation on this strategy described above will], but as the retrospective journal literature brings virtually no revenue, most publishers will agree to author self-archiving after a sufficient period (6 months to 2 years) has elapsed. Moreover, for the really old literature, it is not clear that on-line self-archiving was covered by the old copyright agreements at all" (2001/2003, n.p.). Indeed, some have argued that it should be possible to make all research published before 1996 available open access, as previous to that date no copyright agreements would include a clause relating to the regulation of dissemination through digital means.

But even if publishers *do* respond to such ventures by getting together and agreeing among themselves to try to prevent the self-archiving of either the published version of texts, the refereed but unedited post-prints, or even the preprints, or to restrict self-archiving to internal, institutional, noncommercial use only—although why should they? arXiv.org has been operating for more than fifteen years now without any such difficulty—there is a case to be made for academics cutting out the middle-men and women (that is the publishing houses) and taking the means of production into their own hands and publishing their work for, and by, themselves. After all, as I pointed out earlier, academics often do not get paid, either substantially or directly, for a lot of the writing, editorial work, or refereeing that goes into the production of scholarly texts; publishers often get this work for free. (There are exceptions, particularly in commercial scientific, technical, and medical publishing, where publishers can in fact pay quite well for editing and even peer-reviewing. Still . . .)

There is also, of course, an argument that copyright on the net does not make sense. As Richard Barbrook has maintained, following Tim Berners-Lee: "Technically, every act within cyberspace involves copying material from one computer to another. Once the first copy of a piece of information is placed on the Net, the cost of making each extra copy is almost zero. The architecture of the system presupposes that multiple copies of documents can easily be cached around the network. As Tim Berners-Lee—the inventor of the Web—points out: 'Concepts of intellectual property, central to our culture, are not expressed in a way which maps onto the abstract information space. In an information space, we can consider the authorship of materials, and their perception; but . . . there is a need for the underlying infrastructure to be able to make copies simply for reasons of [technical] efficiency and reliability. The concept of "copyright" as expressed in terms of copies made makes little sense'" (Barbrook 1998, n.p.).

In this respect, perhaps the most sensible default strategy of all is that advocated on the *Self-Archiving FAQ* written for the Budapest Open Access Initiative. This is positioned as being the "one that the physicists have been successfully practicing since 1991 and computer scientists have been practicing since even earlier." It is simply "don't-ask/don't-tell." Instead, self-archive your text, the "preprint as well as your postprint, and wait to see whether the publisher ever requests removal" (*Self-Archiving FAQ*, written for the Budapest Open Access Initiative 2002–2004, n.p.).

2. Judgment and Responsibility in the Wikipedia Era

1. See, for example, John Willinsky's *The Access Principle* (2006). There are also numerous sites on the Web that offer useful introductions, histories, and summaries, including Peter Suber's blog Open Access News (available at http://www.earlham.edu/~peters/fos/fosblog.html), and especially his "Open Access Overview" (available at http://www.earlham.edu/~peters/fos/overview.htm); and the June and July 2006 issues of the online journal *First Monday* 11(6) (available at http://firstmonday.org/issues/issue11_6). For more on the "digital revolution" in academic publishing generally, see John B. Thompson (2005).

2. This anxiety and apprehension is not necessarily misplaced. In a presentation given to a joint British Science Fiction Association/Science Fiction Foundation event in London on 14 May 2006, Bruce Sterling noted how, when his students want to know something about a particular subject, they first Google it, then look for it in Wikipedia at http://en.wikipedia.org. If it isn't in Wikipedia, they start a Wikipedia entry before looking for it on Technorati at http://www.technorati.com or other Web sites. Only rarely do they turn to books: not just because the Web contains more material then any number of paper texts can hope to provide; nor because the material contained in a book is often out of date by the time it has gone through the whole of the publication and printing process (although all of that is sometimes true); but also because they do not assign books and the scholars who write them the same authority as did previous generations. According to Sterling, at least, his students do not give writers authority simply because they have certain qualifications, or have published other

authoritative texts. They are not concerned about that. They are just looking for where the most interesting and exciting work is being produced on a given topic regardless.

This is not to say there are no hierarchies or systems of accreditation operating here, for all that Jimmy Wales, founder of Wikipedia, may think of himself as an "anti-credentialist." "To me, the key thing is getting it right," he is reported as saying, "and if a person's really smart, and they're doing good fantastic work, I don't care if they're a high-school kid or a Harvard professor" (quoted in Lanchester 2006, 18). Rather, these hierarchies and systems of accreditation—the turn to Wikipedia first, for example, or the use of Technorati above other search engines—are operating according to very different criteria from those privileged in the academy.

3. In fact, as it is one of the primary means by which universities and research-funding agencies and councils attempt to measure the quality and value of scholarly work using mechanisms such as the RAE in the United Kingdom, even more importance can be attached to peer review than this.

4. For one account of the "value added" that publishers, and faculty editorial boards in particular, bring to the process of scholarly communication, at least with regard to university presses, see Thatcher (1999).

5. The problem does not arise in the case of those print journals that also offer access to an electronic online version (which according to some reports amounts to almost half of the journals currently available), as their authority and status tends to be vouchsafed to their online versions.

6. This mimicry works both ways. Many paper publications are now imitating their digital counterparts, not in the hope of appearing more legitimate, but to acquire some of their aura of novelty and sexiness and to pitch ideas that are perceived as increasing sales. In 2004 John Sutherland reported in *The Guardian* newspaper that "HarperCollins is releasing a Blitz-barrage of its newly devised PS (More than a Paperback!) editions. . . . The idea originated with the paraphernalia attached to DVDs where, in addition to the feature movie, the home viewer gets interviews, location shots, insider gossip, geeky factoids. In April's first batch of more-than-paperbacks, Douglas Coupland's *Hey Nostrodamus* (fictionalised Columbine) has an appendix with About the Author (biblio info, Q&A, headline reviews), About the Book (reportage from the historical massacre), a Location Feature (where Douglas creates his novels) and if-you-liked-this-you'll-like-that advice" (2004, 4).

7. See http://www.bbc.co.uk. In *Behind the Blip*, Matthew Fuller attributes the predominance of the paper and page metaphors in Web design to the way in which "the techniques of page layout were ported over directly from graphic design for paper. This meant that HTML had to be contained as a conduit for channelling direct physical representation—integrity to fonts, spacing, inflections, and so on. The actuality of the networks were thus subordinated to the disciplines of graphic design and of graphical user interface simply because of their ability to deal with flatness, the screen (though there are conflicts between them based around their respective idealisations of functionality). Currently this

is a situation that is already edging towards collapse as other data types makes incursions into, through, and beyond the page" (2003, 55–56).

8. This is borne out by a report by the Kaufman-Wills Group entitled "The Facts About Open Access: A Study of the Financial and Non-Financial Effects of Alternative Business Models on Scholarly Journals" (2005), in which most online journals are described as being run on voluntary labor, and as having internal peer-review systems, poor copyediting, inconsistent style, etc.

9. For Levinas, we are always confronted by the alterity of the Other. This confrontation is both an accusation and a source of our ethical responsibility, which is why ethics is inevitable and foundational, why it is a first philosophy that precedes ontology (see also my fourth set of metadata). For Levinas, the latter is a philosophy of being in which the other is understood in terms of concepts and categories that belong to the same. Ontology here amounts to ascertaining the extent to which the Other can (or cannot) be recognized as the same, as being like me. Levinas, however, thinks ethics somewhat differently. For him, ethics is a *different* mode of thinking that comes before ontology (albeit not in a linear, temporal sense). Joanna Zylinska—also writing in the context of a discussion of the ethics of cultural studies—succinctly sums up this aspect of Levinas's philosophy: "Instead of attempting to thematize and conceptualize the other as always already known, ethics points to the radical and absolute alterity of the other which collapses the familiar order of Being and calls the self to respond to this alterity. This possibility, as well as necessity, of responding to what Levinas defines as an incalculable alterity of the other is the source of an ethical sentiment. Refusing to assert the self's primacy, Levinas focuses on the vulnerability of the self when facing the other, who is always already 'absolutely other,' and who cannot be fully grasped by the self. This otherness can evoke different reactions in the self. But even though the other can be ignored, scorned, or even annihilated, he or she has to be first of all addressed (responded to) in one way or another" (Zylinska 2005, 13).

10. See chapter 1, n. 17.

11. See Bellamy: "My challenge to those that use Derrida or Bey or Adorno or Bourdieu within their disciplinary frameworks to advance our understanding of new media, is can you enact the ideas of these thinkers in a sophisticated way through new media, or can it only be done through writing books about books? I challenge cultural studies and new media theorists to produce a Derrida engine or a Bourdieu database or a Bey GIS map. I am not aware of any major contribution that cultural studies has made within this medium beyond using it as a publishing and networking mechanism, and beyond writing innumerable valuable books to critique it from a distance. We need more people engaged in building academic resources on-line that help us to look at things in new ways" (2002). For more, see "The Milkbar Challenge" and "Cultural Studies and Online Innovation" strings on the *fibreculture* mailing list, archived at www.fibreculture.org.

12. Witness, to take just one example, the format required for an electronic journal that wishes to be selected and included in Thompson Scientific's Institute for Scientific Information (ISI) Web of Science (WOS), which claims to cover "over 16,000 international journals, books and proceedings in the sciences,

social sciences and arts and humanities": "The *Format of Electronic Journals* is extremely important to ISI. Following are a set of guidelines for Electronic Journal formats. Following these guidelines helps insure correct citation of articles and reduces the possibility of ambiguity in citation of articles. Insure that it is easy to identify the following elements:

- Journal Title
- Year of publication
- Volume and/or Issue Number (if applicable)
- Article Title
- Page Number or Article Number . . .
- A complete table-of-contents for each issue that includes the page/article number for each article (unless journal is being published as single articles).
- Labeling these identifiers in both source articles and in citations helps insure their proper use by those referencing the article and correct labeling by abstracting and indexing firms such as Thomson Scientific. . . .

"References to Your Electronic Journal: Instruct authors to include the following information when citing your e-journal: Journal title (use one standard abbreviation for your journal; avoid acronyms that may be confused with other titles); Volume number (if applicable); Issue Number (if applicable; within parenthesis); Page number and/or article number (clearly identifying the article number as such); Year of publication" ("The Thompson Scientific Journal Selection Process," available at: http://scientific.thomson.com/free/essays/selection ofmaterial/journalselection. Accessed 26 October 2006).

Interestingly, the Higher Education Funding Council for England (HEFCE) intends to use ISI's WOS as the database for its Research Excellence Framework (REF), which is replacing the RAE.

13. For examples of codework, see Mez at http://netwurkerz.de/mez/data bleed/complete/ and http://www.cddc.vt.edu/host/netwurker. A close reading of the latter text is provided by Katherine Hayles in her essay "Deeper into the Machine: The Future of Electronic Literature" (2003).

A partial bibliography for Mez is available at: http://www.hotkey.net.au/ ~netwurker/resume2d.htm.

For more on "codework" in general, see Raley (2001), Sondheim (2001), who invented the term, Wark (2001), and White (2002).

14. Interestingly, as far as the argument I go on to make in this book regarding the importance of developing more open and ethically and politically responsible modes of judging and assessing digitally reproduced scholarship and research is concerned, The Institute for the Future of the Book (http://www .futureofthebook.org) has based its argument for a more open and innovative system of academic publication and peer review (and even peer-to-peer review), at least in part, on a certain conception of the public intellectual. In a posting on the institute's if:book blog on the subject of academic blogging, Ray Cha writes: "I do not mean to suggest that every professor needs to blog. However, on the whole, university presidents and department heads [need] to acknowledge that

they do have an obligation to make their scholarship accessible to the public. Scholarship for its own sake or its own isolated community has little or no social value.

"Therefore, the public university which receives funding from the state government, has a responsibility to give back the results from the resources that society gives it. Further, we also as a society give private higher ed schools protective benefits (such as special tax status) because there is an implied idea that they provide a service to the overall community. Therefore, one can argue that part of higher education's duty includes not only teaching and scholarship, but outreach as well. . . .

"The difficulty has arisen because within the academy there is history of a certain disdain through those who pursued becoming a public intellectual. . . . the web is a much more disruptive force than television in this regard. In that, it has dramatically changed how the university public intellectual can access people. Blogging specifically has lowered the barrier of entry for academics (and anyone for that matter) to interact with the public. Now, they no longer need to rely on traditional media outlets to reach a mass audience" (Cha, 2006).

But I wonder, is there not something rather moralistic, even neoliberal, about this particular stance? After all, The Institute for the Future of the Book is not arguing here that technology should be used to open academic work up to the public on the grounds that they want to develop some kind of "gift economy"; nor out of the sort of belief that motivated many of those who became interested in computer media in the 1960s: that "information wants to be free." Instead, they appear to have adopted a variation on the "taxpayers" argument: that it is important for society to get value for money from academics by making sure the latter's research is accessible to the overall community. In this respect, are they not in danger of promoting ideas similar to those currently being advocated by many neoliberals: that university research only has "value" if its "results" can impact on and be of "service" to prospective users beyond the institution, thus helping to build a more successful and competitive capitalist economy?

15. See Michael Bérubé, Le Blog Bérubé, available at: http://www.michael berube.com.

Jodi Dean, I Cite, available at: http://jdeanicite.typepad.com/i_cite.

Melissa Gregg, Home Cooked Theory, available at: http://www.homecooked theory.com.

Ted Striphas, Differences and Repetitions, available at: http://striphas .blogspot.com.

Gil Rodman, Revolution on a Stick, available at: http://www.comm.umn.edu/ ~grodman/wordpress.

Greg Wise, Ain't Got Time to Blog, available at: http://jmacgregorwise .blogspot.com.

John Beasley-Murray, Posthegemony, available at: http://posthegemony .blogspot.com.

16. See The Chronicle of Higher Education, 28 July 2006. Available at: http:// chronicle.com/free/v52/i47/47b00601.htm. For more on the case of Cole, see Cha (2006).

17. "Free Content" or "Free Expression" is a provisionally titled emerging movement arguing for the same open principles to be applied with regard to content and expression as they are in Free Software and Open Source. Just as software under the free software definition can be freely copied, added to, built upon, reconstructed, and reconceptualized, so, too, under this definition, would a work's content. See Möller and Hill (2006). "The Free Content and Expression Definition" is published in a wiki that can be found at: http://freedomdefined .org/ or http://freecontentdefinition.org.

18. See http://en.wikipedia.org/wiki/Wikipedia and http://digg.com.

19. In an article for the *Chronicle of Higher Education*, Wark is quoted as saying: "Wikipedia is based in sound academic practices to do with peer review—it just changes who those peers are. . . . They're not people who are authorized by Ivy League degrees or anything like that. But there's more of them, and they work faster" (J. R. Young 2006).

20. I am not going into detail regarding any of the examples I am providing here of the kinds of texts that are "born digital." In order to do so in a manner consistent with my argument in this book and its emphasis on singularity and acting tactically, I would need to respond to the specificity and indeed singularity of actual texts. What is more, I would need to do so with an answering specificity, singularity, unpredictability, and inventiveness of my own—in a manner not too dissimilar, perhaps (but still not the same), as the way I have endeavored to respond to open-access archiving here.

21. As Ben Vershbow maintains on The Institute for the Future of the Book's if:book blog with regard to what Douglas Rushkoff apparently calls his "open source dissertation," "[w]riting a novel this way is one thing, but a doctoral thesis will likely not be granted as much license. . . . it's still inordinately difficult to convince thesis review committees to accept anything that cannot be read, archived and pointed to on paper. [At least potentially—although of course a number of universities now require that what are to all intents and purposes paper or at least papercentric theses be submitted in electronic format.] A dissertation that requires a digital environment, whether to employ unconventional structures (e.g. hypertext) or to incorporate multiple media forms, in most cases will not even be considered unless you wish to turn your thesis defense into a full-blown crusade. Yet, as pitched as these battles have been, what Rushkoff is suggesting will undoubtedly be far more unsettling to even the most progressive of academic administrations. We're no longer simply talking about the leveraging of new rhetorical forms and a gradual disentanglement of printed pulp from institutional warrants, we're talking about a fundamental reorientation of authorship" (Vershbow 2006, n.p.).

22. Does my even putting the question of the responsible response to digital academic texts in this fashion not have a performative aspect, in that it establishes the code or terms within which this question can be answered? Does seeing digital publishing in terms of its relation to ink-on-paper publishing not severely limit our understanding of the former? By taking "paper" publishing as a privileged reference point in relation to which e-publishing can be demarcated and elaborated, does this not serve to marginalize or exclude the associations of

e-publishing with a whole host of other technological forms, historical processes and socio-politico-cultural relationships? Film, for example, or photography, video, painting and drawing, animation, graphic design, architecture, music?

23. That said, it is worth noting that in January 2004 arXiv.org initiated an endorsement system. This requires new submitters to supply an endorsement, although existing submitters are not asked to do so, or at least not "for topics in which they have been active." Apparently, this system was introduced to cope with the growth in the number of submitters, and is just one means employed by arXiv.org in an effort to distinguish the parasite from the guest and thus ensure its "content is relevant to current research while controlling costs so we can continue to offer free and open Web access to all" (see http://arxiv.org/new/. Accessed 15 June 2007).

24. At least one version of the etymology of the word *archive* portrays it as deriving "from the Greek word *arkhé* meaning government or order. Found in the word architecture the prefix means a starting point or founding act in both the sense of where something begins, and a legal sense of where its authority is derived" (Richardson and Goffman 2006, 16).

25. An example is provided in Graham Meikle's account of the Sydney Independent Media Centre(IMC). A key idea behind the IMC is open publishing: "There is no gatekeeping and no editorial selection process—participants are free to upload whatever they choose" to the IMC's Web site (Meikle 2002, 89). But as Meikle goes on to acknowledge in an endnote, "this policy is slightly porous, however: of nearly 300 stories posted to the end of August 2000, for example, some five had been removed for being completely off-topic." Now, Meikle goes on to point out that "even these stories are not completely deleted—they are still available on the site in a separate section" (201 n. 3). Nevertheless, we can see that there is still some element of judgment involved, even in explicitly articulated open publishing. What is more, this would be the case even if the IMC had indeed published everything submitted to them. This would still have been a judgment, a decision.

26. *Behavioral and Brain Sciences* (available at http://www.princeton.edu/~harnad/bbs.html) is published by Cambridge University Press; between 1990 and 2002 *Psycoloquy* (available at http://www.princeton.edu/~harnad/psyc.html) was sponsored by the American Psychological Association.

Regarding peer-to-peer review, Fitzpatrick says: "What if peer-review took place not prior to publication but on texts that have already been made public? What if that peer-review happened not anonymously, in back-channel communications with individuals other than a text's author, but in the open, in direct communication between reader and author? Technologies ranging from commenting to . . . a more elaborated P2P system, could be made to serve many of the purposes that current peer-review systems serve (most importantly for institutional purposes, the separating of wheat and chaff), but would shift the process of peer-review from one that determines whether a manuscript should be published to one that determines how it should be received. Such a P2P system raises some potential pitfalls, of course—most notably how to make sure that the new system doesn't simply remanifest the exclusionary manner in which the old sometimes functioned, through a Shirky-esque 'power law'—but . . . such a move of peer-review to a post-publication process would allow for the ongoing discussion and revision necessary to all scholarly thought" (2006a, n.p.).

This leads Fitzpatrick to be quite critical of peer-review and open peer commentary as practiced in the sciences. Writing in the blog of The Institute for the Future of the Book, she reports on "the experiment with open peer review" that at the time was being "undertaken by the journal *Nature*, as well as . . . the debate about the future of peer review" that was hosted by the journal: "The experiment is fairly simple: the editors of *Nature* have created an online open review system that will run parallel to its traditional anonymous review process.

"From 5 June 2006, authors may opt to have their submitted manuscripts posted publicly for comment.

"Any scientist may then post comments, provided they identify themselves. Once the usual confidential peer review process is complete, the public 'open peer review' process will be closed. Editors will then read all comments on the manuscript and invite authors to respond. At the end of the process, as part of the trial, editors will assess the value of the public comments."

Fitzpatrick deems *Nature's* experiment (which has since been suspended) as a "conservative step." She does so for two reasons, both of which again rest on The Institute's championing of their version of the idea of the public intellectual: "First, the journal is at great pains to reassure authors and readers that traditional, anonymous peer review will still take place alongside open discussion. Beyond this, however, there seems to be a relative lack of communication between those two forms of review: open review will take place at the same time as anonymous review, rather than as a preliminary phase, preventing authors from putting the public comments they receive to use in revision; and while the editors will 'read' all such public comments, it appears that only the anonymous reviews will be considered in determining whether any given article is published. . . ."

Fitzpatrick concludes that "*Nature's* experiment is an honorable one, and a step in the right direction. It is, however, a conservative step, one that foregrounds the institutional purposes of peer review rather than the ways that such review might be made to better serve the scholarly community" (2006b, n.p.).

However, could the system of peer-to-peer review Fitzpatrick advocates not be described as being potentially conservative in turn? One of the latter's main goals, for example, seems to be opening up the peer-review process to make it more visible and include a wider public of readers where "texts are discussed and, in some sense, 'ranked' by a committed community of readers" (Fitzpatrick 2006b). But again (as in n. 14 above), does all this talk of increasing transparency and the visibility of the process, and of ranking, not have something of a flavor of neoliberalism about it? (League tables, anyone?) Moreover, will the same not happen in such cases as some people are already intimating has occurred with regard to many social networking sites based on ranking systems? The story here is that, in the beginning, early adopters got involved and made some interesting and informed decisions. As sites have become more popular, however, the influence of these people has tended to be swamped by the crowd and those who are more concerned with promoting their own interests rather than those of these social networking communities. The result is that it is increasingly the more banal, safe, conservative texts that are ranked highest. Gary Marshall cites the example of Digg.com: "The self-proclaimed 'future of news' harnesses the wisdom of crowds to ensure that only the most interesting and important stories rise to the top. . . . These days, the news that rises to the top of the heap is usually trivial, occasionally inaccurate, and frequently followed by flame . . . wars between ill-informed fan boys.

"The future of news? The second most popular World & Business story on Digg this year is *Sexual urges of men and women*—short, badly, written and spectacularly unfunny gag that you'd expect to receive in a forwarded email from an annoying uncle" (Marshall 2006, 17).

There also appears to be an unwillingness on Fitzpatrick's part to assume the kind of radical responsibility I am referring to around questions of judgment and authority. What authority do the members of Fitzpatrick's "committed community of readers" have to rank, peer-to-peer review, or even comment (other than some vague notion of democracy and intellectual collaboration)? And with what legitimacy are decisions made as to which of their reviews and comments are to be incorporated into the text (and its subsequent versions) and its reception and which are not?

The potential conservatism of Fitzpatrick's system of peer-to-peer review is further apparent from its unquestioned reliance on relatively traditional conceptions of the author function, ownership, and the public intellectual, as when she writes: "What this new system of publishing and review implies, however, is less a move away from individual authorship than a recognition that no author is an island, so to speak, that we're all always working in dialogue with others. Even in a radically collective and collaborative electronic publishing system, the individual author would still exist (and would still maintain some form of 'ownership' over her ideas, via some means of Creative Commons licensing), but would do her work in material relation to the work of others, in a process of discussion and revision that now takes place behind the scenes, but that I'd argue is important enough to be moved out in front of the curtain" (2006, n.p.).

Indeed, rather than addressing the radical ethical (and political) questions the digital mode of reproduction raises for such concepts, the height of Fitzpatrick's ambition often appears to be merely for the conventional process of scholarly discussion and revision to be made more visible and transparent.

27. For example, in one of the relatively few discussions of open access to focus on its implications primarily for the humanities, Linda Hutcheon proposes two solutions to the "crisis in scholarly publishing": "The first is the publication of books electronically: in July, an announcement was made that Rice University Press (which ceased publication in 1996) was being revived but would publish only online books—peer reviewed, like all high quality scholarly publications. For disciplines like art history and music, in particular, the savings in the high cost of publishing their books could be immense. The second answer is that uni-

versity tenure and promotion committees in the humanities should move away from the printed book as the measure of success and validate journal articles (in print or online) or electronic books as well, when the same processes of peer review are in place" (2006, n.p.).

28. For more on the specificity of the digital medium, see Hayles (2002, 2003) and my third set of metadata, "The Specificity of New Media."

29. In 2006, Bill Ashraf, a lecturer in microbiology at Bradford University, claimed to be the first in the United Kingdom to eliminate lectures entirely and replace them with podcasts (Stothart 2006, 1, 4). For Second Life, see http://secondlife.com.

30. For more on Weber's work, see Wortham (2003) and Wortham and Hall (2007).

31. Weber himself gives as an example two concepts that have particular importance when it comes to thinking about how texts are to be judged and assessed, but that, as we saw earlier, the digital mode of material support may effectively challenge and place in question. These are the work and the author. He quotes Roland Barthes' "The Death of the Author" by way of illustration: "To give a text an Author is to impose a limit on that text, to furnish it with a final signified, to close writing" (Barthes 1968; cited by Weber 1987, xv). Other examples provided by Weber include the way in which the Judeo-Christian and Platonic tradition of interpretation has "succeeded in playing the game of interpretation all the more effectively for denying that there was any game whatsoever. By concealing its genealogy as interpretation in the names of Truth, Being, Subject and so on, the tradition succeeded in establishing its own authority and driving all competitors from the field" (1987, 5).

32. Cultural studies of course may argue that it is not a discipline, and does not simply dwell unproblematically within the institution, but is in fact an anti- or interdisciplinary field. For a discussion of this claim, and the way in which cultural studies nonetheless continues to think of itself in terms of specific disciplinary limits, see my *Culture in Bits* (2002), especially chapter 6. For a thinking of cultural studies rather differently, see my comments at the end of chapter 3 of the present volume, and also my Conclusion.

33. A brochure I acquired on a visit to Canberra in the summer of 2006 promoting the National Archives of Australia (http://www.naa.gov.au) provides a ready-made example of the aporia that lies at the "origin" of the nation state. According to this leaflet, "the National Archives is one of Canberra's real gems. Nestled in the trees just behind Old Parliament House, it holds a vast collection of valuable Commonwealth Government records including files, photos, posters, maps and film." However, apparently "the most precious document in the archives is Australia's 'birth certificate'—*Queen Victoria's Royal Commission of Assent.*" Yet if it was by means of this document (along with Australia's "original Constitution," which is also contained in the National Archives) that Queen Victoria was able to proclaim the founding of Australia, where did she in turn acquire the authority to do so? Does Great Britain have a similar birth certificate? And if so, was it in turn granted its founding legitimacy by another authority existing outside and prior to its own, as was the case with Australia?

For a reading of another founding national document, see Derrida (2002b).

34. Could this inability to ultimately forget be what motivates Harnad's anxiety with regard to peer review? For an analysis along these lines, see chapter 3.

35. Weber in fact establishes a link between such professionalization and the "institutions and practices which marked the development of the humanities disciplines in general, and those of literary studies in particular" (1987, 27), as the "process of isolating, as constitutive of the establishment of professions and of disciplines, requires itself an isolated, relatively self-contained social space in which to operate. Historically, this space was provided by the university" (31).

36. As we shall see in chapter 3, this is not just confined to the consideration of digital texts. It also applies to cultural studies' relation to its "outside" others, including: those "legitimate" disciplines that have either been marginalized or excluded from cultural studies' interdisciplinary repertoire; and those forms of knowledge that are not, or not yet, regarded as legitimate; as well as those associated with new media technology that are not recognizable as legitimate if judged by the rules and conventions of the paper world.

37. For this relation to the "outside" is not just a feature associated with electronic publishing. The whole idea of the university is based on this relation, as Robert Young makes clear in "The Dialectics of Cultural Criticism" (1996a). The anxiety we have located here when it comes to the institution's dealing with electronic texts is not *just* something that is produced externally to the university by the occurrence of electronic publishing, then; this anxiety is part of what the university is.

Indeed, it is not only disciplines that have been suspended over the aporia of authority I have identified here. I would argue that all the institutions and practices associated with the formation of knowledge—the university, the scholar, the author, the reader, the text, the book and so on—have *always* existed in what could be described as something of a "digital condition." This condition has merely been intensified and made more transparent in what is conventionally referred to as "the digital age."

38. In an interesting article on "Hypercapitalism," Phil Graham endeavors to capture something of what is new about this particular historical moment: "What *is* new about hypercapitalism, what makes it different from past forms of social organisation, is that today's new media facilitate the almost immediate production, consumption, distribution, and exchange of valued categories of thought and language—knowledge commodities—on a planet-wide scale with a mass and immediacy that is historically unprecedented. Further, thought and language have themselves become the primary objects of production, distribution, and exchange within this emergent system" (2002a, 11–12).

39. The example Weber provides is that of the Collège international de philosophie, available at http://www.ci-philo.asso.fr/default.asp. He sees this institution as embodying the "attempt to institutionalize research that might be described as transgressive inasmuch as it questions the defining limits of the established disciplines" (1987,151). For further possible examples, see my *Culture in Bits* (2002, 160 n. 33).

Metadata II. Print This!

1. See the debate between Grossberg (1995) and Garnham (1995).

2. See Morris (1988), McRobbie (1997) and, more recently, du Gay and Pryke (2002) and Hesmondhalgh (2003).

3. A recent collection titled *New Cultural Studies: Adventures in Theory*, edited by myself and Clare Birchall (2006b), does just this, exploring some of the new directions and territories currently being mapped out at the intersections of cultural studies and cultural theory by what we describe as a "post-Birmingham School" generation of writers and practitioners. *New Cultural Studies* looks at the ethics of Alain Badiou and Emmanuel Levinas, the post-Marxism of Michael Hardt and Antonio Negri, the schizo-analysis of Gilles Deleuze and Félix Guattari, the German media theory of Friedrich Kittler and Bernhard Siegert, and the biopolitics of Michel Foucault and Giorgio Agamben, as well as some of the areas where cultural studies is being most interestingly reconceived, such as Rem Koolhaas's Project on the City, and recent work around ideas of the transnational, the post-human, the secret, and the animal.

4. In *Archive Fever*, Derrida privileges the effect on psychoanalysis of "above all E-mail" (1996b, 16). Significantly, the "most important and obvious" reason Derrida gives for doing so concerns not the "major role" letter writing has played in the history of psychoanalysis, but rather the effect of e-mail on "property rights, publishing and reproduction rights" (1996b, 17). This in turn relates to a question Derrida later raises in parentheses in his essay "The Future of the Profession or the University Without Condition" but which he leaves unanswered. This is "the question of the market place in publishing and the role it plays in archivisation, evaluation and legitimation of the academic research" (2001c, 25).

3. IT, Again; or, How to Build an Ethical Institution

1. Just in case I have *not* yet convinced you of this, a list of the many benefits of open-access publishing and self-archiving is provided by Peter Suber (2007b) in his "Open Access Overview" at http://www.earlham.edu/~peters/fos/overview .htm. This list complements and can be placed alongside my own, which I provided in chapter 1. My thanks to Sigi Jöttkandt and David Ottina for originally pointing me in the direction of Suber's work.

2. See http://www.sherpa.ac.uk/repositories.

3. A version of this paper is available at http://www.jisc.ac.uk/publications/ publications/pub_openaccess.aspx. A further list of open-access archives is available on the EPrints site at: http://www.eprints.org.

4. See http://www.opendoar.org.

5. Software for creating e-print archives is available for free at both http:// www.eprints.org/software and http://www.dspace.org. The Online Computer Library Center also provides a list of open-source software designed to help build repositories and harvest data. This is available at http://www.oclc.org/ research/software/default.htm.

6. While I am again turning to Weber in *Digitize This Book!* for help in think-

ing about the digitization of the scholarly research literature, experimenting in the sense we saw Weber refer to earlier in my Introduction (see n. 13) also describes my response to Weber's own writings. Accordingly, my reading of Weber in this book does not come "full circle to produce a concept of itself." Rather it "doubles up into a language that can no longer be assigned to a single, authoritative speaker or to a reliable, truthful voice." In other words, I am not attempting to pin down or otherwise capture the "meaning" of Weber's work here; nor to engage critically or polemically with other interpretations of it; nor even to produce a "deconstructive" reading that shows how Weber's texts put forward irreconcilable positions that are different from, and in many ways opposed to, those they are generally portrayed, or portray themselves, as espousing. I am experimenting, by analysis and performance, with the way in which Weber's own "concepts . . . operate in a singular situation": in this case, that of the development and institution of a cultural studies open-access archive. Indeed, it is with a certain "deconstructive pragmatics" arising out of Weber's ideas on how to (re)think the institution of the contemporary university that this book is experimenting in particular. Weber's writings are thus treated here much as he himself treats those of Jacques Derrida and Paul de Man: as texts "whose import only is accessible to a reading that moves [them] elsewhere"—not least through the notions of repetition, iteration, and iterability Weber discusses in a number of books and articles, among them his own early essay "It."

7. Indeed, the academic economy is dependent for its continuing existence and operation on a certain relation to heterogeneity and excess. I would therefore agree with Willinsky when, in making a case for the increase in the circulation of scholarship that open access can bring, he writes: "What can seem like an excessive number of studies—which produce nonsignificant results, or serve as pilots for larger studies, or prove blind alleys or false leads—have their way of contributing to the knowledge in a field. There is no way of predicting what will at some point spark another researcher, what will add a missing piece to another's work" (2006, 152–53). Willinsky, however, does not pursue the ethical issues raised by this aspect of his analysis for our ideas of scholarship, knowledge, the discipline, and the institution of the university, preferring instead to couch his argument in moral terms. See, for example, Willinsky (2006, 34) and chapter 4, n. 5. Also see chapter 4 for more on the relation between moralism and politics.

8. Lest my shift to the topic of cognition in this chapter seem a little strange, it is worth noting that, for Weber in *Institution and Interpretation*, "[i]nsofar as the institutional role of the humanities is inseparable from the university, it must also be considered in relation to an element it has often tended, deliberately or not, to exclude from its discourse: that of *cognition*" (1987, 135).

9. Later in his essay, Weber cites Derrida: "This 'internal and impure limit' is what makes iterability not simply *a term* designating an object that is self-contained, structured in and of itself, but rather 'itself' a mark, a divided and decisive part of a movement that no one term can decisively determine, i.e., *terminate*. This is why this particular term refers not so much to a 'structure' as to a 'chain,

since iterability can be supplemented by a variety of terms . . .'" (Derrida 1977, 210; cited by Weber 1978, 9).

Indeed, iterability "must be substituted" or supplemented, for Weber, if it "is to avoid the paradoxical fate of becoming, itself, another form of repetition of the same, even as it seeks to delineate 'the logic that ties repetition to alterity'" (1978, 9).

10. Along with the fact that, as I pointed out in my Introduction (n. 13), a lot of this book first appeared in earlier form as e-mails and listserv postings, this is one modest, "minor" way I have attempted to avoid remaining confined solely to the print mode of legitimation; and thus put the legitimacy of my identity and function as an author at risk in order to reimagine, even if to just a small degree, my own authority and "scholarly enterprise" (see chapter 5).

Perhaps a better sense of my efforts to assume (rather than repeat) the ambivalence in authority that make this book possible can be gained by comparing *Digitize This Book!* to John Willinsky's far broader and somewhat more "properly" scholarly (and thus slightly less provisional, speculative, and playful) text on open access, *The Access Principle* (2006). I say this for all that Willinsky's work seems to make something of a nod toward the digital in being composed (like a database?) of a number of short chapters on discrete but related subjects ("Access," "Politics," "History," and so forth); while *Digitize This Book!* is written as an ink-on-paper book replete with an argument that takes the form of a linearly developed narrative, albeit a "broken" one made up of multiple parts.

Granted, the reader may think this attempt on my part to assume some of the academic and institutional ambivalence that makes my own authority and legitimacy as an author possible is not particularly remarkable or radical by the standards of a lot of work in new media, especially when compared to some of the more avant-garde experiments I referred to in the previous chapter (codework, wikified texts, and so on). If so, I would agree, to a certain extent at least. But before reaching any conclusions, it is worth bearing in mind that my efforts to publish an essay arising out of chapters 2 and 3 of this book in a volume on the work of Samuel Weber met with a great deal of resistance. This came both from one of the peer reviewers and also from one of the editors at the particular press concerned, who objected to it on the grounds that, along with the "constant self-conscious narrative," the "language feels more blog-like."

11. This is the metadata contributors to CSeARCH are asked to supply to allow for reasonably efficient searching across the archive. However, of these, only the title, author, and year of publication are compulsory; the rest are entirely optional. For more details, see my fourth set of metadata, n. 5.

12. Since then, arXiv.org has initiated a system that requires new submitters to supply an endorsement (see chapter 2, n. 23).

4. Antipolitics and the Internet

1. See, for example, Zylinska (2001, 2002, 2005, 2006). My emphasis on ethics here constitutes another important difference between my approach and that of

the majority of those who have written on open access to date, who have tended to make a case for open access in moral rather than ethical terms. See Willinsky (2006, 34) for an example.

2. There are a number of other issues I might have raised with regard to Weber's work. These include: how the "authorial function" is "assumed" and performed in his writing, rather than merely "acted out" (1987, xix), and how it is transgressed and thought differently; as well as the extent to which his own texts can be regarded as "institutional practices of a discipline that assume the ambivalent demarcations that make . . . them possible." But for economy's sake let me limit myself to saying that one of the most interesting aspects of Weber's work is undoubtedly the stress he has placed on the importance of thinking about what he calls "the conditions of *imposability*, the conditions under which arguments, categories, and values impose and maintain a certain authority, even where traditional authority itself is meant to be subverted" (1987, 19).

3. For more, see Richard Poynder's (2007) lengthy interview with Harnad. This interview situates Harnad's philosophy of open access in a much wider context: specifically his conception of the evolution of communication and cognition. For Harnad, open access is an important part of the lead up to a fourth revolution in human cognition and communication, the first three revolutions being those of language, writing, and printing.

4. For some of the problems of positioning the Internet in these terms, see chapter 5 and my reading of Mark Poster's essay "Cyberdemocracy: Internet and the Public Sphere." For more on the issues involved in approaching open access specifically in these terms, see my Conclusion.

5. A useful distinction between the neoliberal and the liberal democratic approaches to politics has, however, been provided by Chantal Mouffe. In the first, which Mouffe designates as the "aggregative," "[i]ndividuals are portrayed as rational beings, driven by the maximization of their own interests and as acting in the political world in a basically instrumental way. It is the idea of the market applied to the domain of politics which is apprehended with concepts borrowed from economics" (2005, 12–13). In the second, which she refers to as the "deliberative," the aim is to establish a connection between morality and politics. Advocates of this version of liberal politics thus "want to replace instrumental rationality by communicative rationality. They present political debate as a specific field of application of morality and believe that it is possible to create in the realm of politics a rational moral consensus by means of free discussion" (2005, 13). Politics here, then, is understood not in terms of economics but morality. Obviously the latter comes closest to describing the versions of liberal politics that we have seen Habermas and Willinsky subscribe to.

6. The nonrivalrous nature of digital objects has significant consequences for more than just capitalism's logic of commodification; it also has implications for any presentation of the ethos of digital culture and the net in terms of "sharing" (the peer-to-peer sharing of music and video files, YouTube's video sharing, Flickr's photosharing, and so on). "Sharing" suggests an economy whereby a singular commodity is owned and possessed by one person as their personal property. It is therefore a commodity that cannot be owned or possessed by

someone else unless it is either exchanged with them for money or some other commodity, or a decision is taken to actively share it. However, we can now see that digital objects are not necessarily singular commodities that *can* be owned and possessed by one person as their personal property in that sense. In many instances they may be better thought of as "gifts" that can be owned and possessed by many people simultaneously, and that can be copied and changed into new objects and stored, reproduced, and gifted again.

The dictionary definitions of "share" and gift" appear to support this view. The former is defined as the "allotted portion of something owned by or distributed among several people," and the latter is the "thing given; action of giving" and "something extremely easy to obtain."

7. Barbrook associates the potlatch, the circulation of gifts, with "tribes in Polynesia" in the "The High-Tech Gift Economy." However, the potlatch ritual is more usually associated with the native peoples of the Pacific Northwest Coast of North America.

8. Tribe and Jana attempt to position New Media art as one of the "few historically significant art movements of the late 20th century" (Tribe in Quaranta 2006). To do so they approach it precisely in terms of preestablished frameworks of knowledge and methods of analysis: they understand and interpret New Media art in terms derived from the art movements of the past such as Dada and Constructivism, of which New Media art for them is merely another instance. "The defining characteristics of art movements, in my view, are: self-definition (the artists tend to use a common term, or set of competing terms, to name their practice); the existence of dedicated organizations, venues, publications, and discourse networks; and a common set of artistic strategies and concerns" (Tribe in Quaranta 2006).

9. Full transcripts of both the "good" and "bad" ads are available at: http://www.duncans.tv/2006/aol-internet-discuss. Accessed 16 June 2007. Copies of both ads are available on YouTube at http://www.youtube.com/?v=EfYVMr_hJ4o. Accessed 16 June 2007.

10. Huffington's own blog, *The Huffington Post*, can be found at http://www.huffingtonpost.com/arianna-huffington. Accessed 8 October 2006. For a different take on the relation between blogging and journalism, see Lovink (2006).

11. Rupert Murdoch, in a speech given to the Worshipful Company of Stationers and Newspaper Makers on 13 March 2006, reported in Owen Gibson (2006, 5). More recent reports have indicated that the number of new blogs may now have reached a plateau, and even gone into decline—especially as most blogs have a short life span, with relatively few still being regularly updated more than six months after their initial appearance online.

12. See "The Abu Ghraib Prison Photos," Anti-war.com, 16 February 2006, available at: http://www.antiwar.com/news/?articleid=2444. Accessed 7 May 2006.

Interestingly, the United States army told its personnel to stop posting video clips on the Web after it was revealed that soldiers were swapping images of deceased Iraqis on the Nowthatsfuckedup.com site for nude pictures of other people's girlfriends. More recently, the Pentagon has gone so far as to introduce new rules requiring all military bloggers to submit their entries to their supervising officers for clearance before posting.

13. See *Illuminations: The Critical Theory Project*, available at: http://www.uta.edu/huma/illuminations.

14. See http://www.moveon.org, http://www.internationalanswer.org, and http://www.unitedforpeace.org.

15. In the United Kingdom the leader of the Conservative Party, David Cameron, recently launched a Web site of video blogs modelled on YouTube called "webcameron," available at: http://www.webcameron.org.uk. Even more recently, after the November 2006 Democratic victory in the United States midterm elections—which Dean is credited as having played a large part in through his revolutionizing of his party's campaigning techniques—the British Labour Party is reported to have engaged Dean to do something similar for them.

16. See http://www.apple.com/itunes/download.

17. See http://www.myspace.com, http://www.youtube.com, http://www.flickr.com, http://www.facebook.com, and http://www.bebo.com. Rather than the managers of these sites creating a standard taxonomy of labels and categories, users are able to categorize the contents themselves in any way they wish; these tags are then adopted by the group or replaced by other more popular, useful, or provocative ones.

18. For a $15-per-month subscription, for instance, YouTube has made a limited version of its Web site available for use on Verizon Wireless phones via a service called V Cast.

19. See http://snubster.com.

20. That said, it is important *not* to present the neoliberal global economy as being "driven exclusively by the information revolution." As Chantal Mouffe makes clear, doing so would deprive neoliberal globalization "of its political dimension" and present it as "a fate to which we all have to submit" (2000, 119).

21. Jodi Dean provides her own variation on this theme in "Communicative Capitalism," sketching the oscillations in the 1990s debate over the character of the Internet as follows: "In the debate, Internet users appeared either as engaged citizens eager to participate in electronic town halls and regularly communicate with their elected representatives, or they appeared as web-surfing waste-of-lives in dark, dirty rooms downloading porn, betting on obscure Internet stocks or collecting evidence of the US government's work with extraterrestrials at Area 51 (Dean 1997). In other versions of this same matrix, users were either innocent children or dreadful war-game playing teenage boys. Good interactions were on Amazon. Bad interactions were underground and involved drugs, kiddie porn, LSD and plutonium" (2005, 68).

22. Robert Young has traced the history of the dialectical structure of cultural criticism through the work of Baudrillard, Jameson, Said, Lyotard, and Lévi-Strauss, to as far back in the past as Arnold, Coleridge, and Burke (1996a).

I will return to say more about the way in which both of these "sides" are implicated in each other as their conditions of possibility, and to provide a specific example, in my Conclusion.

23. See http://creative commons.org.

24. To be sure, it is often hard to see just what *yet* another media and cultural studies reading of a film or TV program in these terms is likely to achieve. That said, the attempt within media and cultural studies to shift away from mere negative critique has a tendency to lead to an often uncritical movement from analyses of the allegedly outdated issues of identity and representation to explorations of the media in terms of the supposedly more up-to-date concept of affect (understood somewhat reductively). Unless it is accompanied by a rigorous consideration of the historical and conceptual aspects of this shift, however, this movement from negative critique to the affirmative possibilities associated with affect all too frequently ends up repeating the same kind of structures and problems it is supposed to provide a means of leaving behind.

25. For more on some of the differences between my position and that of tactical media as outlined by Garcia and Lovink, see chapter 5.

26. As Bassett further notes: "Many, like the unfortunate electronic Zapatistas, have had their moment in a cultural studies sun that, at its worst, does more to warm those who *study* forms of resistance, than it does to contribute to a movement. This works the other way around too, since, in so far as contemporary medium theory and medium practice lionise the 'processual as political,' it is in danger of repeating, albeit in the register of medium specificity rather than in relation to media 'content,' both cultural studies' old fondness for the romance of resistance and its incapacity to register the limits of this resistance. This is neither to disparage theory or tacticalism/hactivism. It is to question certain presumed connections between theory and (creative) practice" (2006, 234).

The emphasis Garcia and Lovink place on hybridity as a way of breaking down and moving beyond such dichotomies does not provide a means of eluding such problems. "One of the most well trodden of tactical routes remains hybridisation," they write, "connecting old with new, the street and the virtual. . . . Taking this route we inevitably arrive at the dialectic free zone of Europe's new politics" (Garcia and Lovink 1999, n.p.). Yet as we know from post-colonial theory, hybdridity can be an extremely problematic concept. Is there not a risk here, for example, of Garcia and Lovink suggesting that *before* they become hybrid, these elements—new, old, street, virtual, artist, scientist, technician, craftsperson, theorist, political activist, and so forth—*are* stable, self-identical, pure, somehow non-hybrid; and thus of hybridity, like pluralism, maintaining the very identity of the elements that it is supposedly being employed to challenge?

In this respect I am also somewhat wary of Garcia and Lovink's claim that by taking such a route they will "inevitably arrive at [a] dialectic free zone." This is quite simply not possible. As I have shown elsewhere with an analysis of Hardt and Negri's *Empire* (2000), to try to replace the dialectic with a new, nondialectical alternative is to remain caught in the dialectic. This is why Derrida insists he has "never *opposed* the dialectic. Be it opposition to the dialectic or war against the dialectic, it's a losing battle. What it really comes down to is thinking a dialecticity of dialectics that is itself fundamentally not dialectical" (Derrida 2001a, 33; cited by G. Hall 2006, 42).

Another way of thinking about this—one that would perhaps be more effective, tactically, given that Garcia and Lovink's tactical media has been positioned as an attempt to follow Deleuze's dictum "Experiment, never interpret" that might "free itself from the dialectic"—is offered by Deleuze's "Postscript on the Societies of Control" (1992). For, to paraphrase Deleuze, if we are acting as if we are free of the dialectic, but the result of this freedom is caught in the dialectic, then there is clearly something wrong with our notion of being free of the dialectic.

27. In 2004 Kurtz, who was working on a project to demystify issues around germ warfare, was arrested and accused by the United States government of bioterrorism, although the government has been unable to produce any evidence to this effect.

28. For instance, some people have recently argued there is a possibility that the tactical media approach may continue to be valid in other places, such as Brazil and India, where by comparison the state's ability to co-opt such tactics of resistance is relatively weak and there is still a sense of leftist political possibility and urgency. See Caetano (2006), and the ensuing discussion thread, archived at http://www.nettime.org.

29. For example, Lovink has already raised many of the points I outline above concerning the marginal, subcultural nature of tactical media in a 2002 text written with Florian Schneider that appears almost as a precursor to Dean's analysis of "communicative capitalism": "What comes after the siege of yet another summit of CEOs and their politicians? How long can a movement grow and stay 'virtual'? . . . Today's movements are in danger of getting stuck in self-satisfying protest mode. . . . The strategy of becoming 'minor' (Guattari) is no longer a positive choice but a default option. . . . What if information merely circles around in its own parallel world? What's to be done if the street demonstration becomes part of the Spectacle? . . . A critical reassessment of the role of arts and culture within today's network society seems necessary. Let's go beyond the 'tactical' intentions of the players involved. The artist-engineer, tinkering on alternative human-machine interfaces, social software or digital aesthetics has effectively been operating in a self-imposed vacuum. Science and business have successfully ignored the creative community. Worse still, artists have been actively sidelined in the name of 'usability.' . . . The younger generation is turning its back on new media arts questions and if involved at all, operate as anticorporate activists" (Lovink and Schneider 2002, n.p.).

For one attempt at a more detailed and hospitable reading of tactical media (very much in relation to notions of responsibility), see Stacey (2006). Stacey has also drawn attention to some of the ambivalence and ambiguity of tactical media, especially in relation to the dichotomy they locate with strategy in de Certeau, arguing that: "[T]he most interesting thing about the theory of tactical media . . . is the extent to which it abandons rather than pays homage to de Certeau. This is particularly apposite to the way it develops the notion of tacticality itself, making 'tactics' not a silent production by reading signs without transforming them, but outlining the ways in which active production can become tactical in contrast to strategic, mainstream media" (Stacey, unpublished correspondence).

30. Barbrook's vision of the radical academic gift economy operating within universities is itself in many respects already an old one. Willinsky, for example, refers to a 1942 essay by the sociologist Robert Merton in which the latter was already pointing out "how '"communism," in the non-technical and extended sense of common ownership of goods,' was integral to the scientific ethos" (Willinsky 2006, 41; citing Merton 1968, 610).

31. Dean's bibliography contains no references to any of Gramsci's writings, while it contains one text by Laclau and another by Laclau and Mouffe. For more on the relation of cultural studies to the work of Laclau and Mouffe, see Valentine (2006) and Bowman (2007).

I would like to stress that my discussion of hegemony and post-hegemony in this chapter is not intended as an engagement with the political theory of Laclau and Mouffe (or any of the other readings of Gramsci and of hegemony that have been provided from within cultural studies for that matter, most notably by Stuart Hall). My focus is rather on the sense in which Dean understands the political in "Communicative Capitalism." For Dean, here—very much contra tactical media, as we have seen—"[s]pecific or singular acts of resistance, statements of opinion or instances of transgression," no matter how many or multiple they are, "are not political in and of themselves; rather, they have to be politicized, that is articulated together with other struggles, resistances and ideals in the course or context of opposition to a shared enemy or opponent" (2005, 57).

32. This is why the situation of communicative capitalism cannot be designated as political, for Dean; not even as a different kind of politics to that associated with her reading of Laclau and Mouffe's theory of hegemony. As Dean recognizes politics solely in terms of hegemonic and counter-hegemonic struggle it can only be "post-political."

33. My argument regarding post-hegemony is thus somewhat different from that of John Beasley-Murray, for instance, who also uses the term. See Beasley-Murray (2001); and also his *Posthegemony: Hegemony, Posthegemony, and Related Matters* blog at http://posthegemony.blogspot.com. For Beasley-Murray, we are currently in a post-hegemonic condition. He cites as visible symptoms of this fact: the end of ideology today; the shift that has taken place from (conscious) discourse to (unconscious) affect; and the coming to the fore of the multitude as the privileged subject of society. As far as I am concerned, however, Beasley-Murray's grand narrative is in its own way as antipolitical as Dean's regarding post-politics. Here, too, a decision is being made in advance: in this case that we *are* most definitely now in a post-hegemonic condition; and that, consequently, whatever the nature of a particular "concrete" situation, it can always best be analyzed, understood, and responded to in terms of what Beasley-Murray refers to as post-hegemony. For me, this appears to be too much the product of Beasley-Murray's own affective investments and will to power-knowledge to be convincing as an explanation of the contemporary conjuncture. What I am arguing is that the contemporary conjuncture needs to be subject to much more careful and rigorous analysis; analysis that remains open to the possibility that, yes, we *may* have entered a post-hegemonic condition, at least in the sense I have described, but also that we *may not have*; and that operates on the basis that the

decision as to whether or not a particular "concrete" situation can be best analyzed, understood, and responded to in terms of hegemonic conflict and the articulation of struggles together with other struggles needs to be taken as responsibily as possible, and certainly not decided in advance.

(The 2007 issue of *Theory, Culture, and Society*, which also discusses post-hegemony, appeared too late for me to engage with it here. See *Theory, Culture, and Society* 24[3] [May].)

34. Without doubt it might make things a whole lot easier if politics *could* confirm to that of the past, and we could all unite in hegemonic struggle. The question is, is politics of this kind (always) possible today? Was it even (always) possible in the past?

35. Toward the beginning of *Dark Fiber*, Geert Lovink provides a list that includes Friedrich Kittler, Siegfried Zielinski, Jean Baudrillard, Paul Virilio, Avital Ronell, Vilém Flusser, and Peter Weibel (1996, 24).

36. We can see this even in relatively sophisticated attempts to analyze the horizontal, decentralized networks of the Internet in terms of Gilles Deleuze and Félix Guattari's (currently highly influential) philosophy of immanence, affect, deterritorialization, lines of flight, and so on from the 1980s.

Matthew Fuller provides a recent instance in *Behind the Blip* (2003). Here Deleuze and Guattari's book *What Is Philosophy?* (1994) is used as "an example of where theoretical work presents us with an opportunity to go further" (Fuller 2003, 18), at the same time that it is acknowledged that electronic media constitutes something of a blind spot or "blockage" when it comes to finding a "useable theorisation of media" in Deleuze and Guattari's work. Fuller locates the "beginnings of a useful [interesting this obsession with usefulness, as we shall see in the chapter that follows] theorisation of electronic media" (2003, 34 n. 22) in Guattari's "Regimes, Pathways, Subjects" (1996), and in the chapter "Machinic Heterogenesis" in Guattari's *Chaosmosis: An Ethico-Aesthetic Paradigm* (1995).

Metadata III. The Specificity of New Media

1. If the shifts identified by Ong (1982) and McLuhan (1964) from oral to written cultures, and then from literacy to printing, are two such periods of "drastic technological changes," then the transformation from print to digital we are currently experiencing is unquestionably a third.

Others have identified further moments of transformation that could be added to this three-part model. They include "the invention of the codex, which, in the first centuries of the common era, enabled the transition from the book which one unrolls to the one in which one turns pages . . . ; the invention of the 'author' in the fourteenth and fifteenth centuries . . .; the invention of copyright . . . in the eighteenth century" (Chartier 1997, 11).

2. The latest to do so is the ARHC. See http://www.eprints.org/signup/fulllist.php. Accessed 10 September 2007.

3. I have argued that the ethos of digital culture and the net may often be better thought of in terms of "gifting" than "sharing." See chapter 4, n. 6.

4. When it comes to digital culture, Poster is by no means alone in having such ideas. Many people have put forward similar hypotheses. These include the German Oekonux debate of 2000–2002 (http://www.oekonux.org), which attempted to develop the principles involved in the production and distribution of free software into a plan for the organization of society (see Lovink and Spehr 2006). Brian Holmes's slogan "open source for the operating systems of the earth," and the associated discussion of "open source as a metaphor for new institutions" in Wainwright et al. (2007); as well as Michael Hardt and Antonio Negri's positioning of the decision-making capacity of the multitude as analogous to the collaborative development of the open-source movement, and their arguing toward the end of *Multitude* for a "society whose source code is revealed so that we can all work collaboratively to solve its bugs and create new, better social programs" (Hardt and Negri 2004, 340).

5. Kathleen Fitzpatrick of The Institute for the Future of the Book is just one of those who has argued for the development of a system of peer-to-peer review (2006a). See also chapter 2, n. 26.

6. As was made clear in chapter 1, there are significant divergences even within peer-to-peer file sharing, not least between those networks that are "pure" or decentralized, those that are semi-centralized, and those that are centralized.

7. For example, one cannot simply transfer the situation regarding open access in the academy over to the decentered electronic distribution of films and argue that all films should be given away for free, too. That would raise a number of difficult policy-related questions, such as that concerned with how those involved in the making of films can earn the money to enable them to do so *and* make a living. Issues of this kind do not arise in the case of the majority of academics, since they tend to be employed to carry out research by their institutions. Which is not to say that the problem of developing a future funding policy for creative laborers cannot be resolved, no matter how "precarious" their work; just that it cannot necessarily be resolved in the same way in the case of film production and distribution as it can for the open-access publication of academic scholarship and research.

8. To provide just a couple of brief examples: in contrast to most other instances of Web 2.0, Wikipedia is controlled and run by a nonprofit organization (the Wikipedia Foundation), is funded primarily through private donations, and releases its content under the GNU General Public License. Much of Web 2.0, including Wikipedia this time, tends to be different again from many peer-to-peer file sharing networks, especially those that are peer-run and pure or decentralized in form, as the latter are distributed, commons-based systems that are not owned or controlled by anyone (but rather everyone). This is why more instances of the former than the latter have been turned into a commodity and bought and sold (see chapter 4). Indeed, some have gone so far as to characterize Web 2.0 as "capitalism's preemptive attack against P2P systems": "Success stories of the transition from Web 1.0 to Web 2.0 were based on the ability for a company to remain monolithic in its . . . ownership of that content, while opening up the method of that content's creation to the community. . . . EBay allows

the community to sell its goods while owning the marketplace for those goods. Amazon . . . succeeded by allowing the community to participate in the 'flow' around their products.

". . . The mission of Web 2.0 is to destroy the P2P aspect of the internet. To make you, your computer, and your internet connection dependent on connecting to a centralised service that controls your ability to communicate. Web 2.0 is the ruin of free, peer-to-peer systems and the return of monolithic 'online services'" (Kleiner and Wyrick 2007, 14–15, 18).

9. See http://secondlife.com and http://www.habbo.com.

10. Similarly, for all the broader cultural connotations associated with the term "open source" in particular, the relations of production and distribution associated with peer-to-peer networks are not necessarily appropriate or applicable to culture, or even digital culture, in general. The open, distributed, participatory, cooperative model works well for some things, less so for others. It has been argued that free software, for instance, "has its strength in building software infrastructure: kernels, file systems, network stacks, compilers, scripting languages, libraries, web, file and mail servers, database engines. It lags behind proprietary offerings . . . in conventional desktop publishing and video editing, and, as a rule of thumb, in anything that isn't highly modularized or used a lot by its own developer community. . . .

"Similar rules seem to apply to free information, respectively 'Open Content' development. The model works best for infrastructural, general, non-individualistic information resources with Wikipedia and FreeDB (and lately MusicBrainz) as prime examples" (Cramer 2006, n.p.).

11. This is a reference to, and play on, N. Katherine Hayles's notion of a "media-specific analysis" (see Hayles 2002, 106; and my first set of metadata). For more on "the singularity of new media," see my fourth set of metadata.

12. As Hayles writes with regard to the database: "A database contains only data that is known and instantiated in a particular form. It does not contain other information expressed in modes of organization foreign to its specific structure." Interestingly, from the point of view of my argument in chapters 2 and 3, Hayles proceeds to add, "nor does [the database] contain anything currently thought but unknown in particular, or even more revealingly, anything that is both unthought and unknown" (2005, n.p.).

This argument also applies to standards for preparing metadata, such as that issued by the Open Archives Initiative, so that texts can be easily indexed and searched across a range of open-access archives, journals, and databases. These standards, too, are never neutral: the specific ways in which metadata is selected, organized, and presented helps to produce (rather than merely passively reflect) what is classified as legitimate scholarship—and even more important, what is not. The fantasy of having one place to search for scholarship and research such as a Universal Search Engine or a Global Archive or Virtual Library of fully integrated, indexed, linked, and jointly searchable academic work must therefore remain precisely that: a (totalizing and totalitarian) fantasy.

This is why, when it comes to uploading material into CSeARCH, contribu-

tors are asked to supply only a minimum amount of metadata, with authors being free to index their submissions however they wish (see my fourth set of metadata, n. 5, for more). It is also why I argue that standards for preparing metadata
should be generated in a plurality of different ways and places. In other words,
rather than adhering to the fantasy of having one single, fully integrated global
archive—even if this is made up of a host of distributed, interoperable, OAI-
compliant repositories that can all nevertheless be centrally harvested and
searched (see n. 14 below)—I would argue instead for a multiplicity of different
and at times also conflicting and even incommensurable open-access archives,
journals, databases and other publishing experiments.

13. This is another way of reading my earlier claim in chapter 2 that academic
authority is *already digitized*; that it is in a sense always already in a similar condition to that which is brought about by the process of digitization.

14. This is Stevan Harnad's argument. Harnad has recently advocated that all
universities make it mandatory for staff to deposit their research in institutional
(OAI-compliant) open-access repositories. He has done so because of the low
rate of deposit to central, subject-based open-access archives. "The trouble is
that—except where mandated—most faculty are 'not' depositing their articles
on their Web pages today, and only a few sub-disciplines are depositing in CRs
[Central Repositories]. Hence OA is only at about 15%. . . .

"Right now, the only two CRs with any appreciable content—Arxiv and
PubMed Central—certainly do have 'higher community salience' than IRs [Insti-
tutional Repositories], since IRs are mostly empty. But Institutions need merely
mandate depositing and the 'salience' of their IRs will sail, along with the size of
their contents" (Harnad 2007c, n.p.).

Of course, for Harnad, no open-access repository need be considered insig-
nificant, regardless of how few deposits it contains. OAI compliance and inter-
operability mean that a multitude of distributed repositories—both large and
small—can be indexed and linked, so that their contents can be located by all
the main harvesters and search engines, including OAIster (http://www.oaister
.org), ROAR (http://roar.eprints.org), and Google (Scholar) (http://scholar
.google.com), to form what is in effect one "global," "virtual archive" of jointly
searchable academic work. Indeed, as far as Harnad is concerned: "In our new
era of distributed, OAI-interoperable Institutional Repositories (IRs), all archives
(IRs) are equal and there is no need for, nor any added benefit whatsoever from
depositing in a central archive like the physics Arxiv (which is now merely one of
the web's many distributed, interoperable OAI archives, all being harvested by
central harvesters). Central harvesting and search is the key, not central depositing and archiving.

"On the contrary, having to found and maintain a different central archive
for every field and every combination of fields would not only be arbitrary and
wasteful in the era of central harvesting and search, but it would also be an
impediment rather than a help in getting all the distributed universities (and
research institutions) to get all their researchers to fill all their own IRs, in all
disciplines, by mandating and managing it, locally. (University Research Insti-

tute output covers all of research space, in all disciplines, and all combinations of disciplines.)" (Harnad 2007d, n.p.).

For Harnad, then, the solution to the problem of the low rate of deposit in most subject-based archives is very much the introduction of institutional mandates. And, as I say, of those currently available Harnad considers the Immediate-Deposit/Optional-Access (ID/OA) mandate proposed and recommended by the European Research Advisory Board to be by far the best (see chapter 1, n. 17).

One concern I have with this particular strategy is that I suspect the majority of IRs will find it difficult to address the radical ethical or political issues that are raised by digitization, for precisely the kind of reasons to do with the maintenance of academic and institutional authority and legitimacy I have been discussing in this book. This is partly why, when it came to CSeARCH, a decision was taken to experiment with building a subject-based archive rather than an institutional one: not just because the potential impact of a local repository would likely be restricted to an individual institution and thus somewhat narrower by comparison (as my fourth set of metadata makes clear, one of the ideas behind CSeARCH has been to place the academic institution or community, or at least that part of it associated with cultural studies, in a position where they are called on to respond and to make ethical and political decisions in this respect); but also because it seemed it would be easier for a subject-based archive—and for a cultural studies archive specifically (see below)—to bring to attention and take on, rather than merely act out, such radical ethical and political issues.

Which is not to say it is *impossible* for IRs to do so. Part of what I am trying to suggest in different ways with *Digitize This Book!* and CSeARCH is that interesting and responsible ethical and political decisions *are* possible in relation to both disciplinary and institutional repositories (or disciplinary repositories within universities), if only the opportunity presented by digitization and open access can be taken. This is another reason I have often referred to "open-access archives" here rather than continually distinguishing between subject or disciplinary archives and local institutional repositories (see my Introduction, n. 29).

15. For one version of the story concerning the difficulties involved in the archiving of Derrida's own work, see Bartlett (2007).

5. HyperCyberDemocracy

1. This is the distinction Richard Rorty proposes in *Contingency, Irony and Solidarity* (1989).

2. JenniCam began as an "experiment" by twenty-year-old student Jennifer Ringley in 1996. The site operated for seven years from 1996 to 2003 and became extremely popular. At one stage, according to Ringley, it was receiving 100 million hits a week.

3. This is how Martin Lister et al. present it when they write about the pre-Web Internet (which is, of course, what Poster was concerned with in "Cyberdemocracy") in their *New Media: A Critical Introduction*: "The essentially participa-

tory and interactive elements of the pre-web Internet clearly suggest attractive homologies with Habermas's description of the idealised public sphere. Newsgroups, bulletin boards and email groups all have the facilitation of group communications as their technological *raison d'être*. . . . The pre-web Internet was essentially about dialogue, a fundamental basis for democratic political systems and culture. . . . The participatory nature of the pre-web Internet also answered some of Habermas's critique of mass media—namely, that the mass media had played a key role in the dissolution of a healthy public sphere by replacing a discourse of critical reason with entertainment and spectacle. Here, in the Internet, was a communication system that demanded not channel-flicking passivity but active engagement and dialogue.

". . . the Internet, through democratising the means of media production, revives the participatory nature of the idealised public sphere. It encourages us to take part in debate and offers us the chance to 'talk back' to the media, creating dialogue instead of passivity" (Lister et al. 2003, 176–77).

4. Salter, for instance, notes how, in *Between Facts and Norms*, "Habermas had rejected much of the cultural dopes approach to media studies" of *Structural Transformation*, "arguing instead that citizens adopt strategies of interpretation against media messages" (2003, 125).

5. Interestingly, this question has also been asked in recent years by Paulo Virno (2004a). However, Poster's insistence on the way in which, on the Internet, the "public" and "external" space of technology is always already a part of the "private," "internal" space of human subjectivity and even the body would appear to raise questions for the "public" aspect of Virno's notion of a new public sphere "outside of" the State, too. Consequently, Poster's analysis is in this respect by far the more radical as far as I am concerned. Indeed, rather than rethinking the concepts of public and private, Virno makes it clear that he believes it is possible to "think of a new link between the two," between the public and the private. In fact, for Virno, it is important that a public sphere in some sense is possible. "If the publicness of intellect does not yield to the realm of a public sphere, of a political space in which the many can tend to common affairs, then it produces terrifying effects. A publicness without a public sphere: here is the negative side—the evil if you wish—of the experience of the multitude" (2004a, 40). For Virno, then, the idea of the public sphere has a crucial role to play in the formation and experience of the multitude.

6. See Gary Hall (1996) for an earlier rehearsal of this reading of Lyotard.

Conclusion. Next-Generation Cultural Studies?

1. For more on the advantages of open access according to Peter Suber, see his "Open Access Overview," available at http://www.earlham.edu/~peters/fos/overview.htm.

2. It would be interesting to explore to what extent this is also part of a larger biopolitical digitization of populations in contemporary society, "in the sense that various numerical, statistical and informatic means of managing and 'regu-

larizing' groups of bodies are being established and widely implemented" (Zylinska forthcoming).

3. Available at http://www.codataweb.org/UNESCOmtg/dryden-declaration
.pdf. Accessed 16 June 2007. I am again grateful to Rachel Wilson of RMIT University in Melbourne for informing me of this document.

Koïchiro Matsuura, Director-General of UNESCO (United Nations Educational, Scientific and Cultural Organization), describes their thinking on the
subject as follows: "Science and education are at the very centre of debates on
the challenges and opportunities of knowledge societies. We face a paradox,
however. On the one hand, the accelerating spread of the Internet and new opportunities for free or low-cost publishing are generating real benefits. On the
other hand, the new economic and technological environment is raising concerns about the erosion of access to certain information and knowledge whose
free sharing facilitated scientific research and education in past decades. . . .

"If knowledge societies capable of generating new knowledge in a cumula-
tive, cooperative and inclusive process are to be created, they need to be based
on a foundation of shared principles, particularly that of equitable access to
education and knowledge. . . .

". . . The public domain principle can be conceptually extended by the
assimilation of 'open access' information made freely available by its rights-
holders without cost. One well-known example of open access is the open source
software license by which computer programs are distributed free of charge by
their authors for exploitation and cooperative development. Another is the vast
amount of documentation produced and made available free of charge by the
United Nations and its specialized agencies. Yet another is the movement of
educational institutions around the world to provide their educational resources
on the Internet free of charge for non-commercial usage, typified by the Open-
CourseWare project of the Massachusetts Institute of Technology. The UNESCO
Draft Recommendation urges Member States and international organizations
to encourage open access solutions, and UNESCO itself is strongly committed
to promoting information-sharing in education, the sciences and culture, and
to disseminating information and software for development under open access
conditions" (2003, n.p.).

4. It should be emphasized, however, that open access does not necessarily
enable all research to be made available to everyone. As we saw in chapter 2,
those versions of open access that rely on established paper journals for peer
review only permit that which is (potentially) publishable in ink-on-paper form
to be made available. They thus again take us back firmly into the economy of
the academic publishing market, as we saw with the example of Google Book
Search.

There is also the delimiting effect of funding. For instance, if only that research which is funded by government agencies, policy institutes, research councils, and so on is mandated to be made available through open access, then
that which is not provided for in this fashion either finds financial support elsewhere, and *is* thus able to appear through open access; or, as is increasingly the
case in the United Kingdom, where universities and academics within them are

being "encouraged" more and more to rely on sources of funding external to their institutions for research support, it risks not being conducted at all, and so obviously is not able to appear through open access. This is especially true of the humanities, which find it notoriously difficult to attract money for research from business and industry. Following on from some of the things I said earlier, one could even go so far as to say that open access helps the state control what research is carried out and what is not.

Be that as it may, the above situation is why, for Harnad, "University OA self-archiving mandates are an essential complement to the researcher funder OA self-archiving mandates": because university "mandates cover unfunded as well as funded research" (Harnad 2007b, n.p.). However, this does not entirely re-solve the problem whereby it may be mainly research approved and funded by government agencies that is made available through open access since, as I say, in the humanities at least—because of the difficulty of attracting funding from business and industry—research that is not funded from these sources is increas-ingly at risk of not being carried out (see G. Hall 2008).

5. In the face of such "disintermediation," many in the publishing industry have of course attempted to defend the "value-added" they continue to perceive publishers as offering, beyond what scholars can achieve themselves. See, for example, Thatcher (1999); and, more recently, the "Statement on Open Access" by the Association of American University Presses (2007), and the "Brussels Dec-laration on STM Publishing" by the International Association of Scientific, Tech-nical and Medical Publishers (2007).

6. This is the specific example of the way in which both of these "sides" are implicated in each other as their conditions of possibility I promised I would return to in chapter 4 (see n. 22).

7. Unless otherwise stated, all quotations are from the online version of Terranova's article, available at http://www.uoc.edu/in3/hermeneia/sala_de_lectura/t_terranova_free_labor.htm. Accessed 7 February 2007.

8. Terranova considers "immaterial labor" a more useful concept than "knowledge worker" on the grounds that the former is not "completely confined to a specific class formation" in the way that the latter has often been. Finding a focus on labor more interesting than a search for "the knowledge class," she cites Maurizio Lazzarato's definition of immaterial labor as referring to: "*two different aspects* of labor.

"On the one hand, as regards the 'informational content' of the commod-ity, it refers directly to the changes taking place in workers' labor processes . . . where the skills involved in direct labor are increasingly skills involving cybernet-ics and computer control (and horizontal and vertical communication). On the other hand, as regards the activity that produces the 'cultural content' of the commodity, immaterial labour involves a series of activities that are not normally recognized as 'work'—in other words, the kinds of activities involved in defin-ing and fixing cultural and artistic standards, fashions, tastes, consumer norms, and, more strategically, public opinion" (Lazzarato 1996, 133; cited by Terranova 2000, n.p.).

Accordingly, Terranova follows Lazzarato in seeing this form of labor power as not being restricted to highly skilled workers; rather it is a "form of activity of every productive subject within postindustrial society," thus problematizing "the idea of the 'knowledge worker' as a class in the 'industrial' sense of the word" (2000, n.p.).

Since part of my intention with *Digitize This Book!* is to engage with the dominant neoliberal language and discourses around the "knowledge economy" when it comes to thinking about the institution of the university and open access (rather than categorize knowledge workers as part of a class), I have preferred to employ the term "knowledge worker" here. However, I would agree with Terranova when she says that "the 'knowledge worker' is a very contested sociological category": partly because "knowledge cannot be exclusively pinned down to specific social segments," so it is difficult to know exactly who qualifies as a "knowledge worker" and who does not; and partly because if the constituent population of the Internet is largely seen as being made up of "knowledge workers" (which for me here it is not), there *is* a risk of implying: "that all we need to know is how to locate the knowledge workers within a 'class,' and knowing which class it is will give us an answer to the political potential of the Net as a whole. Therefore if we can prove that knowledge workers are the avantgarde of labor, then the Net becomes a site of resistance (Barbrook 1998); if we can prove that knowledge workers wield the power in informated societies, then the Net is an extended gated community for the Middle classes (Robins 1996)" (Terranova 2000, n.p.).

9. I am of course not the only one to use the term "hyper" in relation to politics. As we saw in my first set of metadata, and will see again in a little more detail in my fourth, Chantal Mouffe also refers to the undecidability that continues to inhabit the decision as a "hyperpoliticization." What differentiates my perspective from Mouffe's is:

First, the way in which, for me, hyperpoliticization raises questions for a number of aspects of Mouffe's own politics, including the nature of some of the political decisions she makes regarding both hegemony and democracy. See my "Hyper-Cyprus: On Peace and Conflict in the Middle East" (2007b) for more.

Second, the emphasis I place not just on hyperpolitics but on hyperanalysis, too—on that which takes us beyond what can be discerned, discovered, and predicted by means of analysis; and thus on the importance of remaining open to performative affects. (What this means in this case is remaining open to the way the politics of open-access archiving cannot be decided in advance but has to be created and invented by its users in a relation of singularity to finite, "concrete" conjunctions of the "here" and "now.") See my fourth set of metadata, "The Singularity of New Media."

10. For a discussion of the way in which cultural studies continues to think itself in terms of specific disciplinary limits, despite Stuart Hall's claims here that it is not "a discipline in its own right; it never has been, and I don't think it should aspire to be. It defines a field of work" (S. Hall 1998, 191), see my *Culture in Bits* (2002), especially chapter 6.

11. This is why I have turned to Poster's "Cyberdemocracy" in chapter 5 as one way of thinking about the politics of cultural studies. I could perhaps have

performed a similar analysis using more conventional, "mainstream" contemporary cultural studies texts, at least as the latter is understood in its more restricted
sense, in which its origins are perceived as lying primarily in Britain with the
New Left, Stuart Hall and the Birmingham School, and before that with Richard
Hoggart, Raymond Williams, and E. P. Thompson. I would have had to work
harder to do so, though. For, as I say, instead of endeavoring to remain open
to new forms of politics and new ways of being political—precisely the kind of
openness, in fact, that one could argue produced the singular work and ideas
that resulted in the emergence and development of cultural studies in the first
place—cultural studies has too often resorted to the fetishization of the politics
associated with its "founding" thinkers, their followers and interpreters, and its
established canon of texts. (All of which is very much in accordance, of course,
with the way in which, following Weber, we have seen how a "discipline" attempts
to overcome the inherently violent, aporetic, and paradoxical nature of its foundation by producing a founding set of principles and procedures for the institution and reproduction of itself and its original guiding idea.)

12. For more on this, see my fourth set of metadata, "The Singularity of New
Media."

13. Hence the way it has previously been possible for me to produce careful readings of certain privileged texts in the cultural studies tradition—by Raymond Williams, Stuart Hall, Meaghan Morris, and Angela McRobbie—readings
that reveal them in their different ways as producing experimental and inventive
interrogations of what it is to be political that are hyperpolitical in that they are
more than political while still being political. See G. Hall (2002; 2004b; 2006).

14. Lyotard of course was not thinking of this in terms of producing a new
form of Habermasian public sphere. Lyotard is in fact very critical of Habermas
in *The Postmodern Condition*, especially the notion that the "goal of dialogue is
consensus"; Lyotard preferred to emphasize dissensus instead (Lyotard 1984,
65, 61).

Metadata IV. The Singularity of New Media

1. For a brief account of some of the differences between my perspective and
that of Mouffe's in respect to hyperpolitics, see my Conclusion, n. 9.

2. Ethics comes first here—i.e., the question is whether ethics can found a
politics and not whether a politics can found ethics—because ethics, for Levinas,
is foundational. It is a first philosophy that precedes ontology (see chapter 2,
n. 9). So, since ethics precedes ontology, it also precedes politics.

3. An ethics of hospitality cannot simply found a politics, then. But as Joanna
Zylinska notes, and as I have being trying to emphasize throughout this book,
what such a Levinasian understanding of ethics "can help us with when it comes
to developing a politics of cultural studies," and of a cultural studies open-access
archive, "is the recognition that the other is always already moral, and thus that
our politics cannot be thought without or outside ethics" (Zylinska 2005, 11).

4. For more on this aspect of Derrida's thought, see his discussion of deci-
sionism in the work of Carl Schmitt in *Politics of Friendship* (1997). For more spe-

cifically on the difficulty of distinguishing ethics from politics, see Bennington (2000), where he writes: "if the third part makes possible the ethical relation as such by instigating an originary and necessary contamination of its purity, then the defining feature of the ethical (the dual figure of the face-to-face, however asymmetrical) tends to be lost in the perspective of a multiplicity of relations introduced by the opening to the third party in general. In which case we might want to say that we are as much in the domain of politics as of ethics" (Bennington 2000, 45).

5. At the moment, when uploading into CSeARCH, contributors are asked to supply a minimum amount of metadata to allow for reasonably efficient searching across the archive: title, author, publication, year of publication, subject area, abstract or description, format or [peer review] status, keywords. Of these, only the title, author, and year of publication are compulsory; the rest are entirely optional. Moreover, although suggestions are provided in an accompanying "help box" that can be viewed by clicking on the question mark at the right-hand side of each section of the submission form, none comes with a compulsory vocabulary. Authors are free to index their submissions in any way they wish.

The idea behind author indexing in such an open way is to encourage, indeed require, contributors to make a decision as to how their work is to be identified, classified, and understood.

I prefer not to think about the manner in which such author indexing systems emerge in the process of actually building and using the archive in terms of what are today often described as "folksonomies." For me, the concept of folksonomies leaves the traditional model for generating taxonomies—the underlying system by which metadata organizes, structures, and presents knowledge—more or less intact, with the hierarchy merely being reversed, from top-down to bottom-up.

6. See chapter 2, n. 26.

7. That said, I am aware that all this creates a rather difficult situation: both because it is impossible to have an institution with no rules; and because my own ethical investments or political commitments do not disappear, even if I often attempt to keep them "veiled" when acting for and as part of the Cultural Studies e-Archive project. This tension is inevitable, though, and it is something which we—as scholars, teachers, and students—experience all the time.

8. For a rehearsal of these ideas in a slightly different context, see G. Hall (2004b).

BIBLIOGRAPHY

Abrahams, Paul, and James Harding. 2002. "The Digital Divide." *Financial Times,* 21 May.

Acland, Charles R., ed. 2007. *Residual Media.* Minneapolis and London: University of Minnesota Press.

Agamben, Giorgio. 2005. *State of Exception.* Translated by Kevin Attell. Chicago: University of Chicago Press.

Aldred, Nannette, and Martin Ryle, eds. 1999. *Teaching Culture: The Long Revolution in Cultural Studies.* Leicester, Eng.: The National Organisation for Adult Learning.

Allen, Katie. 2006a. "Digital Downer: Piracy Hits CD Sales." *The Guardian,* 14 October.

———. 2006b. "No More Big Spenders as Teenagers Switch to File-Sharing." *The Guardian,* 31 October.

Antelman, Kristen. 2004. "Do Open-Access Articles Have a Greater Research Impact?" *College and Research Libraries* 65. Available at: http://www.lib.ncsu.edu/staff/kantelman/do_open_access_CRL.pdf. Accessed 16 June 2007.

Arnold, Matthew. 1868. *Culture and Anarchy.* Cambridge, Eng.: Cambridge University Press, 1932.

Aronowitz, Stanley. 2000. *The Knowledge Factory: Dismantling the Corporate University and Creating True Higher Learning.* Boston: Beacon Press.

Association of American University Presses. 2007. "Statement on Open Access." 27 February. Available at: http://aaupnet.org/aboutup/issues/oa/statement.pdf. Accessed 4 June 2007.

Baker, Nicholson. 2002. *Double Fold: Libraries and the Assault on Paper.* London: Vintage.

Barbaro, Michael. 2006. "Wal-Mart Enlists Bloggers in P.R. Campaign." *New York Times,* 7 March. Available at: http://www.nytimes.com/2006/03/07/technology/07blog.html?_r=1&th&emc=th&oref=slogin.

Barbrook, Richard. 1998. "The High-Tech Gift Economy." *First Monday* 3. Available at: http://www.firstmonday.org/issues/issue3_12/barbrook/. Updated and republished in 2005. *First Monday* (December). Available at: http://www.nettime.org/Lists-Archives/nettime-l-9810/msg00122.html. Republished in *Readme! Filtered by Nettime: ASCII Culture and the Revenge of Knowledge,* Josephine Bosma et al., 1999. Brooklyn, N.Y.: Autonomedia.

———. 2002. "The Napsterization of Everything." *Science as Culture* 11(2) (June).

Barbrook, Richard, and Andy Cameron. 1995. "The Californian Ideology." *Mute*

3 (Autumn). Available at: http://www.hrc.wmin.ac.uk/theory-californian ideology-mute.html. Accessed 6 November 2006.

Barlow, J.P. 1998. *Cybernomics: Toward a Theory of the Information Economy.* New York: Merrill Lynch.

Barthes, Roland. 1968. "The Death of the Author." In *Image, Music, Text.* Translated by Stephen Heath. London: Flamingo, 1984.

Bartlett, Thomas. 2007. "Archive Fever." *Chronicle of Higher Education,* 20 July. Available at: http://chronicle.com/free/v53/i46/46a00801.htm. Accessed 23 July 2007.

Bassett, Caroline. 2006. "Cultural Studies and New Media." In *New Cultural Studies: Adventures in Theory,* ed. Gary Hall and Clare Birchall. Edinburgh: Edinburgh University Press.

Beasley-Murray, John. 2001. "Subaltern Politics: Solidarity and Critique (or, Four Theses on Posthegemony)." Paper presented at the Latin American Studies Association Congress, Washington, D.C., 8 September. Available at: http://www.art.man.ac.uk/SPANISH/staff/Writings/subaltern.pdf. Accessed 22 June 2006.

Bellamy, Craig. 2002. "The Milk Bar Challenge." Posted on the fibreculture mailing list, 22 July. Archived at http://www.fibreculture.org.

Benjamin, Walter. 1973. "The Work of Art in the Age of Mechanical Reproduction." In *Illuminations,* ed. Hannah Arendt. Translated by Harry Zohn. London: Fontana.

Bennington, Geoffrey. 1990. "Postal Politics and the Institution of the Nation." In *Nation and Narration,* ed. Homi K. Bhabha. London: Routledge.

———. 2000. "Deconstruction and Ethics." In *Interrupting Derrida.* London: Routledge.

Bhabha, Homi K. 1994. "The Commitment to Theory." In *The Location of Culture.* London: Routledge.

Black, Edwin. 2001. *IBM and the Holocaust: The Strategic Alliance between Nazi Germany and America's Most Powerful Corporation.* London: Time Warner.

Bolter, Jay David. 1991. *Writing Space: The Computer, Hypertext, and the History of Writing.* Hillsdale, N.J.: Lawrence Erlbaum.

Bowker. 2006. "U.S. Book Production Plummets 18K in 2005; Smaller Publishers Show the Largest Drop in New Titles." Available at: http://www.bowker.com/press/bowker/2006_0509_bowker.htm. Accessed 18 May 2007.

Bowman, Paul. 2006a. "Cultural Studies and Slavoj Žižek." In *New Cultural Studies: Adventures in Theory,* ed. Gary Hall and Clare Birchall. Edinburgh: Edinburgh University Press.

———. 2006b. "Street Fetishism: Ten Theses on Street Politics." Unpublished essay. Available in CSeARCH at: http://rime.tees.ac.uk/VLE/DATA/CSEARCH/MODULES/CS/2006/03/0119/_.docCSeARCH. Accessed 6 November 2006.

———. 2007. *Post-Marxism versus Cultural Studies: Theory, Politics and Intervention.* Edinburgh: Edinburgh University Press.

Breen, Marcus. 2006. "Is There a Cultural Studies Imperative?" *Cultural Currents* 3 (September).

Brown, Wendy. 2001. *Politics Out of History.* London and Princeton, N.J.: Princeton University Press.

Budapest Open Access Initiative. 2002–2004. *Self-Archiving FAQ.* Available at: http://www.eprints.org/openaccess/self-faq/. Accessed 15 March 2008.

Butt, Danny, and Ned Rossiter. 2002. "Blowing Bubbles: Post-Crash Creative Industries and the Withering of Political Critique in Cultural Studies." Paper presented at "Ute Culture: The Utility of Culture and the Uses of Cultural Studies," the Cultural Studies Association of Australia Conference, University of Melbourne, 5–7 December. Posted on the nettime mailing list, 10 December 2002. Available at: http://www.nettime.org/Lists-Archives/nettime-1-0212/msg00057.html.

Bush, George W., and Tony Blair. 2006. "President Bush and Prime Minister Tony Blair of the United Kingdom Participate in Joint Press Availability." White House Web site, 25 May. Available at: http://www.whitehouse.gov/news/releases/2006/05/20060525-12.html. Accessed 16 June 2007.

Caetano, Miguel Afonso. 2006. "Technologies of Resistance: Transgression and Solidarity in Tactical Media." Posted on the nettime mailing list, 30 May 2006. Available at: http://osdir.com/ml/culture.internet.nettime/2006-05/msg00070.html.

Cassy, John. 2003. "Pirates Turn Down the Music." *The Guardian,* 11 February.

Castells, Manuel. 1996. *The Power of Identity.* Cambridge, Eng.: Blackwell.

Centre for Intellectual Property Policy and Management at the University of Bournemouth. 2007. "Counting the Cost of a Writing Career." Available at: http://www.bournemouth.ac.uk/newsandevents/News/march07/counting_the_cost_of_a_writing_career.html. Accessed 12 March 2007.

Cha, Ray. 2006. "Now Playing: Academics in the Role of the Public Intellectual." Posted on the Institute for the Future of the Book's if:book blog, 1 August. Available at: http://www.futureofthebook.org/blog/. Accessed 2 August 2006.

Chartier, Roger. 1997. "The End of the Reign of the Book." *SubStance* 82.

Chun, Wendy Hui Kyong. 2006. "Introduction: Did Somebody Say New Media?" In *New Media, Old Media: A History and Theory Reader,* eds. Wendy Hui Kyong Chun and Thomas Keenan. London and New York: Routledge.

Clark, Timothy. 1999. "Literary Values: Institutional Force." *Culture Machine* 1. Available at: http://www.culturemachine.net.

———. 2005. "Freedoms and the Institutional Americanism of Literary Study." In *The Poetics of Singularity: The Counter-Culturalist Turn in Heidegger, Derrida, Blanchot and the Later Gadamer.* Edinburgh: Edinburgh University Press.

Covey, Denise Troll. 2005. *Acquiring Copyright Permission to Digitize and Provide Open Access to Books.* Washington, D.C.: Digital Library Federation and the Council on Library and Information Resources. Available at: http://www.clir.org/pubs/reports/pub134/pub134col.pdf.

Cramer, Florian. 2006. "The Creative Common Misunderstanding." Posted on the nettime mailing list, 9 October. Available at: http://osdir.com/ml/culture.internet.nettime/2006-10/msg00029.html.

Critical Art Ensemble. 2001. *Digital Resistance: Explorations in Tactical Media.* New York: Autonomedia.

Dean, Jodi. 1997. "Virtually Citizens." *Constellations* 4(2) (October).

———. 2005. "Communicative Capitalism: Circulation and the Foreclosure of Politics." *Cultural Politics* 1(1).

Deleuze, Gilles. 1992. "Postscript on the Societies of Control." *October* 59 (Winter).

Deleuze, Gilles, and Félix Guattari. 1994. *What Is Philosophy?.* Translated by Graham Birchill and Hugh Tomlinson. London: Verso.

Deleuze, Gilles, and Claire Parnet. 2002. *Dialogues II.* Translated by Hugh Tomlinson and Barbara Habberjam. London: Athlone.

Derrida, Jacques. 1977. "Limited Inc." *Glyph* 2.

———. 1979. *Spurs: Nietzsche's Styles.* Translated by Barbara Harlow. Chicago: University of Chicago Press.

———. 1981. *Dissemination.* Translated by Barbara Johnson. London: Athlone.

———. 1982a. "Signature Event Context." In *Margins of Philosophy.* Translated by Alan Bass. London: Harvester Wheatsheaf.

———. 1982b. *Margins of Philosophy.* Translated by Alan Bass. London: Harvester Wheatsheaf.

———. 1983. "The Principle of Reason: The University in the Eyes of Its Pupils." *Diacritics* 13 (Fall). Reprinted in Jacques Derrida, 2004, *Eyes of Philosophy: Right to Philosophy* 2. Translated by Jan Plug et al. Stanford, Calif.: Stanford University Press.

———. 1990. "Sends Offs." *Yale French Studies* 77: *Reading the Archive: On Texts and Institutions.* Reprinted in Jacques Derrida, 2004, *Eyes of Philosophy: Right to Philosophy* 2. Translated by Jan Plug et al. Stanford, Calif.: Stanford University Press.

———. 1992a. "Mochlos; or, The Conflict of the Faculties." In *Logomachia: The Conflict of the Faculties,* ed. Richard Rand. Lincoln and London: University of Nebraska Press. Reprinted in Jacques Derrida, 2004, *Eyes of Philosophy: Right to Philosophy* 2. Translated by Jan Plug et al. Stanford, Calif.: Stanford University Press.

———. 1992b. " 'This Strange Institution Called Literature': An Interview with Jacques Derrida." In *Acts of Literature,* ed. Derek Attridge. London: Routledge.

———. 1994a. *Specters of Marx: The State of the Debt, the Work of Mourning, and the New International.* Translated by Peggy Kamuf. London: Routledge.

———. 1994b. "The Rhetoric of Drugs." In *Points . . . Interviews, 1974–1994.* Translated by Peggy Kamuf et al. Stanford, Calif.: Stanford University Press.

———. 1996a. "Remarks on Deconstruction and Pragmatism." In *Deconstruction and Pragmatism,* ed. Chantal Mouffe. London: Routledge.

———. 1996b. *Archive Fever: A Freudian Impression.* Translated by Eric Prenowitz. Chicago: University of Chicago Press.

———. 1997. *Politics of Friendship.* Translated by George Collins. New York and London: Verso.

————. 1999. *Adieu to Emmanuel Levinas.* Translated by Michael Naas and Pascalle-Anne Brault. Stanford, Calif.: Stanford University Press.

————. 2000. *Of Hospitality.* Translated by Rachel Bowlby. Stanford, Calif.: Stanford University Press.

————. 2001a. "I Have a Taste for the Secret." In *A Taste for the Secret,* ed. Jacques Derrida and Maurizio Ferraris. Translated by Giacomo Donis. Cambridge, Eng.: Polity.

————. 2001b. "On Forgiveness." In *On Cosmopolitanism and Forgiveness.* Translated by Mark Dooley and Michael Hughes. London: Routledge.

————. 2001c. "The Future of the Profession or the University Without Condition (Thanks to the 'Humanities' What *Could Take Place* Tomorrow)." In *Jacques Derrida and the Humanities: A Critical Reader,* ed. Tom Cohen. Cambridge, Eng.: Cambridge University Press.

————. 2001d. "Affirmative Deconstruction, Inheritance, Technology." In *Deconstruction Engaged: The Sydney Seminars,* ed. Paul Patton and Terry Smith. Sydney, Australia: Power Publications.

————. 2002a. *Who's Afraid of Philosophy? Right to Philosophy 1.* Translated by Jan Plug. Stanford, Calif.: Stanford University Press.

————. 2002b. "Declarations of Independence." In *Negotiations: Interventions and Interviews, 1971–2001.* Edited and translated by Elizabeth Rottenberg. Stanford, Calif.: Stanford University Press.

————. 2004. *Eyes of Philosophy: Right to Philosophy 2.* Translated by Jan Plug et al. Stanford, Calif.: Stanford University Press.

————. 2005. *Paper Machine.* Translated by Rachel Bowlby. Stanford, Calif.: Stanford University Press.

————. 2006. *Geneses, Genealogies, Genres and Genius: The Secrets of the Archive.* Translated by Beverley Bie Brahic. Edinburgh: Edinburgh University Press.

Derrida, Jacques, and Bernard Stiegler. 2002. *Echographies of Television: Filmed Interviews.* Translated by Jennifer Bajorek. London: Polity.

Dietz, Steve. 1999. "Memory_Archive_Database." *Switch,* 3.0. Available at: http:// switch.sjsu.edu/web/v5n3/C-1.html. Accessed 23 September 2006.

Directgov. 2006. "Death of the Surfer . . . Birth of the Supersite." Press release, 6 March. Available at: http://archive.cabinetoffice.gov.uk/e-government/ docs/direct_gov/final_tickbx_pr_release.pdf.

Donald, James. 2004. "What's New? A Letter to Terry Flew." *Continuum: Journal of Media and Cultural Studies* 18(2) (June).

Du Gay, Paul, and Michael Pryke. 2002. *Cultural Economy.* London: Sage.

Edu-factory collective. 2007. "edu-factory.org manifesto." Available at: http:// www.edu-factory.org. Accessed 24 February 2007.

Eisenstein, Elizabeth. 1979. *The Printing Press as an Agent of Change: Communications and Cultural Transformations in Early Modern Europe.* 2 vols. Cambridge, Eng.: Cambridge University Press.

Elam, Diane. 2000. "Why Read?" *Culture Machine* 2. Available at: http://www .culturemachine.net.

Evans, Matthew. 2002. Talk presented at "The New Information Order and the

Future of the Archive" conference of The Institute for Advanced Studies in the Humanities, at the University of Edinburgh, 22 March.

Eysenbach, Gunther. 2006. "Citation Advantage of Open Access Articles." *PLoS Biology,* 4(5): e157. Available at: http://dx.doi.org/10.1371/journal .pbio.0040157. Accessed 16 June 2007.

Finkelstein, David, and Alistair McCleery. 2005. *An Introduction to Book History.* New York: Routledge.

Fitzpatrick, Kathleen. 2006a. "On the Future of Academic Publishing, Peer Review, and Tenure Requirements." *The Valve,* 6 January. Available at: http://www .thevalve.org/go/valve/article/on_the_future_of_academic_publishing_ peer_review_and_tenure_requirements_or/. Accessed 9 October 2006.

———. 2006b. "Introducing MediaCommons," Posted on the Institute for the Future of the Book's if:book blog, 17 July. Available at: http://www.future ofthebook.org/blog/archives/2006/07/introducing_mediacommons_or_ ti.html. Accessed 10 August 2006.

———. 2006c. "On the Future of Peer Review in Electronic Scholarly Publishing." Posted on the Institute for the Future of the Book's if:book blog, 28 June. Available at: http://www.futureofthebook.org/blog/archives/2006/06/on_ the_future_of_peer_review_i.html. Accessed 2 August 2006.

Flew, Terry. 2004. "Creativity, the 'New Humanism' and Cultural Studies." *Continuum: Journal of Media and Cultural Studies* 18(2) (June).

———. 2005. "Is Cultural Studies Inherently Left-Wing?" Posted on the CSAA discussion list, 5 January. Archived at: http://lists.cdu.edu.au/mailman/ listinfo/csaa-forum. Available at: http://lists.cdu.edu.au/pipermail/csaa-forum/Week-of-Mon-20050117/000628.html.

Foster, Hal. 1996. "The Archive Without Museums." *October* 77 (Summer).

Foucault, Michel. 1972. *The Archaeology of Knowledge.* Translated by A. M. Sheridan Smith. London and New York: Tavistock Publications.

Frabetti, Federica. 2007. "Technology Made Legible: A Cultural Study of Software as a Form of Writing in the Theories and Practices of Software Engineering." Unpublished paper presented at the "Re-mediating Literature" conference, University of Utrecht, 4–6 July.

Fuller, Matthew. 2003. *Behind the Blip: Essays on the Culture of Software.* New York: Autonomedia.

Fynsk, Christopher. 2004. *The Claim of Language: A Case for the Humanities.* Minneapolis and London: University of Minnesota Press.

Garcia, David, and Geert Lovink. 1997. "The ABC of Tactical Media." Posted on the nettime mailing list, 16 May. Archived at: http://www.nettime.org. Also available at: http://subsol.c3.hu/subsol_2/contributors2/garcia-lovinktext .html.

———. 1999. "The DEF of Tactical Media." Posted on the nettime mailing list, 22 February. Available at: http://www.nettime.org/Lists-Archives/nettime-l-9902/msg00104.html.

———. 2001. "The GHI of Tactical Media: An Interview with Andreas Broeckmann." Posted on the nettime mailing list, 16 August. Available at: http:// www.nettime.org/Lists-Archives/nettime-l-0108/msg00060.html. Also published in *Artnodes*, Universitat Oberta de Catalunya (UOC), December 2002. Available at: http://www.uoc.edu/artnodes/eng/art/broeckmann0902/ broeckmann0902.html.

Garnham, Nicholas. 1992. "The Media and the Public Sphere." In *Habermas and the Public Sphere*, ed. Craig Calhoun. Cambridge, Mass.: MIT Press.

———. 1995. "Political Economy and Cultural Studies: Reconciliation or Divorce?" *Critical Studies in Mass Communications* 12(1). Reprinted as Nicholas Garnham, 1997, "Political Economy and the Practice of Cultural Studies," in *Cultural Studies in Question*, ed. Marjorie Ferguson and Peter Golding. London: Sage.

Garrido, Mario, and Alexander Halavais. 2003. "Mapping Networks of Support for the Zapatista Movement: Applying Social-Networks Analysis to Study Contemporary Social Movements." In *Cyberactivism: Online Activism in Theory and Practice*, ed. Martha McCaughey and Michael D. Ayers. London: Routledge.

Garside, Ryan. 2006. "RIAA Forced to Drop Download Case." *bit-tech.net*, 1 August. Available at: http://www.bit-tech.net/news/2006/08/01/RIAA_forced_ to_drop_download_case/. Accessed 12 August 2006.

Gibson, Ian. 2004. "Scientific Publications: Free For All?" *House of Commons Science and Technology Committee*, 20 July. Available at: http://www.publications. parliament.uk/pa/cm200304/cmselect/cmsctech/399/399.pdf. Accessed 16 June 2007.

Gibson, Owen. 2006. "Internet Means End for Media Barons, Says Murdoch." *The Guardian*, 14 March.

Gitelman, Lisa, and Geoffrey B. Pingree, eds. 2003. *New Media, 1740–1915*. Cambridge, Mass.: MIT Press.

Giroux, Henry A. 1988. *Teachers as Intellectuals: Toward a Critical Pedagogy of Learning*. Granby, Mass.: Bergin and Garvey.

Giroux, Henry, and Kostas Myrsiades, eds. 2001. *Beyond the Corporate University: Culture and Pedagogy in the New Millennium*. New York and Oxford: Rowman and Littlefield.

Graham, Phil. 2002a. "Hypercapitalism: Language, New Media, and Social Perceptions of Value." *Discourse and Society* 13(2).

———. 2002b. "Hypercapitalism: A Political Economy of Informational Idealism." *New Media and Society* 2(2). Available at: http://www.philgraham.net/ HC1.pdf. Accessed 28 November 2006.

Gray, John. 2005. "Mimic, Missionary and a Master of Media Spin." *The Times Higher Education Supplement*, 8 April.

Greenblatt, Stephen. 2002. "Call for Action on Problems in Scholarly Book Publishing: A Special Letter from the President." *MLA Documents and Reports*, 28 May. Available at: http://www.mla.org/scholarly_pub. Accessed 16 June 2007.

Gregg, Melissa. 2002. "Cultural Studies and Online Innovation." Posted on the fibreculture mailing list, 12 December. Archived at http://www.fibreculture .org.

———. 2006. *Cultural Studies' Affective Voices*. Basingstoke, Hampshire, Eng.: Palgrave Macmillan.

Grossberg, Lawrence. 1995. "Cultural Studies and Political Economy: Is Anyone Else Bored with This Debate?" *Critical Studies in Mass Communications* 12(1). Revised and reprinted as Lawrence Grossberg, 1997, "Introduction: 'Birmingham' in America?," in *Bringing It All Back Home: Essays on Cultural Studies.* Durham and London: Duke University Press.

———. 2005a. *Caught in the Crossfire: Kids, Politics and America's Future.* Boulder, Col., and London: Paradigm.

———. 2005b. "Cultural Studies, the War Against Kids, and the Re-becoming of U.S. Modernity." In *Race, Identity and Representation in Education,* ed. Cameron McCarthy, Warren Crichlow, Greg Dimitriadis, and Nadine Dolby, 2nd ed. New York: Routledge.

Guattari, Félix. 1995. *Chaosmosis: An Ethico-Aesthetic Paradigm.* Translated by Paul Bains and Julian Pefanis. Sydney, Australia: Power Publications.

———. 1996. "Regimes, Pathways, Subjects." In *The Guattari Reader,* ed. Gary Genesko. Oxford: Blackwell.

Guédon, Jean-Claude. 2004. "The 'Green' and the 'Gold' Roads to Open Access: The Case for Mixing and Matching." *Serials Review* 30(4).

Guédon, Jean-Claude (with Guylaine Beaudry for the section on SGML). 1996. "Meta-Surfaces or Ends and Means to Grow a Viable Electronic Scholarly Journal." *Surfaces.* Available at: http://pum12.pum.umontreal.ca/revues/surfaces/meta-surfaces.html#AII. Accessed 9 April 2002.

Habermas, Jürgen. 1962. *The Structural Transformation of the Public Sphere: An Inquiry into a Category of Bourgeois Society.* Translated by Thomas Burger. London: Polity Press, 1989.

———. 1986. *The Theory of Communicative Action,* Vol. 1, *Reason and the Rationalization of Society.* Translated by Thomas McCarthy. Cambridge, Eng.: Polity Press.

———. 1989. *The Theory of Communicative Action,* Vol. 2, *Lifeworld and System: A Critique of Functionalist Reason.* Translated by Thomas McCarthy. Cambridge, Eng.: Polity Press.

———. 1996. *Between Facts and Norms.* Translated by William Rehg. London: Polity Press.

Hall, Gary. 1996. "Answering the Question: 'What Is an Intellectual?'" *Surfaces* 6. Available at: http://pum12.pum.umontreal.ca/revues/surfaces/vol6/hall.html.

———. 2002. *Culture in Bits: The Monstrous Future of Theory.* London and New York: Continuum.

———. 2003. "The Cultural Studies e-Archive Project (Original Pirate Copy)." *Culture Machine* 5. Available at: http://www.culturemachine.net.

———. 2004a. "Digitize This." *The Review of Education, Pedagogy and Cultural Studies* 26(1) (January–March).

———. 2004b. "Why You Can't Do Cultural Studies *and* Be a Derridean: Cultural Studies after Birmingham, the New Social Movements and the New Left." *Culture Machine* 6. Available at: http://www.culturemachine.net.

———. 2006. "Cultural Studies and Deconstruction." In *New Cultural Studies: Ad-*

ventures in Theory, eds. Gary Hall and Clare Birchall. Edinburgh: Edinburgh University Press.

————. 2007a. "IT, Again: How to Build an Ethical Virtual Institution." In *Experimenting: Essays with Samuel Weber*, ed. Simon Morgan Wortham and Gary Hall. New York: Fordham University Press.

————. 2007b. "Hyper-Cyprus: On Peace and Conflict in the Middle East." Talk presented at "Communication in Peace/Conflict in Communication," Second International Conference in Communication and Media Studies, Eastern Mediterranean University, Famagusta, North Cyprus, 2–4 May 2007. Revised and published as "WikiNation: On Peace and Conflict in the Middle East." *Cultural Politics* (forthcoming).

————. 2008. "Coca-colonised Thinking?" *The Oxford Literary Review*, 28.

Hall, Gary, and Clare Birchall. 2006a. "New Cultural Studies: Adventures in Theory (Some Comments, Clarifications, Explanations, Observations, Recommendations, Remarks, Statements and Suggestions)." In *New Cultural Studies: Adventures in Theory*, eds. Gary Hall and Clare Birchall. Edinburgh: Edinburgh University Press.

————, eds. 2006b. *New Cultural Studies: Adventures in Theory*. Edinburgh: Edinburgh University Press.

Hall, Stuart. 1992. "Cultural Studies and Its Theoretical Legacies." In *Cultural Studies*, ed. Lawrence Grossberg, Cary Nelson, and Paula Treichler. New York: Routledge.

————. 1998. "Cultural Composition: Stuart Hall on Ethnicity and the Discursive Turn." *Journal of Composition Theory* 18(2).

————. 2003. "New Labour's Double-Shuffle." *Soundings* 24.

Hall, Stuart, Charles Critcher, Tony Jefferson, et al. 1978. *Policing the Crisis: Mugging, the State, and Law and Order*. London: Macmillan.

Hardt, Michael, and Antonio Negri. 2000. *Empire*. Cambridge, Mass., and London: Harvard University Press.

————. 2004. *Multitude: War and Democracy in the Age of Empire*. Harmondsworth, Eng.: Penguin.

Harmon, Amy. 2002. "CD Technology Stops Copies, But It Starts a Controversy." *New York Times*, 1 March.

Harnad, Stevan. 1994a. "I. Overture: The Subversive Proposal." In *Scholarly Journals at the Crossroads: A Subversive Proposal for Electronic Publishing: An Internet Discussion about Scientific and Scholarly Journals and Their Future*, ed. Ann Shumelda Okerson and James J. O'Donnell. Washington, D.C.: Association of Research Libraries, June 1995. Available at: http://www.arl.org/scomm/subversive/toc.html.

————. 1994b. "VI: Reprise." In *Scholarly Journals at the Crossroads: A Subversive Proposal for Electronic Publishing: An Internet Discussion about Scientific and Scholarly Journals and Their Future*, ed. Ann Shumelda Okerson and James J. O'Donnell. Washington, D.C.: Association of Research Libraries, June 1995. Available at: http://www.arl.org/scomm/subversive/sub06.html.

————. 1998/2000. "The Invisible Hand of Peer Review." *Nature*. 5 November

1998. Available at: http://helix.nature.com/webmatters/invisible/invisible
.html. Also available in *Exploit Interactive* 5, April 2000. Available at: http://www
.exploit-lib.org/issue5/peer-review; http://www.cogsci.soton.ac.uk/~harnad/
nature2.html; and http://www.princeton.edu/~harnad/nature2.html.

———. 2001/2003. "For Whom the Gate Tolls? How and Why to Free the Refereed Research Literature Online Through Author/Institution Self-Archiving, Now." Available at: http://www.ecs.soton.ac.uk/~harnad/Tp/resolution
.htm.

———. 2007a. "EURAB's Proposed OA Mandate: Strongest of the 20 Adopted
and 5 Proposed So Far." Posted on *Open Access Archivangelism*, 15 January.
Available at: http://openaccess.eprints.org/index.php?/archives/196-guid
.html.

———. 2007b. "US and EU Both Have Petitions for OA Mandates." Posted on
the BOAI Forum list, 14 March. Archived at http://threader.ecs.soton.ac.uk/
lists/boaiforum/. Also posted on *Open Access Archivangelism*, 14 January. Available at: http://openaccess.eprints.org/index.php?serendipity%5Baction%5D
=search&serendipity%5BsearchTerm%5D=immunise.

———. 2007c. "Re: D-Lib article about Cornell's Institutional Repository."
Posted on the BOAI Forum list, 15 March. Archived at http://threader.ecs
.soton.ac.uk/lists/boaiforum.

———. 2007d. "University of Leicester's Self-Archiving Policy." Posted on the
BOAI Forum list, 8 June. Archived at http://threader.ecs.soton.ac.uk/lists/
boaiforum. Also available at: http://users.ecs.soton.ac.uk/harnad/Hyper
mail/Amsci/6469.html.

Harnad, Stevan, and Tim Brody. 2004. "Comparing the Impact of Open Access
(OA) vs. Non-OA Articles in the Same Journals." *D-Lib Magazine* 10(6) (June).
Available at: http://www.dlib.org/dlib/june04/harnad/06harnad.html.

Harnad, Stevan, Tim Brody, F. Vallières, et al. 2004. "The Access/Impact Problem and the Green and Gold Roads to Open Access." *Serials Review* 30(4).

Harris, Wil. 2006. "Kazaa Cuts Out, Coughs Up." *bit-tech.net*, 27 July. Available at:
http://www.bit-tech.net/news/2006/07/27/kazaa_cuts_out_coughs_up/.
Accessed 12 August 2006.

Hartley, John, and Roberta A. Pearson, eds. 2000. *American Cultural Studies*. Oxford: Oxford University Press.

Hayles, N. Katherine. 2002. *Writing Machines*. Cambridge, Mass.: MIT Press.

———. 2003. "Deeper into the Machine: The Future of Electronic Literature."
Culture Machine 5. Available at: http://www.culturemachine.net.

———. 2005. "Narrating Bits." *Vectors* 1 (Winter). Available at: http://vectors.
usc.edu/narrating_bits/. Accessed 14 November 2006.

Heckman, Davin. 2006. "Re: Query on Modes of Resistance." Posted on
CULTSTUD-L: a listserv devoted to Cultural Studies, 2 June. Available at:
http://osdir.com/ml/culture.studies.general/2006-06/msg00009.html.

Hemmungs Wirtén, Eva. 2004. *No Trespassing: Authorship, Intellectual Property
Rights, and the Boundaries of Globalization*. Toronto, Canada: University of Toronto Press.

Hersch, Seymour M. 2004. "The Gray Zone: How a Secret Pentagon Program Came to Abu Ghraib." *The New Yorker*, 24 May.

Hesmondhalgh, David. 2003. "Cultural Industries and Cultural Studies." Posted on CULTSTUD-L: a listserv devoted to Cultural Studies, 28 February. Available at http://osdir.com/ml/culture.studies.general/2003-02/msg00046 .html.

Hoggart, Richard. 1957. *The Uses of Literacy.* London: Chatto and Windus.

Huffington, Ariana. 2006. "Now the Little Guy Is the True Pit Bull of Journalism." *The Guardian*, 14 March. Available at: http://www.guardian.co.uk/comment/story/0,,1730326,00.html. Accessed 8 October 2006.

Hutcheon, Linda. 2006. "What Open Access Could Mean for the Humanities." *Project Open Source/Open Access*, 13 September. Available at: http://open .utoronto.ca/index.php?option=com_content&task=view&id=389&Itemid=66. Accessed 6 November 2006.

International Association of Scientific, Technical and Medical Publishers. 2007. "Brussels Declaration on STM Publishing," 11 May. Available at: http://www .stm-assoc.org/brussels-declaration/. Accessed 28 July 2007.

Iwata, Shuichi. 2006. "Message from the President." The Global Information Commons for Science Initiative, International Council for Science: Committee on Data for Science and Technology (CODATA). Available at: http://www.codata.org/wsis/GlobalInfoCommonsInitiative.html. Accessed 23 April 2006.

Jacobs, Neil, ed. 2006. *Open Access: Key Strategic, Technical and Economic Aspects.* Oxford: Chandos.

Jeanneney, Jean-Noël. 2007. *Google and the Myth of Universal Knowledge: A View from Europe.* Translated by Teresa Lavender Fagan. Chicago: University of Chicago Press.

Johns, Adrian. 1998. *The Nature of the Book: Print and Knowledge in the Making.* Chicago: University of Chicago Press.

Jöttkandt, Sigi. 2007. "No-fee OA Journals in the Humanities, Three Case Studies." Presentation by Open Humanities Press at "From Practice to Impact: Consequences of Knowledge Dissemination," Berlin 5 Open Access Conference, Padua, 19–21 September. Available at: http://www.aepic.it/conf/viewpaper.php?id=261&cf=10.

Kahn, Richard, and Douglas Kellner. 2005. "Oppositional Politics and the Internet: A Critical/Reconstructive Approach." *Cultural Politics* 1(1).

Kamuf, Peggy. 1997. *The Division of Literature or The University in Deconstruction.* Chicago and London: University of Chicago Press.

———. 2004. "The University in the World It Is Attempting to Think." *Culture Machine* 6. Available at: http://www.culturemachine.net.

Kaufman-Wills Group. 2005. "The Facts About Open Access: A Study of the Financial and Non-Financial Effects of Alternative Business Models on Scholarly Journals." Sponsored by the Association of Learned and Professional Society Publishers. Available at: http://www.alpsp.org/ngen_public/article .asp?id=200&did=47&aid=270&st=&oaid=-1. Accessed 16 June 2007.

Keenan, Thomas. 2002. "Looking Like Flames and Falling Like Stars. Kosovo, the First Internet War." In *Mutations*. Bordeaux, France: Arc en reve, Centre d'architecture and ACTAR.

Kellner, Douglas. 1997. "Techno-Politics, New Technologies, and the New Public Spheres." *New Political Science* 41–42 (Fall). Available at: http://www.gseis .ucla.edu/faculty/kellner/Illumina%20Folder/kell32.htm. Accessed 8 October 2006.

Kelly, Kevin. 2006. "Scan This Book!" *New York Times*, 14 May.

Kingsley, Danny. 2007. "The One That Got Away?: Institutional Reporting Changes and Open Access in Australia." April. Available at: http://dspace .anu.edu.au/bitstream/1885/45158/1/Kingsley-One%20got%20away.pdf. Accessed 5 June 2007.

Klein, Naomi. 2000. "The Branding of Learning: Ads in Schools and Universities." In *No Logo: No Space, No Choice, No Jobs*. London: Flamingo.

Kleiner, Dmytri, and Brian Wyrick. 2007. "Info-Enclosure 2.0." *Mute* 3(4) (January). Available at: http://www.metamute.org/en/InfoEnclosure-2.0.

Kolb, David. 1994. *Socrates in the Labyrinth: Hypertext, Argument, Philosophy*. Watertown, Mass.: Eastgate Systems.

———. 2000. "Hypertext as Subversive?" *Culture Machine* 2. Available at: http:// www.culturemachine.net.

Laclau, Ernesto. 1996. *Emancipations*. London: Verso.

Laclau, Ernesto, and Chantal Mouffe. 1986. *Hegemony and Socialist Strategy*. London: Verso.

Lanchester, John. 2006. "A Bigger Bang." *The Guardian Weekend*, 4 November.

Lawrence, Steve. 2001. "Free Online Availability Substantially Increases a Paper's Impact." *Nature* 411(6837), 31 May.

Lazzarato, Maurizio. 1996. "Immaterial Labor." In *Marxism Beyond Marxism*, eds. Saree Makdisi, Cesare Casarino and Rebecca E. Karl for the *Polygraph* collective. London: Routledge.

Leavis, F.R. 1943. *Education and the University*. Cambridge: Cambridge University Press, 1979.

Lessig, Lawrence. 1999. *Code: And Other Laws of Cyberspace*. New York: Basic Books.

———. 2004. *Free Culture: The Nature and Future of Creativity*. London: Penguin.

Lister, Martin, Jon Dovey, Seth Giddings, et al. 2003. *New Media: A Critical Introduction*. London and New York: Routledge.

Love, Courtney. 2000. "Courtney Love Does the Math." *Salon* 14 June. Available at: http://archive.salon.com/tech/feature/2000/06/14/love/. Accessed 12 August 2006.

Lovink, Geert. 1996. "Essay on Speculative Media Theory." In *Dark Fiber: Tracking Critical Internet Culture*. Cambridge, Mass., and London: MIT Press, 2003.

———. 1997. "Portrait of the Virtual Intellectual." In *Dark Fiber: Tracking Critical Internet Culture*. Cambridge, Mass., and London: MIT Press, 2003.

———. 1999a. "Fragments of Network Criticism." In *Dark Fiber: Tracking Critical Internet Culture*. Cambridge, Mass., and London: MIT Press, 2003.

————. 1999b. "Kosovo: War in the Age of the Internet." In *Dark Fiber: Tracking Critical Internet Culture.* Cambridge, Mass., and London: MIT Press, 2003.

————. 2001. "An Insider's Guide to Tactical Media." In *Dark Fiber: Tracking Critical Internet Culture.* Cambridge, Mass., and London: MIT Press, 2003.

————. 2003. "Introduction: Twilight of the Digerati." In *Dark Fiber: Tracking Critical Internet Culture.* Cambridge, Mass., and London: MIT Press.

————. 2006. "Blogging and Journalism, Cracking the Myth." 8 August. Available at: http://www.networkcultures.org/geert. Accessed 19 November 2006.

————. 2007. "Organic Intellectual: Interview with Andrew Ross [Revised]." Posted on the nettime mailing list, 11 July. Available at: http://www.network cultures.org/geert/interview-with-andrew-ross/.

Lovink, Geert, and Florian Schneider. 2002. "A Virtual World Is Possible: From Tactical Media to Digital Multitude." *Artnodes,* Universitat Oberta de Catalunya (UOC). Available at: http://www.uoc.edu/artnodes/eng/art/lovink_schneider0603/lovink_schneider0603.html.

Lovink, Geert, and Christoph Spehr. 2006. "Out-Cooperating the Empire?— Exchange with Christoph Spehr." Posted on the nettime mailing list, 9 July. Available at: http://www.networkcultures.org/geert/out-cooperating-the-empire-exchange-with-christoph-spehr/.

Lunenfeld, Peter, ed. 2001a. *The Digital Dialectic: New Essays on New Media.* Cambridge, Mass., and London: MIT Press.

————. 2001b. "Digital Grabs: The Digital Dialectic and New Media Theory." In *The Digital Dialectic: New Essays on New Media.* Cambridge, Mass., and London: MIT Press.

Lyotard, Jean-François. 1984. *The Postmodern Condition: A Report on Knowledge.* Translated by Geoff Bennington and Brian Massumi. Manchester, Eng.: Manchester University Press.

————. 1986. "Defining the Postmodern." In *Postmodernism: ICA Documents 4 and 5,* ed. Lisa Apignanesi. London: Institute of Contemporary Arts.

————. 1991. "Re-writing Modernity." *The Inhuman: Reflections on Time.* Translated by Geoffrey Bennington and Rachel Bowlby. London: Polity.

MacColl, John. 2002. "Free Access to Research Publications? The Potential of the Open Archives Initiative." Paper presented at "The New Information Order and the Future of the Archive," The Institute for Advanced Studies in the Humanities, at the University of Edinburgh, 20–23 March. Available at: http://www.iash.ed.ac.uk/proceedings/maccoll/maccoll.html.

MacLeod, Donald. 2003. "Publishers Damned: Free Online Science Service Challenges Established Journals." *Guardian Education,* 7 January.

Madden, Mary. 2004. "Artists, Musicians and the Internet." *Pew Internet and American Life Project,* 5 December. Available at: http://www.pewinternet.org/pdfs/PIP_Artists.Musicians_Report.pdf.

Manovich, Lev. 1998. "Database as a Symbolic Form." Available at: http://www.manovich.net/docs/database.rtf. Revised and reprinted in Lev Manovich, 2001, *The Language of New Media.* Cambridge, Mass.: MIT Press.

————. 2001. *The Language of New Media.* Cambridge, Mass.: MIT Press.

Matsuura, Koïchiro. 2003. "UNESCO's Approach to Open Access and Public Domain Information." Available at: http://www.fao.org/documents/show_cdr .asp?url_file=/DOCREP/006/AD377B/ad377b04.htm. Accessed 6 November 2006.

Marshall, Gary. 2006. "Idiot Wind." *.net* 157 (December). Available at: http:// www.netmag.co.uk/zine/big-mouth/idiot-wind.

Marvin, Carolyn. 1988. *When Old Technologies Were New.* New York and Oxford: Oxford University Press.

McCubbrey, Don, and Rick Watson. 2006. "Call for Participation Global Text Project—IS Book." Posted on the nettime mailing list by Michael Gurstein, 19 May. Available at: http://www.mail-archive.com/nettime-l@bbs.thing.net/ msg03493.html.

McEwan, Ian. 2006. *Saturday.* London: Vintage.

McLuhan, Marshall. 1964. *Understanding Media: The Extensions of Man.* New York: Signet.

———. 1969. *Counterblast.* London: Rapp and Whiting.

McLuhan, Marshall, and B. R. Powers. 1989. *The Global Village—Transformations in World Life and Media in the 21st Century.* New York: Oxford University Press.

McRobbie, Angela. 1997. "The Es and the Anti-Es: New Questions for Feminism and Cultural Studies." In *Cultural Studies in Question,* ed. Marjorie Ferguson and Peter Golding. London: Sage. Reprinted in Angela McRobbie, 1999, *In the Culture Society.* London and New York: Routledge.

———. 2000. "Stuart Hall: The Universities and the 'Hurly Burly.'" In *Without Guarantees: In Honour of Stuart Hall,* ed. Paul Gilroy, Lawrence Grossberg, and Angela McRobbie. London: Verso.

———. 2002. "From Holloway to Hollywood: Happiness at Work in the New Cultural Economy." In *Cultural Economy: Cultural Analysis and Commercial Life,* ed. Paul du Gay and Michael Pryke. London: Sage.

Meek, James. 2001. "Science World in Revolt at Power of the Journal Owners." *The Guardian,* May 26.

Meikle, Graham. 2000. "Interview with Geert Lovink." *M/C Reviews,* 3 May. Available at: http://www.uq.edu.au/mc/reviews/features/politics/lovink.html.

———. 2002. *Future Active: Media Activism and the Internet.* London: Routledge.

Merton, Robert. 1968. "Science and Democratic Social Structure." *Social Theory and Social Structure,* 3rd ed. New York: Free Press.

Miah, Andy. 2003. "(e)text: Error . . . 404 Not Found! Or The Disappearance of History." *Culture Machine* 5. Available at: http://www.culturemachine.net.

Midgley, Simon. 2002. "The End of Books?" *Guardian Education,* 9 April.

Miller, J. Hillis. 1995. "The Ethics of Hypertext." *Diacritics* 25(3) (Fall). Revised and reprinted in J. Hillis Miller and Manuel Asensi, 1999, *Black Holes: J. Hillis Miller; or, Boustrophedonic Reading.* Stanford, Calif.: Stanford University Press.

Miller, J. Hillis, and Manuel Asensi. 1999. *Black Holes: J. Hillis Miller; or, Boustrophedonic Reading.* Stanford, Calif.: Stanford University Press.

Möller, Erik, and Benjamin Mako Hill. 2006. "[cc licenses] A Free Content and

Expression Definition." Posted on the nettime mailing list by Jaroslaw Lip-szyc, 1 May. Available at: http://www.mail-archive.com/nettime-l@bbs.thing .net/msg03457.html.

Morris, Meaghan. 1988. "Banality in Cultural Studies." *Block* 14. An extended revision of "Banality in Cultural Studies" is available in Patricia Mellencamp, ed., 1990, *Logics of Television: Essays in Cultural Criticism.* London and Bloomington: B.F.I. Publishing and Indiana University Press.

———. 1998. "Publishing Perils and How to Survive Them: A Guide for Graduate Students." *Cultural Studies* 12(4).

Mouffe, Chantal. 1996. "Deconstruction, Pragmatism and the Politics of Democracy." In *Deconstruction and Pragmatism*, ed. Chantal Mouffe. London and New York: Routledge.

———. 2000. *The Democratic Paradox.* London: Verso.

———. 2005. *On the Political.* London: Routledge.

Neilson, Brett. 2006. "Cultural Studies and Giorgio Agamben." In *New Cultural Studies: Adventures in Theory,* ed. Gary Hall and Clare Birchall. Edinburgh: Edinburgh University Press.

Neilson, Brett, and Angela Mitropoulos. 2005. "Polemos, Universitas." *Borderlands* 4(1). Available at: http://www.borderlandsejournal.adelaide.edu.au/ vol4no1_2005/neilsonmitropoulos_polemos.htm. Accessed 16 November 2006.

Newman, John Henry. 1858. "University Subjects." In *The Idea of a University: Defined and Illustrated.* London: Longmans, Green, 1929.

Oberholzer-Gee, Felix, and Koleman S. Strumpf. 2005. "The Effect of File Sharing on Record Sales: An Empirical Analysis." Available at: http://www.unc .edu/~cigar/papers/FileSharing_June2005_final.pdf. Accessed 6 November 2006.

Ong, Walter. 1982. *Orality and Literacy: The Technologizing of the Word.* Reprint, London: Methuen, 2002.

Oppenheim, Charles. 2001. "The Legal and Regulatory Environment for Electronic Information." *Infonortics.* Available at: http://www.infonortics.com/ publications/legal4.html.

———. 2004. "Re: Evolving Publisher Copyright Policies on Self-Archiving." Posted on the American Scientist Open Access Forum, 9 November. Available at: http://users.ecs.soton.ac.uk/~harnad/Hypermail/Amsci/4140.html.

O'Shea, Alan. 1998. "A Special Relationship? Cultural Studies, Academia and Pedagogy." *Cultural Studies* 12(4).

Patel, Kam. 2000. "Team Finds Way Round Copyright." *Times Higher Education Supplement,* 12 February.

Phillips, Stephen. 2002. "Take Away Books and the Chairs Collapse." *Times Higher Education Supplement,* 8 November.

Pool, K. 2000. "Love, Not Money." *The Author* (Summer).

Poster, Mark. 1995. *The Second Media Age.* London: Polity.

———. 1997. "Cyberdemocracy: Internet and the Public Sphere." In *Internet Culture,* ed. David Porter. London and New York: Routledge. Reprinted in Mark

Poster, 2001, *What's the Matter with the Internet*. Minneapolis and London: University of Minnesota Press.

———. 2001a. "Theorizing the Virtual: Baudrillard and Derrida." In *What's the Matter with the Internet*. Minneapolis and London: University of Minnesota Press.

———. 2001b. "The Digital Subject and Cultural Theory." In *What's the Matter with the Internet*. Minneapolis and London: University of Minnesota Press.

———. 2005. "Who Controls Digital Culture?" *Fast Capitalism* 2(1). Available at: http://www.uta.edu/huma/agger/fastcapitalism/1_2/poster.html. Reprinted in Mark Poster, 2006, *Information Please: Culture and Politics in the Age of Digital Machines*. Durham, N.C.: Duke University Press.

Poynder, Richard. 2007. "The OA Interviews: Stevan Harnad," 1 July. Available at: http://poynder.blogspot.com/2007/07/oa-interviews-stevan-harnad.html. Accessed 16 July 2007.

Quaranta, Domenico. 2006. "The Last Avant-Garde: Interview with Mark Tribe and Reena Jana." Posted on the nettime mailing list by Domenico Quaranta, 30 October. Available at: http://www.mail-archive.com/nettime-l@bbs.thing.net/msg03865.html.

RAE 2001. "What Is the RAE 2001?" Available at: http://www.hero.ac.uk/rae/AboutUs/. Accessed 12 August 2006.

Raley, Rita. 2001. "Reveal Codes: Hypertext and Performance." *Postmodern Culture* 12(1). Available at: http://www3.iath.virginia.edu/pmc/text-only/issue.901/12.1raley.txt. Accessed 7 December 2006.

Ramírez, Álvaro. 2005. "Narratives in Media and eCommunication: A Blog by Álvaro Ramírez." Posted by Álvaro Ramírez, 5 June. Accessed 6 June 2005.

Raymond, Eric. 2001. *The Cathedral and the Bazaar: Musings on Linux and Open Source by an Accidental Revolutionary*. Sebastopol, Calif.: O'Reilly Media.

Readings, Bill. 1994. "Caught in the Net: Notes from the Electronic Underground." *Surfaces* 4 (104). Available at: http://www.pum.umontreal.ca/revues/surfaces/vol4/readings.html. Accessed 16 June 2007.

———. 1996. *The University in Ruins*. Cambridge, Mass. and London: Harvard University Press.

Richardson, Elvis, and Sarah Goffman. 2006. "Editorial." *Photofile: Contemporary Photomedia and Ideas* 78 (Spring).

Rifkin, Adrian. 2003. "Inventing Recollection." In *Interrogating Cultural Studies: Theory, Politics, Practice*, ed. Paul Bowman. London and Sterling, Va.: Pluto Press.

Rikowski, Glenn. 2003. "The Business Takeover of Schools." *Mediactive* 1.

Robins, Kevin. 1996. "Cyberspace or the World We Live In." In *Fractal Media: New Media in Social Context*, ed. John Dovey. London: Lawrence and Wishart.

Robins, Kevin, and Frank Webster. 1999. "Deconstructing the Academy: The New Production of Human Capital." In *Times of the Technoculture*. London: Routledge.

———, eds. 2003. *The Virtual University? Knowledge, Management and Markets*. Oxford: Oxford University Press.

Rorty, Richard. 1989. *Contingency, Irony and Solidarity*. Cambridge: Cambridge University Press.

Rosenthal, Morris. 2006. "Print on Demand POD: A Lightning Source Example." Available at: http://www.fonerbooks.com/pod.htm. Accessed 16 June 2007.

Ross, Andrew. 2000. "The Mental Labor Problem." *Social Text* 18(2 63) (Summer).

Royle, Nicholas. 1995. "Foreign Body: The Deconstruction of a Pedagogical Institution and All That It Implies." In *After Derrida*. Manchester: Manchester University Press.

[Rumsfeld, Donald.] 2002. "Rumsfeld Warns of Threats Deadlier Than Sept. 11." *NewsMax.com Wires*, 1 February. Available at: http://www.newsmax.com/archives/articles/2002/1/31/163455.shtml. Accessed 16 June 2007.

Rutherford, Jonathan. 2003. "The Private Finance Initiative and the Education Market." *Signs of the Times*, 23 February. Available at: http://www.signsofthe times.org.uk/pfi%5Btextonly%5D.html. Accessed 19 October 2006.

———. 2005. "Cultural Studies in the Corporate University." *Cultural Studies* 19(3) (March).

Sale, Arthur. 2006. "Australia's RQF." Posted on the American Scientist Open Access Forum, 17 November. Available at: http://users.ecs.soton.ac.uk/~harnad/Hypermail/Amsci/5805.html. Accessed 5 June 2007.

Salter, Lee. 2003. "Democracy, New Social Movements and the Internet." In *Cyberactivism: Online Activism in Theory and Practice*, ed. Martha McCaughey and Michael D. Ayers. London: Routledge.

Sayid, Ruki. 2006. "76,000,000 Websites But We Use Just 6." *Daily Mirror*, 6 March.

Sconce, Jeffery. 2003. "Tulip Theory." In *New Media: Theories and Practices of Digitextuality*, ed. Anna Everett and John Caldwell. London and New York: Routledge.

Solomon, David J. 2002. "Talking Past Each Other: Making Sense of the Debate over Electronic Publication." *First Monday* 7(8). Available at: http://first monday.org/issues/issue7_8/solomon/. Accessed 12 October 2006.

———. 2006. "Strategies for Developing Sustainable Open Access Scholarly Journals." *First Monday* 11(6). Available at: http://firstmonday.org/issues/issue11_6/solomon/index.html. Accessed 12 October 2006.

Sondheim, Alan. 2001. "Introduction: Codework." *American Book Review* 22(6) (September/October). Available at: http://www.litline.org/ABR/issues/Volume22/Issue6/sondheim.pdf.

Stacey, Paul. 2006. *New Technologies of Democracy: How the Information and Communication Technologies Are Shaping New Cultures of Radical Democratic Politics*. Unpublished Ph.D. thesis. Middlesex University.

Stallman, Richard. 2002. *Free Software, Free Society: Selected Essays of Richard M. Stallman*. Boston, Mass.: Free Software Foundation. Available at: http://notabug .com/2002/rms-essays.pdf. Accessed 15 January 2007.

Steele, Tom. 1997. *The Emergence of Cultural Studies, 1945–65: Cultural Politics, Adult Education and the English Question*. London: Lawrence and Wishart.

Stiegler, Bernard. 1998. *Technics and Time, 1: The Fault of Epimetheus.* Translated by Richard Beardsworth and George Collins. Stanford, Calif.: Stanford University Press.

———. 2002. "The Discrete Image." In *Echographies of Television: Filmed Interviews,* by Jacques Derrida and Bernard Stiegler. Translated by Jennifer Bajorek. London: Polity.

———. 2003. "Our Ailing Educational Institutions." *Culture Machine* 5. Translated by Stefan Herbrechter. Available at: http://www.culturemachine.net.

Stiglitz, Joseph. 1999. "Public Policy for a Knowledge Economy." Paper presented at the Department for Trade and Industry and Center for Economic Policy Research The World Bank Group, London, 27 January. Available at: http://www.worldbank.org/html/extdr/extme/knowledge-economy.pdf. Accessed 31 October 2006.

Stothart, Chloe. 2006. "Do the iPod Shuffle, But Don't Miss the Lecture." *The Times Higher Education Supplement,* 26 May.

Striphas, Ted. 1998. "The Long March: Cultural Studies and Its Institutionalization." *Cultural Studies* 12(4).

———. 2002. "A Constellation of Books: Communication, Technology, and Popular Culture in the Late Age of Print." Ph.D. diss. University of North Carolina at Chapel Hill.

———. 2003. "Book 2.0." *Culture Machine* 5. Available at: http://www.culturemachine.net.

Striphas, Ted, and Kembrew McLeod. 2006. Special issue on "The Politics of Intellectual Properties." *Cultural Studies* 20(2/3) (March/May). Available at: http://www.indiana.edu/~bookworm and http://kembrew.com/academics/research.html.

Suber, Peter. 2004. "Who Should Control Access to Research Literature?" *SPARC Open Access Newsletter* 79(2) (November). Available at: http://earlham.edu/~peters/fos/newsletter/11-02-04.htm.

———. 2007a. "Balancing Author and Publisher Rights." *SPARC Open Access Newsletter* 110 (2 June). Available at: http://www.earlham.edu/~peters/fos/newsletter/06-02-07.htm.

———. 2007b. "Open Access Overview." Available at: http://www.earlham.edu/~peters/fos/overview.htm.

Sutherland, John. 2004. "Profitable Margins." *The Guardian,* G2, 30 March.

Terranova, Tiziana. 2000. "Free Labor: Producing Culture for the Digital Economy." *Social Text* 18(2 63) (Summer). Available at: http://www.uoc.edu/in3/hermeneia/sala_de_lectura/t_terranova_free_labor.htm. Accessed 7 January 2007. A shorter version of this essay was published in 2003 in *The Electronic Book Review.* Available at: http://www.electronicbookreview.com/thread/technocapitalism/voluntary.

Thacker, Eugene. 2005. "Living Dead Networks." *Fibreculture* 4. Available at: http://journal.fibreculture.org/issue4/issue4_thacker.html. Accessed 21 November 2006.

Thatcher, Sanford G. 1999. "The 'Value Added' in Editorial Acquisitions." *Jour-*

nal of Scholarly Publishing 30(2). Available at: http://128.100.205.43/access/
jour.ihtml?lp=product/jsp/302/302_thatcher.html. Accessed 4 June 2007.

Thompson, E. P. 1970. *Warwick University Ltd.* Harmondsworth, Eng.: Penguin.

Thompson, John B. 2005. *Books in the Digital Age.* Cambridge, Eng.: Polity Press.

Times Higher Education Supplement, The. 2002. "Duo Claims That Physics Website Infringed Their Civil Rights." 6 December.

Tribe, Mark, and Reena Jana. 2006. "Art in the Age of Digital Distribution." *New Media Art.* London: Taschen.

Tschider, Charlotte. 2006. "Investigating the 'Public' in the Public Library of Science: Gifting Economics in the Internet Community." *First Monday* 11(6). Available at: http://firstmonday.org/issues/issue11_6/tschider/index.html. Accessed 17 October 2006.

Turkle, Sherry. 1996. *Life on the Screen: Identity in the Age of the Internet.* London: Weidenfeld and Nicolson.

Valentine, Jeremy. 2006. "Cultural Studies and Post-Marxism." In *New Cultural Studies: Adventures in Theory,* ed. Gary Hall and Clare Birchall. Edinburgh: Edinburgh University Press.

Vershbow, Ben. 2006. "Open Source Dissertation." Posted on the Institute for the Future of the Book's if:book blog, 23 June. Available at: http://www.futureofthebook.org/blog/archives/2006/06/open_source_dissertation.html. Accessed 8 February 2007.

Virno, Paulo. 2004a. "Creating a New Public Sphere, Without the State: Interview with Paolo Virno by Héctor Pavón." Translated by Nate Holdren. Available at: http://www.generation-online.org/p/fpvirno8.htm.

———. 2004b. *A Grammar of the Multitude.* Translated by Isabella Bertoletti, James Cascaito and Andrea Casson. New York: Semiotext(e).

Virno, Paulo, and Antonio Negri. 2003. "Public Sphere, Labour, Multitude: Strategies of Resistance in Empire." Seminar organized by Officine Precarie in Pisa, 5 February. Translated by Arianna Bove. Available at: http://www.generation-online.org/t/common.htm.

Wainwright, Hilary, Oscar Reyes, Marco Berlinguer, et al., eds. 2007. *Networked Politics: Rethinking Political Organisation in an Age of Movements and Networks.* TNI, Transform! Italia, IGOP and Euromovements. Available at: http://www.tni.org/reports/newpol/networkedpolitics.pdf. Accessed 18 January 2007.

Wark, McKenzie. 2001. "Codework." *American Book Review* 22(6). Available at: http://www.litline.org/ABR/Issues/Volume22/Issue6/abr226.html. Posted on the fibreculture mailing list, 22 September. Available at: http://www.fibre culture.org/myspinach/fibreculture/2001-September/000746.html.

———. 2006a. *GAM3R 7H30RY,* Version 1.1. Available at: http://www.future ofthebook.org/gamertheory. Accessed 20 September 2006.

———. 2006b. "The Weird Global Media Event and the Tactical Intellectual." In *New Media Old Media: A History and Theory Reader,* ed. Wendy Hui Kyong Chun and Thomas Keenan. London and New York: Routledge.

Weber, Samuel. 1978. "It." *Glyph* 4.

———. 1987. *Institution and Interpretation.* Minneapolis: University of Minnesota

Press. Revised and reprinted as Samuel Weber, 2001, *Institution and Interpretation (Expanded Edition)*. Stanford, Calif.: Stanford University Press.

———. 1996. *Mass Mediauras: Form, Technics, Media*. Stanford, Calif.: Stanford University Press.

———. 1999. "The Future Campus: Destiny in a Virtual World." *Hydra*. Available at: http://hydra.umn.edu/Weber/text1.html. Accessed 11 August 2006. Reprinted in Samuel Weber, 2001, *Institution and Interpretation (Expanded Edition)*. Stanford, Calif.: Stanford University Press.

———. 2000. "The Future of the Humanities: Experimenting." *Culture Machine* 2. Available at: http://www.culturemachine.net. Reprinted in Samuel Weber, 2001, *Institution and Interpretation (Expanded Edition)*. Stanford, Calif.: Stanford University Press.

———. 2001. "Responding: A Discussion with Samuel Weber." Conducted by Simon Morgan Wortham and Gary Hall. *Culture Machine, InterZone*. Available at: http://www.culturemachine.net. Republished in 2002 in *The South Atlantic Quarterly* 101(3) (Summer); Simon Morgan Wortham, 2003, *Samuel Weber: Acts of Reading*. Aldershot, Eng.: Ashgate Publishing; and Samuel Weber, 2005, *Theatricality as Medium*. New York: Fordham University Press.

Webster, Frank. 2004. "Cultural Studies and Sociology at, and After, the Closure of the Birmingham School 1." *Cultural Studies* 18(6) (November).

White, Michele. 2002. "The Aesthetics of Failure: Net Art Gone Wrong." *Angelaki* 7(1) (April).

Wikipedia. 2006a. "Open Access." Available at: http://en.wikipedia.org/wiki/Open_access. Accessed 13 June 2007.

———. 2006b. "eDonkey Network." Available at: http://en.wikipedia.org/wiki/EDonkey_network. Accessed 6 November 2006.

———. 2006c. "Journal." Available at: http://en.wikipedia.org/wiki/Journal. Accessed 9 November 2006.

———. 2006d. "Metadata." Available at: http://en.wikipedia.org/wiki/Metadata. Accessed 27 February 2006.

Williams, Raymond. 1958. *Culture and Society, 1780–1950*. Harmondsworth, Eng.: Penguin, 1961.

———. 1977. *Marxism and Literature*. New York: Oxford University Press.

———. 1986. "The Future of Cultural Studies." In *The Politics of Modernism: Against the New Conformists*, ed. Tony Pinkney. London: Verso, 1989.

Willinsky, John. 2006. *The Access Principle: The Case for Open Access to Research and Scholarship*. Cambridge, Mass.: MIT Press.

Wortham, Simon. 2003. *Samuel Weber: Acts of Reading*. Aldershot, Eng.: Ashgate Publishing.

Wortham, Simon Morgan, and Gary Hall, eds. 2007. *Experimenting: Essays with Samuel Weber*. New York: Fordham University Press.

Young, Jeffrey R. 2006. "Book 2.0: Scholars Turn Monographs into Digital Conversations." *Chronicle of Higher Education*, 1 August. Available at: http://chronicle.com/free/v52/i47/47a02001.htm. Accessed 16 June 2007.

Young, Robert. 1992. "The Idea of a Chrestomatic University." In *Logomachia: The Conflict of the Faculties*, ed. Richard Rand. Lincoln, Neb., and London:

University of Nebraska Press. Revised and reprinted in Robert J. C. Young, 1996, *Torn Halves: Political Conflict in Literary and Cultural Theory*. Manchester: Manchester University Press.

———. 1996a. "The Dialectics of Cultural Criticism." In *Authorizing Culture*, special issue of *Angelaki* 2(2), ed. Gary Hall and Simon Wortham. Reprinted in Robert J. C. Young, 1996, *Torn Halves: Political Conflict in Literary and Cultural Theory*. Manchester: Manchester University Press.

———. 1996b. *Torn Halves: Political Conflict in Literary and Cultural Theory*. Manchester: Manchester University Press, 1996.

Žižek, Slavoj. 1997. *The Plague of Fantasies*. London: Verso.

———. 1999. *The Ticklish Subject*. London: Verso.

———. 2001. "The One Measure of True Love Is: You Can Insult the Other: Interview with Sabine Reul and Thomas Deichmann." *Spiked* 15 (November). Available at: http://www.spiked-online.com/Articles/00000002D2C4.htm. Accessed 16 June 2007.

Zylinska, Joanna. 2001. "An Ethical Manifesto for Cultural Studies . . . Perhaps." *Strategies: Journal of Theory, Culture and Politics* 14(2) (November).

———, ed. 2002. *The Ethico-Political Issue. Culture Machine* 4. Available at: http://www.culturemachine.net.

———. 2005. *The Ethics of Cultural Studies*. London: Continuum.

———. 2006. "Cultural Studies and Ethics." In *New Cultural Studies: Adventures in Theory*, eds. Gary Hall and Clare Birchall. Edinburgh: Edinburgh University Press.

———. Forthcoming. *Bioethics in the Age of New Media*. Cambridge, Mass.: MIT Press.

GARY HALL is a cultural theorist working in new media, continental philosophy, and cultural studies. He is professor of media and performing arts in the School of Art and Design at Coventry University in the United Kingdom. His books include *Culture in Bits: The Monstrous Future of Theory*, *New Cultural Studies: Adventures in Theory* (with Clare Birchall), and *Experimenting: Essays with Samuel Weber* (with Simon Morgan Wortham).

He is also a new media writer, editor, and publisher. He is editor of the online journal of cultural theory and cultural studies *Culture Machine* (http://www.culturemachine.net), founded in 1999; series editor of Berg Publishers' *Culture Machine* book series; director of the cultural studies open-access archive CSeARCH (http://www.culturemachine .net/csearch); and cofounder of Open Humanities Press (http://www .openhumanitiespress.org). His work has appeared in numerous journals, including *Angelaki*, *Cultural Studies*, *Parallax*, *The Review of Education, Pedagogy, and Cultural Studies*, *The South Atlantic Quarterly*, and *The Oxford Literary Review*. More information about his work can be found at http://www.garyhall.info.